The publisher gratefully acknowledges the generous contribution to this book provided by the General Endowment Fund of the Associates of the University of California Press.

Myths in Stone

Myths in Stone

RELIGIOUS DIMENSIONS OF
WASHINGTON, D.C.

Jeffrey F. Meyer

UNIVERSITY OF CALIFORNIA PRESS
BERKELEY / LOS ANGELES / LONDON

University of California Press
Berkeley and Los Angeles, California

University of California Press, Ltd.
London, England

Library of Congress Cataloging-in-Publication Data

Meyer, Jeffrey F.
Myths in stone : religious dimensions
of Washington, D.C. / Jeffrey F. Meyer.
   p.   cm.
   Includes bibliographical references and index.
   ISBN 0-520-21481-1 (alk. paper)
   1. Washington (D.C.)—Religion   2. Sacred space—
Washington (D.C.) I. Title.
BL2527.W18 M49   2001
975.3—dc21   00-020172
                                        CIP

Manufactured in the United States of America

09 08 07 06 05 04 03 02 01

10 9 8 7 6 5 4 3 2 1

For Cathy, Elsa, Joel, Jonathan, and Julia

Contents

Illustrations

Acknowledgments

I would like to thank some of the many friends and colleagues who helped me to complete this project. First and foremost is Pam Scott, who encouraged me when the idea was still inchoate, then generously assisted me many times as the project developed. Several colleagues read all or part of the book, giving me much valuable criticism and many helpful suggestions, especially Sherman Burson, Joanne Maguire Robinson, and Edward St. Clair. Susan Gardiner, Kathryn Johnson, Edward Linenthal, Jill Raitt, Jim Tabor, and Martin Zimmerman contributed ideas, suggested resources, and gave encouragement along the way. A number of people in Washington offices helped me obtain illustrations, and I am particularly grateful to Sue Koehler at the U.S. Commission of Fine Arts, Denise Liebowitz at the National Capital Planning Commission, and Pam McConnell, curator at the Office of the Architect of the Capitol. At UNC Charlotte, Ron Lewis helped with graphics, and Bob Mundt, dean of the Graduate School, provided financial assistance for illustrations. Thanks also to Ken and Cheri Reynolds for their wonderful hospitality, and to Evelyn Aldridge for years of secretarial help at every stage of this project. Finally, I owe the greatest debt to my wife and daughter, Cathy and Julia, who generously shared me with this book, which, like a demanding and cantankerous family member, got more time and attention than it probably deserved. The book is better for all these friends, colleagues, and family members. I take responsibility for any mistakes and shortcomings that remain.

Introduction

AT A TIME when there were only a few million Europeans in the entire fifteen United States, Pierre Charles L'Enfant conceived a grandiose plan for a national capital to rival the capitals of the great European nations. He convinced President George Washington to support his plan, writing enthusiastically (but inaccurately) that "no Nation perhaps had ever before the opportunity offered them of deliberately deciding on the spot where their Capital City should be fixed."[1] L'Enfant knew he was to direct a great project, often using imperial terms like "vast empire" to describe the American nation and "palace" for the president's future residence. At the same time he was also aware that the city he was planning, as the capital of a *democracy,* was something "wholly new" in the world. Therefore he deliberately located the Congress House, not the president's mansion, as the center in the city plan. Although George Washington and Thomas Jefferson were deeply involved in the process, L'Enfant must be given credit for planning, in only a few months, a democratic capital and a "city for the ages."[2]

In the same letter to Washington he acknowledged that the financial state of the country would not allow the realization of such a plan for many years, but that the city's scale must be such as to allow for future growth. L'Enfant was right on both counts. The city would become a great capital, but it would first pass through a period of one hundred years of painfully slow development. The delay caused nearly a century of disparaging descriptions and snide comments about the American capital. One English visitor in 1806, when told that he was entering Washington, looked in vain for buildings and houses: "Seeing none, I thought I had misunderstood the gentleman who made the remark, and turning round for an explanation, he told me, laughing, that we were almost in the very middle of it."[3] Once called the city of "magnificent distances," Charles Dickens complained in 1842 that it was only a city of "magnificent intentions."

L'Enfant's original plan is still visible in Washington, his gridlike street plan, with diagonal overlays, and his central axial thoroughfares, which define the core of the city. Pennsylvania Avenue remains a main axis connecting the Capitol and White House; the Capitol's vista has become the Mall. The view from the White House now reaches past the Washington Monument to the Jefferson Memorial and the Potomac River. With the passage of time and the gathering momentum of historical events, Washington has finally become the grand capital its creator imagined, the city at the center of the world.

Centrality is a dominant issue in Washington. The city was initially chosen as a compromise among conflicting regional interests and was seen as a midpoint in the geography of the existing states.[4] The District of Columbia was laid out as a perfect square, ten miles on a side (the limits imposed by Article 1 of the U.S. Constitution), with its four corners pointing to each of the cardinal directions, like the ancient cities of Ur and Babylon in Mesopotamia. Instead of a ziggurat at the center, the surveyor "Mr. [Andrew] Ellicott drew a true meridional line, by celestial observation, which passes through the area intended for the Capitol. This line he crossed by another, running due east and west, which passes through the same area."[5] The site for the Capitol building was actually moved slightly eastward, but planners still kept the central symbolism, using the *actual* location of the Capitol to divide the District of Columbia into Northwest, Northeast, Southwest, and Southeast quadrants. The numbered and lettered streets of the city all originate at the Capitol. This aspiration to centrality would increase over time, symbolic and practical factors interwoven.

In 1850, President Millard Fillmore pressed forward with plans to double the capacity of the Capitol. Thomas U. Walter, the architect chosen for the project, seized the opportunity to replace its rather modest dome with a lofty and massive one reminiscent of the great European cathedrals of Saint Peter's in Rome, Saint Paul's in London, and Saint Isaac's in Saint Petersburg. This grander dome, besides being a triumph of architecture and engineering, also assumed immense symbolic importance. Before the project could be completed, the Civil War began and Washington was under threat by Confederate armies. Despite the risk and expense, Lincoln urged the project on: "If the people see this Capitol going on, they will know that we intend the Union shall go on."[6]

Eight years earlier, before the expansion had begun, the American sculptor Thomas Crawford was chosen to create a statue to be placed on the summit of the dome. He submitted a design representing Freedom, the goddess of liberty, wearing a Roman cap called the pileus, like those worn by freed slaves in ancient times. The superintendent of the Capitol expansion project at the time was Secretary of War Jefferson Davis. He did not like the cap, finding it "inappropriate to a people who were born free and would not be enslaved."[7] Some believe that Davis saw in this cap a veiled criticism of the Southern institution of slavery, a threat to the "peculiar institution" in any suggestion of emancipation. Crawford was conciliatory, replacing the Roman cap with a bizarre sort of helmet "composed of an eagle's head and a bold arrangement of feathers, suggested by the costume of our Indian tribes." This is the headgear of the statue today, formally called *Freedom Triumphant in War and Peace*. But the sculptor kept the circlet of stars around *Freedom*'s brow, which he earlier said indicated "her heavenly origin."[8]

The visitor to Washington experiences numerous sites and signs like the Capitol dome, symbolically rich and conveying a variety of messages, some of them paradoxical or even downright contradictory. If the *Freedom* figure, as interpreted by Jefferson Davis, recalls the contentions of slaveholders against abolitionists, there is a counterpoint exactly one mile to the east. In the middle of Lincoln Park stands Thomas Ball's Emancipation monument of the sixteenth president freeing a slave. Ostensibly, both sculptures are dedicated to freedom, yet their histories are filled with ironies. Crawford's *Freedom* was cast in bronze by sculptor Clark Mills, who was sympathetic to the Confederate states and used slaves in his workshop to make the statue. On the other hand, the model for the emancipated slave who crouches below Lincoln in Ball's monument was Archer Alexander. He lived in Missouri, where his emancipation had been declared by military commander John Fremont, only to have the proclamation revoked by Abraham Lincoln. So, in reality, Lincoln had declared Alexander a slave. When Henry Kirke Brown, a Northern abolitionist, proposed a design for the eastern pediment of the House wing in 1855, it was rejected because it included a slave which Montgomery Meigs felt would offend Southern sensibilities. Then, implausibly, when Brown proposed a pediment containing eight slave figures for the lavish statehouse of South Carolina at Columbia, his design was accepted. [9] The Crawford and Ball "freedom" sculptures suggest something of the complexity and paradoxicality of Washington's symbolism as well as the riskiness of any "final" interpretation of its meaning. They also touch on the central issue of individual and communal understanding: who are the "chosen people"? For Davis, the national community was restricted to white Americans. The Lincoln sculpture, despite the ironies just mentioned, offers a different message. Erected in 1876, thanks to contributions of emancipated African Americans, it symbolizes an early step in their long struggle to become part of the "chosen people."

There is a religious message implicit in most of the buildings, memorials,

FIGURE 1 Thomas Crawford,
*Freedom Triumphant in War and
Peace*. Architect of the Capitol.

art, and iconography of Washington that recalls the original conviction so
often stated by the Founding Fathers, that the Almighty stood behind the
American experiment. As the Great Seal of the United States proclaims,
annuit coeptis, novus ordo seclorum: "He [God] gave his approval to these
beginnings, a new world order." This is nowhere manifest more clearly than
in the Capitol building, the "Temple of Liberty." When at last the bronze
head of *Freedom* was formally hoisted into place on December 2, 1863, the
adjutant general's office ordered a ceremony that would rally Union troops
and unmistakably confirm "this material symbol of the principle on which

our government is based."[10] *Freedom* was ritually installed to the thunder of cannons: a thirty-five-gun salute (for the number of states in the Union in 1863) from a field battery on Capitol Hill, which was then answered in succession by a similar thirty-five-gun salute from the twelve forts that encircled and protected the capital. However questionable *Freedom*'s symbolism, since that time the Capitol has possessed the requisite architectural grandeur to be what its designers had always hoped it would be, the moral and ideological center of city and nation.

There are two metaphors that I have found helpful in my attempts to understand the symbolism of Washington, D.C. One is the metaphor of archeology, whose task is to uncover earlier layers of human culture. The second is the metaphor of pilgrimage, the human desire to make journeys to a sacred destination. The first metaphor is principally temporal and requires the investigation of earlier historical epochs, their capitals, and the meaning their architecture conveys. These original meanings, though often hidden and ambiguous, still in some way exert their allure today. They are like a fine vessel or other archeological find from a past civilization. The second metaphor is more spatial, requiring a methodical visitation of Washington's most significant contemporary physical structures. The axial structure of the city invites the visitor to follow a systematic route. So just as traditional pilgrimage centers like Jerusalem, Mecca, and Banaras display a circuit or prescribed route for the pilgrim to follow, I have made a pilgrimage circuit of Washington, beginning at the Capitol, walking the three major axes of the ceremonial core of the city, and ending where I began, at the Capitol.

My two metaphors converge in one description of the pilgrimage experience as "a vertical shaft driven into the past, disclosing deep strata of ancient symbols, potent signifiers (sacred symbol-vehicles such as images, paintings, proper names, and places) which reinforce nationalistic sentiments."[11] The metaphorical first layer is the most obvious and accessible complex of ideas and ideals representing what scholars have called, in recent decades, "civil religion."[12] The expression originates with Jean-Jacques Rousseau. The French philosopher believed that some religion was necessary as an ideology to support any civil society, but he rejected Christianity as inadequate in a revolutionary era. In its place he advocated a generic faith that he called "civil religion." Its general features included belief in an Almighty Power as guarantor of society's morality and civic order, who rewarded the good and punished evil in the afterlife. The Divine Power of Rousseau's civil religion was not the inactive Being of strict Deism but remained interested in human social harmony and provided sanctions to restrain those who might otherwise plot to upset the system. The purpose of civic rituals was to dramatize and celebrate society's values and moral code.

In the America of the Founding Fathers, civil religion was frequently expressed by politicians and preachers and enacted in rituals such as the Masonic rite of laying the cornerstone of the Capitol. Washington, Jefferson, Benjamin Franklin, John Adams, and others believed that the deity was actively interested in the success of the American experiment as a model that could eventually serve as a shining example for the rest of the world. They considered this novel experiment in freedom and democracy an epochal event, calling it a *novus ordo seclorum* (a new order in the world) on the Great Seal they devised for the United States. Nothing like it had been seen before, although there were brief classical foreshadowings in democratic Greece and republican Rome. Already in 1787 Representative James Wilson prophesied that the federal government would "lay a foundation for erecting temples of Liberty in every part of the earth."[13] As he lay dying in June of 1826, Thomas Jefferson wrote to the mayor of Washington, echoing the faith of the Founding Fathers that this new democratic form of government might be "to the world, what I believe it will be, (to some parts sooner, to others later, but finally to all)" a signal to arouse men to burst their chains of slavery.[14] This faith may be seen everywhere in the city but is nowhere more eloquently and fully expressed than in the art and architecture of the Capitol.

Besides the clear expressions of civil religion, there are older and less obvious strands of religious meaning in Washington, which have their roots in the world of biblical thought, both Jewish and Christian. At the foundation of American politics is the deliberate attempt to separate the state from any specific church, while at the same time protecting the right of citizens to freely practice their religions. Still, the Founding Fathers were in certain ways embedded in the world of biblical language and thought because it had, over the centuries, so thoroughly penetrated European and American culture. They spoke the words of the Bible, and they thought by its metaphors. Commenting, for example, on Alexander Hamilton's deft financial strategy that allowed Washington to be built on the Potomac site, lawyer and statesman Daniel Webster said: "He smote the rock of natural resources, and abundant streams of revenue gushed forth."[15] For reasons not difficult to understand, the Christian founders of the colonies found the episodes in the Old Testament more useful than the New Testament to justify their enterprise in the New World. Compelling and ominous images of the New World as the "Promised Land" and the colonists as the "New

Israel" exerted undeniable influence on the minds of settlers as they strove to interpret their experiences in America and justify their conquest of the indigenous peoples they encountered.

At a deeper level, the Bible raised troublesome issues and posed questions that may not have seemed important in other cultures. First, because the Bible revealed a God who acted in history, significant events had to be examined and interpreted in that light. Whereas the great Hindu and Buddhist cultures of Asia might dismiss specific historical events as meaningless, Christian theologians and thinkers labored to make sense of all the major occurrences of human history. A second issue rooted in biblical thought was the tendency to elevate good and evil to transcendent dimensions, sometimes personalizing them as God and Satan. A third might be called "bibliolatry," the worship of specific texts as sacred. Because they considered their holy scriptures to be the very word of God, Jewish and Christian believers were predisposed to venerate such secular writings as the Declaration of Independence and the Constitution as they would divinely revealed documents. These three themes are the most significant for my analysis of Washington because they imply patterns of thinking that not only dictated how questions would be answered but more fundamentally determined which questions would be asked at all.

At the deepest level of investigation the visitor to Washington sees the very beginnings of urbanism. Urban historian Lewis Mumford pointed out long ago that it was the conjunction of the sacred and secular power that first gave rise to cities in the river valleys of the ancient world.[16] Kings and their architects strove to devise ways to express their belief that the gods approved of the ruler and that the royal city was directly related to the heavenly world of the gods and the structure of the cosmos. They built temples and palaces, laid out ceremonial avenues, and designed whole cities to imitate the geometry of the universe as they understood it. These architectural arrangements expressed the belief that heaven and earth should be in harmony, and many of the early methods of expressing this harmony have been repeated in the language of architecture and city planning down through the millennia. That is to say, the vocabulary of architecture and the design of cities have changed very little over the course of urban history. Visitors will find them expressed in the avenues, shrines, memorials, and monumental architecture of Washington today.

Speaking of even more archaic periods, Jacquetta Hawkes has noted that "while civilizations have come and gone we are still born to the identical equipment of body and limbs already shaped a hundred thousand years or more ago," and along with this physical inheritance "highly charged

emotional centers and all the strange furniture of the unconscious mind."[17]
If this is true, then it is not enough to see the sources of Washington's development in Enlightenment views of the world or even in the older biblical
patterns of thought. Our archeology must dig deeper, getting down to unconscious and archaic levels of the human mind, expressed in the search for
sacred centers, for *temeni* (sacred precincts) that are places of connection to
a more real world above, symmetries and axial boulevards, shrines, and
monumental architecture whose underlying purpose is to give a transcendent meaning to the city.[18]

When Pierre L'Enfant proposed a design for the capital to George Washington in 1791, he was certainly not familiar with the concepts of his archaic
predecessors who worked for kings and emperors. But he had been exposed
to the work of André Lenôtre at Versailles, Paris, and elsewhere, the same
"grand style" of planning that subsequently exerted such a strong influence
on other great European capitals, including Rome, London, and Saint Petersburg.[19] The rectangles, circles, and diagonals, the grand vistas, the dramatic highlighting of monumental buildings, and the emphasis on movement are baroque features later reproduced in his plan for Washington. But
it was L'Enfant's genius to transform the royal architecture of monarchy
into a physical plan that was capable of expressing democratic ideals. So
successful was he that architectural historian Norma Evenson could say in
retrospect that "the baroque axis appears sufficiently flexible to represent
any political system."[20] Yet in adapting what had once been monarchic
forms of architecture L'Enfant was at the same time using ideas that had
endured for millennia. Versailles itself, and baroque urban planning generally, were themselves expressions of the same archaic vocabulary of urban
design: centrality, axiality, monumentality, cantonment, and the clever man-
agement of open spaces. If Rousseau was right that every government must
establish its connection with the world of the gods, then the problem for
democracy is even more difficult than it is for monarchy, since in the modern
world the assumed connection between a transcendent being, the earthly
ruler, and his subjects has been severed.[21] Yet even modern rulers who assume office "by the consent of the governed," still make "overt ritual appeals to higher forces and designs, [as when] an American president is at
pains to demonstrate in his inauguration speech the moral leadership that
transforms the electoral choice of this person into something other than an
accident of history."[22]

Washington is a fusion of the secular and sacred, a uniquely modern
blend of politics and religion that is nevertheless grounded in the archaic
past. Politics and religion have always engaged the deepest convictions and

commitments of human life, but of the two, religion is probably the more powerful. When they become yoked, as they normally have been throughout human history, the resultant combination is potentially explosive. The ancient fusion of secular and sacred, which gave birth to cities and to the first large-scale political entities, still functions to enlist commitment, enflame passions, and create bonds of loyalty beyond anything one could rationally explain. All of us are implicated in ways of thought and modes of feeling that have ancient roots in cultural transformations that occurred many thousands of years ago and may be, for the foreseeable future, an inevitable feature of that "strange furniture of our unconscious mind."

Yet the archeology metaphor alone is not sufficient, suggesting as it does ancient and unchanging meanings and eternal verities. This immutability is an illusion because of the transience of mythic meanings and the "super-abundance of architectural forms, that is, the way in which even the apparently simplest buildings invariably both transcend and subvert the deliberate intentions of their designers."[23] Because the meaning of capital cities is not static, I use the metaphor of pilgrimage as a corrective to this possible misapprehension. We do not know when the religious practice of pilgrimage first began, but it is a feature of all the major religious traditions—Hinduism, Buddhism, Taoism, Judaism, Christianity, and Islam. Perhaps it is universally attractive as a natural and powerful analogy of the human passage through life.[24] Going on a pilgrimage reassures pilgrims, in a concrete way, that their lives are not just an aimless wandering about, but a movement toward a sacred destination. The act of going on a pilgrimage suggests that life has meaning.

One scholar of political religion claims that "one's first pilgrimage to Washington can be a blinding religious experience, a rite of communion."[25] Although I doubt that Washington produces such a powerful effect on most visitors, the city lends itself to such an analysis, at least as an interpretative device. The axial structure of Washington invites visitors to follow specific routes in exploring the city's significant buildings and monuments. I do just that in the reflective narratives that begin the three sections of this book.[26] I did not take off my shoes, crawl on my knees, or kiss the ground, but I did find my walks conducive to reflections on the nation's now mythic Founders and the events of its sacred history, memories awakened at sites along the way. As Freud noted, "the monuments and memorials with which cities are adorned are also mnemonic symbols."[27]

A careful analysis of pilgrimage traditions reveals useful concepts that facilitate an understanding of the national mythology.[28] Pilgrimages organize space in a sophisticated and complex way, beginning at a sacred center but extending beyond it to eventually delineate a universal or cosmic system. Pilgrimages also structure time and history through the creation of pilgrimage calendars, and many sites are conceived as the place where creation took place and time began. Each of the most famous pilgrimage cities—Jerusalem, Mecca, and Banaras—is held by believers to be the center of the world and connected with creation. One can see the centrality theme developing in the growing ambition of Washington first to be the nation's center, and then the center of the world. As Chapter 1 documents, there was even a movement to restructure the world's time meridian so that it would pass through Washington instead of Greenwich.

Ritual complexity is another feature of pilgrimage centers, involving traditions that embrace continuity and change, predictability and surprise, order and chaos. Washington has its rituals to reaffirm the unity of the nation, to celebrate victory, and to commemorate noble deaths. It has exemplary liturgies that reaffirm the nature of the three branches of government and their interrelationship, most prominently the inauguration of the president every four years. On the "chaotic" side there are the popular rituals enacted on the Mall, on Pennsylvania Avenue, and in Lafayette Park that bring protesters and supporters to Washington to dramatize and debate their causes. Symbolic complexity is also a feature of pilgrimage, with multiple interpenetrating levels of meaning and symbolism. Evidence of this complex network of symbols may be found throughout the city, but chiefly in the monuments and spaces of the core area.

Finally, pilgrimage is usually a behavior that develops at the "bottom" and moves up. By that I mean that it is not devised and ordained by ruling powers but is the collective behavior of free individuals. Once established, of course, it may achieve official sanction, be co-opted by a clerical hierarchy, and even become a criterion of orthodoxy. But it is not so in its origin. Washington bears the imprint of many hands: the original planner L'Enfant, Washington, and Jefferson; architects Benjamin Latrobe, James Hoban, Charles Bulfinch, and Thomas Walter; superintendents, sculptors, and painters such as Luigi Persico, Thomas Crawford, Augustus St. Gaudens, Constantino Brumidi; landscapists Andrew Jackson Downing and Frederick Law Olmsted Jr.; and the architects of the United States Senate Park Commission (better known as the McMillan Commission), to name only a few of the more prominent. But in many ways "the people" have shaped Washington, not only through their congressional representatives but also simply by choosing which memorials they like and which they do not, which they frequent and which they ignore. In so doing, they are "voting with their feet,"[29] ; they have simultaneously created the basis of the "pilgrimage route" I adopted. For example, the memorial to Ulysses S. Grant, though vast in scope, centrally placed, and skillfully executed, has never captured the allegiance and affection of most visitors to the capital. Other sites, including the Washington Monument, the Lincoln Memorial, and the Vietnam Memorial, are continually sought by throngs of visitors.

Pilgrimage is always set against the background of the story or stories that engendered it. But new narratives may enhance or change its meaning. I call these stories myths, the foundational narratives that form a community and shape the identity of individuals. To visit Washington is to experience the retelling of a story of mythic proportions, whose roots have a complex past, going back to Europe, to biblical lands, and even to the African and Asian river valleys where civilization began. The strangeness of this mythology is well captured in Lincoln's second inaugural address as the "mystic chords of memory." Mythology is communal poetry, the human attempt to make sense out of the chaos of human life, to connect what is disconnected, and to gain some hold on mysteries that defy rational figuring. As Robert Penn Warren pointed out, "if poetry is the little myth we make, history is the big myth we live, and in our living, constantly remake."[30] The chaos of events and persons, exemplifying justice and injustice, wavering loyalties and fierce commitment, the succession of peaceful achievements and bloody disasters—all of these cry out for understanding. The poet Elizabeth Bishop hails a great artist who is able to combat the destructiveness of mere history:

> Minimal, incoherent fragments:
> the opposite of History, creator of ruins,
> out of your ruins you have made creations.[31]

In that regard, at least, poetry and mythology are the same. We, the American people, call upon the myths of the past, reinterpret them, and recreate them to make sense out of the confusion of our uncommon history. Now "we" are no longer limited to the circle of white male gentry who founded the nation and first uttered the words "We the people," but are increasingly a rainbow of colors and ethnic diversity. The more democratic character of U.S. citizenship has brought changes in the interpretation of the national myth. This enterprise of myth-making may begin when visitors to Washington experience the planning, the buildings, the spaces, and the iconography of the city. But as they "reflect on, and 'play with' the built structures in their environment, they endlessly disrupt old meanings and awaken fresh ones" in the effort to find a place for themselves in the national mythology.[32] Though Pierre Charles L'Enfant's plan provided the initial impetus, the myth of Washington has been shaped through the contributions and objections, the support and obstructions of presidents, commissions, architects, engineers, superintendents, and U.S. senators and representatives, and by us, the people. Together over time, we have continued to create the myth in stone that is today's Washington. Myth-making remains. "We," however, keep changing.

PART I

The Axis of Power

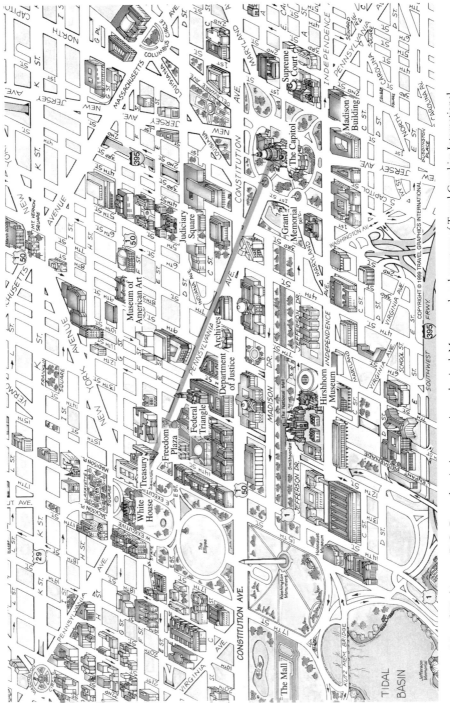

FIGURE 2 Map of Washington, D.C., Pennsylvania Avenue axis emphasized. Map reproduced courtesy of Travel Graphics International.

On Pennsylvania Avenue from the Capitol to the White House

I am Louis XIV, the Sun King, standing on the west terrace of the Capitol gazing at the Mall. It is early morning, and the shadow of the great dome sweeps down the lawn toward the Grant Memorial below. Beyond the reflecting pool, the Mall stretches toward the Washington Monument, which bisects the Lincoln Memorial behind it. Across the Potomac River, in the distant background, are Arlington Cemetery and the hills of Virginia. Major L'Enfant knew what he was doing when he created this grand vista for citizens of a democracy. He recreated the commanding view of Versailles, where the domain of the king stretched as far as the royal eye could see (see Figures 2 and 3). For a moment I feel like that king.

But I am an ordinary citizen of the United States standing on the Capitol terrace on a fresh summer morning. My imagination does not hear the regal music of the French court but Aaron Copland's "Fanfare for the Common Man." I turn my head and catch the Capitol guard eyeing me. Perhaps he has sensed my momentary illusion of grandeur and wants to see if I plan to do anything about it. Instead I look down at the white marble railing in front of me, where I see graffiti—"A & R" scratched inside a lopsided heart, the name "Tim," and to remind me of our increasing multiculturalism, "Renata" and "The Kha family." Minor vandalism executed at a time when the guard was not so alert. This is the center of the grand plan, the Congress House where our representatives, often with very little grandeur, wrangle over the creation of our laws and policies.

I stroll down the steps on the northwest side of the Capitol and cross over to the Grant Memorial. It is immense, one of the largest monuments in the world. But my fellow citizens do not flock to it as they do to the Washington Monument and to the Jefferson, Lincoln, and Vietnam Memorials. Although Ulysses S. Grant was the general who finally saved the Union, his subsequent presidency was marred by serious scandals. Today it is the Lincoln Memorial that speaks to the meaning of the Civil War.

FIGURE 3 U.S. Capitol with Mall vista. Architect of the Capitol.

The Grant Memorial is designed with great artistic skill. On the southern pedestal is the vivid tableau of the caisson charging through swampy terrain. On the northern pedestal is a cavalry group. One horse and rider have fallen into the mud. The horses, every vein, tendon, and muscle realistically depicted, look powerful. I have read that Henry Shrady, the sculptor, had real horses hosed with water to enhance their features and that he literally worked himself to death over the ten years it took to complete this monument. Immense skill has gone into this memorial, yet it is not completely successful. Why?

Grant is correctly placed, facing west toward Virginia like a sentinel, protecting the capital from Confederate troops (see Figure 4). He is hunched over against the wind and cold, a simple and determined man. There is something incongruous, though, about this battered general looking out over the sparkling water of a neoclassical marble reflecting pool. The sculp-

FIGURE 4 Ulysses S. Grant Memorial. Photograph by the author.

tures would seem more appropriately placed in a field of blood and gore. Grant led the union to victory in the dirtiest, bloodiest war in U.S. history—the first one to be documented by photography. The names of its battles—Antietam, Chancellorsburg, Manassas, and Gettysburg—conjure up sepia images of fields littered with corpses.

More than anything else, photography has changed our view of war. My adolescent images of the Revolutionary War are taken from American Heritage histories, which describe tidy troops dressed in bright colors and shining buttons and heroic action, like the description of the battle of Germantown: "By three A.M. Washington and Sullivan were inside the British picket lines. As dawn approached, an autumn mist rose with the sun, wrapping the whole sloping countryside in a ghostly, glowing pall. . . . The American striking force surged ahead, suddenly buoyant with the elixir of seldom-tasted victory. Musketry banged and crackled, adding its smoke to the sticky dawn mists."[1]

Photographs of the Civil War do not depict "the elixir . . . of victory." Nowhere does one find elegant leaders like Washington and Cornwallis, perfect gentlemen in victory or defeat. The Civil War generals are scruffy and unshaven; the troops have torn and muddy uniforms, their faces look vacant, their eyes hollow. Glory leaks out like blood in the field littered with mangled and rotting bodies.

I put this scene out of my mind and begin my walk up Pennsylvania Avenue to the White House. I am on the lookout for some sort of epiphany, some symbol that will capture the meaning of this axis. Since its creation in

the head of L'Enfant, from the time when Jefferson planted Lombardy pop-
lars along its edge, this has been the most important avenue in Washington.
It is the corridor of power, linking the legislative, executive, and judicial
branches. Millennia earlier, ancient cities in Mesopotamia had similar avenues linking the royal palace and the temple of the priests at the core of the
city. Such links proclaimed to the world that the gods approved the government of the king. The relation between religion and secular power is much
more nuanced in Washington, but it is on this avenue, between Capitol and
White House, that the connections are made.

Just beyond the intersection where Constitution and Pennsylvania Avenues diverge, I come to an important crossroads, Judiciary Square between
Fourth and Fifth Streets. On L'Enfant's original plan, double-wide blocks
show that this was to be an important axis. His notes show that this was
to be the site for the Supreme Court. I turn north and enter the southern
end of what is now called Marshall Park, passing federal and district court
buildings. At the northern end I stop before the classical columns of the
Superior Court of the United States, once Washington's City Hall. I turn
around on the front steps and make a discovery: L'Enfant's plan is still visible. Below me, beyond the standing statue of Abraham Lincoln and the
seated figure of John Marshall, the axis sweeps down the hill, crosses the
Mall, and continues on toward the Potomac.

The Supreme Court is now east of the Capitol, its Beaux Arts classicism
in stark contrast to the Victorian Library of Congress on the opposite side
of East Capitol Street. I know that L'Enfant wanted this city to reflect the
Constitution that had just been ratified by the states. But the Court's role
was not clear to him or to the Founders until Chief Justice Marshall began
to define it in the early years of the nineteenth century. The judicial branch
has now clearly taken its place with the executive and legislative branches,
and if the Supreme Court's place in the city plan seems an afterthought, it
now at least makes a monumental statement by its size and magnificence.

I return to Pennsylvania Avenue and continue walking toward the White
House, crossing another important axis at Eighth Street, where L'Enfant had
planned a "national church." His axis began in the north at the intersection
of New York and Massachusetts Avenues, two of the fifteen radial avenues
named for the then-existing states. From there, Eighth Street ran due south,
passed through the site for the national church, crossed the Mall, and extended all the way to the Potomac River, where a square with "naval itin-
erary columns" was to be located. This north-south axis stands midway
between the Capitol and the White House but is now nearly invisible, interrupted by the National Archives building and the Smithsonian's Hirsh-
horn Sculpture Museum on the south side of the Mall.

Religion has always been a contentious issue in the nation, with some citizens struggling to build up "the wall of separation" between church and state and others dedicated to lowering it. Both sides sanctify their efforts by invoking the Founding Fathers. These men, led by Thomas Jefferson and James Madison, succeeded in cutting the connection between the new government and any specific church. Yet their work seems to have stimulated religion rather than inhibiting it. I walk around to the Constitution Avenue side of the National Archives and see a line of faithful pilgrims stretching down the massive front stairs to the street. Inside there is an atmosphere of hushed reverence like that in a church or synagogue. Parents whisper to their children as they pass by the hallowed scriptures.

Returning to Pennsylvania Avenue, I walk northwest, the massive buildings of the Federal Triangle on my left—"seventy acres of bureaucrats" someone has called it. One of the buildings in this ensemble of structures is the Department of Justice. I walk around to the front of it, on Constitution Avenue, and there is my epiphany. The building has two pediments, one at each end, and inscribed on the west pediment are the Latin words *ars aequi*—the art of equity, or justice. But, suddenly conscious of all the potentially contending powers in this form of government, I take these words to mean the art of equalizing, balancing. I notice that the panels above every other window, for the length of the building, show the balanced scales of justice. On this avenue of power, *ars aequi* sums it up accurately: the justice of this system of government depends on the art of balance.

This avenue reminds me that the United States polity is based on a system of checks and balances as complex as a clock among the legislative, executive, and judicial branches, between religion and secularity, between the states and the federal government, the Senate and the House, the practical and the ideal, and all the other elements of effective government. Here was the great discovery of the Founding Fathers. Although they disagreed fiercely with each other on many issues, what they agreed upon was more important: namely, that power had to be divided. As soon as power became too concentrated, liberty vanished. Too much power in the executive would create despotism. Too much power in the people would lead to chaos. Too much power in the legislature would foster corruption. "It is a melancholy reflection that liberty should be equally exposed to danger whether the Government have too much or too little power," said Madison. Their answer was the delicate balance, *ars aequi*. A little too much weight on either side of the scale and the equilibrium was destroyed. Miraculously, they appear to have succeeded.

I continue my walk and in a few minutes arrive at Freedom Plaza, which runs between Thirteenth and Fifteenth Streets. Before me, laid out in white marble on a gray granite ground, is the core of L'Enfant's famous plan. Around the perimeter is a selection of famous visitors' comments on the capital, inscribed on the pavement. Three are by African Americans and one by a Native American, reminding me that "We, the people" now has a more inclusive meaning. As I read, I realize that these words create a conversation. One person poses a question; another answers it. James Fenimore Cooper comments that Washington has "an air of more magnificence than any other American town . . . . [It is] mean in detail, but the outline has a certain grandeur about it." Bruce Catton muses over the purposes of American pilgrims to Washington: "whatever we are looking for, we come to Washington in millions to stand in silence and try to find it." What is this "something?" Joel Sayre responds: "Our capital city, born in the Potomac marshlands, has grown by feeding on an indestructible idea." (He must mean freedom or democracy.) Herbert Hoover speaks in straightforward Quakerly words: "Washington . . . is the symbol of America. By its dignity and architectural inspiration . . . we encourage that elevation of thought and character which comes from great architecture." Thomas Jefferson would have quickly agreed.

Crossing the plaza, I begin walking the last few blocks to the White House but immediately encounter the old Treasury building, which effectively blocks the sight line between the White House and the Capitol. This aspect of L'Enfant's ideal plan was thwarted. It is said that the irascible and impatient Andrew Jackson marched out of the White House one day, plunged his cane into the ground, and said of the Treasury building, "it will be built here!" He probably never spoke those words, but this particular "mistake" in the urban plan serves to remind visitors that the distance between the ideal and the real, especially in Washington, is often considerable. I look at the statue of a youthful Alexander Hamilton and recall that he used financial control to strengthen central government. He and his building, like an awkward elbow, intrude into the smooth flow of Pennsylvania Avenue. Someone once called Hamilton a "porcupine," a comment that reminds me how often in the city's history the prickly reality of "the bottom line" has deflated ideals and destroyed lofty plans. The reminder seems appropriate as I pass the offending Treasury building and arrive at the East Gate of the White House, terminus of the first axis.

CHAPTER 1

Capital and Capitol

City at the Center of the World

GEORGE WASHINGTON first came to know Pierre Charles L'Enfant as his staff officer in the Revolutionary army, then later admired his work as the designer of Federal Hall in New York, where Congress first met. Growing up in France, L'Enfant had received artistic training from his father. He was familiar with the design of Paris and Lenôtre's brilliant plan for the gardens of Versailles. These designs, especially Versailles, with its grand vistas, dynamic diagonal avenues, and parklike ambiance, exerted a powerful influence on his later plan for the federal capital. Washington could think of no one else capable of planning a federal city worthy of the destiny he imagined for the new nation.

For the brief period of one year L'Enfant had the intoxicating experience of creating a grand federal city. He had the ear of Washington, and no one could successfully challenge his plans.[1] Thomas Jefferson gave Washington a sketch for a modest city covering about three hundred acres, laid out like a grid along the north shore of Tiber Creek near Georgetown (see Figure 5). L'Enfant immediately rejected it, calling for a city designed on a grand scale and condemning any grid plan as "at last tiresome and insipid," the product of "some cool imagination wanting a sense of the real grand and truly beautiful."[2] The fiery imagination won. Washington gave his approval to L'Enfant's ambitious plan.

L'Enfant won this skirmish and a few others, but ultimately lost the war. His greatest enemy was not Jefferson, but his own haughty intransigence. The French planner resisted submitting his ideas to the judgment of the three commissioners Washington had appointed to oversee the building of the new capital. And astonishingly, L'Enfant tore down the foundation walls of a half-completed house that stood in the way of one of his future avenues. The house belonged to Daniel Carroll of Duddington, an influential citizen of Maryland and a nephew to one of the commissioners. Thus tensions increased over the fall and winter until even the patient George Washington

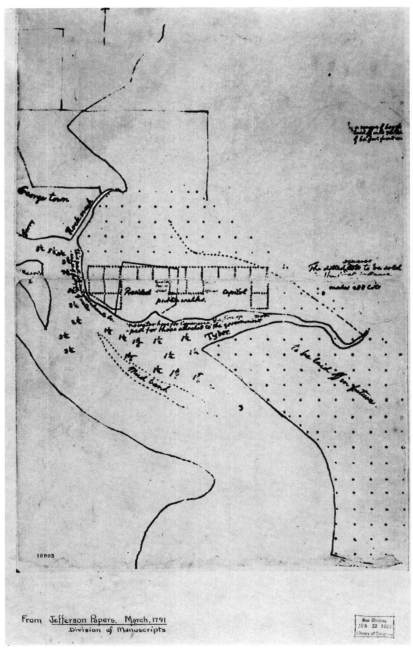

FIGURE 5 Thomas Jefferson's plan for Washington, March 1791. Courtesy of the Library of Congress.

had had enough. On February 27, 1792, on Washington's instructions, Jefferson wrote to L'Enfant that his services would no longer be required.

The fire of L'Enfant's genius had blazed for a moment and quickly burned out. Yet the work he did during that one year was so compelling that if he could see the city today he would recognize in it the embryo of his original plan. Of course he would not like the results. Over the intervening two hundred years there have been many changes in the design of the city that would offend him. L'Enfant resented *any* changes to his plan. He was as accepting of criticism as Thomas Jefferson was of changes in his draft of the Declaration of Independence. Yet many of L'Enfant's core ideas remained to guide future development. The location of the Capitol and the president's house, the grand vistas, the diagonals imposed upon a gridwork of streets, sunburst intersections with streets radiating outward, and a parklike quality—all these current features of the city are derived from L'Enfant's original ideas (see Figure 6).

In 1967, Edmund Bacon, architect of the rebirth of Philadelphia, wrote that "the building of cities is one of man's greatest achievements." He then added the warning: "The form of his city always has been and always will be a pitiless indicator of the state of his civilization."[3] Pitiless, yes, and in the case of Washington perhaps a relentless reminder, as the city's history unfolded, of the truth about the evolving American experiment. In this sense, every culture lives on in the "glass houses" of its cities. A perceptive observer should be able to infer something about the inner spirit of a civilization that produced the cities. This chapter begins the exploration of the national capital as a repository of myths in stone, asking what can be learned about the nature of the new republic that built it and the evolving national government that guided its development.

Today we take for granted the existence of a permanent national capital. But before the ratification of the Constitution in 1788 it was simply one possible solution to the problem of where the government would reside. The Continental Congress had moved from place to place since 1774 for its periodic meetings: from Philadelphia, to Baltimore, Lancaster, and York during the war, then to Princeton, Annapolis, Trenton, and finally New York.[4] Representatives explored the idea of having a continually moving capital or dual capitals. During this period, terms like "residence of Congress," "seat of government," and "federal town" were all used. Only at the end of the 1780s did the grander terms appear: "federal city," "capital," and even "imperial seat" or "imperial city."[5] Up to that time in America the word "capital" had referred to the seat of a colonial or state government.

The idea of a federal district exempt from state control was also a novelty.

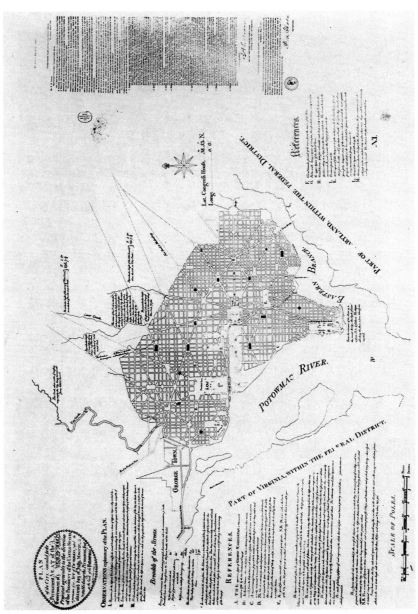

FIGURE 6 L'Enfant's plan for Washington. Library of Congress.

But as they realized the economic advantages, various states offered grants of territory that would allow an independent federal jurisdiction within their borders. By the time the Constitution was ratified in 1788, it was not a question of *if* but *where,* and the document included the following provision: Congress would "exercise exclusive Legislation in all Cases whatsoever over such District (not exceeding ten Miles square) as may, by Cession of particular States, and the acceptance of Congress, become the Seat of the Government of the United States." These words determined the existence of a federal district and a national capital. Yet even after the Constitution was ratified, it was unclear where such a district and capital would be located. The issue was contentious from the beginning, with the urban areas along the East Coast ranged against the western (inland) areas, and northern, middle, and southern states in blocks of self-interest. They combined to advocate their own favorite locations, split, recombined in different alliances, and carried on a long struggle to settle on the place of the federal district and capital. Beginning before the ratification of the Constitution and continuing after it, some fifty sites advanced their claims, from as far north as Newburgh, New York, as far south as Norfolk, Virginia, and as far west as Marietta, Ohio.[6] The debates were so bitter, inconclusive, and confusing, even after the Constitution had been ratified, that with the change of a vote or two in the House or Senate the outcome might have been entirely different.

Although a site on the Potomac River was always one of the leading contenders, sites on the Delaware and Susquehanna Rivers also had strong advocates. An enthusiast for the Potomac called it the "most noble, excellent, and beautiful river . . . in the universe." Propagandists shamelessly rhapsodized its virtues. The Thames, Seine, and Rhone, said one, were mere rivulets in comparison. Another confidently asserted that Providence had chosen the river and created a father (Washington) to render it navigable. (He was alluding to the fact that Washington had been president of the Potomac Navigation Co. in the 1780s, with the aim of building locks and canals to open water transport to the Ohio valley.) One well-known Potomac booster and local landholder, George Walker, declared that Providence had not only chosen the Potomac but had also designated the specific site between Georgetown and Alexandria, because it was the central point between the northern and the southern states of the Union. The Potomac had its detractors as well. Benjamin Rush, a signer of the Declaration of Independence and physician in Philadelphia, wanted the capital located at Philadelphia; he wrote to Vice President John Adams in 1789: "You will probably be dragged in a few years to the banks of the Potomac, where negro slaves will be your servants by day, mosquitoes your sentinels by night, and bilious fevers your companions every summer and fall, and pleurisies every spring."[7]

In the end, thanks to seven years of work by Madison and Jefferson, and especially the stolid and tactful persistence of George Washington, Congress chose the Potomac site. The turning point came at a dramatic moment, just when it appeared that Congress would never reach an agreement. The two issues before Congress that seemed insoluble were the question of debt assumption and the location of the national capital. Hamilton wanted the federal government to assume the states' Revolutionary War debts in order to enhance the young nation's financial reputation overseas and to create a stronger federal union. The northern states, with larger debts and a greater comfort level with a strong central government, favored assumption. The southern states (except South Carolina), fearing encroachment on states' rights, generally opposed it. So intractable were the positions that it seemed likely that the newly formed union might fall apart.

This crisis set the stage for a chance meeting between Thomas Jefferson and Alexander Hamilton. As Jefferson tells it, he came upon Hamilton in front of George Washington's mansion in New York, "sombre, haggard, and dejected beyond description." Hamilton urged the importance of assumption with Jefferson, asking him to seek southern support. Jefferson promised to think it over: "I proposed to him however to dine with me the next day, and I would invite another friend or two, bring them into conference together, and I thought it impossible that reasonable men, consulting together coolly, could fail, by some mutual sacrifices of opinion, to form a compromise which was to save the union."[8] The description exudes the sweet reasonableness of the Enlightenment and perhaps some of the haze of self-serving hindsight. The support of Virginia, which had already retired most of its debt, was crucial. Madison joined them for the meal, and the three worked out a compromise whereby Madison would temper his opposition to debt assumption if the northern states would accept the Potomac site for the federal city. Although there was some further maneuvering in Congress, the Potomac site was thus determined.[9]

Washington quickly selected as the city's planner his former staff officer, Major L'Enfant, who came equipped with a grand vision, limitless self-confidence, and an almost filial veneration for his former commanding officer. As though oblivious to the years of heated congressional arguments about the location of the capital, he had written an enthusiastic letter to President Washington ten months before the Potomac site was chosen:

Sir: The late determination of congress to lay the foundation of a city which is to become the Capital of this vast Empire, offers so great an occasion of acquiring reputation, to whoever may be appointed to conduct the execution of the business, that Your Excellency will not be surprised that my Ambition and the desire I have of becoming a usefull citizen should lead me to wish a share in the undertaking.

No nation perhaps had ever before the opportunity offerd them of deliberately deciding on the spot where their Capital city should be fixed—or of combining every necessary consideration in the choice of situation.[10]

In fact many past capitals had been built from scratch. Most recently, Peter the Great had built Saint Petersburg at the swampy estuary of the Neva River. What was new was the republican political system, the penniless condition of the treasury, and the sparse population of the nation desiring to build such a grandiose capital.[11]

Still, L'Enfant rightly regarded the project as an unprecedented task. Could he use his repository of architectural ideas derived from a monarchic government to build a capital for a democracy? L'Enfant was clearly aware of the problem, even as he wrote to Jefferson on April 4, 1791, asking for plans of great European cities the secretary of state might have in his possession. As if to forestall Jefferson's concern, he added that he would "reprobate the Idea of Imitating." He would rather "delineate on a new and original way the plan the contrivance of which the President has left to me without any restriction soever."[12]

Jefferson responded a week later, sending plans for twelve Europeans cities that he had collected while minister to France. Although Jefferson was worried that L'Enfant was planning an imperial capital, he took the risk of advising for its most important building "the adoption of some one of the models of antiquity which have had the approbation of thousands of years."[13] Thus with L'Enfant's vision and Jefferson's preference coinciding, the revolutionary republican government was to have a capital whose architectural treatment resembled those of the monarchic governments of Europe yet expressed the new political system. "It was my wish," L'Enfant wrote to Washington, "to delineate a plan wholly new and which combined on a grand scale will require more than ordinary exertions but not more than is within your power to procure." With these words he called upon the president to "pursue with dignity an undertaking of a magnitude so worthy of the concern of a grand empire."[14]

Why did the new republic adopt the architecture and planning tradition so long connected with monarchy? However that question is answered, it was a decision that has always brought the capital its share of critics.

Mumford, in his famous *City in History*, asserts that L'Enfant brought forth
in the new capital the same forms that "architects and servants of despotism
had originally conceived," a "static image that had been dictated by cen-
tralized coercion and control." In the usual baroque way, every other urban
function in the plan of Washington, wrote Mumford, was sacrificed to
"space, positional magnificence, and movement."[15] More recent critics have
taken up the same theme. Consider L'Enfant's grand avenues, the largest
160 feet wide. The architect had devoted more acreage to them than to all
the land remaining for public buildings and private residences together!
What could be the purpose of such extravagance, asked a later critic, other
than to provide courses for the fast-moving carriages of the aristocracy, the
display of "the daily parade of the powerful," while the common herd stood
by gaping from the sidewalks. Another more ominous rationale suggested
for such gigantic baroque thoroughfares was to provide avenues for displays
of military equipment and columns of marching men.[16]

Both L'Enfant and Jefferson would have been horrified by such interpretations. Although he imported much of the vocabulary of monarchic
architecture and planning, L'Enfant believed he could reconfigure it to
clearly express the new political system. For Jefferson, the important thing
was to adopt styles with classical precedents, and "classical" meant the
purity of Greek and Roman forms, not the more elaborate elegance of the
baroque period or even the Georgian style then popular in England. Jefferson thought the Greek and Roman architecture was a natural, simple,
and perfect expression of the inner nature of things, the opposite of the
merely decorative and therefore unnatural additions of subsequent architecture.[17] They were the perfect examples of cultural simplicity and expressions of the plain virtues that should characterize Americans and their
republican government. The new public buildings "would be lectures on
moral philosophy."[18]

Although L'Enfant's plan recalls the heroic landscapes of kings and emperors, "the salient lessons of mathematics, triumphal architecture, and
green avenues were absorbed by the city's designer, Pierre L'Enfant, and
transplanted to the frontiers of democracy."[19] That transposition was the
real magic of L'Enfant.

One may still ask why Washington and Jefferson went along with
L'Enfant's grandiose plan to lay out such a vast city from the beginning.
Why not begin modestly with the essential buildings required by the executive, legislative, and judicial functions and let the city grow naturally
around them? Would this not be far more expressive of the nature of the
new republic than the pretentious prospects and vast spaces of the L'Enfant

design, which would require about a hundred years to finally "fill out"? Jefferson's own sketch indicates just such a modest plan, but he offered his design tentatively and quickly abandoned it when it was clear that Washington favored L'Enfant's grander scheme.

The reason for Washington's acceptance of the L'Enfant plan reveals much about the ideals of the Founding Fathers. While they espoused the rhetoric of republican virtue and simplicity, they envisioned at the same time a magnificent future for the new government. They knew the power of ideas and believed that the United States would become a model destined to influence nations all over the world. They were firmly convinced that the new nation, from its first plantations, had been under the hand of Divine Providence. Its "mission," to bring the blessings of liberty to every land, was a politicized version of the Christian missionary project, carrying some of the same religious intensity and dedication. Without this faith the design for a vast capital would have been foolish and pretentious. The audacious actions of Washington, L'Enfant, and Jefferson in planning the capital made "the rather presumptuous claim, which over the long stretch of time miraculously turned out to be nearly true, that this pseudometropolis was the epicenter of a political earthquake destined to topple all monarchs and despots on the planet."[20] That is what their plans were all about.

Though the population of the new nation was small, all the Founders believed in this mission. Thomas Paine had written in *Common Sense,* "The cause of America is, in a great measure, the cause of all mankind." Benjamin Franklin wrote from Paris in 1777, " 'Tis a common observation here that our cause is *the cause of all mankind; and that we are fighting for their liberty in defending our own.*"[21] "The world has its eye on America. . . . The influence of our example has penetrated the gloomy regions of despotism," said Hamilton.[22] Madison said, "we are teaching the world the great truth that governments do better without Kings & Nobles than with them. . . ." [Ours is the] "government for which philosophy has been searching, and humanity been fighting, from the most remote ages."[23] The culminating and validating experience of this belief was the Revolution, which one historian says "was *in itself* a religious experience," a revelation of the Divine Will manifested and received, "which provided the fundamental basis for American civil religion as we know it."[24] Historian Joseph Ellis describes Jefferson looking back to this event as "something magical and spiritual." What had happened at that founding moment was "a kind of primal encounter with political purity that all the original participants experienced as a collective epiphany."[25]

Just as he was completing his second term and preparing to leave

Washington for Monticello, Jefferson wrote a circular letter "to the Citizens of Washington," relating this vision to the development of the capital:

> I see the true character of the national metropolis. The station we occupy among the nations of the earth is honorable, but awful. Trusted with the destinies of this solitary republic of the world, the only monument of human rights, and the sole repository of the sacred fire of freedom and self-government, from hence, it is to be lighted up in other regions of the earth, if other regions of the earth ever become susceptible of its genial influence. All mankind ought, then, with us, to rejoice in its prosperous, and sympathize in its adverse fortunes, as involving everything dear to man. . . . I shall ever feel a high interest in the prosperity of the city, and an affectionate attachment to its inhabitants.[26]

It is difficult to summarize ideals and motivation in a complex endeavor like the creation of the national capital, but they may be seen in microcosm in the process of creating an appropriate "Great Seal" for the United States, a kind of compendium of national mythology writ small. Congress considered the task so important that in 1776 it appointed its most prominent thinkers, Franklin, Jefferson, and Adams, to "bring in a device for a seal for the United States of America" for their approval. The process was not easy. Three committees and six years later Congress was still not satisfied with the results.[27] The history of this effort provides important insights into the central conceptions of the founders and their understanding of the American experiment.

While Adams suggested a rendition of "The Judgment of Hercules," which emphasized virtuous and honorable endeavor, Franklin suggested a depiction of Moses calling the Red Sea to overwhelm pharaoh and his armies. He added the motto "Rebellion to Tyrants Is Obedience to God." Jefferson liked this so well that he too suggested it for the obverse, or front, of the seal, while adding two mythical Anglo-Saxon heroes, Hengist and Horsa, for the reverse side. Jefferson held to a Romantic notion that early Saxons were governed by a simple form of democracy until they were conquered by the monarchist Normans. The episode at the Red Sea reaffirmed two essential points: the legitimacy of the revolution and the validity of the fathers' claim that God favored their endeavor. Following the Founders' suggestions, Pierre Eugene du Sumitière, the first committee's technician and artistic adviser, developed a shield design that emphasized two kinds of unity: that of six different northern European peoples who came as colonists and that of the thirteen states they founded. He incorporated the motto *E pluribus unum*, "Out of many, one."

Congress tabled the first proposed design. It appointed two later committees that eliminated some of its elements and added new ones. But the idea of Divine Providence guiding the new government was retained. The third committee added the phrase *deo favente* (with God's favor) on the reverse side, which now showed a Masonic thirteen-stepped pyramid surmounted by the all-seeing eye of the Architect of the Universe.[28] Congress finally gave the responsibility for designing the seal to its secretary, Charles Thompson. He added the symbol of the eagle, its talons clutching the olive branch of peace and the arrows of war, as the prominent image on the obverse, while maintaining the Masonic pyramid and all-seeing eye on the reverse. This was the design approved by Congress on June 20, 1782.

Thompson's report included his explanations of the symbols. He first described the obverse side, with the eagle and escutcheon, as indicating the unity of the thirteen states, the powers of war and peace, and sovereignty indicated by the constellation of thirteen stars. For the reverse side, "The pyramid signifies Strength and Duration: The Eye over it & the Motto allude to the many signal interpositions of providence in favour of the American cause. The date underneath is that of the Declaration of Independence and the words under it signify the beginning of the New American Aera, which commences from that date."[29] His final sentence refers to the fact that he had removed *deo favente* and added two other mottoes in its place, *annuit coeptis* ("He [God] approved their undertakings") and *novus ordo seclorum* ("a new world order," or "a new age").[30] The Latin word *seculum* refers to both a "world" and an "age" in space and time, although the temporal dimension is primary. Applying this thought to the plan of Washington, the city and the Capitol were designed unequivocally to be placed at the center of a new world and to signal a crucial turning point in human history. According to historian Perry Miller, American colonists believed that "God governed the universe not only in space but also in time, and as there was intelligent purpose in each enactment, so all events were connected in a long-range program which men call history."[31]

The later history of the Great Seal reaffirms the meaning of its designs and mottoes. President William McKinley delivered an address on the Great Seal on October 9, 1899. The only president to speak on the topic, he focused his remarks on the meaning of the reverse side and expressed his faith that Providence was still guiding the United States as it had from the beginning. This belief, reaffirmed by nearly every president, is a central tenet of American civil religion. McKinley explained the symbol in words similar to those of Charles Thompson:

On the reverse side of the Great Seal of the United States . . . is the pyramid,
signifying strength and duration. The eye over it and the motto allude to the
many signal interpositions of Providence in favor of the American cause. The
date underneath, 1776, is that of the Declaration of Independence, and the
words under it signify the beginning of a new American era which commences
from that date.[32]

Since the 1930s, more Americans have seen the Great Seal on the back
of the dollar bill than anywhere else. In 1935, according to Vice President
Henry Wallace, it was he who suggested to President Franklin Roosevelt
that the Great Seal be put on the obverse and reverse sides of a coin. The
president, as a thirty-second-degree Mason, was struck with the representation of the "all-seeing eye" on the reverse side. He was further "impressed
with the idea that the foundation for the new order of the ages had been
laid in 1776 but that it would be completed only under the eye of the Great
Architect." Roosevelt then suggested that the Seal be put on the dollar bill
rather than on a coin.[33]

The L'Enfant plan for the capital was accepted, then, because Washington
and Jefferson found it an appropriate physical expression of America's grand
destiny. Jefferson did not blush to call the planned Capitol "Athenian" in
taste but embellished for a nation "looking far beyond the range of Athenian
destinies."[34] Adopting biblical patterns of thought, perhaps unconsciously,
the Founders saw their revolution as a decisive event in human history,
initiating a kind of "millennium." The past could be interpreted as a prologue to the present and future of America, a series of events that "in some
manner mark the world's progress toward its present condition of liberty."[35]
This conviction became stronger as the United States grew in power over
the nineteenth century. McKinley expressed it in that same speech on the
Great Seal:

It is impossible to trace our history since [1776] without feeling that the Providence which was with us in the beginning has continued to the nation his
gracious interposition. . . .
    May we not feel assured, may we not feel certain tonight that, if we do
our duty, the Providence which favored the undertakings of the fathers, and
every step of our progress since, will continue his watchful care and guidance
over us, and that "the hand that led us to our present place will not relax his
grasp till we have reached the glorious goal he has fixed for us in the achievement of his end?"[36]

John Wilson explained this sort of rhetoric as emerging from the Hebraic
sense of historical destiny allied with the Christian image of the millennium.

The yoking of these two religious perspectives has provided the basic form of identity for the American community.[37] The United States was a new Israel leading the world toward a messianic destiny. Although they may not have recognized its Hebraic character, the Founding Fathers' Enlightenment thought shared the same sense of mission.

The "sacred fire of freedom" had to be preserved in the city at the center of the nation if it was later to be "lighted up in other regions of the earth." Jefferson's fire image suggests something like an Olympic torch, to be carried everywhere. L'Enfant had this global vision from the beginning. He designed Washington to be not just a national center but a great capital that would enlighten the world. He created a prospect for the Capitol that looked toward the Virginia hills and the distant West. The president's house looked down the Potomac, toward the Chesapeake Bay and the sea, embracing the world beyond. The capital would be the center of both space and time, the engine for exporting freedom and democracy.

An anonymous writer, who published his views in the *Gazette of the United States* in 1795, clearly grasped the central symbolism of the city, which he said would be a "temple erected to liberty." L'Enfant, he said, had fixed the Capitol as

> the center of the city, as the city is the center of the American Empire, and he rendered the edifice accessible by more than twenty streets which terminate at this point. Each street is also an emblem of the rays of light which, issuing from the Capitol, are directed toward every part of America . . . . Each street is also an emblem of the facility with which the Capitol may be approached, in every respect and at all times, by every individual who shall live under the protection of the Union.[38]

The centrality of Washington in space and time should not be taken in a literal sense. It is a mythic center. Edward Shils described the intimate connection between individual leadership and "active centers of social order" where such leaders exercise their dominion. These centers "have nothing to do with geometry and little with geography" but are places of serious acts, points where a society's leading ideas come together with its leading institutions to create an arena in which the events that most vitally affect its members' lives take place. There the power or "charisma" of the ruler becomes evident, a sign "not of popular appeal or inventive craziness, but of being near the heart of things."[39] One can hardly imagine a better description of the function of Washington as the center and physical expression of American ideals.

L'Enfant's intuitive grasp of the capital's symbolism as "the heart of things" had been echoed in more practical calls for centrality. Delegates from the southern states argued that the future development of the new nation would move to the south and west and that the location of the future capital should be moved in that direction. Northern delegates pointed to the possible admission of Canada to the Union and argued for a northerly site. The final decision on the capital's location tilted toward southern desires, but soon came to be rationalized as central to the entire nation.

James Madison insisted on the centrality of the capital for practical reasons. Just as there is a natural limit for a democracy—"that distance from the central point which will just permit the most remote citizens to assemble as often as their public functions demand"—there was also a limit for a republic—"that distance from the centre which will barely allow the representatives to meet as often as may be necessary for the administration of public affairs." Then he proceeded to exactly measure the distances between the U.S. boundaries set by the peace treaty with Great Britain, concluding that no boundary was so far away as to render an effective republic impossible.[40] By a stroke of luck (or the dispensation of Providence, according to the more religiously inclined), the Potomac site chosen was exactly at the midpoint between the Saint Croix River, which formed the northern boundary of the United States at that time, and the Saint Mary's River, which formed its southern boundary. And if George Washington was the mythic founder of the new nation, that was added reason for the new capital to be located near his home at Mount Vernon.

In 1809, William Lambert proposed to the House of Representatives that a prime meridian be established "through the dome of the Capitol in Washington" to replace that of Greenwich, "since the calculation of longitude from the meridian of a foreign nation . . . implied a 'degrading' 'dependence,' and was 'a shackle of colonial dependence.' "[41] The meridian issue had been important enough for Andrew Ellicott, the surveyor of Washington, to write to Jefferson: "I have taken the liberty of sending you an almanac for the year 1993, which I calculated . . . . The Astronomical part is adapted to the meridian, and latitude of the City of Washington."[42] Lambert's proposal received support from some in Congress, from some cartographers, and from James Monroe, who would become president seven years later. Monroe said that the establishment of a meridian had become "an appendage, if not an attribute of sovereignty."

Lambert's proposal was opposed by Herbert Vaughan, a merchant, politician, and Enlightenment thinker, who wanted a *universal* meridian rather than an *American* prime meridian. Grounded in Enlightenment conceptions, Vaughan argued that if we praise the human wisdom that has discovered the laws of nature (e.g., Newton) "still more emotion ought we feel toward that power by which they were both invented and executed." Thus correct mapping was a religious act discerning and acknowledging God's plan and design. Vaughan's "natural meridian" was to pass through the Canary Islands, thus dividing the world into two hemispheres, the Old World with its three continents and the New World with its two. Using a different meridian plan, he, like Lambert, could highlight the New World as supplanter of the Old, the new model for humankind generally. And though opposed to making it the prime meridian, he too believed that Washington should be in the geographic center of the United States.[43]

There are so many symbols of centrality in Washington that Gutheim calls it a "multicentered city."[44] Besides the Washington Monument, which is now the geometric center of the ceremonial core, there is the "Zero Milestone" at the north end of the Ellipse, from which road distances in the United States are measured. There is also the "Jefferson Pier," which can still be seen just northwest of the Washington Monument. It marks the spot where the monument should have been, where a perpendicular line from the center of the White House drawn south intersected a line drawn due west from the center of the U.S. Capitol. There was a legend among some older inhabitants of the city that President and Mrs. Jefferson were present when the foundation of the pier was being laid and that Mrs. Jefferson gave her thimble to be placed under the foundation. (But Martha Jefferson died in 1782, and the pier was not built until 1804.) Later it was discovered that this pier had been used as a benchmark from which several old surveys of land on the Potomac were made. This was the location L'Enfant planned for the equestrian statue to honor George Washington, and it might have been the site for the Washington Monument had soil conditions not made a solid foundation there questionable. It became more important a century later at the hands of the McMillan Commission. Instead of being one of three focal points (with the president's house and house of Congress) in the core of Washington, it became the center of a new grand design by Charles McKim, Daniel Burnham, and Frederick Law Olmsted Jr. Senator George F. Hoar of Massachusetts, speaking at the centennial of Washington as capital in 1900 called the Washington Monument "a prime meridian," not a geographic one like Greenwich, but "the prime meridian of pure, exalted, human character" will be marked forever by the obelisk.[45] Although the Washington Monument was placed off actual center, the pier marking the intersection may still be seen a short distance from its huge marmoreal neighbor.[46] Only recently, a century later, with the 1996 report of the National Capital Planning Commission, has there been an attempt to restore

L'Enfant's intention to have the Capitol as the center of the Washington plan.[47]

While L'Enfant was planning his city, Major Andrew Ellicott and African American mathematician Benjamin Banneker were surveying the area and laying out the perfect square that would form the District of Columbia. Conceptually, it was a simple process. Banneker did the astronomical calculations by tracing a meridian through Jones Point near Alexandria, which would mark the southern terminus of the square. They then laid off an angle of forty-five degrees to the northwest, which continued exactly ten miles to the western terminus in Virginia, and completed the other three sides of the square in the same fashion (see Figure 7). Engraved milestones were erected to mark each mile along the perimeter, most of which still exist.[48] The result was two somewhat conflicting diagrams for the city, and two potential meridians. The center of the Ellicott/Banneker square was a little to the southwest of the president's house, while L'Enfant chose Jenkins Hill, the most prominent elevation, as the conceptual center of his design, the site of the Capitol.[49]

The implementation of L'Enfant's original design hit an immediate snag for lack of funds. Virginia and Maryland ceded land and promised, respectively, $120,000 and $72,000, but a far greater sum would be needed to begin to realize the grand plan. Washington apparently thought that if he asked Congress to provide the money it might reverse its decision and move the capital elsewhere. Although L'Enfant opposed the method, Washington decided to ask the landholders to donate half their lots to the government and keep the other half for themselves, with the tantalizing promise of an immense profit as their land appreciated in value. The lots ceded to the government would then be sold to bidders, and the funds collected would finance the construction of the capital and its public buildings. The president's decision put the future of the new capital into the questionable hands of private land speculators. Benjamin Henry Latrobe, architect of the Capitol from 1803 to 1817, later complained that the landowners opposed "every project which appears more advantageous to his neighbor than to himself. Speculators, of all degrees of honesty and of desperation, made a game of hazard of the scheme."[50]

There followed a ten-year period of lotteries, stock jobbing, sales to individuals and consortia of buyers, and other schemes that failed to raise sufficient money for the task. The speculators usually borrowed money, often using land purchased elsewhere as collateral. These holdings were also mortgaged. The speculators were frequently unable to meet either their financial commitments or their promises to build homes on the lots they had

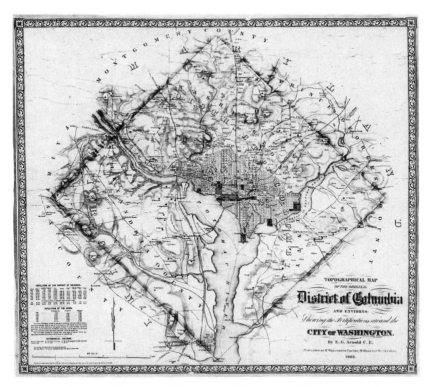

FIGURE 7 Topographical map of the District of Columbia, 1862. U.S. Commission of Fine Arts.

purchased. By the end of the decade, all the major speculators—John Nicholson, Robert Morris, James Greenleaf, and Thomas Law—were in debtors' prison, and the land could not be sold because of all their encumbrances.[51] As the time for moving the federal government to Washington drew near, John Adams's son Thomas visited the city in May 1799. He was "bowed and scraped to, & feasted & flattered," but described the city to his parents as follows:

> The affairs of that city have been unfortunately managed; the title to a considerable portion of the soil is liable to dispute; private speculation has so interwoven itself with every thing relating to the concerns of the city, that no one, who does not court difficulty and embarrassment will venture to purchase there, and in my opinion a reformation must take place in the plan and entire scheme, or nothing honorable, useful, or decorous will ever result from it.[52]

By 1800 such a reformation had been made. The federal government had committed itself to appropriating money to build the city and from that time on "assumed the full cost of the development of the capital."[53]

But congressional appropriations were small, barely enough to continue work on the two main buildings, the Capitol and the president's house. These structures stood nearly a mile apart, with little in between but swamp, wasteland, muddy paths, and a few houses. The agonizingly slow development of Washington led visitors, foreign and domestic, to ridicule the city unmercifully, as Charles Dickens did, calling it the "city of magnificent intentions." One English visitor wrote sarcastically in 1803: "The first notice you have of this embryo London (or to be more in tone with the American modesty this embryo Rome) is a small stone between two stumps of trees upon which is inscribed 'The boundary of the City.' This is proper enough for you have got about two miles to go before you fall in with a single inhabitant to tell you so."[54] In 1816, Henry Cogswell Knight wrote of a few straggling flocks of sheep, "small scraggy animals," grazing around the Capitol. He compared the unfinished city to "a rough chariot wheel, horizontal on the ground, with nothing but the nave, and three or four spokes, yet apparent."[55]

Robert Mills's Treasury building just east of the White House, begun in 1836, was still not completed in 1867. The Washington Monument, begun in 1848, was only finished some forty years later. In the winter of 1861–62 Anthony Trollope was still calling the city "a ragged, unfinished collection of unbuilt broad streets, as to the completion of which there can now, I imagine, be but little hope." Even after the Civil War there was still sentiment to move the capital somewhere to the west, to Chicago, Cincinnati, or St. Louis.[56] When Washington was proposed as the site of the World's Fair in 1871, one long-suffering senator objected, "Let us have a city before we invite anybody to see it."[57]

At last, in the late nineteenth century, the city began to "fill out." With the McMillan plan of 1902, the pretensions of the capital to be a world center finally began to be credible. To aid the members of the McMillan Commission in their plans to aggrandize the city, there existed the immense and impressive Capitol, which stood as the center of Washington and as a compendium of its symbolism. Major L'Enfant had located it at the center of the four quadrants of the city. The numbered (north-south) and lettered (east-west) streets of Washington begin at the Capitol, extending in the four directions to form the urban gridwork. The diagonal streets, named for the fifteen earliest states (Vermont and Kentucky had joined the union by the time L'Enfant was planning the capital) lie in relation to the Capitol much as the actual states lie in relation to the District of Columbia. The streets named for the New England states are generally to the north, the mid-Atlantic states in the center, and the southern states generally in the southern sector of the city plan, thus creating a microcosm of the nation. Just as Washington was situated at the center of the states, so the Capitol occupied the same position in relation to the rest of the city (see Figure 8).[58] Even the fastidious Henry James acknowledged the impressiveness of the building: "I had found myself from the first adoring the Capitol . . . . The ark of the American covenant may strike one . . . as a compendium of all the national standards, weights and measures and emblems of greatness and glory and indeed as a builded record of half the collective vibrations of a people."[59]

The Capitol is exactly oriented to the four cardinal directions. It faces east, according to the Masonic traditions of Solomon's Temple, signifying to the monarchs and people of Europe the dawning of "a new order of the ages."[60] From the earliest version of the building to the current one, the rotunda was meant to visually suggest the ideal unity sought by the new nation, the place where the two houses of Congress are united, where the ordinary people can join with their representatives, where the three branches of government come together on ceremonial occasions. Standing in the rotunda the visitor may have the feeling of being in a cosmic center, with four doors opening to the cardinal directions on the horizontal plane and the vertical axis connecting the "three worlds" (see Figure 9). Standing on the earth, one looks up at Constantino Brumidi's *Apotheosis of Washington*, showing the Founder raised to the status of a heavenly being in the world above. Below, where there were once plans to bury Washington, lies the crypt. It is marked by a compass rose. As Nathaniel Hawthorne said, "It is natural to suppose that the center and heart of America is the Capitol."[61]

Visually, the Capitol commands a prospect of all the important buildings of the city. Ignoring what would be the center of Ellicott's square, L'Enfant wrote that he could discover no more advantageous site for erecting the "Federal House" than the western end of Jenkins Hill, which "stands ready as a pedestal waiting for a monument."[62] From this dominant location he created a grand avenue leading to the president's house and a vista looking directly west toward what would later become the Mall and southwest down Maryland Avenue. From the west terrace of the Capitol today, the visual dominance of the Capitol is unmistakable.

L'Enfant's plan for the city made use of two organizational devices, both originating from the center point of the Capitol. One was the common orthogonal grid of north-south and east-west streets that has been characteristic of planned cities since urbanism first appeared in ancient Mesopotamia.

THE CITY OF WASHINGTON.

BIRD'S-EYE VIEW FROM THE POTOMAC, LOOKING NORTH.

FIGURE 8 Bird's-eye view of Washington, D.C., Nathaniel Currier and James Merritt Ives, 1892. Courtesy of the Library of Congress.

FIGURE 9 Constantino Brumidi, *Apotheosis of Washington*, U.S. Capitol Rotunda dome. Architect of the Capitol.

This organizing principle is a human imposition upon the landscape that dominates whatever natural forms and features may stand in its way. The other was a system of diagonal or radial streets, which L'Enfant meant to use to celebrate the most important buildings and provide visual and transportation links between them. This system of radials was not rigidly imposed; it was dictated by the features and elevations of the existing landscape: "Having determined some principal points to which I wished to make the others subordinate, I made the distribution regular with every street at right angles, North and South, east and west, and afterward opened some different directions, as avenues to and from every principal place."[63] The squares thus created by the intersection of gridwork and radial streets are "all proportional in magnitude to the number of avenues leading to them."[64]

As the anonymous observer quoted above saw clearly, the diagonal streets are like rays of light, the more important the site, the more streets radiate out from it. L'Enfant's plan had twenty streets radiating from the Capitol, fifteen from the president's house.

Fifteen of the squares were dedicated to the states, another of the many indications that at this early point of political development the unity of the states was an overriding concern to the creators of the new government. The states were to develop the squares to honor revolutionary events and heroes particular to their own histories. Other squares were to be occupied by major buildings and monuments—the national church, the president's house, the judiciary, and most important, the Federal or Congress House.

It has to be said that Thomas Jefferson's quick sketch for the federal city lacked the central symbolism. L'Enfant's plan harmonized better with the political system of the new government by giving clear precedence to the Congress House, while Jefferson's showed the "Capitol," as he called it, occupying a square equal in size and balancing the square designated for the president's house, the two connected by a road and public walks. L'Enfant said of the president's house: "The spot I assigned [for the presidential palace] I chose somewhat more in the wood, and off the creek."[65] The two men seemed to have corrected each other. Later when Jefferson was shown L'Enfant's plan, he crossed out "presidential palace" and wrote in pencil "president's house."

Jefferson chose republican Rome as the model for the American experiment in democracy. Besides being a political model, Rome's urban plan and architecture, with their strong emphasis on centrality, became models for the new capital. Tiber replaced Goose Creek as the name of the stream that passed by, and the term "Capitol" was soon used to designate the building where Congress would meet.[66] Rome's greatest national temple, dedicated to Jupiter Maximus, was located on the highest of the city's seven hills, the Capitoline. Jefferson wanted to express republican symbolism but at the same time capture the grandeur of Rome as the center of the classical world. Some decades later, Senator Charles Sumner recalled this imagery as he described how the Capitol's situation "may remind you of the Capitol in Rome, with the Alban and Sabine hills in sight, and with the Tiber at its feet. But the situation is grander than that of the Roman Capitol."[67]

The colonies had called the meeting places of their representatives "state-houses." But in 1699, when the House of Burgesses transferred the capital to Williamsburg from Jamestown, it decreed that "for ever hereafter [the building will] be caled and knowne by the name of *Capitoll*." This was the first time the term "Capitol" was used to designate the main government building, and the name and its symbolism took hold. On the earliest manuscript map of Washington, Jefferson replaced L'Enfant's designation "Congress House" with "Capitol."

The symbolic importance of the Capitol was acknowledged from the beginning, its meaning conveyed by the same religious complex of centering symbols used in the capital as a whole. Still, between the initial plans and the eventual realization of them stood many decades of painfully slow development. Both capital and Capitol should be considered "[not] a creation but a growth . . . . The evolution of both city and building was accomplished through long and trying years."[68] Henry Adams later described the process as follows: "Congress doled out funds for this national object with so sparing a hand, that their Capitol threatened to crumble in pieces and crush Senate and House under the ruins, long before the building was complete."[69] Yet the symbolic meaning survived. As Capitol historian Pamela Scott points out, "Washington and Jefferson's idea that the Capitol should convey America's new political, social, and cultural order was so strong that it survived continual revisions and major additions to the design they had sanctioned in 1793." The earliest design, separate wings joined by a domed rotunda, represented the ideas of national union, the bicameral legislature, and accessibility to all citizens.[70] All of these symbolic characteristics are still visible in the much-enhanced and enlarged building of today.

Secretary of State Jefferson suggested a competition for the best design for the Capitol, and Washington approved of the plan. They offered the winner a lot in the new city and five hundred dollars or a medal of the same value. Some fourteen entries were received, but only one of the applicants, Stephen Hallet, was a professionally trained architect. Benjamin Latrobe, an architect not in the United States when the competition was held, judged that no self-respecting architect would enter a competition "with such motley companions," and George Hadfield, an English-trained architect judged the entries a "pile of trash."[71] In the end the prize went to an amateur, William Thornton, but because of Thornton's inexperience Hallet had to be hired as the superintending architect.

As befits a structure of great symbolic significance, the laying of the cornerstone was planned as an elaborate Masonic ritual. Special ceremonies at the initiation of grand building projects like temples and palaces have been recorded since ancient times, including such cruel practices as killing and burying human beings under the foundation. All the more necessary here, it was thought, that there be a ritual recognition of the welcoming of a new age, a turning point in human history. Architectural metaphors abounded, comparing the building of a national character to the formation of a new and revolutionary government. Washington talked of the infinite care and attention that must be given to forming a new government: "if the foundation is badly laid, the superstructure must be bad."[72]

In the effort to devise a grand rite with deep religious resonance in a nation without an established church, the Masonic tradition of holding a ceremony to lay the first cornerstone seemed an obvious choice. The implements used in the early rites, such as Washington's trowel and gavel, became hallowed objects in later ceremonies enhancing their sacred character and the awe surrounding them. (A similar process of historical enrichment may be seen in the use of George Washington's Bible in subsequent presidential inaugurations.) Len Travers notes that this first cornerstone ritual helped to establish the Freemasons as a kind of republican priesthood, who alone possessed the secret knowledge and spiritual authority for endowing architectural rituals with patriotic significance.[73] Similar rites were planned for each of the three later cornerstone ceremonies at the Capitol (in 1818, 1851, and 1959). They were used at the Washington Monument in 1848 and at the beginning of construction for many other important buildings in Washington, and the practice spread throughout the new nation. Just a month after the Capitol ceremony, similar rites were devised for the cornerstone laying at the University of North Carolina, and less than two years later Masonic lodge members Paul Revere and Governor Samuel Adams set the cornerstone of the Massachusetts State House with similar rites.[74] The Masons' priestly role lasted until the 1830s, when an anti-Masonic party formed to attack their privileges, secrecy, and elitism.

The later history of the Capitol is similar to that of the city as a whole, with a large gap between lofty intentions and the stark realities of a nation that was weak both militarily and financially. Hallet was forced to resign in 1794, and his replacement, English architect George Hadfield, lasted only three more years. Beginning to work with Jefferson in 1803, Latrobe was given the task of repairing and completing the flawed wings of the Capitol as planned by Thornton and Hallet.[75] He had to gut the interior of the Senate wing to stabilize its foundations. The outspoken Latrobe had a running battle with Thornton, who continued to take a proprietary interest in the Capitol. Then the war of 1812 saw a British army burn Washington's few monumental buildings: the president's house, the executive offices, the Capitol. "In the north wing," reported Latrobe, "the beautiful doric columns which surround the Supreme Court room, have shared the fate of the Corinthian columns of the Hall of Representatives, and in the Senate Chamber, the marble polished columns of fourteen feet shaft, in one block, are burnt to lime, and have fallen down. All but the vault is destroyed. They stand a most magnificent ruin."[76] The buildings were saved from total destruction only by a heavy thunderstorm that doused the fire.

If some patriots found the rain providential, Latrobe later had reason to regret it, feeling that the buildings would have been better if rebuilt entirely. He was called back to oversee the reconstruction, but he resigned after a few more years' struggle, forced out in 1817, he said, by "an aggressive D.C. Commissioner, an aloof President Monroe, and a suspicious Congress."[77] The development of the Capitol was plagued by the same lack of funds, congressional incomprehension, and petty intrigues that slowed the development of the city as a whole. Latrobe described his years of frustration as chief architect:

> [I am] bidding an eternal adieu to the malice, backbiting, and slander, trickery, fraud, & hypocrisy, lofty pretensions & scanty means, boasts of patriotism & bargaining of conscience, pretense of religion & breach of her laws, starving doctors, thriving attorneys, whitewashing jail oaths, upstart haughtiness, & depressed merit, & five thousand other nuisances that constitute the very essence of this community [Washington] . . . the more you stir it, the more it stinketh. . . . And, in general, honest & right intentioned as is our cold-blooded President [Madison], you might as well stroke an armadillo with a feather by way of making the animal feel, as try to move him by words from any of his opinions or purposes.[78]

George Hadfield, looking back on the history of the building in 1820, wrote that if Washington had simply hired an eminent European architect at the beginning, "the Capitol would have been long ago completed for half the sum that has been expended on the present wreck."[79] The task of finishing the building was entrusted to Charles Bulfinch, who completed the central rotunda, giving the building its dominant symbol of national unity: two houses of Congress joined together by a domed center that "belonged to the people." It was finally completed in 1826.

Since that time, the Capitol has been twice expanded (in 1851–1860 and 1959–1964). Millard Fillmore appointed Thomas U. Walter as Capitol architect in 1851. Because the greatly expanded building would have dwarfed the Bulfinch dome, Walter designed the present great iron dome to restore the symmetry, an impressive feat of engineering at the time it was completed. Jefferson would not have liked it. Not only did it have a cupola or lantern on its top, but it was modeled on such ecclesiastical structures as Saint Peter's in Rome, Saint Isaac's in St. Petersburg, and Saint Paul's in London. Chief Engineer Montgomery Meigs chose Thomas Crawford to design a Liberty for the tholus, compromising on the Indian head piece to mollify the criticisms of Jefferson Davis (see introduction). Thus, despite aesthetic and structural problems, the Capitol gradually grew to assume the iconic status it holds today. It became so potent a symbol that "forty-seven of fifty state capitols unmistakably emulate it, not to mention innumerable county courthouses and city halls." It has now risen to the status of "a transcendent national icon," says Wilbur Zelinsky, "so that we find it in advertisements, posters, business logos, folk crafts, souvenirs, and all manner of places."[80]

Walter carefully articulated the symbolic program for the new dome. Thirty-five pillars support the dome, the number of states at the time the expansion was planned. The cupola has thirteen small pillars, the number of original colonies. The symbolism of *e pluribus unum* is as important in the Capitol as in the city as a whole. Within the building, Statuary Hall may be seen as conveying the message of the unity of the states under the federal government. Each state was encouraged to contribute statues of two native sons (or daughters) to the national pantheon of heroes. The House chamber displays the seals of all the states on its ceiling.

The essential symbolic message was spelled out by Bulfinch in 1926, though later additions expanded and reinforced it. Lincoln's devotion to the completion of the dome, despite the hardships of war, was a lasting confirmation of its meaning. But it was already clear at the time of the Capitol expansion that the building was the physical symbol of the Constitution and the union of the states. Daniel Webster, at the laying of the third cornerstone on July 4, 1851, under the cloud of sectional strife, had said in his oration:

> If, therefore, it shall be hereafter the will of God that this structure shall fall from its base, that its foundation be upturned and this deposit brought to light, BE IT KNOWN, that on this day the Union of the United States of America stands firm; that their Constitution still exists unimpaired. . . . All here assembled . . . unite in sincere and fervent prayers that this deposit, all the walls and arches, the domes and towers, the columns and entablatures, now to be erected over it may endure forever! God save the United States of America![81]

Capital and Capitol are both a compendium of symbols meant to reflect republican ideals expressive of the *novus ordo seclorum,* political unity, freedom, and democracy. The issues of centrality and new beginnings were important in both the Capitol and the city as a whole, and behind these grand ideas the conviction that the deity would providentially guide the nation toward its destiny. Biblical phrases resounded: the capital was the "city on the hill," center of "the promised land," where the "new man" could live virtuously and innocently in the new Eden (as Bronson Alcott called it). The United States began a new order that would supplant the degenerate and fallen old world (Crevecoeur had called the American the "New Man" in contrast to the "Old Man" of Europe). The trajectory of the national history was toward a millennium when the American example of liberty would renew the whole world: "There were visions of new Edens wherein men, emerging with regained innocence from baptism in infinite spaces, might begin all over again."[82] "The presumption of newness, which constituted the innocence of Americans, constituted also the core of their myth."[83]

Considering deeper layers of symbolism, we cannot ignore the resemblance of Washington and its architecture to the earliest urban centers in Mesopotamia, the Nile valley, the Indus, the Yellow River, Southeast Asia and Mesoamerica, and western Africa. These ancient sites reveal their builders' concern with the location of the city, orientation to the four cardinal directions, central monumental architecture like temples, palaces, pyramids, ziggurats, and raised altars, and processional boulevards connecting these places of power. The designs of these ensembles indicate a desire to proclaim the connection between the gods and their rulers, between the world above and the royal city on earth.[84]

Paul Wheatley, who has given such impetus to the study of royal capitals and early urban development, singles out, among other factors, cardinal orientation, axiality, and central symbolism as characteristic of these sacred ceremonial centers, all of which are clear features in the planning of Washington.[85] Although the builders of Washington had rejected the religious and political bases of these archaic governments, they built a city that is remarkably like them in its physical appearance. The "modern city," said Charles Long, is built on "the residual structures of this pattern," or is the extrapolation of one of the functions of its domestication.[86]

The ubiquity of central symbolism has been interpreted by many scholars as expressing the human longing to establish a connection between earth and heaven, to claim divine approval for their undertakings, and to secure permanence in a world so obviously marked by instability: "The city symbolized the majesty and predictability of the cosmos. The ritual center, and later the city, expanded man's horizons beyond the immediate, the local, and the fleeting to the stabilities of the universe."[87] Urban monumentality was the effort, conscious and unconscious, to participate in the permanence of the order of the universe, creating the illusion, the great *maya* that all such cities project, that their power and order is eternal.

The notion that a city and its architecture could concretely express abstract ideas was an Enlightenment concept that Jefferson wholeheartedly endorsed. He clearly felt that the structure of architecture reflected the order of the cosmos, "that the mathematical ratios of Palladio were as much a part of nature's order as the relations of a man's head to his torso or the relation of Venus to the sun."[88] A contemporary anthropologist has noted that there must be a "set of symbolic forms" used by any governing elite to justify their existence and order their actions. These must include "a collection of stories, ceremonies, insignia, formalities, and appurtenances that they have either inherited or, in more revolutionary situations, invented. It is these—crowns and coronations, limousines and conferences—that mark the center as center and give what goes on there its aura of being not merely important but *in some odd fashion connected with the way the world is built*."[89]

The conclusion that emerges from this line of thought is simple. The capitals and their great monuments, in their symbolic articulation, reflect the geometry of the universe, "the way the world is built." The plan of the city and the structure of its buildings reflect social, political, and even cosmic order. The rulers, because they live in an order that reflects the nature of things, have a claim, in their disposition of space, their buildings, and their ceremonies, to have touched the heart of reality. Their subjects will then be expected to conform to that reality.

Jefferson apparently never gave a thought to encouraging an original, native style of architecture. Rather, he felt the classical style was best able to express the republican ideals of the new nation. At the same time, this grand style of architecture and urban planning made an implicit claim for the new democracy. Its ideal of representative government and human freedom would create a nation every bit as magnificent as older forms of government dominated by royalty and clergy, and far surpass them in liberty, virtue, and justice. His choice of style enabled him to hold these disparate ideas together. He wrote to the directors in charge of building the Virginia capitol that they had two choices: to choose an architect who might have a thousand-to-one chance of hitting on a pleasing design or to go out and find an existing building, proven by time, and use it as a model. He chose the *square*, for Virginia, exemplified in the Maison Carrée, "the most perfect and precious remains of antiquity in existence," one that "has pleased universally for near 2000 years." For the Capitol he preferred the *circle*; the Pantheon. Square and circle represented the simplest and purest forms, evoking the perfection implicit in a new and revolutionary beginning.

There is an obvious parallel between the extravagant physical plans of

L'Enfant and the visionary political dreams of Thomas Jefferson. Jefferson was "the clear voice of America's revolutionary ideology, its purest conscience, its most brilliant expositor, its true poet."[90] Both he and L'Enfant peered into the future, one seeing more vividly a grand city, the rival of the great European capitals, the other seeing clearly a grand political system that would replace corrupt forms of government and offer other nations a model for imitation. The two men reached into the ancient past to plan a capital for the future, one that they hoped would be ageless. They chose pure classical forms: squares, circles, rectangles, arches, triangles, columns—forms that have been used in world cultures since ancient times to express perfection and stability. Sometimes the visitor to Washington can be overwhelmed by it all—the innumerable stately columns, the endless colonnades, the ubiquitous pediments, the bundles of fasces, the numerous female figures representing yet another abstract virtue—liberty, democracy, plenty, hope, justice, and so forth. But it is hard to imagine any other architectural style then available that could have expressed the ideals of the new republic so well: "The architects of Greece and Rome created only simple shapes. . . . The portico, the pediment, the dome, the square forum, and the oval arena—cube, hemisphere, cylinder, cone—each has its quiet and immediate access to the understanding, not of one people, but of all peoples." These elemental forms become "screens through which reality, beyond that revealed by the senses, is made known to us. There is an architectural Platonism which is so nearly religious that one hesitates to comment on it for fear of being ill mannered."[91]

If, as historian Norma Evenson said, the baroque axis is flexible enough to represent any political system, then L'Enfant's plan is exonerated. The nature of baroque planning is to highlight and celebrate important sites, where lines of sight intersect and avenues converge. On the ancient gridwork plan, found since the beginning of urbanism, it superimposes a pattern of diagonals. That is, it isolates and elevates significant buildings, memorials, and sites, placing them in a hierarchy. This type of plan can be used to glorify a monarchy or facilitate a despotic government like Hitler's Third Reich. But it can also be used, as it is in Washington, to highlight the U.S. Capitol and subordinate the president's house. As we shall see in the next chapter, L'Enfant's capital became a faithful reflection of the structure of American politics.

Washington and Jefferson had lost something, certainly, in not choosing a previously existing city, like New York or Philadelphia, as the national capital. It has been said that without the vibrancy of life found in an organically growing urban center where people work and play, the remote site on the Potomac could never generate a unique American culture.[92] But what the city lacked in urban liveliness it has gained in symbolic clarity. Images such as "temple," "altar," "shrine," "stage," and "theater" have been frequently used to interpret its meaning. It is a myth in stone, whose meaning is not fixed but has continually changed in the two centuries since its founding. Whether a visitor fully accepts the regnant myth or not, there is no doubt that the city makes a clear and powerful statement. As Alfred Kazin wrote, other cities represent money, energy, push. Washington alone had "a touch of the transcendent." It had, in the end, what the Founders had hoped for, and it manifested "perhaps the only thing that the wildly heterogeneous America of the late twentieth century could look up to—a *center*."[93]

On August 22, 1820, John Law—called a "rising young man of the city," and son of Thomas Law, one of the land speculators—gave the major address at the laying of the cornerstone of the new City Hall in Judiciary Square. He played to the crowd by blaming the slow progress of the capital on Congress. Their representatives, he said, acted as though "there was a magic power in the term Metropolis, which, when applied by Congress of the United States, to a houseless heath, would immediately convert it into a splendid city." He then contrasted the stinginess of Congress with the "power and resources of the Autocrat of Russia," who had built a grand Saint Petersburg on the banks of the Neva River in nine short years.[94] Law failed to mention that between thirty thousand and a hundred thousand workers had been driven to their deaths or died of disease in the process. The more leisurely pace in Washington, besides being easier on the laborers, had other advantages. It grew by a sort of benevolent, participatory form of democracy that blundered along in the construction of the city, missing some opportunities but also allowing time for correcting potential mistakes. In this way, too, the evolution of the city reflects national history—two steps forward, one step back. Certainly not perfect, but it is the way the system has always worked.

CHAPTER 2

A Balancing Act

Pennsylvania Avenue and Power

BENJAMIN RUSH once asked Thomas Jefferson to comment on great Americans he had known since 1774. Jefferson chose James Madison as "the greatest man in the world." Washington Irving, in contrast, later remarked of the fourth president: "Poor Jemmy Madison," he is "but a withered little apple-john." In fairness to the memory of Madison, it must be said that Jefferson's comment came in 1790, shortly after Madison's triumph with the Constitution and Bill of Rights. Irving saw him many years later, in a social gathering dominated by the scintillating Dolly Madison, who would have made most men seem like poor little "apple-johns."[1]

Madison's dominant role as a Founding Father has long been acknowledged, yet it was only in 1980 that a major piece of architecture was built in Washington to honor him. The James Madison Building of the Library of Congress was a tardy and dubious tribute to the great architect of the U.S. Constitution. It cost $130 million and was the second largest building on Capitol Hill, just after the enormous Rayburn Building. The James Madison Memorial Hall, dominated by a life-size seated statue of the fourth president, is just inside and to the left of the main entrance to the building. The rest is utilitarian space devoted to the needs of the library. Architectural critic Ada Huxtable calls this building "Brobdingnagian," a "stillborn behemoth." It was "dead on arrival," she said, completely lacking in character, no different from "any speculative office building behind a Mussolini-modern facade."[2] Another irony for the diminutive Madison, that he be celebrated by this enormous and undistinguished structure.

In many respects James Madison seemed ill-suited to the dominant role he would play in American life: Founding Father, framer of the Constitution, secretary of state, and president. He was barely 5'5" tall, often sickly, perhaps even hypochondriacal, and spoke so softly that his words were barely audible in public. He did not fight in the war and worried incessantly that travel would injure his health. When Congress met at Philadelphia he would remain there after adjournment, suffering the hot and humid summer weather rather than risk the trip home to Montpelier in Virginia. Once when he was boarding at an inn in Williamsburg someone stole his hat. He had only about a mile to walk to reach the governor's palace, but "I was kept from going to the latter for two days, by the impossibility of getting a hat of any kind." Finally, he was able to obtain a parson's-style black hat, with small crown and large brim, which he admitted was "a subject of great merriment to my friends." Thus protected, he courageously set forth.[3]

There is a wonderful irony that this physically frail man was the Founding Father most involved with determining the disposition of power within the Constitution. But after all, who better than a weakling to know that freedom requires the restraint of power? His strength was mental, his manner of thinking tough, methodical, penetrating, and comprehensive; he had what Bernard Bailyn called a "hard, quizzical, grainy quality of mind."[4] The word "grainy" suggests the quality of wood that indicates a clear direction and implies the futility of going against the grain. Although he may have hesitated to exercise his body, he made exhaustive mental preparations for his work at the Constitutional Convention. While Jefferson talked breezily of not having to search the musty documents of the past as he wrote the Declaration of Independence, Madison took on the drudging scholarly work of exploring the history of ancient and modern confederacies to learn what might or might not work as the delegates labored to frame a new Constitution. Madison may have been afraid to expose his head to the sun, but he was not afraid to argue for his ideas at the convention, even if the delegates had to strain to hear his words. When power is at stake, emotions run high and tempers flare. Madison never flinched. He walked into the convention with the Virginia Plan and fought for it. He did not get everything he wanted, but no one played a more central role in the outcome. He sought at each step an exquisite balance. "Every word of [the Constitution]," he said, "decides a question between power and liberty."[5]

"It is a melancholy reflection," Madison wrote to Jefferson, "that liberty should be equally exposed to danger whether the Government have too much or too little power."[6] Madison's task, clearly a delicate one, was the disposition of political power. It was generally accepted among the Enlightenment thinkers that the British system of government was the most successful the world had ever seen, precisely because it had learned how to distribute power: "The political thought of the eighteenth century began with one governing assumption underlying everything else . . . . the irreconcilable antinomy of liberty and power." The British were successful because of the balance of their mixed constitution of king, lords, and commons, which prevented any ultimate seizure of power (royal despotism, aristocratic oligarchy, or mob rule) and preserved the liberties of the nation.[7] Led by Madison, the framers of the Constitution adopted this principle, adapting it to their own condition.

Visitors to the James Madison Building will find inscribed on the wall a quotation from the fourth president that includes the words "the essence of government is power." Power, the subject of this chapter, is closely related to centrality, the subject of the previous one. By centering, one conquers territory and does it with the blessing of the gods. As Mircea Eliade said so often, religious centers of whatever kind become the organizing principle for all habitable space.[8] In most political systems of the past, religion had therefore always played a central role in the disposition of political power. Yet though most assertions of sovereignty had been founded on some transcendent religious principle, it would be a mistake to conclude that religion has always supported the established power. It was an opiate at times, but at other times it stimulated riots and rebellions that overthrew the established order. It may have inspired love and compassion, but it also aroused hatred. It counseled peace but just as frequently brought war (as the Founders were well aware). It may have brought strangers into unsuspected communities of caring, but it had also excommunicated heretics and rejected the "unrighteous." With a potential for good or evil influence, the Founders understood that religion was a power to be dealt with carefully. Madison and Jefferson, ever sensitive to its darker potential, sought to control it through the same principle of balance.

Since ancient times, royal and priestly power has been allied, confirming political systems thought to be reflections of the eternal order of things. Gerardus Van der Leeuw, a historian of religions, has postulated that the most primal religious experience is the confrontation with unusual power in all its guises.[9] The object of this experience is not necessarily ethical or spiritual, although it is often found in conjunction with beliefs in gods, spirits, and ghosts. Van der Leeuw wrote his "interpretation of the Universe in terms of Power" in 1933, yet it still provides a useful way to discuss the sacral dimensions of politics and a corrective to the common tendency to see sharp distinctions between sacred and secular. A contemporary writer says, in confirmation of Van der Leeuw's thesis, that religions "become the most finely tuned examples of power *structures,* patterns of force which control human lives and dictate how they are to be conducted. Make no mistake about it: religions are about power, about the power to be given you and about the power which controls you."[10]

Although the Founding Fathers were able to create a system based on clear distinctions between religious and state functions, they wanted at the same time to maintain the connection between the new political system they were founding and the will of the Divine Being upon whom it depended. They saw religion as a power necessary to the good order of society, giving the revolutionary political arrangements their validity. To ignore or cut this connection would have been unthinkable. Their problem was how to encourage the practice of religion without allowing it to oppress the people. Their solution was the same for both religious and political power: divide and conquer. By not establishing a church, they would control the dangerous potential of religion while encouraging the beneficial powers and moral impulses that arise from it. They would temper sectarian religions by balancing one church against another, believing thus that no single one would become dominant enough to oppress people's minds as they had done in Europe. The religion of the Enlightenment, "natural religion," in contrast, was the very basis of political existence. Divine Providence, in their minds, not only approved of the American experiment but willed its spread to the rest of the world.

In appealing to "natural religion" the Founders were articulating a modern revision of the commonplace insight, traceable through the course of human history, that the political power that rules nations and the cosmic power that rules the universe are intimately connected. This insight is manifested not only in ancient writings but also in the art and architecture of cultures for which no written history exists: "Virtually everywhere the generation of power in the city has been expressed in religious terms."[11] The human power of kings and emperors derived its validity from its connection with the dominion and will of the god or gods. Mumford had said that cities were born precisely in the coming together of religion and "secular" power, and without the transcendent power behind the secular, the human assumption of power would seem to be merely arbitrary.

Satisfied that they were blessed by the powers above, kings and emperors directed their architects to build cities to reflect and express this divine-human relationship, to celebrate and commemorate their connection to the ultimate source of authority. In ancient Mesopotamia, in fact, the gods announced to kings, through dreams and portents, that they wished a city and its temple to be built or rebuilt.[12] The founders of ancient cities developed vocabularies of architecture and urban design that we now take for granted because they have changed so little between then and now. Some of the most important elements in this urban lexicon were monumental palaces and temples that housed the earthly and heavenly powers; vertical structures like ziggurats, obelisks, and pyramids that physically pointed to the world above; and grand avenues and axial boulevards that articulated the connections between these major structures and made clear the nature of their relationships.

Babylon provides a good example. The Founding Fathers had read about its tower in the Bible, and Herodotus had described it as an exact square, with wall and moats, divided into two sections; in the center of each was a sacred precinct, one the royal palace and the other the temple of the god Zeus Belus.[13] Actually the shape of the city was more like an irregular rectangle, with its corners oriented to the four cardinal directions. Nearby was the city of Borsippa, itself nearly a perfect square, with corners similarly oriented and marked by gridwork streets. From the central temple compound the " 'Processional Way' led to the Borsippa Canal, which linked the city with Babylon."[14] There were three monumental centers in Babylon, the royal palace, the Etemenanki (with the ziggurat), and the Esagila (temple of Marduk), all connected by a grand processional boulevard that began at the Ishtar Gate in the north and ran directly south, linking the three compounds. The plan of the city demonstrated the structure of the cosmos. Marduk, the god of the city who was worshiped in the temple, was the basis of Babylonian political power.

When the Spaniards arrived in Central and South America, they found similar architectural orientations and forms in the Aztec, Mayan, and Incan sites: platforms, stepped pyramids, monumental buildings, and axial boulevards. Best documented is the city of Tenochtitlan, conquered by the Spanish, where archeological remains have been uncovered and eye-witness accounts were written down from the time of the conquest.[15] More recent European capitals employ a similar vocabulary in their urban planning. In Paris, Madrid, Vienna, Berlin, London, and Saint Petersburg, "grand processional axes, long, imposing facades, enormous squares, and converging diagonals provided a common design repertoire for the European capital city."[16]

The best example, however, is Beijing, the most recent Chinese capital. Its buildings and structure reflect a tradition that goes back more than three millennia and whose traditional character lasted until the early twentieth century. Extensive textual materials testify to its meaning. Parallels with Washington are intriguing, though ultimately the differences are far more significant than the similarities.[17]

As with Washington, centrality was a factor of overriding concern. Chinese tradition called the empire Zhongguo, "the central kingdom," reflecting the belief that it was the center of the lower world. The capital was also conceptually the center of the empire, even though its location changed many times over the course of Chinese history. The building of Beijing followed patterns prescribed for more than two thousand years. Its outer walls formed a square, like the District of Columbia, but it was aligned to the four cardinal directions by its sides rather than its four corners. Inside the outer walls were more restricted walled areas that protected an "imperial city" of government buildings and inside that the "Forbidden City," where the emperor and his family lived. Like Washington, Beijing had a monumental core and was laid out orthogonally, with a regular pattern of gridwork streets. There were no diagonal thoroughfares. Both cities were "horizontal" in character, with codes prohibiting buildings above a certain height. Both had large open spaces, the Mall and parks in Washington, religious altars and compounds in Beijing.

The Chinese capital was designed as an earthly reflection of a heavenly city in the region of the pole star where the deity (called "Heaven" or "Emperor Above") ruled the universe. Ancient Chinese astronomical maps named stars and constellations in the polar region for persons, buildings, and structures of a heavenly capital. As the heavenly deity ruled the celestial regions, the emperor, called the "son of heaven," was believed to rule the earth by heaven's divine authority. The Chinese called his authority to rule the "mandate of heaven." The power of the deity therefore "flowed south" from his throne in the pole star capital to the earthly capital, creating a celestial meridian. The emperor sat on a majestic throne in the Hall of Supreme Harmony in the Forbidden City, facing south, his mandated authority also "flowing south" to the human world and creating an earthly meridian. Confucius used this imagery in his well-known description of an ideal sovereign: "What action did he take? He merely placed himself gravely and reverently with his face due south; that was all."[18]

This archaic conception of the relations of divine and human power was expressed clearly in the architecture and planning of Beijing. Like other royal capitals in the ancient world, it used the architectural vocabulary mentioned above: gates and walls marking sacred terrain, huge buildings and altars where intercourse with the transcendent world took place, and a grand avenue along which the emperor and his retinue made their way in elaborate processions to the religious sites of worship. The graphic expression of power and authority was the north-south axial boulevard, which visually confirmed that ultimate power was bestowed upon the emperor by Heaven. The celestial and earthly meridians were aligned in a seamless flow. There was no balance of power, but a single monolithic continuum that reached from heaven to emperor, and from his throne to the people of the earth he ruled.

This axial way is the most obvious thoroughfare in Beijing (see Figure 10). It begins at the bell and drum towers in the north and runs from there through the central palaces and halls of audience, continuing southward through a series of nine gates until it reaches the last gate in the center of the southern wall. From there it continues on imaginatively as the extension of the dominion of heaven to the entire human world. It connects the imperial palaces with the altars and temples of worship: the Altar of Heaven, the Altar of the Spirits of Land and Grain, the Ancestral Temple, the Altar of the First Cultivator.

Two of the nine gates were most important, places of interdiction and communication. Meridian Gate (Wumen) was the ceremonial point of contact between the emperor and his officials, and Heavenly Peace Gate (Tiananmen) the symbolic place of contact between the imperial government and the people. From Tiananmen imperial edicts were promulgated in a dramatic ritual: they were lowered in the beak of a golden bird to the waiting officials below. Mao Zedong seized on the symbolic meaning of this gate, using it as the site for his major pronouncements and rallies. Chinese students also took advantage of its symbolic potential on four major occasions in the twentieth century, occupying the square in front of it to protest government policies and challenge the disposition of political power.

The power structure in traditional China was therefore conceived as a seamless whole. There was no distinction between religious and political power, or any between the power of heaven and the emperor. Yet there could occur a rift in this seamless flow of power. If the emperor somehow failed in his sacred duty to rule responsibly heaven took away his mandate. He was said to have failed before heaven and before his imperial ancestors and lost the right for himself and his descendants to govern the empire. At the end of the Ming dynasty (1368–1644 C.E.), the last emperor wrote a suicide note expressing his guilt in just such terms. A plaque marking the spot where he hanged himself may be seen today just north of the Forbidden City. Yet when the new Qing dynasty (1644–1911 C.E.) took over, the old unilinear power relationship was restored.

The axial thoroughfare defined power in the traditional Chinese capital, articulating the relationships between the major centers of combined religious and political power. When in 1989 the students occupied Tiananmen Square they used this symbolism, taking over a space that had always signified the locus of communication between rulers and subjects. When the army was finally ordered to remove them and crush the "rebellion," the tanks and troop carriers moved in along Changan Boulevard, which did not exist in traditional times but now runs perpendicular to the old axial way,

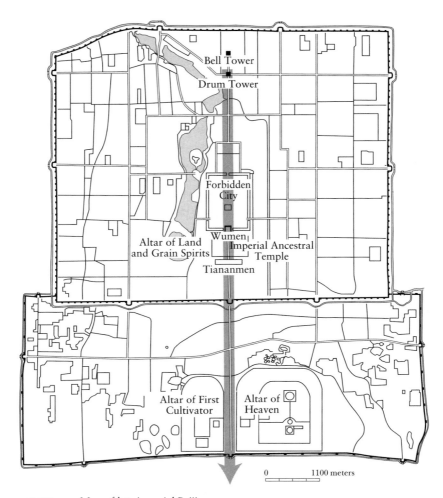

FIGURE 10 Map of late imperial Beijing.

crossing it at Tiananmen Square. The language of avenues and architecture
continues to be suggestive.

We can see clearly the same dynamic relationship of architecture and
power in a twentieth-century guise in Adolf Hitler's plans for Berlin. He,
too, strategically located all the major powers at the center of his grand
plan: his own palace, the chancellery, and a grand boulevard that linked
them with a triumphal arch and the quasi-religious hall that symbolized the
glory of the German people. Though his plans are a caricature, in their very

exaggeration they clarify the principle of axiality and its function to delineate the distributions of power.

The Führer was fascinated by the opportunity to use architecture and urban design to achieve his purposes. At first he dreamed of building a new capital but soon pronounced that capitals like Washington and Canberra, which he had never visited, were "lifeless." And so he turned his attention to a thorough rebuilding of Berlin. He was much impressed with the Arc de Triomphe and the Champs Elysées in Paris, but he wanted to surpass them in size, making his axial boulevard longer and wider, his triumphal arch higher. He spent countless hours with Albert Speer, his chief architect, discussing the shape a reorganized Berlin should take. He became so involved that Speer speculates that the future of Europe might have been entirely different if Hitler had found a wealthy patron as a young artist or architect in the 1920s. But in the end, Speer comments, for Hitler politics and architecture were inseparable.

Early in the Third Reich, Speer redesigned the *old* chancellery for the Führer, creating a quarter-mile "pilgrimage" walk for diplomats and visitors through grandiose rooms to a reception room where Hitler presided. "On the long walk from the entrance to the reception hall they'll get a taste of the power and grandeur of the German government," Hitler boasted.[19] In the redesigned Berlin, however, the *new* chancellery building was to be twice as long. Diplomats and supplicants to the Führer would have a half-mile of halls and corridors to traverse! The capital core was built along an immense axial avenue 400 feet wide, modeled on the Champs Elysées in Paris but much wider. At one end of it, Hitler wanted to build his grander Arc de Triomphe. At the other end of the avenue he had Speer design an immense domed hall, with the dome 825 feet in diameter. Had the plan been realized, this hall would have been seventeen times the size of Saint Peter's in Rome. It was here that Hitler attempted to make contact with the religious, or pseudo-religious. Speer calls the hall "a place of worship," for even he sensed that a sheer display of power was not sufficient. "Without some such essentially pseudo-religious background the expenditure for Hitler's central building would have been pointless and incomprehensible," comments Speer.[20]

If the gigantic domed hall was to evoke the mystical nationalistic feeling of the German "Volk," Hitler's plans for his own palace left no doubt where power resided in the Third Reich. His residence was to be 22 million square feet, 150 times larger than the residence of former chancellor Otto von Bismarck, almost twice as large as the immense new chancellery described above. These were the main structures to be linked by the grand axial avenue. Speer describes a lowering of morale in Germany in 1939, at which

time Hitler began looking at the immense space he was planning from another perspective. He realized that riots were a real possibility and called
for iron gates, steel doors, and bullet-proof shutters for windows along the
axial way. And as for the wide avenue itself, Hitler saw new possibilities.
He would build barracks for the army nearby, and said, "If they should
come rolling up here in their armored vehicles the full width of the street—
nobody will be able to put up any resistance."[21]

In the end, rising war costs forced Hitler to abandon his plans for Berlin's
reconstruction. His romantic megalomania in architecture stands only as an
exaggeration of traditional elements, overblown and imitative. Although not
original, Hitler had a kind of insane perspicacity, and his plans provide food
for thought about both positive and negative potentials of axiality and monumentality. He was working with the same vocabulary of archaic urban
planning, the same compendium of forms and spaces used in Washington,
China, and European capitals. As one architectural historian has pointed
out: "there was little difference between Fascist taste, Communist taste and
democratic taste in the ways which the various regimes, claimed to be so
vastly different in their social and political philosophies, actually expressed
themselves architecturally in the 1930s."[22] Or, as Ada Huxtable said, commenting on Mussolini's plans for Rome, "forms in themselves are innocent,"
but they can be used "to seduce the spirit."[23]

While the fascists and Soviets were erecting their own monumental buildings, Washington saw the construction of the massive Federal Triangle, the
National Archives, the Supreme Court, the National Gallery, and the Jefferson Memorial. All were calculated to present political ideas, glorify patriotic heroes, and inculcate prevalent national myths. Yet monumental architecture does not have to be oppressive. Daniel Patrick Moynihan, who
as assistant secretary of labor was involved with the rehabilitation of Pennsylvania Avenue in the Kennedy administration, tells of walking through a
particularly grim vista in New York City, "past the gauntlet of looming,
indifferent towers toward the sacrificial pyramid at the far end." The message of the architecture, thought Moynihan, was: "Man, in the Presence of
the State, Thou Art Nothing." In redeveloping the capital's major axis, he
observes, "This is what we wanted to prevent, and we did."[24] Whether they
succeeded or not, the viewer may judge.

Compared with the monolithic power strategies of Hitler, the intricate
calculations that created Washington seem modest indeed. The problem—
articulating power relationships—was the same, but the ideology much different and its articulation far more nuanced. In one sense, the creators of
the Constitution and the builders of Washington were engaged in the same

delicate task, defining powers and setting them in relation to each other. I will briefly summarize some of the theoretical discussions about the division of power in the new republic, then examine how the new order was incorporated in the planning of Washington.

Washington presents an axial structure far different from that in traditional China and Hitler's imagined Berlin, based not on the emphatic concentration of power but on its careful dispersal. It is therefore multi-axial. The vistas of dominion are already clear in L'Enfant's original plan, the primary one looking west from the Capitol, the secondary looking south from the president's house. They symbolize an imaginative extension of empire, democracy, and liberty to the rest of the world and correspond in their suggested universality to the single axis of Beijing. But it is Washington's third axis, today's Pennsylvania Avenue, that suggests the special articulation of power developed by the Founders of the new republic. Like the Chinese gates Wumen and Tiananmen, this avenue called attention to issues of power in the interface between the people and their "rulers." Instead of a simple hierarchical system that smoothly subordinated ministers to the emperor and people to both, the power relationships in Washington are more complicated and required more delicate articulation.

Washington developed slowly, mostly because of economic limitations. In addition to lack of funds, however, the shape of the U.S. government, though generally prescribed in the Constitution, had to be worked out in painstaking particulars. How would the executive and legislative branches relate? How would the national and state governments interact? What was the actual role of the Supreme Court? On these and many other issues the Constitution was not specific. So it was not a matter of simply grasping the power structure defined in the Constitution and reproducing it in the plan of Washington. In fact it took some decades to work out the shape of that power structure.

At the most general level, there was agreement. The Founding Fathers, like the Chinese, believed that a Divine Being was the source of order in this world and the foundation of government. As Madison said of the work of the Constitutional Convention in *Federalist 37*, "It is impossible for the man of pious reflection not to perceive in it a finger of that Almighty hand which has been so frequently and signally extended to our relief in the critical stages of the revolution."[25] Instead of channeling power through the ruler to the people, they believed that the Almighty had done the reverse, vested the power primarily in the people. The new republican form of government was not a rejection of the religious source of political power but a reinterpretation of how it operated. The president and representatives were to be chosen by, and would derive their authority from, the people. Scholars trace this radical change of mind about the source of political power not only to secularizing Enlightenment thought but also to indigenous religious events like "the Great Awakening." Before the Awakening,

> most individuals gladly yielded their judgment and conscience to the superior claims and knowledge of their "betters," the ruling elite in church and state, who derived their authority from God and as his vicegerents administered the ordinances of government for the good of the people. After the Awakening this order of things became reversed: the state and church were considered by increasing numbers of Americans to be the creatures of the people, and subject to their authority. . . . The people considered themselves better able than any elite to interpret God's will and expected their elected officials to act as *their* vicegerents under God.[26]

From this point of view, the Founding Fathers did not so much lead uneducated citizens as articulate sentiments and attitudes that were already commonly accepted.

Although the ultimate source of authority was a matter of general agreement, arguments raged in the Continental Congress and later in the Constitutional Convention over how the power derived from it should be distributed. This was the central issue between Federalists and Republicans throughout the 1790s. Unlike Hitler, who was comfortable with power, the Founding Fathers fully agreed that it was not to be trusted. (They had seen in Europe how power was abused by kings, nobles, and churchmen, and they wanted none of that in their republic.) They worried about how to keep power from being too concentrated, fearing that to the extent it coalesced in any one party liberty would be lost. Madison said in *Federalist 47*: "The accumulation of all powers, legislative, executive, and judiciary, in the same hands, whether of one, a few, or many, and whether hereditary, self-appointed, or elective, may justly be pronounced the very definition of tyranny."[27] It was a delicate balance Madison sought, as he said categorically: "Every word of [the Constitution] decides a question between power and liberty."[28] Lincoln would pose the same question seventy years later: "Must a government, of necessity, be too strong for the liberties of its own people, or too weak to maintain its own existence?"[29] The issue has remained a subject of debate throughout American history.

John Adams and James Madison thought more deeply about the issue of power than any of the other Founders. Although Adams agreed with most of Thomas Paine's ideas about democracy, he attacked Paine's *Common*

Sense for its simplistic notion of government by a single assembly, holding that only a Congress with "complexity and balance" could succeed.[30] Adams's first serious writing, in 1763, was a meditation on how government could restrain man's dark desires by creating a balance among monarchy, aristocracy, and democracy.[31] "Balance" became his "ruling dogma": "In that current of eighteenth-century English opposition thought upon which the American Revolution itself had been justified, an insistence upon balance was the central element."[32] No individual, party, or faction could be trusted unless set against another to restrain it. He made the striking pronouncement that "power must be opposed to power, force to force, strength to strength, interest to interest, as well as reason to reason, and passion to passion."[33] For Adams, this meant combating any excessive accumulation by distributing power among three branches of government: the presidency, the Senate and the House of Representatives. Even late in life he returned with frequency to this initial insight. Newly reconciled with Jefferson, he wrote in 1813 to his former antagonist with some asperity: "Checks and balances, Jefferson, however you and your Party may have ridiculed them, are our only Security, for the progress of Mind, as well as the Security of Body."[34]

For the American system, there were two primary balancing acts: first, among the three branches of government, and second, between the sovereign states and the national government. John Locke had emphasized the need for separated powers in *Two Treatises of Government*, but it was Montesquieu who first clearly stated the modern theory of the three powers: legislative, executive, and judicial.[35] His theory was embodied in the Constitution, but the powers of the third party, the judiciary, remained ambiguous until gradually expanded for the Court by Chief Justice John Marshall in the early nineteenth century.[36]

For some ultra-Federalists like Alexander Hamilton, for whom politics was the supreme power struggle, the second balancing was central, setting up "an indissoluble union in which the states should be "in perfect subordination to the general authority."[37] For his fellow *Federalist* author Madison, there were many more troubling complexities, even beyond the tripartite government and federal-state issues. There was the question of the rule of the majority in a democracy to be balanced against the rights of minorities. The issue most troubling to Madison is a nonissue today: how to protect the rights of a property-owning minority from a property-less majority. But the problem is still with us in other guises. It gains currency when it is posed in terms of a racial majority oppressing a minority, or a religious majority trying to establish its own version of the truth in some facet of public life. There were, in addition, other important balances that engaged the deeper thinkers among the framers: between regional interests—North and South, Eastern states and Western states; between the disestablishment of religion and the encouragement of its free exercise; between political parties (which they hoped to do without); and between what the founders called "energy" in government (i.e., a strong central authority) and freedom. At the Virginia Ratification Convention, one observer described the divisions of opinion as follows: "one half of her crew hoisting sail for the land of *energy,* and the other looking with a longing aspect on the shore of liberty."[38]

It was Madison's realization of the importance of balance that gave him an answer to Montesquieu's warning that a stable republic could safely operate only over "a contracted territory," which seemed to preclude its success in so large a territory as the United States. "Brutus," one of the anonymous writers who opposed the Constitution in 1788, made the same point. Madison, however, saw some hope in the expansion of the United States because the society would become "broken into a greater variety of interests, of pursuits, of passions, which check one another, whilst those who may feel a common sentiment have less opportunity of communication and concert."[39]

The complexity of achieving the requisite balances in government is expressed in the metaphors used to describe the process of composing the Constitution. Madison spoke of an "exquisitely balanced middle" and used the image of a "Swiss watch" to describe the constitutional government of the United States, formed by "delicately balanced wheels and cogs."[40] Using similar language, Adams wrote to Jefferson in 1821: "I may refine too much. I may be an Enthusiast. But I think a free Government is necessarily a complicated Piece of Machinery, the nice and exact Adjustment of whose Springs Wheels and Weights are not yet well comprehended by the Artists of the Age and still less by the people."[41] Although such mechanistic metaphors may be unappealing today, they were the common currency of the Enlightenment. Since Newton, mechanical models had provided the major images for understanding the universe the Creator had constructed. In that sense, the metaphors could not have been loftier, implying as they did that the framers were imitating and applying the work of the Divine Being to the sociopolitical world.

What is not traceable to Enlightenment thought is the reason Madison, Adams, and other framers found such delicate and intricate balances necessary. For that we must turn to Christianity. Although the Founders are occasionally, and unfairly, accused of being romantic in their attitudes toward human nature, they were quite the opposite. Rousseau may have been romantic in his views of humanity, but the Founders were not. The Americans were schooled in a realistic Calvinism that entertained a dark view of humans as fallen creatures. Among the Founders, only Paine and Jefferson could be justly accused of having a romantic view of human nature, and even they had absorbed some of the pessimistic strain pervasive in American culture since the Puritans. Jefferson, though he was confident that Americans could overcome the past and create an agrarian paradise in their New World, could say: "In truth I do not recollect in all the animal kingdom a single species but man which is eternally and systematically engaged in the destruction of its own species. What is called civilization seems to have no other effect on him than to teach him to pursue the principle of *bellum omnium in omnia* on a larger scale."[42] While this may have been a departure from Jefferson's normal optimism, Adams and Madison always took into account the dark side of human nature. Elkins and McKitrick locate this characteristic pessimism in Adams's inner conflicts with his own passionate nature, struggles that he usually lost. The checks and balances he had to summon to control himself were mirrored in those he suggested were necessary in the body politic.[43] Unlike Jefferson, Adams had no thought that Americans in their "promised land" were a special case. He had the melancholy conviction that human nature was everywhere the same, and that Americans would repeat all the follies and the errors of the past.[44]

Madison's best-known statement on the subject came in *Federalist 51*. Although it may be a sad reflection on human nature, he describes the separation of power as a necessary device to control the abuses of government.

> But what is government itself, but the greatest of all reflections on human nature? If men were angels, no government would be necessary. If angels were to govern men, neither external nor internal controls on government would be necessary. In framing a government which is to be administered by men over men, the great difficulty lies in this: you must first enable to government to control the governed; and in the next place oblige it to control itself.[45]

Although their theory of government assumed the consequences of the fallen human state (what Christians called "original sin"), the pessimism of the framers should not be pushed too far. Even the Federalists, who took human depravity more seriously than Jeffersonian Republicans did, were not overwhelmed by it. "If depravity, ambition, and lust for power were the ruling passions of mankind," they observed, "no set of checks and balances could long preserve any government." If humans were irremediably and invariably evil, all projects aiming to establish any form of government would be doomed to fail. As North Carolina Federalist James Iredell commented, "the possible depravity of *all public officers,* is one that can admit of no cure."[46]

Relying on the better angels of human nature, the framers completed their work on the Constitution and offered it to the states for ratification in 1788. The fact that they had been able to come to an agreement among themselves seemed amazing in itself. When New Hampshire became the ninth state to ratify the Constitution, it seemed almost a miracle. It was certainly something without precedent in the world. As both Madison and Tocqueville stated, the United States was neither a pure confederation (of allied sovereign states) nor a single national government. There was no word in the language to describe it.[47] As a revolutionary act the founding event quickly took on a mythic cast. Adams called the creation of the Constitution "the greatest single effort of national deliberation that the world has ever seen." Jefferson said that the Convention was an "assembly of demi-gods." Of course, neither of them was present, so their enthusiasm may have been based on ignorance. But even Madison, who suffered through the emotions of the convention, making painstaking notes of its struggles and conflicts, said that "there was never an assembly of men, charged with a great and arduous trust, who were more pure in their motives, or more exclusively or anxiously devoted to the object committed to them, than were the members of the Federal Convention of 1787."[48]

Like Adams and Jefferson, Madison seemed well aware that originating events like the Declaration of Independence and the Constitution can assume a mythic character. That was why he wanted a Bill of Rights attached to the Constitution as soon as possible, so that the document and its first amendments would be perceived as a seamless whole. This would allow the Bill of Rights to gain "efficacy as time sanctifies and incorporates it with the public sentiment." The two together would then acquire "that veneration which time bestows on every thing, and without which perhaps the wisest and freest governments would not possess the requisite stability."[49] I consider the sacralization process of the Declaration and the Constitution in the next chapter. The rest of this chapter is devoted to examining how the urban structure of Washington mirrors the political structure set forth in the Constitution.

It was James Stirling Young who first noticed the remarkable congruity between articles of the Constitution and the layout of the capital. As he remarked in the preface to his book on Washington in the early nineteenth century, the new capital was a company town, "owned by the government, occupied by the government, conceived and created by the government. . . . The plans and provisions the rulers made for Washington were projections of the rulers' own ideas and images of government. Thus, the physical arrangement of Washington was the structure of government expressed in terms of space."[50] Young explains the phrase "structure of government expressed in terms of space" as principally referring to the three branches: executive, legislative, and judicial. Each is given its separate location, at some distance from the others, so as to avoid "mutual confrontation." Young sees the three sites situated so as to both relate and separate what would become contending powers.[51] Young describes the separation of powers as reflected in the physical structure of the capital as well as in the social patterns of its nineteenth-century inhabitants. Eventually, officials connected with the executive, legislative, and small and shadowy judicial branches lived in different areas, and ate and took their leisure in different places, creating a sort of social segregation that reflected their separate functions: "Legislators with legislators, executives with executives, judges with judges, the members gathered together in their extra-official as well as in their official activities, and in their community associations deepened, rather than bridged, the group cleavages prescribed by the Constitution."[52] Young writes almost as an anthropologist in depicting the executive and judicial branches as more culturally sedentary, bringing families to the city, buying homes, and settling. The legislators were more like roving nomads, living in boarding houses with no families and thus adding a cultural clash to their already divergent interests.

Insightful as Young's analysis was, the correlations between Constitution and capital are more extensive and subtle than even he realized. On the map of L'Enfant's Washington, the houses for Congress and the president are most prominent, each astride one of the two dominant axes in the plan, and each enjoying a prominent vista. Oddly, L'Enfant does not indicate the place for the Supreme Court, although he recognizes the importance of the judiciary elsewhere in his writings. The universal assumption is that he meant to locate it at a prominent site in the plan, the place that in fact has become Judiciary Square.[53] Following this interpretation, the executive and legislative branches are then connected by the important axial thoroughfare that would later be called Pennsylvania Avenue. The fourth important axis, which runs through the site L'Enfant selected for the "national church," is discussed in the next chapter. The most prominent elements in the original plan as well as its later development are the four major axes and three major building sites. The core is the central triangle connecting the president's house, Congress, and the planned equestrian statue to General Washington.

In many ways the judiciary seems the stepchild of the plan, a situation
that correlates with its ambiguous status in the Constitution, which simply
states: "The judicial Power of the United States, shall be vested in one supreme Court, and in such inferior Courts as the Congress may from time to
time ordain and establish." The Judiciary Act of December 1789 provided
some initial clarity about the U.S. system of courts, but the Supreme Court
of the United States did not meet until 1790 in New York, with "a crowded
courtroom and empty docket." Only three of the five appointed justices were
present, Chief Justice John Jay and Justices William Cushing and James
Wilson. For its first three years the Court "had almost no business at all."[54]
In fact, Jay was in England during most of his incumbency and resigned
from the Court to become governor of New York in 1795. During the first
decade of its existence, the Court followed a prudent and tentative path as
it began to define its own status, a process of creation and discovery.

Most commentators believe that a major turning point came in 1803 with
the *Marbury vs. Madison* case, heard under Chief Justice John Marshall.
William Marbury was one of John Adams's last-minute appointees, and his
commission as justice of the peace for Washington, D.C., somehow got lost
in the chaos of the transition from the Adams to the Jefferson administration. Ignored by the new secretary of state, James Madison, Marbury appealed to the Supreme Court, whose response was one of the most adroit
imaginable. The Court first agreed that Marbury's commission was being
illegally withheld but stated that it was legally impossible for the Court to
issue the writ to help Marbury. In fact, the Judiciary Act of 1789 clearly
gave it the right to do so. Just at this point emerged what the chief justice's
cousin and constant antagonist, Thomas Jefferson, called Marshall's "cun-
ning." The chief justice declared, as an aside (*obiter dictum*), that the Judiciary Act was, by the way, unconstitutional, and therefore the Court could
not employ a power with which it was endowed by an unconstitutional act
of Congress. Marshall thereby asserted for the first time the Court's power
to declare a law passed by Congress unconstitutional, but because the Republicans were more interested in the Marbury case itself, they did not push
the issue at the time. It is no wonder that Jefferson complained much later
that nothing could exceed the "impropriety of this gratuitous interference,"
this "perversion of the law." Though Marshall's words were clearly *obiter
dictum,* he grumbled, this case is now "continually cited by bench and bar,
as if it were a settled law."[55] And so it was.

Despite Jefferson's animadversions, the right of judicial review, thus initially stated, became an accepted weapon in the Court's arsenal. It later
acquired other powers and jurisdictions, but none to equal this one. Often

using similar tactics throughout the nineteenth century, the Court gradually acquired the power to put it on an equal footing with the legislative and executive branches. To state the case baldly, the Court became a "policy-making agency of the American government," like the other two branches. Americans do not like to admit this. They want to believe that the Supreme Court is doing nothing but "its mythic business of consulting the oracle" when it interprets the Constitution.[56] In a similar vein, religious believers often do not acknowledge the power wielded by their priests or ministers in interpreting the meaning of sacred scriptures. They wish to believe that their clergy simply explain the literal meaning of the text. But official interpreters, whether priests or justices, create meaning as they compose their interpretations. "We are under a Constitution," said Charles Evans Hughes (later chief justice) in 1907, "but the Constitution is what the judges say it is."[57]

The religious metaphor has not escaped historians. Legal historian Robert McCloskey uses Christian vocabulary to explain the meaning of the Court, calling it "a kind of secular papacy." He claims that the American belief that the Constitution embodies a higher law gives it an "odor of sanctity" and allows the Supreme Court justices "to assume the priestly mantle."[58] Citing Max Lerner, Zelinsky uses Jewish terms to make the same point, calling the justices of the Supreme Court "high priests" who "proclaim dogma and explicate talmudically the hidden sense of divine writ."[59] And according to Bellah and Hammond, "No single church evokes the breadth of respect enjoyed by the Supreme Court." Because of the separation of church and state, the function of chief moral arbiter fell to the courts, which were called upon to "articulate ultimate purpose and justice; and judges felt little ambivalence in doing so."[60] Their experience dealing with the Bible and its interpretation in the churches prepared the American people to venerate the Supreme Court and its explanations of the Constitution.

The changing physical headquarters of the Court provide a remarkable parallel to its gradual accretion of this religio-political power. First meeting on the second floor of the Royal Exchange in New York, it soon joined Congress in Philadelphia, meeting in the Old City Hall until moving to Washington in 1801. Although the decision was made in 1791 to build a separate structure for the Court, insufficient funds dictated that the judiciary be housed temporarily with Congress.[61] At the beginning, therefore, the Court met in various temporary quarters in the Capitol, finally landing in the basement in 1810.[62] One foreign commentator noted that meeting in such "cellar-like" circumstances created "the impression of justice being done in a corner . . . while the business of legislation is carried on with . . . pride, pomp, and circumstance."[63] Yet the truth is that the Supreme Court room, with its vestibule, dynamic roof lines, arches, and curved shapes was a triumph of the skill of Benjamin Latrobe, "the most magnificent suite of rooms then existing in America primarily through their shapes and spatial arrangements"(see Figure 11).[64] In 1860 the old Senate Chamber on the first floor was redesigned for the Court's use, and the Court remained there until 1935 when it moved to its present location.

William Howard Taft was the chief justice who in 1926 spurred Congress to authorize the building of a separate structure for the Supreme Court. He suggested Cass Gilbert as architect, who was subsequently chosen. Gilbert, along with John Russell Pope, was an exponent of Beaux Arts classicism in the last decade of its existence as a viable monumental style, and the two architects left their indelible stamp on Washington with several important buildings. Gilbert created the Court building as a stylistically pure Roman temple, which he hoped would "cause some reaction against the silly modernistic movement that has had such a hold here for the last few years."[65] His love for the classical tradition probably explains Gilbert's ill-considered admiration for Benito Mussolini. Having met him in 1927, Gilbert sent Mussolini photos of his designs for the Court in 1932, with "cordial wishes for your health and the prosperity of your great regime and the glory of Italy." Henry Taft, William Howard's brother, praised Gilbert's design as appropriate because it evoked the Rome whose laws "lasted down through the centuries." Ironically, he spoke just at the time the rule of law in Rome was about to crumble before the will of the fascist autocrat.[66]

Court, Capitol, and White House are both connected and separated by America's grand thoroughfare, Pennsylvania Avenue. In L'Enfant's original plan, as in Jefferson's sketch, the Congress and the president's house enjoyed preeminence. Because the judiciary had not yet assumed its powerful role, neither plan designated a site for the Supreme Court. But if scholars are correct that L'Enfant meant for the Court to be located at the present site of Judiciary Square, just north of Pennsylvania Avenue between Third and Fourth Streets, then L'Enfant's plan seems remarkably perceptive. The Court is one of the three powers, appearing to be third in rank in both the Constitution and in the city plan. And while the first two powers are directly connected by an axial boulevard, the third is placed off the axis, observing, as it were, the traffic of power between the two and sitting in judgment on their actions.[67] It would be difficult to imagine a more accurate depiction of the dynamics of political power in the early republic, and now.

Beyond the static disposition of these three centers of power, there are periodic rituals that celebrate their interrelatedness and the central values these buildings represent. Pennsylvania Avenue has become the ceremonial

FIGURE 11 Old Supreme Court Room, U.S. Capitol. Architect of the Capitol.

axis of Washington and the nation, America's "Main Street." L'Enfant deliberately made it the longest and most important street in the capital: "These avenues I made broad. . . . The first of these avenues and the most direct one begins at the Eastern Branch and ends over Rock Creek at the wharves at Georgetown."[68] Pennsylvania became the parade route for the celebration of national heroes and the route of mourning for funerals.

The first grand funeral was for President William Henry Harrison, who died shortly after taking office in 1841. His funeral procession moved from the White House, where the viewing had taken place, along the avenue to the Capitol and Congressional Cemetery. There were twenty-six pallbearers, a procession of marshals of the District of Columbia, political dignitaries, a Marine band, and some 10,000 mourners. Harrison, who made no mark on U.S. policy, provided at least a paradigm for the funerals of later presidents: "The ceremonials surrounding the death of this President of 30 days have been revived, in a sense, whenever one of his successors has died in office."[69] These are sorrowful occasions of national convocation, continuing to resonate in the memories of those who have experienced them. A contemporary writer describes himself at the inaugural parade of Lyndon

Johnson, his memory becoming blurred "because a melancholy impulse had taken me back to the spot on Pennsylvania Avenue, near the National Gallery, where I'd stood for the funeral procession the year before. When I try now to picture a triumphant LBJ going by, I see instead the riderless black horse"[70] —the powerful symbol of loss in the Kennedy cortege.

Together with the funerals, the celebration of heroes and national triumphs have found their natural expression on Pennsylvania Avenue. Admiral George Dewey's victory parade was held there in 1899. General John Joseph Pershing received the same honors in 1919, passing under a model of the Arc de Triomphe. Lindberg was honored in 1945. The avenue has also been the venue for protests and demonstrations, beginning in 1894 with the long march of Jacob Coxey's "army" to Washington from Ohio; they were protesting unemployment and lobbying for legislation to employ them on public works projects. Women's suffragists paraded on the avenue in 1913. Between 1920 and 1926, demonstrators ran the gamut from the "Be Kind to Animals" parade to a march of the Ku Klux Klan. In 1932 the "Bonus Army" (so-called because these army veterans held government bonus certificates that were due years in the future) came to ask Congress for advance pay to help get them through the Depression. Eventually, led by General Douglas MacArthur and Major Dwight Eisenhower, a column of tanks rolled down Pennsylvania Avenue, routing the army veterans with tear gas. Two died in the attack and some fifty were injured.[71] After World War II large demonstrations moved to the Mall, as we shall see in Chapter 8.

Without doubt, however, the most important and symbolically weighted ritual of Pennsylvania Avenue is the inauguration of the president. "Democracies—and especially ours in the United States," says Daniel Boorstin, "—despite many strengths, are conspicuously weak in ritual. . . . In our country the only ritual required by our Constitution is the president's inauguration."[72] As outlined in that document, the inauguration was a minimal ritual that has subsequently grown to meet a felt need. The text simply states that before the president "enter on the Execution of his Office, he shall take the following Oath or Affirmation:—'I do solemnly swear (or affirm) that I will faithfully execute the Office of President of the United States, and will to the best of my Ability, preserve, protect and defend the Constitution of the United States." Because of the dearth of rituals to define and affirm the nature of the national community, the presidential inauguration has grown in importance to fill this need.

Ironically, the tradition of an inaugural parade was begun by Thomas Jefferson, though at the time he was making every effort to destroy the ceremonials of the Adams and Washington presidencies, which he considered royalist. According to the story, he rode down Pennsylvania Avenue from the president's house accompanied by his secretary and a groom and took the oath of office in the Capitol.[73] Great trees from little acorns grow, and from this simple act grew the elaborate ceremonial occasion celebrated at the inauguration of each president. As Zelinsky notes, "arch-democrat" Thomas Jefferson, who achieved so much with his "casual, throwaway performances," made his historic mark here as well, the inaugural event later becoming "an extraordinarily ornate, costly, and imposing affair, truly imperial in grandeur. Symbolically, it now far outshines the vestigial glow of July 4."[74] Since Jefferson's simple oath-taking, nearly all American presidents have proceeded down Pennsylvania Avenue to be sworn in by the chief justice at the Capitol.

Though the inauguration begins with a parade, it acquires its stature from the grand ceremony of the oath-taking and the inaugural address at the Capitol. At the moment he takes the oath, the president presides at a renewal ritual, connecting himself and his contemporaries with the first inauguration of George Washington and with the founding of the nation. Washington, in his first inaugural address in New York, had sounded what became a perennial theme, echoed in different words by most of his successors:

> No people can be bound to acknowledge and adore the Invisible Hand which conducts the affairs of men more than those of the United States. Every step by which they have advanced to the character of an independent nation seems to have been distinguished by some token of providential agency; and in the important revolution just accomplished in the system of their united government the tranquil deliberations and voluntary consent of so many distinct communities from which the event has resulted can not be compared with the means by which most governments have been established without some return of pious gratitude, along with an humble anticipation of the future blessings which the past seems to presage.

Standing in the center, the president serves as the focal point of a microcosm of the entire nation. With the members of Congress as witnesses, the chief justice of the Supreme Court administers the oath of office, bringing into balance for one ritual moment the three powers of government. Nearly every president has referred in his inaugural address to the oath to defend the Constitution, thus reaffirming loyalty to the sacral founding document. The entire government is present: the vice president, the remaining justices of the Supreme Court, Congress, cabinet officers, the military, the diplomatic corps, and dignitaries foreign and domestic. The entire nation is virtually present: millions watch on television, represented at the event by tens of thousands of ordinary visitors. Some are local residents and others have come "on pilgrimage" from all the states of the union.

The presidential inauguration is a ritual enactment of what the plan of Washington and the Constitution express in architectural and literary terms, the exquisite balance among the powers that make up the body politic. Madison has been honored, even extravagantly praised, for his work in creating a Constitution that works, and L'Enfant should also be credited with a feat almost as delicate and perceptive. With little outside help, he created a plan for the capital that honored all the factors in the political equation embodied by the Constitution. His design placed the three powers in their proper structural relationship; but L'Enfant was also skilled enough to acknowledge other problems of balance that are part of the complex equation. He acknowledged the "distinct communities" Washington referred to, dealing with the problem of church and state, religion and secularity in creating an important place for a national church, separate from but related to the centers selected for the three powers. He saw the problem of states versus national government, so he provided fifteen squares for the fifteen states in the plan for the city. He recognized regional differences, with street names of the New England, mid-Atlantic, and southern states clustered in their respective sections of the city.

A famous, perhaps apocryphal, story brings out the major function of Pennsylvania Avenue—to separate the powers and at the same time to connect them. When John Tyler assumed the presidency after Harrison's death, it was widely assumed that he would be "malleable." Henry Clay repeatedly tried to establish his influence over Tyler, but the latter continued to resist. Finally, after a heated exchange at the White House, Tyler stormed at Clay: "Go you now then, Mr. Clay, to your end of the avenue where stands the Capitol, and there perform your duty to the country as you shall think proper. So help me God I shall do mine at this end of it as I shall think proper."[75]

Commenting on the lack of rituals in the United States, Daniel Boorstin noted that "in our democratic New World society architecture can and does play the role of ritual."[76] This comment is true of Washington more than anywhere else, particularly if one realizes that architecture is *placement* and order, not just buildings. The stones and the spaces they define create a mythic arena for ritual. The moments in national life when one of the three powers, as institutions, touches another are protected by ritual. The formality of these exchanges is a reminder of the uses of ritual—to establish distance and at the same time to allow contact, to prevent conflict by preserving respect. This is as true at the gates of Beijing as it is on the streets of Washington, where the buildings and the rites maintain the delicate art of balance. We have L'Enfant and Madison to thank for that.

CHAPTER 3

A "National Church" and Its Holy Scriptures

In 1882 a young scholar named J. Franklin Jameson made his initial visit to the library of the State Department in Washington, D.C., to undertake research in American constitutional history. Three years later, in the introduction to his first published monograph, Jameson explained that he had noticed a curious phenomenon: "The constitution of the United States was kept folded up in a little tin box in the lower part of a closet, while the Declaration of Independence, mounted with all elegance, was exposed to the view of all in the central room of the library."[1]

My point in recalling Jameson's observation is that the Constitution is far more than the "charter" or "instrument" embodied in the plan of Washington. It is not just a dry legal document that defines how power should be distributed and exercised by the various branches of government. Shortly after Jameson's experience, the physical document began to assume a new aura of sanctity that would ultimately lift it to "biblical" status. Ever more reverently treated and gloriously enshrined, it would end up an icon in the National Archives, where it is viewed today by millions every year in a hushed atmosphere of solemn public veneration. It has taken its place as a part of the national cult in its Washington temple.

This chapter examines the fate of Pierre Charles L'Enfant's plan to develop an important site for a national church, creating a prominent square for the location on an axial street that was arguably second in importance only to Pennsylvania Avenue. Although the national church was never built and the axial street (Eighth Street) was interrupted at several intersections, declined in importance, and gradually almost disappeared, the church's functions have been parceled out to other locations. In a strange way, the original site of the Patent Office (now shared by the National Portrait Gallery and the Museum of American Art), built where L'Enfant had sited the national church, has assumed some of the functions he had intended for it.

The National Cathedral, though nominally Episcopal, has acted the role of L'Enfant's church in some instances. And more recently, the National Archives, built astride the intended Eighth Street axis at Pennsylvania Avenue, has become a clear surrogate for the church in at least one of its functions. It is the repository of the nation's "biblical" texts, the Declaration of Independence and the Constitution.

The Founding Fathers uniformly acknowledged the importance of religion for a viable society. While wishing to disestablish any specific religion, they had to face the problem of how the benefits of religion might be retained in the new republic. As Kammen notes, "church disestablishment in the late colonies and new states was not demanded by libertarian atheists but by evangelical pietists concerned with the freedom of religion." It was undertaken "to free America *for* religion and not *from* religion."[2] This issue faced all the Enlightenment thinkers, compelling most of them to favor some type of religious foundation for the new forms of representative government they advocated, as a guarantor of the order and security they knew every society must have. Rousseau's *Social Contract,* for example, included a chapter entitled "Civil Religion," which asserts that "it is very important for the state that every citizen should have a religion that will make him love his duty." The dogmas of this religion will be quite simple, said the French philosopher: "The existence of a mighty, intelligent, and beneficent Divinity, possessed of foresight and providence, the life to come, the happiness of the just, the punishment of the wicked, the sanctity of the social contract and the laws; these are the positive dogmas."[3] There was only one "negative dogma," and that was intolerance.

All of these ideas were acceptable to the Founding Fathers. Using a different term with the same meaning, Benjamin Franklin had earlier spoken of "the Necessity of Publick Religion" in his "Proposals" of 1749, and his *Autobiography* contains a summary of his religious beliefs that might have been almost exact rephrasing of the tenets of Rousseau's civil religion.[4] It was a close approximation of the religious views of Washington and Jefferson as well. Washington had said in his first inaugural address that "the propitious smiles of Heaven can never be expected on a nation that disregards the eternal rules of order and right which Heaven itself has ordained." As two scholars have recently pointed out, the Founders, "even those who had little use for the Christianity that was preached in the churches of the time believed that a moral citizenry was necessary to democracy, and that morality often rested on religious conviction."[5]

Robert Bellah, almost single-handedly, brought the term "civil religion" back into the arena of scholarly debate in 1963 when he wrote his famous

Daedalus article on the subject of civil religion in the United States. Like Louis XVI, he could well say *"après moi le déluge,"* for a flood of scholarly analysis followed, in books, articles, seminars, and conferences devoted to exploring the rediscovered concept of civil religion.[6] These ranged from the strictly academic and theoretical to a few who followed the earlier startling admonition of J. Paul Williams that the U.S. government "must teach the democratic idea *as religion.*"[7]

From the earliest monarchic centers in Mesopotamia, where urbanism began, down to the twentieth century, all traditional societies had a specific religious ideology. Even in modern Europe of the past few centuries, only one theoretical exception suggests itself—Machiavelli, the political thinker who cut away, "root and branch," all the medieval theocratic ideas that were the foundation of scholastic politics. But though he was an opponent of the church, "he was no enemy of religion," convinced that it was one of the necessary elements of social life and could become "the chief source of the greatness of the state."[8] More striking still, in the most rabid period of bloodshed in the French Revolution, there was the attempt to hang on to a religious ideology, a modern worship of abstract patriotic qualities like liberty, equality, and brotherhood. Altars, ceremonial ritual, and days of observance imitated the liturgical traditions of the Roman Catholicism the revolutionaries rejected.

Even in its most attenuated modern formulations, there is abundant evidence of the conviction that a nation needs religion, some transcendent authentication for the exercise of power that is part of every political system. Outside of systems of established religion, nearly every nation must appeal to this "higher court" to sanction its coercive policies and to authenticate its existence. As Walter Lippmann put it, most generally, the state needs some belief that "there was a law 'above the ruler and the sovereign people . . . above the whole community of mortals.'" Or more crisply, John Stuart Mill: "In politics as in mechanics the power which is to keep the engine going must be sought outside the machinery."[9] Even Hitler made vague appeals to a kind of mystical Germanic "Volksgeist" as a rationale for the Third Reich, although when he was presented with the problems of real people, like transportation and recreation, he showed little interest.

L'Enfant, sharing the Enlightenment vision of a new religion for the State, made the site for his national church a place of strategic importance. He located it in one of the most prominent squares of his design, east of the president's house, equidistant from it and the Capitol. The legend on his map describes the grand square as follows:

This Church is intended for national purposes, such as public prayer, thanksgiving, funeral orations etc. and assigned to the special use of no particular Sect or denomination, but equally open to all. It will be likewise a proper shelter for such monuments as were voted by the last Continental Congress for those heroes who fell in the cause of liberty, and for such others as may hereafter be decreed by the voice of a grateful Nation.[10]

The north-south axis on which he placed the church was also a dominant one, passing through three of the fifteen squares dedicated to the use of the states, another set aside for a display of "grand fountains," and terminating on the banks of the Potomac at a plaza with a monument devoted to naval accomplishments. Only the locations chosen for the Capitol, the president's house, and the Supreme Court equaled or surpassed it in importance.[11]

As far as I can discover, this aspect of L'Enfant's plan was never even seriously discussed. His church was the victim of total disinterest on the part of the poverty-stricken new republic. Washington and Jefferson (Adams was not interested in the Potomac site) could barely raise enough money to continue the ongoing work on the president's house and the Capitol. Yet L'Enfant's perceptions of the need for religious functions in the republic were accurate, and various places were later found for "public prayer, thanksgiving, funeral orations etc.," including the White House and the Capitol rotunda. In a curious way, the building eventually constructed on the commanding Eighth Street square did fulfill L'Enfant's hopes. The Patent Office, designed by William P. Elliot Jr. and Robert Mills, was "a splendid and appropriately scaled structure for this commanding, elevated site." It has been called "a shrine celebrating American mechanical ingenuity."[12] This descriptive phrase incorporated a belief that later took its place in the network of dogmas defining American public religion: that this system of government enshrined the condition of liberty necessary to unlock the doors of creativity, American "know-how," and general prosperity.

Early in its history, the Patent Office was a precursor of the Smithsonian, "a showcase of the nation's resources, economic productivity and historical achievements, including thousands of American inventions, examples of manufactured products, the Declaration of Independence, George Washington's uniform and military gear, and tens of thousands of natural history specimens."[13] The building now houses two Smithsonian museums, the National Portrait Gallery and the National Museum of American Art. Taken together they enshrine the history, patriots, heroes and heroines, and artistic genius of the country, performing functions similar to those envisioned in L'Enfant's description. Most of the second floor of the National Portrait

Gallery is dedicated to the Hall of the Presidents and the Galleries of Notable Americans. There are displayed some of the iconic images of the Founders with which citizens are so familiar, the works of Gilbert Stuart, Charles Wilson Peale, Jean-Antoine Houdon, and others.

If there is a substitute for L'Enfant's church in the most literal sense, it is the Washington Cathedral, more properly the Cathedral of Saints Peter and Paul, which is on Saint Alban's hill, outside the monumental core. Although Congress granted the Protestant Episcopal Cathedral Foundation a charter for the "promotion of religion and education," it is not directly affiliated with the federal government. Strictly speaking, it is the seat of the Episcopal Diocese of Washington, established in 1893, but it has always attempted to transcend sectarian status and was meant to be "open to all," to use the phrase from L'Enfant's plan.[14] The bishops of the cathedral have continued to emphasize this point. The first, Henry Satterlee, was determined that it should be "a 'House of Prayer for all People' . . . a spiritual home to which men of every class, rich and poor, statesman, tradesman and laborers, may come without money and without price, with the consciousness that it is their common Father's house." African American bishop John T. Walker wrote in 1983: "Whoever you are, wherever you live, whatever your religion, race or national background, you will find a warm welcome here. Washington Cathedral stands as the great symbol of the religious heritage and foundation of the nation."[15] This spirit of tolerance has allowed it to become one of the primary sites of the nation's civil religion.[16]

Its art and iconography reaffirm the connection. "The artistry of the Cathedral's stained glass windows powerfully conveys events and insights of biblical and national history," says a guide to the cathedral. Stones on the floor of the narthex are etched with the seals of the fifty states, the Great Seal of the United States, and the seal of the District of Columbia. There is an equestrian statue to Washington across the street, and a bay dedicated to him inside the church contains a heroic statue of the first president. On the wall behind him are Masonic symbols, including his Masonic gavel with an image of the Capitol (1793) on one side of it and of the cathedral tower on the other side. The intimate connection between religion and politics could hardly be clearer. Underneath is the date 1907, when Theodore Roosevelt used the historic gavel to tap the cornerstone of the cathedral into place.[17] On the south side of the bay is a door to the Rare Book Library, which contains two portraits of Washington, one by Gilbert Stuart and another by Rembrandt Peale.

Another bay is dedicated to Robert E. Lee and Stonewall Jackson, indicating the desire to transcend regional differences. There is a War Memorial

Chapel, including the seals of all five armed services, which is dedicated to all the men and women who have given their lives in the nation's wars. American political figures, inventors, artists, writers, and humanitarians are remembered in various ways throughout the cathedral. There is a Lincoln bay as well, with a bronze statue of the sixteenth president. Behind him, carved in stone, is his farewell address to the citizens of Springfield, Illinois, on February 11, 1861. His words recall the central tenet of U.S. civil religion, the conviction that the Divine Being was with America's great leaders: "I now leave, not knowing when or whether ever I may return. With a task before me greater than that which rested upon Washington. Without the assistance of that Divine Being who ever attended him, I cannot succeed. With that assistance I cannot fail."[18] And as great British figures are buried in Westminster Abbey, American notables are and will continue to be interred at the Washington Cathedral.[19] Among those already buried there are Cordell Hull, Helen Keller, and Woodrow Wilson. Funerals and memorial services were held there for Dwight Eisenhower, Harry Truman, General Omar Bradley, Anwar Sadat, and Martin Luther King Jr.

But the building with the greatest claim to function as L'Enfant's "national church" is the National Archives, located on his Eighth Street axis on the northern edge of the Mall. It was completed in 1935, the work of neoclassicist John Russell Pope, who would later design the Mellon Gallery of Art and the Jefferson Memorial. The building has two entrances. The lesser known, on the Pennsylvania Avenue side, allows public access to the reading rooms and archives. More important is the main entrance on Constitution Avenue, with its grand monumental staircase leading into "a half-domed room in which documents sacred to the American republic are on exhibit."[20] This building, more than any other, is the unequivocal temple of the American State because it houses the scriptural basis of this form of government, preserved in the Declaration of Independence and the Constitution. In a culture grounded in bibliolatry, nothing has the authority to legitimate actions like "scriptures." As Kammen has pointed out, Americans tend to think of the problem of legitimacy with kings, popes, and Old World aristocracies. But "modes of legitimacy are even more important in a democracy than in a traditionally hierarchical society because they are less visible and cannot be taken for granted. Hence the importance of our having a written Constitution."[21]

As this chapter's initial anecdote makes clear, the Declaration of Independence and the Constitution were not always treated like sacred scriptures. There is a clear distinction between the *content* of the two documents, which together were highly revered from the beginning as the charter of the new form of government, and the physical documents themselves. Lance Banning has said, for example, "The quick apotheosis of the American Constitution was a phenomenon without parallel in the western world."[22] He was referring to the *ideas* embodied in the documents. The inscribed parchments themselves were treated rather carelessly at first. They were kept in the office of the secretary of state, along with other documents important to the nation, but received no special treatment. Since the secretaries of state did not want to be bothered with their care, they relegated that duty to "petty functionaries."[23] Only in 1922 were the two major documents transferred to the Library of Congress, where they began to receive the veneration due them as the "scriptural" foundation of American democracy.

The fact that the Declaration achieved this status earlier than the Constitution should come as no surprise. The committee of John Adams, Roger Sherman, Benjamin Franklin, and John Jay asked Jefferson to write it because they sought lofty prose. As Adams later said, "he brought with him a reputation for literature, science, and a happy talent for composition. Writings of his were handed about remarkable for their peculiar felicity of expression."[24]

The Declaration is addressed at least to the feelings, if not to the heart. It creates its own inspired character through apophatic statements—that is, oracular, declarative pronouncements. Its powerful assertions, brushing aside all doubts, are characteristic of many sacred writings. The words are portentous: "When in the course of human events"—the very first phrase already locates the moment of its creation as one of the great events in the long sweep of human history. "We hold these truths to be self-evident: that all men are created equal"—no tortuous reasoning, no argument, however compelling, no "proofs" given, but a direct and simple enunciation of truth. "That they are endowed by their Creator with certain unalienable rights"— an assertion that grounds the Founders' rebellion in the highest and most unarguable region, the Creator's design. "And for the support of this declaration, with a firm reliance on the protection of divine providence we mutually pledge to each other our lives, our fortunes and our sacred honour"—relying on the same unassailable sacred ground, the signatories find this cause worth the supreme sacrifice of all they hold dearest: their lives, wealth, and most crucial, their reputation.[25]

Yet the history of the Declaration of Independence is not a simple uninterrupted rise from neglect to sacral veneration. During the first fifteen years of its existence, the Declaration was all but forgotten. As historian Pauline Maier points out, "considering how revered a position the Declaration of Independence later won in the hearts and minds of the American people, their disregard for it in the earliest years of the new nation verges on the incredible."[26] Even the memories of the Founding Fathers grew fuzzy about certain factual matters relative to the document. Adams, Jefferson, and Franklin all stated that they had signed the document on July 4, whereas it was really almost a month later, August 2, when they began to sign it.[27] Perhaps their memories faded because of the aura of glory associated with the date of July 4. The divine confirmation came when both Adams and Jefferson died on July 4, 1826, fifty years after the "signing." As Caleb Cushing said in his eulogy of the two men, "Had horses and the chariot of fire descended to take up the patriarchs, it might have been more wonderful, but not more glorious."[28]

A decade later, the Declaration had completed its ascent to revered status. With the Federalist Party dead, both Whigs and Jacksonians claimed fealty to Jefferson and his Declaration. The document became a flashpoint at mid-century, however, as tensions rose between slave and free states. Politicians began to shift the central focus of the document from justifying the "right of revolution" to arguing for "the equality of all men." All Northern states eventually accepted the logic and abolished slavery. But some slavery advocates took the position that "all men" simply did not apply to blacks, others that the assertion of equality was simply wrong. John C. Calhoun, as the most eloquent defender of the South's "peculiar institution," wished to go back to the earlier focus. He said that the Declaration's assertion of equality was a "hypothetical truism" about men in the state of nature but was inapplicable in a real society of men. The equality issue had lain dormant for a long time, he said, but was now germinating and spreading its "poisonous fruits." The equality statement was unnecessary in the first place, he said, since separation from Britain could be justified without it.

Lincoln read the document literally. He pointed out in his debates with Stephen Douglas that if, as Douglas maintained, the document referred only to males of European ancestry and their rights, then the document must be consigned to the trash bin of history. If it was only a justification of American Independence, the document was "of no practical use now—mere rubbish—old wadding left to rot on the battle-field after the victory is won," nothing more than an interesting memorial of a dead past. In that sense, he and Calhoun agreed that the equality statement was unnecessary to the assertion of American independence. But, said Lincoln, once having introduced the idea into "a merely revolutionary document," Jefferson had declared "an abstract truth, applicable to all men and all times, and so to embalm it there, that to-day, and in all coming days, it shall be a rebuke and a stumbling-block to the very harbingers of re-appearing tyranny and oppression."[29] Garry Wills and others have claimed that Lincoln almost single-handedly changed the meaning of the Declaration, pulling off what Wills calls "a giant (if benign) swindle, . . . one of the most daring acts of open-air sleight-of-hand ever witnessed by the unsuspecting," thereby changing the national future. Whether true or not, when the Civil War settled the Lincoln-Douglas (and Calhoun) debate, the meaning of the Declaration of Independence had been finally determined. It would be a living and growing document, as Lincoln insisted, later called upon in the women's suffrage movement and many other struggles for equality.

In 1943 and 1944, during the dark days of World War II, readings about patriotic heroes and events were broadcast during the intermissions of the Sunday concerts of the New York Philharmonic, "to lift the spirits of Americans by recalling to them heroic things done and wise things said in the American past." If this scenario sounds like that of a believer turning to the Bible, Torah, or Qur'an in time of adversity, Carl Van Doren and Carl Carmer left no doubt about their intention when they later gathered the readings into a book entitled *American Scriptures*.[30] In the preface they announce that they will not fabricate the past but let the documents speak for themselves: "The *American Scriptures* assumed that nothing can be quite so interesting as the truth." Van Doren warns the nation neither to remember only "old misfortunes," which leads to despair, nor to remember only "old triumphs," which leads to heedlessness and arrogance: "Let it remember the truth, honestly yet vividly."

It is an interesting thought—that documents speak the straightforward truth, with no need for interpretation. In *American Scriptures,* however, only a single set of readings, those on the Alamo, recalls anything but a triumph. Because the authors include Patrick Henry's "Give me liberty or give me death" speech, which he probably did not deliver, and the Revolutionary hero Lafayette's letter to his wife, which says "In America, there are no poor," it becomes clear that the "truth" of the anthology is chiefly mythic rather than historical. In assembling these texts about American heroes, great events, and revered documents, the compilers do what the creators of Washington, D.C., have done: they present Americans with a summary of the patriotic "truths," the major threads creating a tapestry that is the national mythology.

It is surely excusable to tone down critique during a time of national danger. Still, it is interesting to note the different ways that the Declaration of Independence and the Constitution are treated in *American Scriptures*. It quotes the Declaration of Independence up to the point where Jefferson began his litany of the offenses of King George against the American colonies. The segment ends with Jefferson's words to the mayor of Washington just days before his death, in which he urges the annual recollection of Independence Day. In contrast, although the Constitution is honored in a chapter of the book, its actual words are never quoted. Rather, Benjamin Franklin's address in support of the Constitution is provided, presumably because it is more inspiring than the document itself. Even here, Franklin expresses his hope for the ratification of the Constitution "because I expect no better, and because I am not sure that it is not the best." Hardly a ringing endorsement, yet it probably reflects the feelings of most of the delegates—as a compromise it was the best they could hope for. Franklin's most memorable and moving words came when he looked at the carved sun motif on the back of Washington's chair: "I have often, in the course of the session, looked at that sun behind the President, without being able to tell whether it was rising or setting. But now, at length, I have the happiness to know that it is a rising and not a setting sun."[31]

The words may be a clue to why the Constitution assumes scriptural status for Americans. Simply stated, it was the revered foundation for a system of government that has worked. The Constitution is the oldest document that still serves as a charter for government in the world. Over the past two hundred years dozens of constitutions adopted elsewhere have landed on the scrap heap. Only the U.S. Constitution has lasted.[32] It marked the beginning of the *novus ordo seclorum,* the guarantor of the most cherished rights of Americans (each reader may here fill in the blank: freedom of religion, political liberty, security, the freedom to make money without too many governmental regulations, etc.). To mirror the rising-sun image, Thomas Paine wrote a few years later in Part II of *The Rights of Man:* "There is a morning of reason rising upon man, on the subject of government, that has not appeared before." It would spread everywhere, to the benefit of all nations: "From a small spark kindled in America, a flame has arisen not to be extinguished. Without consuming, like the *Ultima Ratio Regum,* it winds its progress from nation to nation, and conquers by a silent operation."[33]

The Constitution was the practical embodiment of the revolutionary ideal, but its elevation to sacral status in the twentieth century went beyond its intellectual content—perhaps despite its intellectual content. There have been periodic efforts to popularize the document and to make it a part of the process of public education. Yet surveys have repeatedly shown that few Americans have anything but the vaguest idea what the Constitution actually says. At the same time that the readings from *American Scriptures* were being broadcast, a survey of 2,560 Americans revealed that 20 percent had simply never heard of the Bill of Rights, and 39 percent said they had heard of it but could not identify it in any way.[34] The results of these and similar surveys again pose the question: why has the Constitution assumed scriptural status? It is, after all, a dry legal document, as acknowledged even by its most ardent supporters. "We the people of the United States," it begins, "in Order to form a more perfect Union, establish Justice, insure domestic Tranquillity, provide for the common defense, promote the general Welfare, and secure the Blessings of Liberty to ourselves and our Posterity, do ordain and establish this Constitution for the United States of America." Citing this preamble, James M. Beck, a "Constitution worshiper" of the 1920s, explained that it only "seemed to be" a dull, legal document. "To illustrate the great interest of the subject," he continued, "if the student has a little imagination he need only take the Preamble. There is a noble dignity about it," and like the lofty truths of Shakespeare and Scripture, "the more one reads it, the more one is impressed with its majesty."[35] Majesty, perhaps, but Beck was leading with his only ace. After that card was played, it was all downhill, at least in terms of rhetoric, loftiness, inspiration. The text of the Constitution is covered by the dusty footprints of James Madison and Gouverneur Morris. It is addressed to the human head, methodically going through the division of power for the new government: Article 1—the legislative power; Article 2—the executive power; Article 3—the judicial power; Articles 4 to 7 covering certain powers dealing with the states, how the Constitution may be amended, who is bound by it, and how it shall be ratified. It ends with the ringing phrase: "In Witness whereof We have hereunto subscribed our Names."

Some parts of the original Constitution have been superseded by amendments, but with little improvement of the prose. The 12th amendment presents a modification of the electoral process in a single, run-on sentence:

The Electors shall meet in their respective states and vote by ballot for President and Vice-President, one of whom, at least, shall not be an inhabitant of the same state with themselves; they shall name in their ballots the person voted for as President, and in distinct ballots the person voted for as Vice-President, and they shall make distinct lists of all persons voted for as President, and of all persons voted for as Vice-President, and of the number of votes for each, which lists they shall sign and certify, and transmit sealed to the seat of government of the United States, directed to the President of the Senate;—The President of the Senate shall, in presence of the Senate and House of Representatives, open all the certificates and the votes shall then be counted; —The person having the greatest number of votes for President, shall be the President, if such number be a majority of the whole number of Electors appointed; and if no person have such a majority, then from the persons having the highest numbers not exceeding three on the list of those voted for as President, the house of Representatives shall choose immediately, by ballot, the President.

This passage requires unwavering determination even to reach its end, whether comprehending or uncomprehending. But the document was not meant to inspire; it was meant to outline a new form of government in the most unambiguous prose possible. It was not to be oratorical, moving, or emotional, but just the opposite. Here is the outline of government, it says, the rules we shall operate by. Given the requirement for sober, legal prose, it is all the more fascinating to follow the process by which this dry charter made its journey from a dusty box in the bottom of a closet in the Department of State to its apotheosis, like an enshrined copy of the Torah, in the National Archives. Like Sleeping Beauty, it was touched with the kiss of patriotic veneration and wakened to a new life.

There was, at the beginning, a sense of the miraculous that those assembled for the Constitutional Convention could agree on a charter of government at all. How could the competing interests of thirteen states and contending regions ever reach agreement? Washington was so skeptical that he almost did not attend; yet he so longed to establish the new government on a solid footing that he not only went but also put his prestige on the line by accepting the position of president of the convention. As he wrote in a letter to General Henry Knox:

I must candidly confess, as we could not remain quiet more than three or four years in time of peace, under the constitutions of our own choosing . . . I see little prospect either of our agreeing upon any other, or that we should remain long satisfied under it if we could. Yet I would wish any thing and every thing essayed to prevent the effusion of blood, and to avert the humiliating and contemptible figure we are about to make in the annals of mankind.[36]

Four months of secret debates ensued. Washington sat like a god in the president's chair, listening but rarely speaking. At one point, to head off some wrangling and disagreement, according to the *Records of the Convention of 1787*, Franklin got up and proposed that the sessions begin with a prayer: "If a sparrow cannot fall to the ground without His notice, is it probable that an empire can rise without His aid?"[37] The delegates finally signed the new Constitution on September 17, 1787, a conclusion that Washington found "little short of a miracle." Then the work began to obtain its ratification, and again, to the amazement of many, the states ultimately approved it. Washington never forgot his sense of the improbability of this series of events. In his famous Farewell Address in 1796 he asked Heaven's continued blessings "that your union and brotherly affections may be perpetual—that the free constitution, which is the work of your hands, may be sacredly maintained."[38]

Others of the Founding Fathers saw the hand of God in the Constitution as well. Benjamin Rush, friend of Adams and Jefferson, thought it "as much the work of a Divine Providence as any of the miracles recorded in the Old and New Testament were the effects of a divine power." It was compared to Noah's ark as a vessel of safety. In 1834 Representative Caleb Cushing called it "our Ark of Covenant," and William Howard Taft did the same in 1922.[39] Once the Constitution had been ratified and the new government was in place, even the anti-Federalists accepted its legitimacy, and arguments turned to the question of how to interpret it.

This may seem surprising, in view of the strength of anti-Federalist sentiment. Jefferson had written a letter to Samuel Kercheval in 1816, commenting, "Some men look at constitutions with sanctimonious reverence, and deem them like the arc of the covenant, too sacred to be touched." Although "not an advocate for frequent and untried changes in laws and constitutions," he does finally suggest that we "provide in our constitution for its revision at stated periods."[40] Yet in practice this never happened, and Jefferson never seriously proposed it. Instead of challenging the authority of the Constitution, the Jeffersonian Party focused on its interpretation.

The Constitution has been discussed, and often in reverential terms, in nearly every presidential inaugural address since Washington's. This is probably natural, since each president has just sworn allegiance to the Constitution before beginning his address. John Quincy Adams, after taking his oath to preserve, protect, and defend the Constitution, called it "that revered instrument." Van Buren referred to it in the atmosphere of growing animosity arising from the slavery issue. He promised strict adherence to its letter and spirit: "Looking back to it as a sacred instrument carefully and not easily framed . . . I shall endeavor to preserve, protect, and defend it by anxiously referring to its provision for direction in every action." It was the touchstone of Lincoln's initial stance as he took office, and his first inaugural address was a long meditation on the relationship of the Constitution and the Union of the States. Acknowledging the right of Congress to amend the Constitution, Lincoln also reaffirmed his oath to defend it. "*You* have no oath registered in heaven to destroy the Government," he said, addressing the seceding states, "while *I* shall have the most solemn one to 'preserve, protect, and defend it.'" It was Lincoln who lent a mystical quality to the ideal of the unity of the states and reaffirmed that as the central idea of the Constitution.

In the early period of the republic, therefore, union and unity were paramount, and the Constitution was venerated as the charter that guaranteed them. That had been the substance of the miracle, the agreement of delegates from so many states with different histories, economies, mores, and cultures. Gradually another factor, prosperity, intruded and became a leitmotif of the eulogies to the document. Beginning in the first schoolbook to discuss the Constitution, *A Plain Political Catechism,* was the message that the document provided for the happiness and prosperity of the country. The connection between the Constitution and financial prosperity was never clearly explained; it was simply assumed.

It is tempting to see a parallel between American attitudes toward the Constitution and Jewish attitudes toward their Covenant, the Mosaic Law, or Torah. Both are chiefly legal documents, not inspiring in their content so much as in their function as the charter of a community, a people. For Jews, the Exodus and the Covenant were inspirational events that were duly celebrated during the annual Passover feast. Yet it was the laws of the Torah that provided direction in their everyday lives. As such they have become more than mere legal codes determining the dynamics of society. Over the course of centuries the Torah actually embodied Jewish society and created strong communities. It was in these latter functions that the laws engendered the most extreme expressions of loyalty.

In cultures less fixated on "the Word" as truth, scriptures have a somewhat different meaning. But in American Protestant culture, the dominant orientation of the Founding Fathers, the culture is not only founded on "the Word," but so steeped in the discourse, words, metaphors and ideas of Old and New Testament that they were simply taken for granted as the vocabulary of ordinary discourse. As Perry Miller said of the biblical context, it was "so truly omnipresent in the American culture of 1800 or 1820 that historians have as much difficulty taking cognizance of it as of the air people breathed."[41]

For this reason I borrow Martin Marty's notion of *creencias* to explain the elevation of the Constitution and the Declaration of Independence to canonical status. *Creencia,* literally "belief" or "creed," is a term Marty takes from Spanish philosopher José Ortega y Gasset to explain the biblical "hold" upon American sensibility. *Creencias,* he says, "are the ideas that we are, and not merely those we hold. They are the small pool of constitutive beliefs that are so deep they seem to be part of us." They are to be contrasted with *vigencias,* "the binding customs of the culture, the habits and manners, the ethos and style that become characteristic of wide elements in it."[42] The latter are influenced, of course, by the former, and they are more easily identified and dealt with, accepted or rejected. But the *creencias* lie at a deeper level. I suggest, as an example of a *creencia*, the conviction of Enlightenment thinkers that the highest truths could be conveyed by words. Although they might have argued about what those truths were, they never doubted that their spoken and written words could clearly communicate them. This *creencia*, of course, goes back to the origins of Western culture, to Greek rationalism and Hebrew scripturalism.

In a 1959 essay entitled "The Discovery of What It Means to Be an American," James Baldwin relates that he went to live in Paris because he hated America. But as he tried to relate his own experience to "that of others, Negroes and whites, writers and non-writers," he says, "I proved, to my astonishment, to be as American as any Texas G.I. And I found my experience was shared by every American I knew in Paris." Baldwin's analysis of his experience shows that he had found the existence of *creencias:* "Every society is really governed by hidden laws, by unspoken but profound assumptions on the part of the people." Realizing that he shared these with Americans, both black and white, he says, "I was released from the illusion that I hated America" and "I was able to accept my role—as distinguished, I must say, from my 'place'—in the extraordinary drama which is America."[43]

Marty's analysis of the Bible as an "icon" in American society may be applied to the Constitution, as he himself suggests.[44] "If this is 'a nation with the soul of a church,'" he says, quoting Tocqueville, "that soul is fed by documents." Besides the Declaration of Independence and the U.S. Constitution, enshrined in its archival heart, "the Bible is there too." He admits that there are some dangers in speaking of the Bible as an icon but believes that the effort to do so will "lead beyond merely rational analysis to the root emotions of people in a culture"— that is, to the realm of the *creencias.* One salient quality that marks a document as an icon is the partial irrelevance of its content. I have pointed out already that few Americans read the Constitution or know what it says, even the part that has provided grist for the mill of two hundred years of controversies and Supreme Court decisions, the Bill of Rights. Marty finds the same to be true of the Bible. In fact there seems to be a strange inverse relationship: the more a person reads and studies the Bible, the less it can be considered an icon. And vice versa.

The principal function of "book as icon," therefore, is not to give knowledge and understanding to the devotee, but to provide comfort and security. To use Marty's description, the icon functions as a carapace, a shell that protects a person's most fundamental beliefs and basic commitments. That this carapace should be "the written word" in American society is not at all surprising. It is rooted in cultural patterns nourished for centuries, including the conviction that God has spoken through the words recorded in a book. Ronald Reagan, during a presidential campaign, pointed to the Bible and said to his listeners, "It is an incontrovertible fact that *all* the complex and horrendous questions confronting us at home and worldwide have their answer in that single book." If one accepts that statement, the Bible is indeed a carapace, if not a bomb shelter! One can imagine the retort of Henry David Thoreau: "It is remarkable that, notwithstanding the universal favor with which the New Testament is outwardly received, and even the bigotry with which it is defended, there is no hospitality shown to, there is no appreciation of, the order of truth with which it deals. I know of no book that has so few readers."[45]

And that is just the point. Grover Cleveland's attitude toward the Bible may be taken as a clear example of belief in the book as icon. He wanted "the plain old bible book without criticisms or cross-references, which were unnecessary and confusing."[46] In this regard his thoughts on the subject lead naturally to Warren Harding, for whom religion, "like the Constitution," was something to be honored and let alone.[47] Jefferson represents the opposite attitude. His viewpoint was aniconic, and he was an iconoclast toward both Bible and Constitution. He took the Bible's meaning not literally, but so seriously that he spent weeks in the White House poring through the text, reading the criticisms and cross-references, comparing the Greek, Latin, and French translations. The outcome was his "Philosophy of Jesus" and some years later, "The Life and Morals of Jesus." Both of these redactions present Jesus as the foremost moral reformer in human history and at the same time relentlessly excise all supernatural elements from the Gospel accounts. Jefferson's life of Jesus jumps from Mary laying Jesus in a manger to his circumcision eight days later, then quickly to his twelfth year. The account ends with disciples rolling a great stone to the door of his sepulchre. The life omits shepherds, magi, choirs of heavenly angels, accounts of the resurrection and ascension—everything, in short, that most Christians remember and celebrate each Christmas and Easter as the very heart of their faith.[48] Jefferson's "tampering" with sacred texts was academic and rational, according to Enlightenment standards of judgment. Cleveland's iconic approach, however simplistic, had the power to move people that Jefferson's lacked.

Following this analysis, then, the Constitution and Declaration of Independence have become icons, not because of their content, but as symbols that, like the flag, are the focus of feelings about the meaning of the American experiment. Thurman Arnold wrote a sardonic description of "Constitution Worship" in the 1930s: "Like the Bible, the Constitution became the altar whenever our best people met together for tearful solemn purposes. . . . Teachers in many states were compelled to swear to support the Constitution. No attempt was made to attach a particular meaning to this phrase, yet people thought that it had deep and mystical significance, and that the saying of the oath constituted a charm against evil spirits."[49] Arnold was reacting to the treatment of the document as "fetish," a word that had begun to be used in criticism of a worshipful attitude toward the Constitution some years earlier. Senator William E. Borah had warned against constitutional "fetishism" in 1912. A year later Brooks Adams spoke of lawyers worshiping it as a "fetich." Against the movement to disparage or change the Constitution, the National Association for Constitutional Government was formed in 1916. One of its purposes was "to secure a popular realization of the vital necessity of preserving the nation's basic law unimpaired." With that, "the 'fetich' was well under way," remarks Kammen.[50]

The canonization of the two texts received added impetus during the sesquicentennial celebrations of 1937 and 1938. Senator Borah tried to allow for the possibility of changing the Constitution through the amendment process, while still insisting that it was sacred. It was reported that one of his speeches placed the story of the 1787 Convention "in the realm of sacred history." The rhetoric of the sesquicentennial years constantly used religious terminology like "sacred," "sacred history," "pilgrimage," "shrine of the Constitution." Representative Sol Bloom, who headed the planning commission for the celebration, once asked his staff in preparing a talk for him to broadcast on NBC "to include references to Providence and the Almighty." He began his talk to the Daughters of the American Revolution convention of April 1938 with the sentence, "Worship is the core of all things."[51]

One of the clearest expressions of the iconic status of the Declaration and the Constitution can be studied in the phenomenon of the "Freedom Train," which has been called "the most elaborate ideological undertaking of the early postwar years" and "one of the, if not *the,* greatest patriotic campaigns in American history."[52] The story of this endeavor begins, in fact, in the National Archives on a day in early April 1946. William Coblenz, assistant director of the Department of Justice's Public Information Division, decided to spend his lunch hour there viewing the current exhibit. He was deeply impressed. Thinking that the vast majority of Americans would never have the opportunity to see America's cherished documents, he conceived the idea of taking them around the country on a kind of patriotic tour. He took the idea up the chain of command, receiving encouragement at every level and finally the endorsement of President Harry Truman.

This was the beginning of the Cold War period, and Attorney General Tom Clark reflected the enthusiasm of many when he spoke of the opportunity as a "means of aiding the country in its internal war against subversive elements and as an effort to improve citizenship by reawakening in our people their profound faith in the American historical heritage." Meetings were held, committees formed, and substantial funds raised with the help of movie and media leaders, such as Barney Balaban, president of Paramount Pictures, Philip Graham of the *Washington Post*, and Spyros Skouras, president of Twentieth Century Fox. They promised to help with an enormous publicity campaign to dramatize the "American way of life through the travelling exhibition of the most impressive collection of original American documents ever assembled." At a meeting in Tom Clark's New York office on January 7, 1947, the committee decided to transport the documents around the nation on a train.

Later that same month, Winthrop W. Aldrich, chairman of Chase National Bank, assembled a group of donor organizations and corporations that pledged $150,000 for the project and organized the American Heritage Foundation to plan the tour of what had come to be called the Freedom Train. To ensure that the meaning of the event would not be lost, the foundation planned a full week of meetings in each city to be visited, during which "the American heritage and good citizenship would be discussed and promoted." These weeks were called Rededication Weeks, with the goal of preparing hearts and minds to see the 126 cherished documents. Among the most important were Jefferson's copy of the Declaration of Independence, the Bill of Rights, and Washington's annotated copy of the Constitution. (The handbill distributed by the Advertising Council listed these three first on the list of eight documents.)[53] The publicity campaign was nationwide. Irving Berlin wrote a song called "The Freedom Train," recorded by Bing Crosby and the Andrews Sisters. Fawcett Publications brought out an issue of the *Captain Marvel* comic book in which the hero saved the Freedom Train from "the world's wickedest scientist . . . Sivana." The foundation made a film with the help of Dore Schary at RKO Pictures, which was narrated by Joseph Cotton and shown in theaters throughout the country.

Ripley did a "Believe It or Not" cartoon of the signing of the Declaration, which stated: "There were 56 signers of the Declaration of Independence. Though they differed in background and political and religious belief, they agreed upon one of the greatest revolutionary statements in the history of mankind . . . that all men are created equal and endowed with unalienable rights, and that governments derive their just powers from the consent of the governed."[54] Approximately 250 national magazines and thousands of other publications carried features about the Freedom Train and the foundation's programs. *Reader's Digest* reprinted 3.5 million copies of an article on the Bill of Rights that was given to visitors to the train.

The Freedom Train began its tour at Philadelphia on September 17, 1947, the 160th anniversary of the signing of the Constitution. Its engine was christened "The Spirit of 1776" and designated specifically for this noble task. The locomotive had been ceremonially baptized a few weeks earlier with a bottle containing water from the Atlantic and Pacific Oceans, the Great Lakes, the Gulf of Mexico, and the Mississippi and Potomac Rivers. The tour made stops at 322 cities in all forty-eight states, traveled 37,000 miles, and was visited by 3.5 million people. All were encouraged to sign a "rededication scroll" to be placed in the Library of Congress. It is estimated that some 50 million people participated in Rededication Week events and activities. The tour ended January 22, 1949.

A number of ironies were associated with the Freedom Train endeavor. For example, as the documents enshrining freedom were being selected, some wanted to include the Truman Doctrine, the Wagner Labor Act, the President's Committee on Civil Rights Report, and Executive Order 8802, which established the Fair Employment Practice Commission. But the foundation decided it would not include documents that were "the subject of current legislative consideration or were deemed to be of a partisan or controversial nature." An ironic event occurred when the train reached New England, where organizers urged participants in Rededication Week to take the "Freedom Pledge":

> I am an American. A free American.
> Free to speak—without fear
> Free to worship God in my own way
> Free to stand for what I think right
> Free to oppose what I believe wrong
> Free to choose those who govern my country.
> This heritage of Freedom I pledge to uphold
> For myself and all mankind.

Perhaps emboldened by this heady proclamation of freedoms, some citizens, "primarily communists and conscientious objectors" according to Bradsher, protested the contrast between the Freedom Train documents and the actual state of democracy in America. Bradsher's article notes that the FBI "kept track of them," and between September 20 and October 24, J. Edgar Hoover sent the attorney general nine reports on the protesters.

The final leg of the Freedom Train's journey was a swing through the South, where many cities and states had laws enforcing segregation in public gatherings. Would the crowds visiting the train to view the Emancipation Proclamation be segregated? The foundation issued a press release saying that it would not tolerate such practices and requiring each of the forty-nine southern cities to be visited to declare their policies ahead of time. All complied except Memphis and Birmingham, and although many believed that the foundation would back down, it did not, and the train bypassed those two cities. Walter White, president of Tuskegee Institute, later wrote that the train had made clear the difference between democracy and bigotry: "If the Freedom Train has accomplished nothing more than that, it has been worth all the time and money put into its creation." The foundation's historical consultant, Frank Monaghan, stated that the train "did more to bring the basic documents of our American heritage to the enraptured attention of the American people that any other single operation." And even if they were not quite "enraptured" by the documents, the Freedom Train represented an outpouring of patriotism rarely seen before or since.[55]

It is impossible not to see parallels here between the Freedom Train, with its sacred objects, and similar religious practices, such as the processions when statues of saints, holy relics, or even the sacred host are carried through the streets for the adoration of the crowds. Consistent with this "objectification" of the actual documents, historian Catherine Albanese calls the Constitution the "greatest sacramental sign of the new republic."[56] The documents had clearly become icons.

The Declaration of Independence and the Constitution have indeed come on a long journey from neglect to veneration. The two documents are now encased in massive bronze bullet-proof glass containers filled with inert helium gas to prevent contact with damaging oxygen. Water vapor is introduced into their environment to keep the old parchment (which was not of particularly good quality in the first place) from becoming brittle. Yellow light and special filters prevent fading.

During the day the documents are displayed in glass cases, but at night they are lowered into a vault of reinforced concrete and steel. According to a National Archives brochure, it is twenty feet deep and weighs fifty-five tons. Once the documents are in the vault, "massive doors on top . . . swing shut, and the documents are safe." John Russell Pope's neoclassical building provides an awesome setting for the documents. Outside, the structure is ringed by massive Corinthian columns (seventy-two of them, weighing ninety-five tons each). The main doors are bronze, forty feet tall and one foot thick. Inside the vaulted ceiling rises ninety feet high and draws the visitor's vision toward the "altar" opposite the main doors. It is flanked by two huge painted murals, one of Jefferson presenting the Declaration to John Hancock as president of the Continental Congress, the other of James Madison presenting the Constitution to George Washington as president of the Constitutional Convention. The atmosphere is hushed and reverent, reminiscent of a mausoleum, or at least some structure of religious worship. The interior perhaps resembles a synagogue more than a church, with the two documents enshrined like a Torah in its "arc" (Hebrew *aron*, referring to the arc of the Covenant).

The religious, almost ecclesiastical, atmosphere created is deliberate. In 1922, when the Constitution and Declaration of Independence were first taken to the Library of Congress, officials of the library wanted to create a display location that would function "as a sort of 'shrine,'" which visitors to Washington could tell about on their return home (see Figure 12). They hired Francis H. Bacon (his brother was Henry Bacon, designer of the Lincoln Memorial) to design a display case that resembled "a conventional altar piece." The Declaration was in an upright case and the five pages of the Constitution in a horizontal glass case in front of it. Around the assemblage was a marble balustrade "suggesting the chancel rail before an altar," which "pilgrims" could enter, single-file, for a close look at the charters.[57] The same sort of assemblage was used in the National Archives building. There is no chancel rail, but the display case is placed on a three-tiered "altar." For the sesquicentennial celebration, replicas of this shrine were available in two sizes, a large one for public places and a smaller version for private homes.[58]

Constitutional expert Pauline Maier expresses her irritation at the process by which the Declaration of Independence became a sacred text after 1815, its enduring truths often described with words borrowed from the vocabulary of religion. Its current shrine in the National Archives reminds her of the "awesome, gilded, pre–Vatican II altars of my Catholic girlhood." Sanctifying these documents, she complains, "strikes me as idolatrous, and also curiously at odds with the values of the Revolution." Yet she admits that the shrine of the National Archives, rather than making connections with the period of the Revolution, seems "part and parcel of the 1940s and 1950s, an assertion of American values . . . against fascist and communist enemies, with the vault and its massive closing doors, an assurance to the fearful that those values could not be destroyed."[59]

FIGURE 12 National Archives, interior. Courtesy of the National Archives, photo no. 64-NA-1-462.

In the end, the National Archives is not about Revolutionary values at all. It is a church or cathedral that enshrines the icons of American identity. The fact that both major documents worshiped there have been the subject of unending contention over their two hundred-plus years of history, between Federalists and anti-Federalists, Jacksonian Democrats and Whigs,

Republicans and Democrats, liberals and conservatives, in no way detracts from their functioning as sacred scripture, charters of American society and politics. Quite the reverse. "It is essential to Constitutionalism as a vital creed," points out Thurman Arnold, "that it is capable of being used in this way on both sides of any question, because it must be the creed of all groups in order to function as a unifying symbol."[60] In that regard it is quite like the Bible, to which it has so often been compared.

These two documents are not only a collection of ideas and principles but also a compendium of images and symbols by which a people has constructed and maintained its world: "If worlds are invented, therefore, it is a long and collective process of invention and one that is inherently conservative. It is, in other words, one that we are always inclined to rely on, and at the same time to forget."[61] It is in contemplating the element of "forgetting" that we come to realize that the Declaration and Constitution embody a *creencia,* an expression not of what Americans believe, but of who they are.

PART II

The Axis of Enlightenment

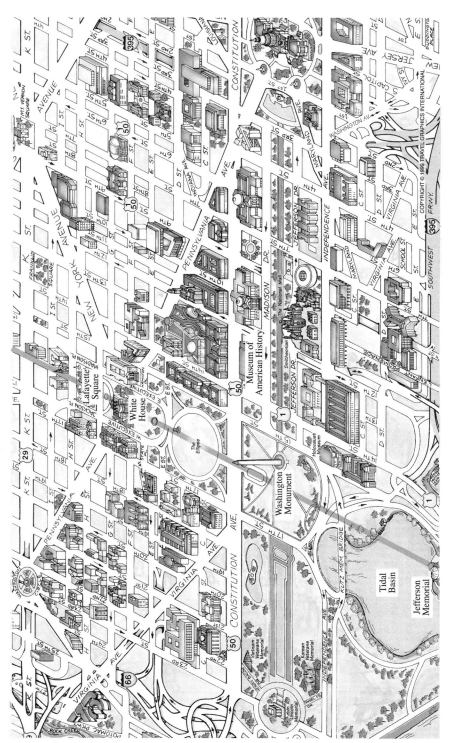

FIGURE 13 Map of Washington, D.C., White House–Jefferson Memorial axis emphasized. Map reproduced courtesy of Travel Graphics International.

From the White House
to the Jefferson Memorial

I begin my walk of the second axis in Lafayette Square, just across Pennsylvania Avenue from the White House on its northern side (see Figure 13). Back in the spring of 1790, the land rose gradually from the banks of the Potomac to this general site, which L'Enfant had chosen for the "President's Palace." Washington was not completely happy with the location and moved it a bit west to the exact spot it occupies today.

I want to see the vista that L'Enfant chose for the second-most-important building in the city. But without an invitation to the second floor of the White House, I think it will be impossible. Then I hit upon an idea. There are a few tall buildings on the north side of Lafayette Square, and I walk into the lobby of one of them, the Hay-Adams Hotel, asking at the desk if it is possible to go up to the roof. It is not, says the concierge. Then, "Of course if you talk with hotel security . . . but it probably won't do any good." I ask the desk to call security. A Mr. Haines appears immediately, and I explain what I want to do. He is surprisingly agreeable, warning me that he must first let White House security know that someone will be on the roof of the Hay-Adams with a camera.

We take the elevator to the rooftop, and voila!, there is just the spectacular view I expected. Although L'Enfant made this axial vista shorter than that from the Capitol, it meets the Potomac just where the river turns south. He has made use of what landscape architects call "borrowed scenery." I see security agents moving about on the roof of the White House (one of them, alerted by Mr. Haines, is looking at me with large binoculars). Just east of the axis is the Washington Monument. Across the tidal basin I can see the Jefferson Memorial, and beyond that the stretch of the Potomac flowing south toward Alexandria and the Chesapeake Bay. I am sure that L'Enfant was aware of all of these picturesque advantages as he analyzed the topography of his future city.

I return to ground level and Lafayette Square. Here, from his home on the square, Henry Adams watched the rites of political power. Here also, sitting on a park bench almost every day for four months, Charles Guiteau darkly observed the comings and goings of President James Garfield. Then, on July 2, 1881, Guiteau shot Garfield. I walk past the equestrian statue of Andrew Jackson to the south end of the park at Pennsylvania Avenue, now closed to traffic because of the bombing of a federal building in Oklahoma City on April 19, 1995. Here I find the nomadic encampments of Concepcion Picciotto and W. Thomas, two veteran protesters who have maintained an antinuclear peace vigil since 1981. Times have changed, and these two with them. Concepcion hands me her card, complete with website address.

Their homemade signs recall the 1960s: "Live by the bomb, die by the bomb," and "Ban all nuclear weapons or have a nice doomsday." W. Thomas looks like John Brown, with wild hair, a full beard, and a glittering eye. Concepcion is au courant in her views of the house across the street. "All they are interested in over there," she says, nodding her head toward the White House, "is orgies. Corrupt, corrupt." Like an anchorite of old, she sleeps sitting upright, so that the police will not have an excuse to haul her away for "camping." "People have beat me up at night," she says, showing me a newspaper clipping on her display board. It shows her with a bloodied face. "Now they're using lasers," she adds, pointing to a red spot on her cheek. This is a war zone!

The president and his home are above all a *focus*. They draw tourists as well as zealots, beautiful people, whiz kids, spin doctors, the insane, assassins. Picciotto and Thomas are on to something—this is an ideal place to lodge a protest. The official response is heightened security. Security at the Capitol, in contrast, seems lax. There are no fences, no guard houses. No protesters are camped permanently on the premises. In Congress, power and viewpoint are diffused. The presidency creates a focus, like a magnifying glass drawing the sun to a pinpoint of heat and light. The president is the "One Man," as the Chinese used to call their emperor. Though not a monarch, he is still the focus of passions. They don't shoot representatives or senators. They shoot presidents.

I walk toward the White House. The north face is rather modest, considering the occupant. But on the southern side I find a more impressive view. Some Japanese sailors are taking turns posing in front of the iron fence that surrounds the grounds. The White House, with its semicircular bay and high pillars, is prominent in the distance up the sweep of lawn. One nineteenth-century visitor, I recall, considered it on a par with the homes of England's middle nobility. Abigail Adams hung her laundry to dry in one of its rooms, and until the time of Lincoln, presidents used to meet with plain folks for an hour or two every day. The White House has always been both impressive and ordinary at the same time.

I follow the arc around the Ellipse and cross Constitution Avenue; as I walk onto the Mall, I feel as if I have stepped into a gigantic park. I would not know where I am but for the city signature, the Washington Monument just ahead. It is slightly off-axis, and like the Treasury building, offensive to the geometry that marks every other aspect of the ceremonial core of Washington. But in the place where it should have stood is the "Jefferson Pier," a stone marker. A perpendicular line drawn south from the White House would intersect the line of the Capitol vista exactly at this spot. Thomas Jefferson, they say, placed the marker here, where he and L'Enfant wanted the equestrian statue of Washington. I am grateful it never got built. And I am grateful that Robert Mills's complex design for the Washington Monument, with its colonnade and busy sculptural relief, never got built either.

I admire the clarity and simplicity of this obelisk, rising unadorned straight from the earth, a classically simple form, pure and elemental. In Egypt the obelisk was originally erected in honor of the sun god, and every element of its form directs the attention to the sky. Likewise in Washington, the Washington Monument is part of every vista in the core area of the capital. In its plainness, strength, uprightness, immovability, and dominance, it is a good symbol of the Father of the Country. Jokes have been made about it, but I will go along with Freud and his cigar here: sometimes an obelisk is just an obelisk.

I continue toward the Jefferson Memorial and reach the edge of the tidal basin, which is lined with cherry trees. The trees are not blooming, and I have seen them only in photographs, but now I imagine them in flower because this image, in its beauty and evanescence, is my epiphany for this axis. The hope and promise of the Enlightenment—rationality, beauty, wisdom, clarity, and light. It was the Founders' idea that men (only men) can use their God-given minds to discern the truth and establish a government based on those truths that are inherent in nature and in their own hearts. As Jefferson said, they did not have to search the musty records of the past to discover their principles: "We hold these truths to be self-evident."

I have seen this bright belief inscribed all over Washington, not just on the walls of the Jefferson Memorial, but also on the walls of the Library of Congress, the Museum of American History, and elsewhere. That freedom requires knowledge became a central tenet of the American creed. An educated citizenry preserves democracy, a democracy protects individual freedom. Despite all the political wrangling in the last twenty-five years of the eighteenth century, all participants agreed on these essential points. The enemies were authoritarian monarchs who controlled bodies and ecclesiastical hierarchs who controlled minds. Authoritarian power had to be resisted, vigilance maintained, lest freedom be diminished. The best weapons were education and knowledge.

With the hindsight of the late twentieth century, these beliefs seem naive, a product of that springtime period that marked the birth of the nation. Soon enough the elevated principles ran afoul of reality, the darkness of history, the recalcitrance of human nature. Something died. But that is the theme of another reflection.

I walk along the east side of the tidal basin to the Jefferson Memorial, the youngest of the major monuments of the capital. I think Jefferson would have liked it, for it follows the classical model of the Pantheon, which he used for the library at the University of Virginia, an enduring form to transcend the vagaries of time and the uncertainty of architectural genius. Even more than his own buildings, this memorial is penetrated by light, from all directions.

A young Jefferson stands strong and tall, square-jawed and confident, holding in his hand the scroll of the Declaration of Independence. He is the embodiment of the Founding Fathers, who dared to declare their separation from Britain, dared to defend the deed with arms, dared to shape a confederation of states, and finally, dared to distribute power in a Constitution that would bind the states together in a unity. This is what God-given reason, guided by untarnished moral sentiment, can do.

This pantheon is not a shrine of deities, but of texts, each of the four inscribed on these walls religious in content or allusion. "All men are created equal, that they are endowed by their Creator with certain unalienable rights" is the key phrase, the leitmotif. "Almighty God hath created the mind free. All attempts to influence it by temporal punishments or burthens . . . are a departure from the plan of the Holy Author of our religion" is from the Virginia Statute for Religious Freedom. The southeast wall proclaims Jefferson's belief that laws and constitutions must change as the human mind matures: "Institutions must advance also to keep pace with the times. We might as well require a man to wear still the coat which fitted him when a boy as civilized society to remain ever under the regimen of their barbarous ancestors." We can hear, behind these words, the Pauline metaphor: "When I was a child I thought as a child . . . when I became a man I put on the things of a man."

On the northeast quadrant are the haunting and prophetic words from Jefferson's letter to George Washington: "God who gave us life gave us liberty. Can the liberties of a nation be secure when we have removed a conviction that these liberties are the gift of God? Indeed I tremble for my country when I reflect that God is just." These words hang there uncomfortably, like a thundercloud. I find myself imagining Jefferson on a sweltering summer night at Monticello, in physical and mental discomfort, listening at dusk to the songs of his slaves.

These reflections carry my thoughts ahead to the next axis, which asks whether a nation "so conceived," but falling far short of that perfect conception, can continue to endure. The Founders chose Jefferson to frame those words because of his facility with language. He wrote the eloquent words, describing it as a land of persons equal and free, at the same time that his own lands were being tended by slaves. But his words, with whatever limitations and mental reservations he circumscribed them, like the most powerful of the biblical texts, took on a life of their own. They became a mythic charter that gathered power like a river, like the Potomac gliding slowly toward the sea. I stand here before the graven eloquence of the prophet of freedom, feeling uneasy on this artificial island between city and river, between ideal and reality, between what should have been and what is.

CHAPTER 4

The White House and Presidential Religion

ON DECEMBER 5, 1782, His Royal Majesty King George III made a formal appearance in Parliament. A peace treaty with the United States had been signed five days earlier, and the king, adorned in flowing burgundy-and-blue robes, wished to inform his former colonies that "he did not hesitate to . . . offer to declare them free and independent States." He closed his prepared speech with a prayer that the United States should not suffer unduly from its want of a monarchy.[1]

The king's prayer sounds quaint today, even ludicrous. But at the time it raised a serious question. Today, with socialism and international communism in full retreat, it is easy to assume the inevitable triumph of democracy, or more accurately, some form of republican government. But such an outcome would have been considered impossible in the eighteenth century. At that time, most thinkers were skeptical that ordinary human beings could govern themselves. In fact, all the evidence was on the other side. With few exceptions in human history, nations had been ruled by the monarchic government of kings, queens, and imperial sovereigns.

The men of the Enlightenment were aware of only two brief moments in human history when ordinary men, in Greece and later Rome, had attempted to rule themselves. The outcomes were not auspicious.[2] These ephemeral attempts at democracy were immediately succeeded by despotic, power-driven conquerors—Alexander and Caesar. A few years later the same phenomenon would follow the French Revolution in the person of Napoleon. As John Adams commented morosely, "there never was a democracy yet that did not commit suicide."[3]

All the Founding Fathers had acknowledged that true democracy was impossible in a large and populous nation. Jefferson had even wistfully admitted that the American Indian form of government was best, though unfortunately impractical for the large population and vast territories of the

American states. Madison had carefully considered historical examples of confederacies in the ancient past—the Amphictyonic council and Achaean league, for example—and Switzerland and Holland in more recent European history. He found them seriously lacking in governing principles and disappointing in outcome.[4] He too rejected simple democracy as unworkable in a large nation with a numerous population.

With the euphoria of the Revolution behind them, the Founders had to face the practical task of constructing a new government out of whole cloth. Like most other participants in the historic endeavor, Madison supported the work of the Constitutional Convention in spite of many misgivings. Once committed, he and Hamilton undertook an active propaganda campaign, writing the *Federalist Papers* to convince their fellow citizens that the Constitution was the best charter that future Americans could hope for. In *Federalist 14*, dated November 30, 1787, Madison wrote that the republican form of government chosen by the delegates "accomplished a revolution which has no parallel in the annals of human society," a fabric of government "which had no model on the face of the globe."[5]

The new form of government was so bold and unprecedented that even its creators were assailed by doubts and fears. Jefferson and Adams were ministers to France and Great Britain when they received drafts of the new Constitution of the United States. Both had serious doubts about its viability. Jefferson said, on November 13, 1787, in a letter to Adams, "there are things in it which stagger all my dispositions to subscribe" to it. He was most worried that it would soon produce a hereditary monarchy. Adams wrote from London three weeks later, confessing that he too had serious reservations, but of a different sort: "You are afraid," he accused Jefferson, "of the one—I, of the few. We agree perfectly that the many should have a full fair and perfect Representation.—You are Apprehensive of Monarchy; I, of Aristocracy. I would therefore have given more Power to the President and less to the Senate."[6] Washington would later be accused of leading the country toward a monarchy, and while Jefferson defended him against that charge, he confessed that Washington had "often declared to me that he considered our new constitution as an experiment on the practicability of republican government, and with what dose of liberty man could be trusted for his own good; that he was determined the experiment should have a fair trial, and would lose the last drop of his blood in support of it. . . . I do believe that General Washington had not a firm confidence in the durability of our government."[7]

To contemporary Americans with two hundred years of hindsight, the form of government constructed by the Founders may seem inevitable. But many of their compatriots feared that George III would have the last laugh. When the representatives gathered in 1787 to write that Constitution, they had considered a variety of alternative government institutions to replace the Articles of Confederation and strengthen the union of the states. As recently as January of the same year, John Jay wrote to Washington, asking in all seriousness, "Shall we have a king?"[8] A few months before his exchange with Adams, Jefferson fretted about the role of the executive in a republic. On August 4, 1787, he wrote from Paris to Edward Carrington, a leading citizen of Virginia and delegate to the Continental Congress. He stated his view on the importance of separating the legislative and executive functions of government and advised Congress, if the Convention failed to do so, to establish an "executive committee."[9] Many had no idea how to provide the executive function. James Madison, the "Father of the Constitution," had admitted to George Washington a few months earlier: "A National Executive must also be provided. I have scarcely ventured as yet to form my own opinion either of the manner in which it ought to be constituted or of the authorities with which it ought to be clothed."[10]

When the Convention did act, approving the Constitution on September 17, 1787, they chose a single executive officer, a president, not an executive committee. Article 2, section 1, states: "The executive Power shall be vested in a President of the United States of America. He shall hold his Office during the Term of four Years." It is difficult to imagine how different the history of the country would have been if a committee instead of one individual had performed the executive function—or whether it would have worked at all. As Boorstin remarks, "Jefferson was abroad at the time of the Constitutional Convention, and it is doubtful if the Constitution was much the worse for it."[11]

Madison, in writing the *Federalist Papers* with Hamilton, had strongly supported the Convention's choice of a unitary and powerful executive. The turning point in the Convention had come when James Wilson first proposed that the executive consist of a single person, whereupon, according to Madison's notes, "a considerable pause" ensued.[12] Finally Randolph described Wilson's plan for a single executive as "the foetus of monarchy," a misguided attempt to take the British constitution "as our prototype."[13] The delegates gulped, perhaps, but forged ahead. In the end, Madison had joined Wilson and Gouverneur Morris in pushing for a single executive officer, "a Magistrate," said Morris, who is "not the king but the prime minister. The people are the King." As floor leader for the effort, Morris was expressing the idea that all three were fighting for, that political powers were the people's, the royal prerogative resided with them.[14] In fact, after the Convention completed its work, the authors of the *Federalist Papers* were more worried that the legislative branch would be "everywhere extending the sphere of its activity, and drawing all power into its impetuous vortex."[15]

On the other side, Jefferson's concerns were of a different sort. After he had had time to carefully consider the text of the proposed Constitution, despite misgivings, he was willing to give it his general approval if two criteria could be satisfied. He strenuously objected to its lack of a Bill of Rights, which was, of course, later added. "The second feature I dislike, and greatly dislike," he said in a letter to Madison, "is the abandonment in every instance of the necessity of rotation in office, and most particularly in the case of the President."[16] He spelled out what he specifically feared in a letter to George Washington in May of 1788. Without term limits in the Constitution, the presidency, he feared, would become

> an office for life first, then hereditary. I was much an enemy to monarchy before I came to Europe. I am ten thousand times more so since I have seen what they are. There is scarcely an evil known in these countries which may not be traced to their king as its source, . . . I can further say with safety there is not a crowned head in Europe whose talents or merits would entitle him to be elected a vestryman by the people of any parish in America.[17]

Jefferson was clearly worried that the states had fought a war to free themselves from monarchy, only to allow its gradual and subtle reemergence in the guise of the presidency. He was not alone in this worry. Patrick Henry too feared "a great and mighty President" with powers of a king. "We shall have a king; the army will salute him monarch; your militia will leave you, and assist in making him king and fight against you."[18] The question was strenuously controverted during the last decade of the eighteenth century: What is the nature of the office and the man called the president of the United States? Predictably, some participants in the debate feared the concentration of power in a single individual, while others worried that a weakened executive would mean feeble and ineffective government. Gradually the extreme positions were rejected. The president was not to be a king, but neither was he simply to be an ordinary citizen temporarily administering the will of Congress during his set term of office. But between those two extremes there was still room for substantial disagreement.

The debate on the nature of the presidency was played out on two tracks. Both had to struggle with the power of symbols, one focusing on ideological debates about the *person* of the president, and the other on more material things, such as the executive mansion and the style of living of the person who was to live there. George Washington had said that the president's house should be built on a scale far superior to any other in the country. Pierre L'Enfant called it "the President's Palace" on his plan for the city of Washington. Jefferson promptly crossed out the last word and wrote "House," thus neatly setting the terms for the debate. At the beginning of the experiment, Washington and Hamiltonian Federalists leaned more toward the regal and Jeffersonian anti-Federalists (or Republicans) leaned more toward the egalitarian conception.

The Founding Fathers had rejected a parliamentary system of government. By vesting supreme executive power in the hands of a single individual, they did create a model of leadership susceptible to development in the direction of monarchy. In more recent times, critics of that tendency have even used the term "imperial presidency." That was always the risk, as Jefferson clearly foresaw. He wrote to James Madison from Paris on March 15, 1789, that he was aware that some Americans were hoping to edge the country toward a monarchy: "We were educated in royalism; no wonder if some of us retain that idolatry still."[19] He and the anti-Federalists would fight this tendency at every turn.

But the choice of a single executive also had some psychological advantages, for which other Founders had a better sense than Jefferson. Among these advantages was the ability to call upon the resonance of ancient beliefs and feelings ordinary people may have toward the person who rules them. People are more likely to respond to a solitary figure of eminence than to a large and cumbersome congressional plurality. If they stand in awe of this president, giving their respect and obedience, their compliance may promote a general state of harmony and peace in society.

In fact, so strong is the inveterate human tendency to follow hallowed patterns that some historians have suggested that the model for the U.S. presidency was in fact the reviled figure of George III. John Adams was in no doubt about the exalted status of the presidency: "The office, by its legal authority, defined in the Constitution, has no equal in the world, excepting those only which are held by crowned heads; nor is the royal authority in all cases to be compared to it."[20] In other words, by explicitly rejecting the traditional religious model of kingship, the exalted figure of the president could, if carefully managed, evoke some of its aura without risking the development of monarchism.

Merrill Peterson hints at the same human need when he says that Americans, "without kings, nobles, or armies [this was in the Jefferson period]; without church, traditions, and prejudices," had a greater need for the heroic element than the European nations.[21] Again, it was Adams who had a sense of the potential power of this natural human feeling, evidence of this particular piece of "the strange furniture of the human mind." He said it straightforwardly: "There is a strong and continual effort, in every society of men, arising from the constitution of their mind, towards a kingly power."[22]

The stage on which this drama of role definition was enacted was the president's house (Jefferson won the naming competition), later to be called the White House. It is the oldest historical structure in Washington. The site for the future building was marked off by architect James Hoban in the presence of the district commissioners on July 19, 1792. Hoban had come from Ireland, and most historians assume that his model for the building was the Lienster House, near Dublin, a mid-ranking domicile of British nobility. The cornerstone was laid on October 13 of the same year, three hundred years and one day after Columbus's 1492 landing in the Bahamas, with an elaborate Masonic ceremony. Since then, the character of the building has evolved in a way parallel to the evolution of the presidency, as its physical, material partner in the two-hundred-year dialogue on the nature of the office, steering a course in the gray area between a royal monarch and a plebeian executive. From the powdered-wigged, sword-girted John Adams to Jimmy Carter with his sweater and Bill Clinton in his jogging suit, both the character and the vestments of the occupants of the White House have continued to change. Whatever individual styles they brought to the position, the residence of the presidents has marked its occupant as someone set apart, neither king nor commoner, but a *tertium quid*.

By engaging in this ongoing dialogue, American presidents, whether in sword or sweater, continued to define the nature of executive leadership. Being presidential could mean nothing more than doing mundane administrative tasks. It could also mean leading exalted State rituals, like those of Inauguration Day, when the president's role scaled ceremonial heights. In the background of the discussion lurked the ancient figure of the sacred king, a conception of ruling power that had for millennia given authority to imperial and royal governments. Implicit in the sacral status of the traditional ruler was the belief that this person exercised sovereignty under the authority of the gods, that the world above and the world below were somehow related in the central figure of the sovereign. This fundamental religious ideology gave legitimacy to government in traditional cultures. The ruler had authority not because he was powerful enough to destroy any opposition, but because the gods wanted him to rule.

Once human societies had evolved into civilizations or cultures based in cities, sacral kingship appeared. Lewis Mumford has written that it was the coalescence of sacred and secular power that gave birth to cities in the first place.[23] The earliest known examples are Egypt and the Mesopotamian city-states, but similar patterns of regal sacred authority developed in India, China, Southeast Asia, sub-Saharan Africa, and Mesoamerica. In all of these places, the political vision was expressed in monumental architecture and elaborate city-planning. In its fully developed forms, the functions of the sacred king were comprehensive. He was mediator between the world above and the people below; source of all power, authority, and order in the human society below him; cause of fertility among crops and animals; miraculous healer of the sick and bringer of all blessings. Over the past thousand years, some of these powers fell away as societies, especially those in Europe, became more rationalized, but the one royal function that was never discarded was that of mediator between the two worlds. Even in nineteenth-century Europe, some kings and queens were still believed to rule by God's will and with his authority.

Though the Founding Fathers turned sacral kingship on its head by insisting on the people's right to choose their rulers, they believed that the source for their revolution was found in nature and "nature's God." The Creator of the Universe was still the ultimate authority, but the flow chart was changed. Rather than authority coming from God to the king, as in the European Divine Right of Kings, the American Founders saw power and authority coming through the people, whose free choice expressed the Divine Will. This was the correct order of nature, in their view, an expression of the laws of nature and "nature's God."

Those presidents whose behavior was closer to the regal more directly evoked the ancient history of sacral status. Since sacral kingship was always found in highly structured, hierarchical societies, it is not surprising that those with monarchist leanings in the United States tended to be the more aristocratic Federalists. They believed that national unity and public order were somehow directly related to their own elevated status and prestige. But even those of a more republican leaning could not avoid the inevitable connection between their person and the welfare of the country. Because the Constitution invested power in a single individual and balanced it against two plural bodies, Congress and the Supreme Court, the destiny of the president and the nation became inextricably entwined. The president became the living symbol of the nation. As a magnifying glass gathers and focuses the rays of the sun to a point of light, the Constitution elevates the "temperature" in the figure of the single individual who is placed at the head of the nation.

Without thinking in such conceptual terms, Washington nevertheless realized that as first president he would set precedents that would determine the role of the office for those who followed him. He understood that public behavior and ceremony would create the symbolic meaning of the office and dramatize its status. He also worried constantly about his own "image," how he would be perceived by his contemporaries and remembered by posterity. If this sort of self-conscious anxiety now seems unworthy, the desire for virtuous glory and the "fame" that came with it was considered admirable in the Enlightenment period. As James Wilson, a delegate to the Constitutional Convention, said: "The love of reputation and the fear of dishonour are, by the all-gracious Author of our existence, implanted in our breasts, for purposes the most beneficent and wise."[24] John Adams wrote to his friend Benjamin Rush in 1806 of an incident that occurred during his presidency. The Federalist newspaper editor William Cobbett had said to Adams's private secretary: "There never was a greater difference between two men than between Washington and Adams in one point, the desire of fame. Washington had an enormous, and insatiable thirst for it; but Adams was excessively careless of it!" Adams then remarked to Rush: "He did not, I presume, intend it, and I certainly did not consider it, as a compliment."[25] The perfection of the public persona was not just an individualistic concern, but a duty that patriotic leaders owed to their fellow citizens.

For both public and private reasons, Washington gave a great deal of his attention to the role he was to play as president. "It is my wish and intention to conform to the public desire and expectation with respect to the style proper for the Chief Magistrate to live in."[26] At the same time that he was planning the city of Washington and the president's house with a view to the future rituals to be performed there, he was already setting precedents of behavior in New York, as he did later in Philadelphia. He sent a message to the New York *Gazette of the United States,* prompting the editors to publish an article that stated: "The President has assigned every Tuesday and Friday, between the hours of 2 and 3 for receiving visits; and that visits of compliment on other days, and particularly on Sunday, will not be agreeable to him."[27]

Advised by Adams and especially Hamilton, Washington developed a presidential etiquette that was partially modeled on court practice in Great Britain. Hamilton wanted him to make it as "high toned" as he could get away with. Adams, in view of his intuition about the uses of the human tendency to revere kings, advised: "Neither dignity, nor authority can be supported in human Minds . . . without a splendor and Majesty, in some degree proportioned to them." He wanted the president's official title to be "His Highness the President of the United States of America, and Protector of the rights of the same." On another occasion he urged the title "His Most Benign Highness."[28] Unlike Jefferson, Hamilton and Adams were less worried about a monarchy than they were about a weak nation—one that had barely emerged from the loose Confederation to become a feeble constitutional government, unable to keep peace at home or win respect in Europe. For them a strong, regal presidency was a necessity.

There was an important psychological truth behind all the concern about ceremony and domestic behavior. Washington sensed that everything he did was significant. From the procedures to be observed in high government rituals down to questions of domestic etiquette—how the president should relate to leading citizens and to ordinary citizens, what kind of house he should occupy, and what clothes he should wear. All of these issues, he realized, were expressive of the status of the president. He understood that all these items would, to use contemporary jargon, "make a statement."

It was therefore decided, during Washington's first term, that the president was not to be expected to accept social invitations. He would host a few large annual entertainments each year and more frequent small informal dinners. Then there would be the staged levees, or receptions, modeled on British royal ceremony. These afternoon gatherings were stiff and formal, requiring appropriate clothing and powdered hair. When guests entered, they found a tableau: Washington standing before the fireplace, one hand holding a hat, the other resting on his sword. For fifteen minutes the honored visitors were announced in a low voice by a presidential aide; each one then bowed and retired to his or her assigned place. No talking was permitted. On the quarter-hour, the doors were closed, and Washington made the rounds of the guests, addressing each in turn with some pleasantry or congratulatory remark. He bowed but never shook hands. When he had finished making the rounds, he returned to the mantel, and the guests went to him, one by one, bowed, and left without speaking.[29]

While Washington was defining his presidential persona in such fashion amid the gentile urban circumstances of New York and Philadelphia, the construction of the executive mansion had commenced in the wilderness on the banks of the Potomac. Pierre L'Enfant had grown up in the monarchical splendor of Versailles and Paris. He loved the rituals of the French court and planned a palatial house for the president. William Seale, historian of the White House, speculates that the L'Enfant plan called for a "President's Palace" of enormous dimensions, approximately 200 by 700 feet, although his actual drawings for it, if there were any, have not survived.[30] These dimensions would indicate an edifice about five times larger than the mansion that was constructed. He certainly gave it locational importance in the overall plan, second only to the House of Congress. Washington himself chose the exact spot, slightly west of the site L'Enfant had indicated. The residence of the president was to have had five grand streets radiating from an extensive square on the north side of the building. On the opposite side, the planned edifice would have commanded a view of the Potomac flowing south toward Alexandria and Mount Vernon.

In a letter to the commissioners dated March 8, 1792 (just before he was fired as director of the project) L'Enfant presented the following idea: "For the President's house I would design a building which should also look forward but execute no more of it at present than might suit the circumstances of this country, when it shall be first wanted. A Plan comprehending more may be executed at a future period when the wealth, population and importance of it shall stand upon much higher ground than they do at present."[31] L'Enfant followed the same approach, therefore, that he employed for the capital as a whole: a plan of grand scope that would begin modestly but could be expanded as the financial circumstances of the young republic permitted. Soon, however, L'Enfant's arrogance lost him the good will of his patron, President Washington, and his services were terminated. Jefferson, worried all along that the imperious Frenchman was planning a royal city instead of a capital for democracy, wrote the letter of dismissal, probably with some sense of relief.

But L'Enfant was no monarchist, though his terminology sometimes misrepresented him. (Even Jefferson had once, at least, slipped and called the presidential mansion a palace.) His plans, though grand, were devised with the republican nature of the young democracy in mind. He had been careful to give precedence to the Capitol, planning for a House of Congress that had precedence over the president's "palace" in at least four respects. It was planned for a higher elevation and sited in the city's central location. There were more radiating streets emanating from it and it had a longer vista than the president's house. On this point L'Enfant and Jefferson agreed. Although Jefferson's own simple sketch for the capital showed squares of approximately the same size, he noted in a paragraph of a proclamation amending the bounds of the federal district that "the highest summit of lands in the town heretofore called Hamburg, . . . shalle be appropriated for a Capitol . . . and such other lands between Georgetown . . . and the stream heretofore called the Tyber . . . as shall be found convenient . . . shall be appropriated for the accommodation of the President of the U.S."[32]

Shortly after L'Enfant's dismissal, the commissioners of the federal district announced a competition for the designs for the Capitol and the president's house. Notices appeared in major newspapers throughout the country. Five hundred dollars, or a medal of that worth, was offered to the person who designed the "most approved plan" for the president's house. The announcement still shows L'Enfant's influence, noting, "It will be a recommendation of a Plan if the Central part of it may be detached and erected for the present with the appearance of a complete whole and be capable of admitting the additional parts in future."[33] Washington controlled the process from beginning to end, even helping to judge the competition. The prize was awarded to James Hoban, whom Washington had met in Charleston and introduced to the commissioners. After Hoban's design was selected, Washington immediately decided it was too plain and small. He added embellishments and increased the building's dimensions by one-fifth, in length and width.

Overall, the design of the house reflected the president's inclination toward the ceremonious and regal. The oval room in the center of the mansion on the south side was likely intended to accommodate the formal levees mentioned above. The grand room that took up the entire east end of the house would have been called a "saloon" in England and was probably larger than any similar "great room" in America at the time: "Fluted columns, balustrades, rich window reveals, a broad sweeping stair bursting from the doorway and passing bridgelike over a sunken light well—all indicate that this house was intended to be magnificent." In specifying a larger scale for the mansion and enhanced ornamentation, it is clear that Washington was still enamored of the royal style of his dismissed French architect.[34]

John Adams approved of Washington's presidential style. He "sought to make the presidency not just an office of dignity and authority but one with an aura of the regal, the potentate, the distant and lordly suzerain."[35] He continued the practice of the levees (models of which he had seen at the Court of Saint James in London) at the capital in Philadelphia. It was nearly the end of his term in 1800 when he and his family moved to the new capital in Washington. Although the executive mansion was not yet completed, the government moved to the Potomac according to the agreement reached in Congress ten years earlier. The Adams family moved into a president's house that was unfinished. The grounds were not landscaped. Pits and piles of rubbish dotted the area amidst roughly cut areas of weeds. Inside only half of the thirty-six rooms had been plastered. Many rooms were empty of furniture, and the house was damp and cold, unable to be comfortably heated. Abigail Adams complained that there was "not a single apartment finished . . . the principal stairs . . . not up . . . not the least fence, yard, or other convenience without, and the great unfinished audience-room I make a drying-room of, to hang the clothes in."[36] The executive mansion at 1800 Pennsylvania Avenue was too cavernous for a home, too shabby for a palace.

Adams's cultivation of a regal style was partly intentional and partly a feature of his own personality, which a biographer describes as follows: "He maintained a stiffly formal and aloof demeanor, what one acquaintance called a habitually 'ceremonious' manner." Abigail once scolded him for his "intolerable forbidding expecting Silences[s]," for "tis impossible for a Stranger to be tranquil in your presence."[37] Adams purchased a large coach, had his coat of arms painted on its door, bought a team of horses, and was attended by footmen in livery. For his apparent affectations, Adams was derided by Republicans as "the Duke of Braintree" and "His Rotundity,"[38] but his behavior was as much dictated by his political views as by his personality.

Shortly after his arrival in Washington, he addressed a ceremonious meeting of House and Senate on November 22, 1800, and during the next week, first the Senate and then the House returned the visit with a formal procession down Pennsylvania Avenue (then "a sea of mud") to pay elaborate respects to the president and his wife. Addresses were read to the president, expressing the most flattering sentiments. The president formally responded, then led the guests to state rooms on the west end of the mansion for refreshments. This was the first and only time such formalities were observed in Washington.[39]

The Republicans often spoke of "the Revolution of 1800," which they saw as a rejection of the Federalist monarchic tendencies of the two previous presidents. Jefferson certainly changed the personal style of the presidency, altered the official persona, and modified the etiquette of the chief magistrate. He immediately eliminated the levees and established the practice of hosting informal dinners with guests seated at a round table in no order of precedence or hierarchy.[40] He sold Adams's carriage and horses, keeping only a one-horse market cart for domestic use and riding around Washington on his own horse, accompanied by a single servant.[41] This act was but one minor detail of Jefferson's concerted effort, as a Republican, to undo what he considered the harmful monarchical policies of the Federalist governments of Washington and Adams. Jefferson, the agrarian utopian, had not liked cities to begin with. His plan for the new capital, submitted to Washington, had been a small gridwork plan with only two prominent features: the Congress Hall and the president's house. He so disliked the grandeur of the president's house that one could almost have imagined him refusing to move in, choosing instead some humbler dwelling elsewhere in the city.

This did not happen. The architect in Jefferson was stronger than the populist. He could never resist the challenge of remodeling a structure to his own uses, and soon he was at work at it, reenlisting James Hoban to take charge of the project. Ironically, along with some simplifications to the design of the house, Jefferson wound up enriching the interiors, adding neo-classical decorations to the architraves and cornices of the doors, new glass doors, transoms, chair rails, and fancy baseboards. His handsome $25,000 annual salary was used to stock a gourmet board, and Jefferson's own papers document "his staggering expenditures on wines."[42] As usual, Jefferson's rhetoric and behavior made an ambiguous mix of the revolutionary and traditional, republican innovation and the preservation of federalist forms. Jefferson was no "log cabin" president, as Seale remarks drily.

The later history of the White House (the name began to be used when the exterior was painted white after the burning of the building by the British in the War of 1812) is a history of the pendulum swinging between the poles of regality and republican populism. All the early presidents realized that they had the privilege and responsibility of setting patterns that would de-termine future practice. Madison said that "precedents, once established, are so much positive power."[43] His administration brought back a degree of grandeur in social events, though Dolly Madison had a knack for making people comfortable at grand parties. James Monroe, the last of the Virginia dynasty, though a Republican, bought elegant interior furnishings and brought back more formality to social ceremony. He presided over the "Era of Good Feelings," and believed he was returning to an early Washingtonian era when partisan conflicts were at a minimum. He pushed for a grand reconstruction of the White House after its burning by the British, including an enormous expenditure on imported French furnishings. Having restored more grandeur to what the Federalists had built, Monroe reigned from the house his Republicans had denounced as monarchic twenty years earlier. One representative from New York called Monroe's stiff levees an "or-deal."[44]

Andrew Jackson returned to the Jeffersonian populist model and carried it even further. Washington's elite were shocked by what happened at his postinauguration party.

> The motley crowd clamored for refreshments and soon drained the barrels of punch. . . . A great deal of china and glassware was broken, and the East Room filled with a noisy mob. . . . Such a scene had never before been wit-nessed at the White House, and the aristocratic old Federalists saw, to their disgust, men whose boots were covered with the red mud of the unpaved

streets standing on the damask satin-covered chairs to get a sight at the President of their choice.[45]

The contrast with Martin Van Buren, Jackson's hand-picked successor, could not have been greater. Van Buren was constantly accused of adopting a kingly style for the presidency and creating an extravagant White House. For three long days, Whig representative Charles Ogle held forth in the House of Representatives on the "palatial" White House, "a PALACE as splendid as that of the Caesars, and as richly adorned as the proudest Asiatic mansion."[46] And so the cycles have continued, down through the history of White House and presidency.

Although much of what occurred during the first third of the nineteenth century seems a function of both the personalities and the politics of the various presidents, systemic modifications also changed the nature of the presidency and the balance of power in Washington. Although their styles were different, Washington and Jefferson ruled by a charismatic aura acquired by their mythic roles in the Revolution. But, according to James Stirling Young, something occurred during the final year of Jefferson's presidency that reduced the power of the presidency drastically. Because of the widespread antagonism toward his embargo policy, he lost all the power he had acquired in Congress through his charisma and personal diplomacy.

From then on, through the rule of John Quincy Adams, the presidency was very weak. Contrary to Jefferson's worries about the gradual accretion of presidential power, the sources of political energy and initiative were congressional factions. There was no party unity or discipline, and Madison's prophetic fears about the "impetuous vortex" of the legislature were realized. Justice Joseph Story reported in 1818 that the "Executive has no longer a commanding influence, the house of representatives has absorbed . . . all the effective power in the country." Congress lined up against the presidents, from Madison to Adams, and won almost every battle. "I have never known such a state of things," Monroe wrote to Madison after a series of reverses, "nor have I personally ever experienced so much embarrassment and mortification." It can be said of John Quincy Adams, says Young, "that the last Jeffersonian President could not have played a less significant role if he had been absent from Washington altogether. He retreated to private hobbies and office routine, waiting second-term defeat." [47] Though peerless in legal and social status, living in a grander house than any other person in the capital, and with a salary quadruple that of his highest ranking subordinate in the political system, the post-Jefferson presidents reigned without ruling. Each was a "King without a court."[48]

Andrew Jackson enormously enhanced presidential power during his two terms in office. The issue he used to gain ascendancy was his titanic struggle with the Bank of the United States, which one scholar calls "the single most important event during the entire middle period of American history."[49] He finally destroyed the bank, and with that victory Jackson spawned the Democratic Party and its opposition, the Whig Party, congealed party loyalty, turned the veto power into a political tool, and established the direct connection to the people as his source of political power. Jackson accomplished his vast expansion of presidential power, ironically, by going directly to the people and trumping their elected representatives in Congress.[50] The Founding Fathers had blurred the connection between the people and the president, especially through the device of the electoral college. Jackson revitalized the connection and by doing so opened a source of executive power never previously utilized.

As single heads of government, therefore, American presidents have wielded power as leading actors on the stage of history and in their roles approximated the status of the sacred king. At the same time, they played a more contemplative and conceptual role, acting as theologians for the nation. Presidents exercised this theological role on scripted ceremonial occasions as well as at moments of crisis.

In traditional societies, a corps of priests usually acted as both ritual experts and diviners. As part of the structure of the government, these men presided at ceremonies that reaffirmed the connection between the ruler and the Divine Being or beings, sought the expression of the divine will through procedures of divination, and interpreted events according to the corporate understanding of their political destiny. The high priest was a mediatorial figure who stood between the heavenly and human worlds explaining the will of the gods to their subjects below.

Little of this protocol of priesthood applied directly to eighteenth- or nineteenth-century American political life. Besides rejecting kingship, sacred or secular, American democracy severed the formal relationship between religion and government, explicitly rejecting priestly functions. The priesthood was one part of Jefferson's hated triad—kings, nobility, and clergy—which he stigmatized as the cause of all the miseries and ignorance of the third estate in Europe. But in separating institutional religion and politics, the U.S. system of government left a vacuum. Traditional functions of leadership were in danger of being ignored under the new system. Sensing the need to play these roles, American presidents often had to improvise their parts, thereby setting precedents. They had to become ritual masters for important government ceremonies—state funerals, victory celebrations, proclamations of prayer and fasting, and so on. Beginning with Washington, the presidents declared days of thanksgiving and proclaimed times of fasting and humiliation. John Adams, for example, proclaimed May 9, 1798, to be a day of humiliation to "satisfy" divine displeasure (revealed by the threat of war with France). James Madison declared two days of humiliation during the War of 1812.[51] The practice of declaring such days, as well as proclaiming days of mourning for slain presidents, has continued to the present.

Perhaps the best expression of the interpretative function of the presidents' roles may be found in the long history of presidential inaugural addresses. In these orations they played the part of theologians, "explaining the ways of God to men." Although the annual State of the Union messages focused more on more practical and political matters, the inaugural addresses allowed the presidents to think more generally about their status, to express the direction of their hopes and plans for the approaching term, and to explain how they related to previous presidencies and fit into the evolving myth of the American nation. The inaugural addresses are the expression of the public persona of each president. He demonstrates his personal and individual qualities (usually in the form of humility, real or feigned), and also reflects on his political role—that is, the accumulating sense of who the president is in his relation to his predecessors. In these, their most solemn pronouncements, the presidents have used the opportunity to reflect on the history of the nation in the light of America's proclaimed ideals and its presumed destiny as the instrument of the Divine Being.

As he did in so many other respects, Washington set a precedent in his first inaugural address, framing his speech with references to the religious significance of "the experiment intrusted to the hands of the American people." After indicating his own diffidence at undertaking the presidency, he asked the blessing of "that Almighty Being who rules over the universe" upon the new government, since it was clearly His hand that guided the new nation into being. Unlike the stereotype of Deism, which understood God as remote from his creation, Washington saw the "Almighty Being" as intimately involved in the world. At every step, said the first president, by which the United States

have advanced to the character of an independent nation seems to have been distinguished by some token of providential agency; and in the important revolution just accomplished in the system of their united government the tranquil deliberations and voluntary consent of so many distinct communities from which the event has resulted can not be compared with the means by which most governments have been established without some return of pious gratitude, along with an humble anticipation of the future blessings which the past seem to presage. These reflections, arising out of the present crisis, have forced themselves too strongly on my mind to be suppressed.[52]

These words betray Washington's sense of the miraculous—an amazement that the revolution should have succeeded against the most powerful nation in the world, and that the Constitution should have been agreed upon in an "unparalleled unanimity" after so much wrangling by the disparate states and their representatives. Upon its acceptance by the state he wrote to his friend Lafayette: "It appears to me, then, little short of a miracle, that the delegates from so many different states, . . . in their manners, circumstances, and prejudices, should unite in forming a system of national government, so little liable to well-founded objections."[53]

Still, Washington knew that the euphoria would pass and that the blessings were temporary. Soon after assuming the presidency he became painfully aware of the "party animosities" already appearing. He therefore added, in his first inaugural address, that "the propitious smiles of Heaven can never be expected on a nation that disregards the eternal rules of order and right which Heaven itself has ordained." The success of the nation so auspiciously founded would in the end be "staked on the experiment intrusted to the hands of the American people." In closing, Washington again invoked "the Parent of the Human Race" to bless the deliberations of Congress that were about to begin.

Washington's use of Deist expressions such as "Almighty Being," "Great Author of every public and private good," and "Parent of the Human Race" reflects Enlightenment religiosity. In omitting any reference to Jesus Christ, he and other early presidents attempted to place their "priesthood" on a higher plane, above the level of a sectarian Christianity to a height where he could speak for any and all religions. This deliberate choice then and later allowed presidents to honor the principle of freedom of religion by speaking from a lofty universalist position.

John Adams spoke more briefly about religion in his inaugural address of 1797, delivered in Philadelphia. Although he mentioned his veneration of Christianity and a respect for that religion as one of the best recommendations for political office, he began his address with a typical invocation to "an overruling Providence which had so signally protected this country from the first." The ending is almost a litany of universal religion: "And may that Being who is supreme over all, the Patron of Order, the Fountain of Justice, and the Protector in all ages of the world of virtuous liberty, continue His blessing upon this nation and its Government and give it all possible success and duration consistent with the ends of His providence."

Jefferson also spoke of the role of religion in his inaugural address, which was the first delivered at the newly built Capitol in Washington. He invoked an enlightened religion "practiced in various forms," all of them "inculcating honesty, truth, temperance, gratitude, and the love of man; acknowledging and adoring an overruling Providence, which by all its dispensations proves that it delights in the happiness of man here and his greater happiness hereafter." At the conclusion, the third president again called upon "that Infinite Power which rules the destinies of the universe" to guide the nation's political leaders. Four years later, concluding his second inaugural address, he shaped his thought with biblical metaphors. He again invoked the help of the "Being in whose hands we are,"

> who led our fathers, as Israel of old, from their native land and planted them in a country flowing with all the necessaries and comforts of life; who has covered our infancy with His providence and our riper years with His wisdom and power, and to whose goodness I ask you to join in supplication with me that He will so enlighten the minds of your servants, guide their councils, and prosper their measures that whatsoever they do shall result in your good, and shall secure to you the peace, friendship, and approbation of all nations.

The biblical allusion to America as "the Chosen People" is as old as the first colonists, but it is highly unusual in the early presidential inaugurals. Substantial use of biblical language and metaphor was not to be heard again until the time of Lincoln.

The tone of inaugural addresses having once been set by Washington and his immediate successors, the subsequent presidents followed in what became well-worn patterns of expression. James Madison, James Monroe, John Quincy Adams, Andrew Jackson, and their successors continued to use Enlightenment names for God: "the Almighty Being," "Heaven," the "Divine Author of Being," "Overruling Providence," and similar appellations.[54] The national faith as expressed by the presidents in these formal addresses might be summarized as follows: An overruling Providence willed the success of the American experiment in the first place, intervened to ensure its success, and still watches over it. The purpose of God is to eventually extend this democratic government to the whole world.

As time went on, however, the religious references seemed to become perfunctory; they stereotypically invoked Providence or Almighty God to watch over and care for the United States and expressed the chauvinistic faith that "God is on our side." After Washington's, the inaugurals rarely even hinted at a conditional nature of the Divine Will until William Henry Harrison spelled it out once again, in the context of U.S. policy toward the

American Indians: "I can conceive of no more sublime spectacle, none more likely to propitiate an impartial and common Creator, than the rigid adherence to the principles of justice on the part of a powerful nation in its transactions with a weaker and uncivilized people whom circumstances have placed at its disposal." These are somewhat surprising sentiments coming from the old warrior who gained his heroic status and established his qualifications for the presidency at the battle of Tippecanoe!

Yet they bring out clearly that other aspect of the presidential role, as national moral theologian, and recall again the warning of Washington that "the propitious smiles of Heaven can never be expected on a nation that disregards the eternal rules of order and right which Heaven itself has ordained." From that time on, presidents have interpreted historical events and called Americans to consider those "eternal rules of order and right." In doing so, Washington and the many subsequent presidents who invoked them were implicitly adopting what biblical scholars have called the "Deuteronomic theology." Put most simply, it stated that God's blessings were conditional.[55]

> And if you obey the voice of the Lord your God, being careful to do all his commandments which I command you this day, the Lord your God will set you high above the nations of the earth. And all these blessings shall come upon you and overtake you. . . . But if you will not obey the voice of the Lord your God or be careful to do all his commandments and his statutes which I command you this day, then all these curses shall come upon you and overtake you.[56]

Though the presidents occasionally alluded to it, the conditional character of divine blessings did not receive serious attention until the crisis of the Civil War. The genteel tradition of referring to Providence, and the requisite nod to the Almighty, who was presumed to guide the fortunes of the United States, continued to be invoked in the inaugurals of Van Buren, James K. Polk, Zachary Taylor, Franklin Pierce, and James Buchanan. Finally, up against the explosive issue of secession and facing a mortal threat to the continued existence of the United States, Lincoln raised the theological question once again. For his recognition of the mystery of the Divine Will, Reinhold Niebuhr called him the foremost American theologian of the nineteenth century. With Lincoln, as with Washington, religious issues were prominent in his inaugurals. But now there was a difference. Lincoln no longer used Enlightenment phraseology but found his metaphors in the world of biblical thought and expression.

In his first inaugural address, Lincoln used all his powers of reason and persuasion to deal with the impending crisis of secession. His major purpose was to avert war and to preserve the Union. He did not believe that as president he was constitutionally empowered to interfere with the "right of each State to order and control its own domestic institutions according to its own judgment exclusively." But he did oppose any efforts to secede from the Union as equally unconstitutional. He urged caution and professed his faith in the revolutionary creed of the Founding Fathers, that divine authority comes from the will of the people, not through a divine right of kings. Lincoln's faith was based on "the ultimate justice of the people," which would, in the end, indicate the will of God: "If the Almighty Ruler of Nations, with His eternal truth and justice, be on your side of the North, or on yours of the South, that truth and that justice will surely prevail by the judgment of this great tribunal of the American people." But the burden of the future would rest on the South: "The Government will not assail *you*. You can have no conflict without being yourselves the aggressors. *You* have no oath registered in heaven to destroy the Government, while *I* shall have the most solemn one to 'preserve, protect, and defend it.' "

Four years later, chastened by the shedding of so much blood and rejecting any simplistic analysis of the tragedy, Lincoln gave the brief inaugural that would take its place with the Declaration of Independence as a great charter for the future of the nation, though the directions it laid out went unheeded at the time. Half of this short address is a religious meditation on the mysterious will of God and a questioning of Deuteronomic theology and its simplistic axioms: "Both sides read the same Bible and pray to the same God. . . . The prayers of both could not be answered. That of neither has been answered fully. The Almighty has his own purposes." Lincoln was both prophet and theologian, engaging in what is technically called theodicy, the attempt to vindicate the justice of God. There had been no inaugural address like it.

Since the Civil War was a direct challenge to the faith upon which the nation was built—the belief that this nation, under God, was to be an exemplar of freedom and democracy for the whole world—Lincoln was forced to wrestle with the issue forthrightly. He chose to do so in religious terms, concluding that, "as was said three thousand years ago, so still it must be said 'the judgments of the lord are true and righteous altogether.' " The address was an honest struggle with the challenge to the American creed, whose foundations appeared to be crumbling. The address continues to resonate—today, schoolchildren are required to memorize it, and its harmonies have become part of the way Americans interpret the national experience.

After Lincoln, perhaps partly because the crisis of national faith had receded, the level of eloquence in inaugural addresses was also much diminished. In his first inaugural, Grant reaffirmed the American credo that "our own great Republic is destined to be the guiding star to all others." But he also remarks, like a child with his hand in the cookie jar, "Why, it looks as though Providence had bestowed upon us a strong box in the precious metals locked up in the sterile mountains of the far West," and in a stroke, the great mysterious God of Lincoln's agonizing was suddenly reduced to a surrogate Santa Claus! The president did, however, call the nation to a moral consideration of the problem of the Amerindian tribes.

There was a significant change in the specific form of religious expressions used in the inaugurals after the Civil War. Perhaps encouraged by Lincoln's biblical musings, subsequent presidents adopted a more recognizably Christian (or at least biblical) terminology. Grant asks "the prayers of the nation to Almighty God," and similar straightforward invocations are made in the inaugural addresses of James Garfield, Grover Cleveland, William McKinley, William Howard Taft, Woodrow Wilson, and later presidents.

Unmistakable biblical imagery appears in the addresses of Garfield, Harrison, Cleveland, McKinley, and Warren Harding. McKinley seems almost nonplussed by the acquisition of the Philippines and suggests we must therefore do our best by the natives and make them Christians. The conclusion of Calvin Coolidge's inaugural takes up this theme. It not only uses Christian language but also celebrates the zeal of American Christian missionaries to other nations: "America seeks no earthly empire built on blood and force. . . . The legions which she sends forth are armed, not with the sword, but with the cross. The higher state to which she seeks the allegiance of all mankind is not of human, but of divine origin. She cherishes no purpose save to merit the favor of Almighty God." By this time in American presidential history, the Enlightenment appellations for the deity have almost entirely been displaced in inaugural addresses by the simple word "God," and religious thoughts offered by the presidents reflect conventional piety.[57]

Dwight Eisenhower began his first inaugural invoking "Almighty God" with what he called "a little private prayer of my own." Like Lincoln, he confronted what he saw as a serious threat to the American faith, the communism that dominated nearly half the world. And like Lincoln, he drew on religion to cope with the dangers. Religious metaphors and terminology pervaded his first inaugural address. Are we, on our long pilgrimage, nearing the light, he asked, or "are the shadows of another night closing in on us?"

Eisenhower used the term "faith" nine times in the following paragraphs, holding Americans to their principles as the only sure hope in the struggle with their opponents: "Freedom is pitted against slavery; lightness against the dark." He reaffirmed the traditional understanding of the American mission: "The faith we hold belongs not to us alone but to the free of all the world."

George Bush also asked for the help of God and led the nation in a prayer, recalling that in taking his oath he was placing his hand on the same Bible that Washington had placed his hand on two hundred years earlier. "My first act as President is a prayer. I ask you to bow your heads." He then led the nation in the following prayer:

> Heavenly Father, we bow our heads and thank You for Your love. Accept our thanks for the peace that yields this day and the shared faith that makes its continuance likely. Make us strong to do Your work, willing to heed and to hear Your will, and write on our hearts these words: "Use power to help people." For we are given power not to advance our own purposes, nor to make a great show in the world, nor a name. There is but one just use of power, and it is to serve people. Help us to remember it, Lord. Amen.

This prayer indicates how deeply the theology of the inaugurals has changed since the days of the Founding Fathers. Not just more conventionally pious and monotheistic in tone, it is unabashedly Christian, using terms like "Lord" and "Heavenly Father" and stressing the love of God. It suggests that very personal, almost familiar, relationship between the believer and God that is characteristic of some forms of Christianity.

The inaugural addresses are very limited in their scope. They occur only every four years, at most, and are not long enough to allow presidents to do much more than express their religious views and roles in a cursory way. Except at times of serious national threat, they became rather stereotyped. The only memorable oratory and rhetoric was delivered at the founding of the republic and by Lincoln. Yet taken as a whole, they do reveal agreement about the religious significance of the presidency and a consistency of belief about the meaning and destiny of the United States: that the Divine Being chose this nation to bring the good political news to the world by being a shining example of freedom, justice, and democracy among nations, and that God has guided the nation to that destiny. This untroubled and mostly unreflective faith has rarely been questioned by its high priests and theologians, the presidents. Lincoln is the exception. And even in the late 1960s, when this faith was challenged by radical protesters against the Vietnam disaster, Nixon simply chose to ignore Vietnam and the protests in his inaugural address of 1968, as Pierce and Buchanan had ignored the impending civil war in the ominous 1850s.

According to a historian of the U.S. presidency, "The democratic element of our tradition has not dismantled the monarchical element of the Constitution. . . . We remain perhaps closer to a constitutional monarchy than it is comfortable for a democracy to admit."[58] The inhabitants of the White House have come and gone, exerting their powers and interpreting events according to their own understanding of the American faith. Their personal power has grown, and at the same time their eminence and vulnerability have increased. In their persons, the United States may be praised and glorified, or blamed and attacked.

The phenomenon of presidential assassinations and assassination attempts appeared first during the reign of King Andrew I. That should not be surprising. Assassination is a kind of shadow correlate of the enhancement of executive power that began with "Old Hickory," perhaps a social expression of the law of action and reaction. As presidential power increased, so did resistance to it. Subsequent presidents, up to Lincoln—Van Buren, Harrison, John Tyler, Millard Fillmore, Pierce, and Buchanan—were unable to effectively appropriate the new lever of power that Jackson had discovered. During this period, only Polk, or "Little Hickory," came close to doing so. With the Civil War as his necessary crisis, Lincoln asserted executive power once again to preserve the union. It is impossible not to see in his assassination the beginning of a reactive trend. After Garfield and McKinley had been shot (in 1881 and 1901, respectively), U.S. Circuit Judge LeBaron Bradford Colt said to the New Hampshire Bar Association, "The record is appalling, in thirty-seven years three Presidents of the United States have been assassinated, an average of one every twelve years. The history of Europe for a thousand years furnishes no parallel."[59] Then an attempt was made on Teddy Roosevelt's life during his run for president on the Bull Moose ticket in 1912, on FDR's life in 1933, and on Truman's in 1950. After Kennedy was assassinated in 1963, others attempted to take the lives of Nixon (in 1974), Ford (twice in 1975), and Ronald Reagan (in 1981). The record is now far more appalling than that lamented by Colt. Although a public task force concluded in 1970 that presidential assassination was "typically anomic"— undertaken for private rather than public reasons— the increasing frequency still calls for an explanation.[60]

In 1996, after two clumsy attacks on the White House, Pennsylvania Avenue was closed to vehicular traffic, the section north of the executive mansion becoming almost an extension of Lafayette Park. The perimeter of defense was thereby increased, as was the distance between the president and ordinary citizens. Accounts of days when presidents strolled about Washington talking informally to bystanders seem like a utopian fairy tale. Although President Clinton occasionally ran on the streets in a jogging suit, he was surrounded by a formidable phalanx of Secret Service agents. His human surroundings bristled with security personnel. The president's house is now more like L'Enfant's "palace," and his status edges closer to that of the sacred Chinese emperor, whose ritual processions were veiled with blue cloth to prevent common eyes from seeing him, and whose subjects, if they looked directly at him, were to be slain on the spot.

If the U.S. sovereign has now wrested from Congress the power to wage war, he is also becoming as remote as an emperor of China or Japan. Catherine Bell notes that the "restriction of admittance to the ruler's presence and the decorous regulation of behavior required of all those given admittance create relationships that actually empower the ruler. . . . The distinctive status and power of the ruler are predicated in part on the distance separating him or her from other people."[61] His invisibility in the great white house, surrounded by fences and security guards, enhances presidential power and mystique, though we ordinary citizens are deceived by the media, with its film clips, sound bites, and other forms of virtual reality, into believing that he is with us, a man of the people.

CHAPTER 5

The Washington Monument

Enigma Variations

AT THE CEREMONIAL core of the capital, it is ironic that the least accessible of the Founding Fathers is Washington himself. Visitors who see the Lincoln Memorial, with Daniel Chester French's colossal seated statue and the Great Emancipator's own words engraved on the walls, believe that they have learned something about his basic character. In Rudulph Evans's pantheon and statue of Jefferson on the tidal basin they can read Jefferson's own words and believe that they understand something of what the third president means for Americans. Each shrine projects the personalities and significant qualities of its subject and makes him accessible to the visiting public. But for Washington, there is only the mute obelisk, without image, words, or explanation. A recent book on the engraved inscriptions in Washington, D.C., states, in bemused surprise, "Of note is that no inscriptions were found at the Washington Monument."[1]

He may be "first in war, first in peace, and first in the hearts of his countrymen," as Henry Lee said at his death, but the first president remains a mystery for most Americans. "Although the life of George Washington has been abundantly chronicled," says a recent book on the first president, "it remains an enigma."[2] "Washington eludes us," says Garry Wills, "even in the city named for him."[3] Although there are paintings and sculptures of him elsewhere in the city, the obelisk remains his main symbol. But it is mere geometry, a stone tower whose height is precisely ten times its base measurement. When one stands at its foot, the shaft of marble soars heavenward and is capped by a pyramid, its summit lost in the sky. What appears intelligible at a distance, even obvious, seems to evaporate close-up, where the visitor is overwhelmed by its sheer size. The highest vertical structure in the United States until the 1920s, it is still the tallest masonry structure in the world. Visitors who draw close to the Jefferson and Lincoln Memorials learn more; those who draw close to the Washington know less. What does it mean?

As an architectural creation, the obelisk first appeared along the rim of the Libyan desert before the alabaster altars of Ra, the Egyptian sun god. Later, Romans erected one in the Circus of Caligula, and later still in Saint Peter's and other locations inspired by classical revivals during the Renaissance.[4] The Egyptologist Alexandre Moret defines an obelisk as "a needle of stone on a square plan, terminating in a pointed pyramidion, with four faces, each of which is an isosceles triangle." The classical obelisk often had a gilded or polished copper pyramidion as its cap. This is exactly what visitors see in Washington, even to its shining metallic tip.

The earliest obelisk was found at the temple of Sesostris I at Heliopolis, the city of the sun, and it has always been considered a solar symbol. Pliny the Elder said that obelisks were "petrified rays of sunlight."[5] When one looks at the obelisk from a distance, this explanation is puzzling. But stand at its base and Pliny's words are convincing. Because of its tapered shape, the Washington Monument, obeying the laws of perspective, recedes into some imaginary point in the heavens. As Ra was the sun god, the obelisk built to him must certainly represent some human attempt to reach the god above. Look up from the base of the monument on a sunny day with the sun directly above it, and it does look like a needle pointing to the sky, the reflecting planes of the sides like "petrified rays of sunlight" (see Figure 14).

The question of what the obelisk may tell us about the first president does not have an easy answer. If you look for his image elsewhere in the capital you will find no single painting or sculpture that can be taken as the standard image of Washington. Although acknowledged by everyone as the most important of the Founding Fathers and foremost among the heroes of the nation, he is the hardest to fathom. Americans can quote Jefferson: "We hold these truths to be self-evident . . ." They can quote Lincoln: "Four score and seven years ago, our Fathers brought forth on this continent . . ." But how many Americans could quote a single line written or spoken by George Washington? Their dollar bills are at hand, but the image gazing out from them is little more than a mask, an icon, conveying nothing except, perhaps, a certain remoteness.

Children play a game with the dollar bill in which the money is folded so that the horizontal middle range of the bill disappears and Washington's portrait turns into a mushroom—his jabot (neck ruffle) becomes the stem of the mushroom and the top of his head the cap. Not known as a prankster, the first president would not have been amused. The real Washington is as distant from the images we have of him as a mushroom is from a man. Search as we may, there is no adequate representation of the man, but only a mythic and cultic image. Comparing him with Shakespeare, Cunliffe admits that "both men are baffling figures to us, prodigious and indistinct."[6]

FIGURE 14 Washington Monument. Photo by the author.

In many ways, the reason for the Washington enigma is itself a puzzle. Washington was certainly a simpler and more straightforward man than either Jefferson or Lincoln. His thoughts are not complex or difficult to understand. And he was easily the most frequently painted and sculpted figure of the entire eighteenth century, in both Europe and America. Some of the most competent artists of the time produced literally hundreds of original portraits of him. He spent long hours posing for painters, including Charles Wilson Peale, his son Rembrandt Peale, John Trumbull, and Gilbert Stuart. At first impatient about sitting like "patience on a monument," he described himself as restive as a colt newly saddled. But by 1785 he had learned to reconcile himself to the requirements of prominence: "No dray-horse moves more readily to his thill than I to the painter's chair."[7]

Washington was also the subject of countless popular images, book and magazine illustrations, almanacs, broadside cuts, and ornamented music. His likeness was reproduced on Liverpool pitchers, on cotton textiles, and in Chinese reverse paintings on glass, coins, medals, mirror knobs, tavern signs, and other ornamented crafts and manufactures: "It was the first time in America that the likeness of a public figure was disseminated so broadly to so varied an audience."[8] Images of Washington were kept like the icons of saints. An article in the *American Magazine* in 1836 noted that "prints of Washington dark with smoke are pasted over the hearths of so many American homes." And a Russian visitor, Pavel Svinin, had earlier seen a religious analogue in this practice: "It is noteworthy that every American considers it his sacred duty to have a likeness of Washington in his house, just as we have images of God's saints."[9]

In addition to the hundreds of two-dimensional renderings of Washington, there was the three-dimensional work of sculptors Jean-Antoine Houdon, Giuseppe Ceracchi, Horatio Greenough, Clark Mills, Thomas Crawford, and numerous others. Of course some of these sculptures are so idealized that they convey no realistic idea of what he looked like. For example, the Italians Giuseppe Ceracchi and Antonio Canova produced statues that portray Washington as a classical figure; they are literal renditions of the frequent comparison of Washington to such figures as Cincinnatus, Fabius, Cato, and other Roman heroes.

But not all the sculptures were so conventionalized. Horatio Greenough's statue of Washington, a massive seated figure modeled on the Zeus of Phidias, took its facial features from Houdon's bust, which is considered the most accurate sculptural representation of Washington. The statue is so much larger than human scale, however, that it raises the hero to the pantheon of the gods. Greenough had been commissioned in 1832 to do the statue for the rotunda of the Capitol, where it was to reside just below the dome. Its enthusiastic promoters believed it would become the premier and signature image of Washington in the capital. But Greenough's choice of model, toga-clad with chest bare, proved unfortunate. When it was installed in the rotunda ten years later, citizens were outraged. They were more than willing to see Washington deified, but what shocked ordinary Americans was seeing the Father of the Country naked from the waist up, "as though he were entering or leaving a bath" (see Figure 15).[10]

Montgomery Meigs, the chief engineer in charge of the expansion of the Capitol in the 1850s, said that though the immense statue could be appreciated by "a few scholars," it was "unsparingly denounced by the less refined multitude."[11] But Nathaniel Hawthorne was probably closer to the truth when he exclaimed: "Did anybody ever see Washington nude? It is inconceivable. He had no nakedness, but I imagine he was born with his clothes on, and his hair powdered, and made a stately bow on his first appearance in the world."[12] Hawthorne saw clearly that Washington had already been sacralized as a mythical figure and was no longer subject to human standards. In 1843, too imposing for popular taste and too heavy for the rotunda floor (the colossal statue weighed twenty tons), Greenough's work was moved to a location outside on the Capitol grounds. When it began deteriorating in the weather, it was again moved, this time to a niche in the Smithsonian in the Museum of American History, where it remains today next to an escalator, a monumental afterthought unrelated to nearby museum exhibits.

Greenough was trying to create an idealized image of Washington that would transcend time. Other sculptors had as their major aim a realistic representation of Washington. In 1784 the legislators of the Commonwealth of Virginia voted to erect a statue of Washington, their most eminent native son, in the state capital. They formed a committee and contacted Jefferson and Franklin, then ministers of the victorious colonies to the French government in Paris. The two, empowered to choose a sculptor, settled on the forty-four-year-old Jean-Antoine Houdon, famous already for his busts of Voltaire, Diderot, Rousseau, Franklin, Lafayette, and many other Enlightenment figures. Franklin obliged by personally escorting Houdon from France to America, where the sculptor made studies for the commission for the State of Virginia and a bust that has become the most famous sculptural likeness of Washington. In order to achieve perfect verisimilitude, he traveled to Mount Vernon, relying on exact measurements of the general and a life-mask taken from Washington's face.[13] The life-mask still exists, preserved in the Pierpont Morgan Library in New York City.

FIGURE 15 Horatio Greenough, sculpture of George Washington. Courtesy of the Library of Congress.

Houdon, based on this mask and exact measurements he himself took, produced the Washington bust that is "without doubt the most precious sculptured relic of Washington. By many it is considered the standard by which Washington's features, at the time of his maturity, should be judged by sculptors."[14] It is probable that no more accurate image of the first president can be found. The original is on display at Mount Vernon, and a copy is in the National Portrait Gallery in Washington (see Figure 16).

Houdon's standing statue, commissioned by the Virginia legislature, now

FIGURE 16 Jean-Antoine Houdon, bust sculpture of George Washington. Courtesy of the Mount Vernon Ladies' Association.

stands in the rotunda of the Virginia statehouse (see Figure 17). There is also an exact replica of it in Statuary Hall in the U.S. Capitol, where it is accessible to large numbers of tourists. Of this standing statue of Houdon's, Lafayette is quoted as saying that it was "a facsimile of Washington's person." And if it be objected that Lafayette made similar expostulations of admiration every time he was shown an image of his old friend, we may listen instead to Washington's good friend and appointee Chief Justice Marshall on the Houdon statue: "Nothing in bronze or stone could be a more perfect image than this statue of the living Washington."[15] But most convincing is the statement of Rembrandt Peale, himself an artist, who together with his father, Charles Wilson Peale, painted some of the best-known portraits of the president. The Peales lived on the same square in Philadelphia as Washington during the latter's second term as president and saw him almost every day. Says Peale: "Now if you will stand in the southwest corner of the rotunda [in the Virginia statehouse, Richmond] and look at this statue on a level with it you may well think you are beholding Washington himself. That is the man, sir, exactly."[16]

One enigma of Washington in the capital is therefore not that it is impossible to find accurate images of him, although it may be difficult for the hurried tourist to do so. It is rather the opposite. Beginning in the early nineteenth century, it became clear that Americans *did not want to see* the real Washington but demanded that all images of him, whether visual or verbal, conform to the mythic paradigm that existed in their imaginations.

A brief look at the work of Gilbert Stuart supports this interpretation. Stuart painted seventy to eighty portraits of Washington (originals and copies), some bust portraits, others full length, seated and equestrian. Stuart's bust portraits of Washington are divided by Gustavus Eisen, the foremost authority on the portraits of Washington, into three major types or series: the Vaughn, the Brook, and the Athenaeum. These designations are the names of the owners of the principal painting in each series when Eisen was doing his exhaustive studies of these portraits. According to Eisen, the earliest bust portraits, the Vaughn type, are most true to the president's actual appearance. But in consulting with the two Peales, Stuart came to the conclusion that Washington's appearance was "too aged," with too personal a look on his face, not showing "that dominance and leadership which the public demanded in a portrait of their leader." In other words, the real Washington did not look as heroic as he ought to. As a result, Stuart gradually eliminated traces of age and infirmity.

If this deliberate distortion is true of the later portraits in the Vaughn series, the Athenaeum series was even more idealized. In this last series of

FIGURE 17 Jean-Antoine
Houdon, sculpture of George
Washington, standing, Virginia
Statehouse, Richmond. The
Library of Virginia.

bust portraiture, "the subject is greatly idealized, dignified, mysterious, and somewhat aloof. . . . A general sphinx-like air has made this portrait very popular, although it could have resembled Washington but little" (see Figure 18).[17] As Daniel Boorstin remarks, "lasting popular devotion significantly fixed on Gilbert Stuart's unfinished portrait (the 'Athenaeum')," and it is this portrait that is most thoroughly "suffused with an unworldly haze."[18] A young Sylvia Plath described the image that gazed down at her from a classroom wall as having a "lamblike granny-face . . . between neat blinders of white curls."[19]

Stuart and others made countless reproductions of this portrait, among them the engraving on the U.S. one-dollar bill. When most Americans think of Washington, this is the image that comes to mind. And it has become so thoroughly conventionalized that were it to be reduced to a mere featureless oval with the familiar triangular "wings" of hair, most people would still

FIGURE 18 Gilbert Stuart, bust painting of George Washington. U.S. Senate Collection.

be able to identify it as representing Washington. One wag, novelist John Neal, was quoted as saying that "if Washington were to rise from the Grave, and not be found to resemble Stuart's Portrait, he would be rejected as an Impostor."[20]

As the honor and adulation paid to Washington increased during the early nineteenth century, Americans continued to profess their desire to know exactly what the great man had looked like. John Marshall said that "it is impossible to contemplate the actions and character of Washington, his early and steady adherence to the cause of Liberty and his devoted patriotism, without feeling an ardent desire to know the exact appearance of so great and excellent a man, and how far his corporeal features correspond with his acknowledged mental greatness."[21] Artists obliged with literally hundreds of original attempts and thousands of reproductions. It is certain that some of these artists were motivated to produce an exact likeness of the hero, yet some mysterious shadow always seemed to intervene between the intention and the act.

Take Rembrandt Peale. He literally made a career of the effort to paint a perfect simulacrum of Washington. He had his first sitting with the great man when only seventeen years old, and he was so nervous that he asked his father to paint Washington at the same time, to take some of the pressure off his own efforts. His uncle, James Peale, also seized the opportunity to capture Washington's portrait, so the hero was surrounded by three Peales. This incident gave rise to Gilbert Stuart's quip to Martha Washington when she expressed her amusement at the situation: "Watch your husband. He is in danger of being 'Pealed.'" Rembrandt Peale continued in his efforts through later years, and toward the end of his life, in the 1850s, he traveled all over the nation, delivering a lecture about his efforts to capture the authentic Washington. It began with these lines: "It is impossible to contemplate the actions & character of Washington—his zealous adherence to the cause of Liberty, and his self-sacrificing Patriotism, without feeling an ardent desire to know him, as it were, *personally*, and to judge how far his Corporeal features corresponded with his acknowledged mental & moral greatness."[22]

Peale told his audiences of his own acquaintance with Washington, of his own efforts and those of other painters—John Trumbull, Gilbert Stuart, Charles Wilson Peale (his father), and others—to capture the likeness of the president. He was satisfied with none of their portraits, not even his own. Finally in 1823 he resolved to make one last-ditch effort to capture the great likeness and believed he had finally met with success. The remaining two-thirds of what must have been a very long and tedious lecture recounts many self-serving "depositions" from a list of luminaries, all testifying that Peale's was the most perfect likeness of the great man in existence. Among his "expert witnesses" were John Marshall, Bushrod Washington (nephew of the first president and a Supreme Court justice), George Washington Parke Custis (Washington's adopted grandson), Lafayette, and a group of original members of the Society of the Cincinnati, as well as his own father, Charles

Wilson Peale. "If his [Washington's] Relatives and Friends have given it preference over any other Portraits, I may be pardoned for being induced to coincide with them—they have been the Jury who have tried the Case, and I, at least, am bound to submit to their Verdict," he said, humbly acquiescing to their accolades.

After this buildup, one is disappointed to read the following description of this most ballyhooed of all the portraits of Washington, now in the Senate Chamber of the Capitol: "The portrait is highly artificial, and while it is 'heroic' it is not a good likeness of Washington as we know him now. Above all, it is patriotic and impresses us, but also overawes us, with its enormous size and its oval oak leaf frame painted directly on the canvas."[23] It seems that Rembrandt Peale, seeker after the true likeness, was in the end captive to the same overriding mythology that doomed the efforts of all his contemporaries (see Figure 19).

In the end, there is no one image of Washington that has received general approbation. The Houdon bust was criticized by Bushrod Washington. The vaunted standing statue in the Richmond statehouse was criticized by Eisen as portraying "a French gentleman . . . pompous and ostentatious instead of dignified." The face, he continued, is "coarse, crude, unintellectual, lacking sympathy, force, and thoughtfulness."[24] The clay life-mask taken by Houdon would have to be acknowledged as the best likeness of the first president. It is complete with hair marks and skin texture, yet it seems among the *least* expressive images we have of Washington. It is more like a death-mask, concealing the man under the surface of an entirely unexpressive face. One imagines that even if photography had been available and there existed a photograph of the first president, many would say about it, as they might say about the photograph of a friend, "it doesn't capture him." Hundreds of the painted and sculpted portraits of Washington in the three volumes of Eisen provide a good general, if composite, sense of what he looked like. Thus the enigma of Washington is rooted not in the absence of a perfect likeness, but in two other factors.

First, Washington's character is opaque because he was by nature and intention reserved, stiff, and somewhat remote even to those who knew him. As Jefferson once remarked: "His heart was not warm in its affections." A Dutch visitor to Mount Vernon in 1784 arrived with a desire to appreciate Washington but reported that he "could never be on familiar terms with the General—a man so cold, so cautious, so obsequious." Another European visitor said of him: "There seemed to me to skulk somewhat of a repulsive coldness, not congenial with my mind, under a courteous demeanor."[25] Among his military companions, it was probably his officers who admired

FIGURE 19 Rembrandt Peale, bust painting of George Washington as *Patriae Pater*. U.S. Senate Collection.

him the most, not ordinary soldiers. He did not have the common touch, and no one ever give him a nickname, even on the British side. His adoring but saucy hagiographer, Parson Weems, at his most familiar, merely calls him "old George." To ordinary soldiers, reports one biographer, "he was a stern, awe-inspiring figure. He attended to their wants, he shared their dangers and discomforts, but he was not one of them. He kept a distance, and emphasized it in a host of orders of the day that have a rigid, monitory sound; they are full of rebuke and prohibition, and where they are appreciative they are still a little glacial. They do not *give* praise; they *bestow* it."[26] Samuel Downing, a soldier under Washington during the Revolution, was interviewed many years later as one of the last living links with the great general. He spoke of the soldiers' love for and devotion to Washington, but said, "Oh! But you never got a smile out of him."[27]

Eisen notes that Washington never, during the years he was president, shook hands with anyone.[28] In a casual age like ours, Washington's formality is bound to be regarded as repellent. Ever since the presidency of Andrew Jackson, U.S. politicians have felt compelled to display the "common touch" of populism as the avenue to power. The point has often been made that contemporary Americans are not comfortable with heroes: "In America at the end of the [twentieth] century, no one is admirable, no one unblemished, no one on a pedestal . . . our children are denied permission to admire. We have given free rein to envy, to our desire to tarnish and tear down; and shortchanged our instinct to emulate, to build up, to admire. Not finding heroes, we have succumbed to scorn."[29]

It is difficult to return to the thought world of the eighteenth century, when exactly the opposite sentiment was prevalent. What Washington said about the new nation at the end of the war could apply equally to his own life: "We are a young nation and have a character to establish."[30] At the age of thirteen he was already striving to do so, copying a set of 110 "Rules of Civility and Decent Behavior in Company and Conversation." Such maxims as the following appeared: "Let your countenance be pleasant but in serious matters somewhat grave"; "And in all Causes of Passion admit Reason to Govern." To his nephew Bushrod Washington, later to become a Supreme Court justice, he wrote "Be courteous to all, but intimate with few; and let those few be well tried before you give them your confidence."[31]

In all his behavior, he reflected the classical ideal of honor. Love of glory, in a good cause, was considered a virtue in the Enlightenment, a conscious rejection of the humility and self-effacement of monkish Christianity.[32] As Washington said in a letter to Henry Lee in 1786, "Example, whether it be good or bad, has a powerful influence, and the higher in Rank the officer is, who sets it, the more striking it is."[33]

Washington's favorite play was Joseph Addison's tragedy *Cato,* in which the author contrasts the heroic protagonist, who represents the old order of Roman democracy, with the power-hungry Caesar, about to triumph in a civil war and seize the status of emperor. (Washington once wrote to an early romantic interest that he would "play Juba to her Marcia," referring to the young lovers in the drama.) The play had enormous influence in America during the Revolutionary period. Washington had it performed at Valley Forge.[34] The line "What pity is it / That we can die but once to serve our country!" may have been the source of the famous exclamation attributed to Patrick Henry. For Washington, the play delineated the nature of true honor and nobility of soul. The heroic young Juba recommends Cato's virtues to his Numidian countryman Syphax:

> There may'st thou see to what a godlike height
> The Roman virtues lift up mortal man,
> While good, and just, and anxious for his friends,
> He's still severely bent against himself;
> Renouncing sleep, and rest, and food, and ease,
> He strives with thirst and hunger, toil and heat;
> And when his fortune sets before him all
> The pomps and pleasures that his soul can wish,
> His rigid virtue will accept of none.[35]

This passage could be a description of Washington's behavior during the Revolutionary War, sharing the hardships of the army, refusing any pay other than his bare expenses, and most emphatically rejecting the assumption of power. In fact, when informed that the troops wanted to acclaim him king, he became enraged: "No occurrence in the course of the war has given me more painful sensations, than your information of there being such ideas existing in the army, as you have expressed, and I must view with abhorrence and reprehend with severity."[36] This was "his rigid virtue" speaking. Washington was frequently eulogized after his death, for unlike Napoleon, he was able to resist the temptation to seize autocratic power. This was the quality Lord Byron so admired in his Washington poem "Cincinnatus of the West." Washington's sense of honor was so absolute that it erected a facade that effectively masked his own feelings. But this too is part of the code, as Juba points out:

> Honour's a sacred tie, the law of kings,
> The noble mind's distinguishing perfection,
> That aids and strengthens virtue where it meets her,

And imitates her actions, where she is not:
It ought not to be sported with.[37]

In an age like ours, which prizes spontaneity and "naturalness," Washington's behavior appears excessively calculating. From the time he was appointed commander-in-chief of American forces in the Revolutionary War, Washington realized that his own character was somehow merged with the destiny of the newly emerging nation in the minds of Americans. His image was its image. From that point on, his behavior and speech became even more cautious as he realized that everything he said or did would redound to the credit or discredit of the new nation. When, early in the Revolutionary War, the British commander-in-chief General William Howe tried to communicate with him, he addressed the letter to "George Washington, Esq." Washington returned the letter to him unopened. Again Howe tried with "George Washington, Esq., &ca, &ca." Again it was refused. Finally, Howe sent an officer who obliged with a request to see "His Excellency, General Washington." He was received.[38]

The story is told that the emperor Vespasian muttered, as he was about to expire: "*Vae, puto deus fio*" (Alas, I think I am becoming a god!) For Washington (who of course would never have uttered such world-weary sophistry), the phrase should read: "*Vae, puto monumentum fio,*" for he knew long before his death that he was becoming a monument. Here is the second reason why Washington is so hard to find in the U.S. capital or anywhere else. He has become a myth, the subject of adoring hagiography and pious legends among both the learned and ordinary folks. He is saint, savior, and even god, and finding the "real Washington" behind all the sacred mythic elaborations is almost impossible. It is also beside the point, for his importance to most Americans was not his humanness, but his mythical, semi-deified status as the chosen vessel of Providence to establish the great experiment of democracy. To such transcendent beings as Washington we create statues and build memorials. We do not "get to know them."

What is most important to Americans is not that he wore false teeth or raged at General Charles Lee for his cowardly retreat at Monmouth, not that he wept in the presence of Elias Boudinot, grew wheat rather than tobacco on his plantation, got furious at "that rascal Freneau" (whose Republican newspaper mercilessly criticized him during his second term), or sometimes laughed at Gilbert Stuart's off-color jokes. Washington is important to Americans as their central figure of self-understanding, the mythic embodiment of the ideals Americans consider their highest and best.

His biographers are reluctant to allow him any expression of what they consider unseemly emotion. Although General Lee's actions at Monmouth enraged him and he cursed his subordinate officer passionately, Parson Weems bowdlerizes the event. Washington spoke to Lee, he says, with "great warmth." The general is said to have wept at his farewell to his troops. His early biographer Jared Sparks hastens to describe this as "the tear of manly sensibility," lest we erroneously suspect the hero of any (feminine) weakness.[39] He was the revolutionary military hero, wise patriot, Founder of the nation through his quiet guidance of delegates to approve a practical Constitution, and first leader of the fledgling government as president. There must be no trait open to criticism. In short, Americans revered him not for his human qualities but as a compendium of their most cherished virtues.

The heroic status shaped by these virtues is grand enough, but the American imagination has enhanced them tenfold by conflating their civic and patriotic character with age-old religious paradigms. The power of Washington as a symbol is directly linked with overt and covert religious models that have lifted him above the human realm. Because this religious dimension of his significance was sometimes hidden under an apparent "secularity," it becomes all the more powerful for being not consciously detected. Within a few years after his death he had become a virtual saint, a sacred figure on a par with the great founders of religions.

It is easy to see how this transfiguration occurred. Officially an Episcopalian, Washington was no zealot about organized religion, though he eventually came to hold a firm belief in Providence. His early Anglicanism had provided him with a strict moral code, but he seemed to be comfortable with the Deism of the Enlightenment—of Franklin, Jefferson, and even Tom Paine. He was tolerant of a great range of religious opinion, never once using the word "Christ" in his public utterances. He had a gentrified tolerance of religious differences, although most Americans were in fact sectarian Christians. They incorporated Washington into their inner pantheon not as Deists, but according to their own religious mode of thinking. By the end of the Revolutionary War, he was "about half way to Olympus." In 1800 America was in need of a hero to unify warring political factions. "Divested of most of his personal traits, made into an abstract catalogue of virtues, he was straight way elevated to the Valhalla of national heroes."[40] Several authorities traced Washington's forebears to the time of William the Conqueror, but "one intrepid genealogist produced a four hundred page tome tracing Washington's progenitors back to Odin, the Norse god."[41]

The major agents of Washington's transformation into a religious figure were popular political orators and preachers, and the difference was often hard to discern. Beginning with the many who seized the occasion of his death to "interpret" his significance to their listeners, funeral orations nearly all speak of his being chosen by Providence. Although they drew classical comparisons (with Cincinnatus, Cato, and Fabius) the preachers especially dwelt on comparisons with well-known biblical figures such as Moses, Cyrus, Joshua, and even Jesus, a model of piety for young and old. The pulpit and courthouse orators "played a major role in the canonization of Washington, and they lent it their continual support through the years." These sentiments were not merely the ravings of uneducated pulpit thumpers. The Reverend David Tappan, professor of divinity at Harvard College, proclaimed: "Well may he be ranked among Earthly Gods, who, to other great accomplishments united a 'humble,' yet near resemblance of HIM who is the standard of human perfection, and the express IMAGE of divine glory."[42] One unconventional scholar, Moncure D. Conway, observed that the Washington family had passed into "a conventionalization curiously resembling that of the Holy Family: the savior of his country has for his mother a saintly Mary; his father is kept in the background like Joseph; he is born in a mean abode."[43] How a prosperous Virginia plantation can be called a "mean abode" is hard to imagine, but such details were mere quibbles to Washington's earnest orators and preachers. They began to employ these biblical allusions because they knew they had a powerful resonance for their listeners. Sometime later, J. N. Danforth, trying to shame those who, he claimed, had not built a fitting memorial to "Mary, the Mother of Washington," intoned his belief that "we owe all the mighty debt due from mankind to her immortal son."[44] One U.S. senator asserted that George Washington was untempted by evil: "The devil is an ass. But he never was such an ass as to waste his time tempting George Washington."[45]

Comparisons of Washington to Jesus Christ strike the theme of the hero as religious founder, placing him in the exalted company of Jesus, Muhammad, the Buddha, Moses, Zoroaster, and others. Though such comparisons may seem extravagant, Americans needed a figure who could transcend parties, as well as partisan and sectional interests, and bring the new nation together in a "more perfect union." Without Washington's prestige there would have been no one to accomplish that delicate task. Weems's famous biography recounts the tale of Washington's mother's dream, a familiar mythic motif in the lives of great religious figures. In the dream, with detail too complicated to relate here, Mary Washington sees a house burst into flame, and when all, including her husband and the servants, are too afraid to do anything, five-year-old George runs up, calling: "Oh, Ma! don't be afraid: God Almighty will help us, and we shall soon put it out." It is a dream about George Washington saving the new nation, and as Weems adds, it "needs no Daniel to interpret it."[46]

If these early responses to Washington seem inflated, Frances Whittemore recounts the events surrounding the installation of the Washington monumental pillar in Baltimore. When the sixteen-foot statue of the hero was elevated to its place, she says that the enthusiasm of the crowd, "a cloud of witnesses," broke forth in loud shouts while tears ran down the faces of many veterans present. Just as the statue was settled into its place, it is said, "a shooting star dashed across the sky and an eagle alighted on the head of Washington."[47] In just such miracles are legends born and saints canonized.

In religious traditions, the function of "founder" figures is to announce to the world the messages that Divine Power has communicated to them. Founders bring the transcendent truths to earth, embodying them in their own lives. Although themselves figures of power, they must at the same time be humble and self-effacing. The purpose of this humbling is to acknowledge the gulf between themselves and the greater reality they have come to represent and the truths and ideals it is their mission to convey. So they must surrender themselves in acknowledgment of it.[48] The self-emptying theme of Christianity is given a secular expression in Washington's frequent resignations.[49] "He was a virtuoso of resignations," says Garry Wills, and used them as ways to achieve even greater power, but in a way consonant with the ideals of the new democracy.

Writers and artists sensed this aspect of Washington's role. Greenough explained his ill-fated statue to Lady Rosina Wheeler Bulwer-Lytton, as follows: "I have made him *seated* as *first magistrate* and he extends with his left hand the emblem of his military command toward the people as the sovereign—He points heavenward with his right hand. By this double gesture my wish was to convey the idea of an entire abnegation of Self and to make my hero as it were a *conductor* between God and man." In another letter, to Edward Livingston, he makes the same point more briefly: "I wish while I impress the beholder with the idea of Washington, to remind him that Washington was an agent."[50] Power, in other words, must be rejected in order to be achieved. He who would be first must take the last place.

Washington himself struck this theme of humility at the end of his long letter to the governors of the states on disbanding the army:

> I now make it my earnest prayer, that God would have you, and the State over which you preside, in his holy protection; . . . that he would most graciously be pleased to dispose us all to do justice, to love mercy, and to demean ourselves with that charity, humility, and pacific temper of mind, which were the characteristics of the Divine Author of our blessed religion, and without an humble imitation of whose example in these things, we can never hope to be a happy nation.[51]

The founder figure's human personality is subsidiary to his religious and mythic role. His image becomes a mask through which something more important is conveyed. The mask-like quality of so many paintings of Washington, especially Gilbert Stuart's, are perfectly appropriate therefore, and inevitable, for a figure who is more important as a symbol than as a human being with faults and foibles. Sigfried Giedion notes that some of the earliest representations of real human beings discovered by archeology are masks (such as those found at Hassuna and Uruk in Mesopotamia, from the fourth and third millenniums B.C.E.): "What are today called masks were, for primitive and primeval man, a means of transformation into another being, another nature, and a means of contact with supernatural powers."[52]

In the classical period, masks were called *persona*, objects through (*per*) which voices sounded (*sonare*). That is, the mask was nothing in itself, but it took on the power of exemplary or supernatural beings. The mask represented the mediator through whom the transcendent ideas or ideals were made known to the people. The reality represented was important, not the physicality of the mask. The mask hides individual differences, idiosyncrasies, eccentricities, and all other specific features that would detract from the idea it attempts to convey. This is exactly the function of Stuart's Athenaeum portrait of George Washington. In fact the Athenaeum portrait was often severed from its torso by other artists and reinstalled as needed. John James Barralet did it for his *Commemoration of Washington,* and Stuart himself did it, placing it incongruously on the heads of his images of standing Washington, where its iconic quality often looks out of character on the more active bottom half of the full-length figures. Grant Wood makes a humorous comment on this tradition by putting the Athenaeum head on the body of Washington as a boy in his painting of the legend of the cherry tree.

Though paintings, especially Stuart's, were an important constituent of the mythical Washington, a single work of literature did the most to canonize Washington for later generations of Americans. This is *The Life of Washington* by Mason Locke Weems, better known as Parson Weems. Weems was an insinuating but somehow likable character, always brimming with schemes to make money and at the same time accomplish some moral good in the world. Unhappy with the stiff, tedious, five-volume official biography of Washington's life produced by John Marshall, Weems wrote his own shorter and livelier version of the hero's life. Along with a generally accurate account of the main events of Washington's life, Weems added (most critics would say "fabricated") some colorful incidents that have become more significant to the Washington myth than the more sober events of documented history. Weems's intent in writing the biography should have been obvious to anyone reading the frontispiece of his 1809 edition:

THE LIFE
of
GEORGE WASHINGTON
with
CURIOUS ANECDOTES
Equally Honorable to Himself
and
Exemplary to His Young Countrymen

The most important of these exemplary and "curious anecdotes," of course, is the tale of the cherry tree, told to him, Weems claims, by "an aged lady, who was a distant relative, and when a girl spent much of her time in the family."[53] It is amusing to think that this story, without a doubt the tale most used to inculcate honesty in the mendacious children of America, is itself a fabrication.

Some sense of Weems's sentimental style may be gathered from the passage he puts into the mouth of George's father, Augustine, after the youth has admitted hacking at the tree: " 'Run to my arms, you dearest boy,' cried his father in transports, 'run to my arms; glad am I, George, that you killed my tree; for you have paid me for it a thousand fold. Such an act of heroism in my son, is of more worth than a thousand trees, though blossomed with silver, and their fruits of purest gold.' "[54] Yet Weems was no prude, occasionally introducing racy elements to spice his narration. He describes the general in a social situation in which the young ladies present allow their minds to wander from the readings of a preacher "to catch a livelier devotion" from Washington's "mind-illumined face." At such times "sighs of sentiment too delicate for description" are seen to "heave the snowy bosoms of the noble dames."[55]

Weems's greatest success came from his ability to enliven Washington's life with anecdotes whose concreteness left an indelible impression on the minds of his readers and made the "catalogue of virtues" for which Washington was eulogized come alive. For example, it is clear from many of his writings that Washington believed Providence had guided him and the fate of the new nation. He wrote to Benjamin Harrison on December 18, 1778: "Providence has heretofore taken me up when all other means and hope seemed to be departing from me in this. I will confide."[56] Weems elaborates this theme by telling how the boy Washington was astonished to discover some plantings in the family garden that spelled his name. They were cabbage sprouts carefully planted by his father to teach him that Providence, the "Great Designer," created the world and watches over it. Another deception in the interest of moral instruction. Weems then demonstrates Washington's belief in divine Providence by showing the general praying at Valley

Forge. Like the cherry-tree story, this praying tableau has had a long after-life, appearing for example, on the cover of the *Saturday Evening Post* in 1935. The scene now appears in stained glass on the window of the prayer room in the U.S. Capitol.[57]

Weems describes the disaster of General Edward Braddock's defeat, while Washington himself was "protected by Heaven." He quotes a famous Indian warrior after the battle as saying, "Washington was not born to be killed by a bullet! For I had seventeen fair fires at him with my rifle, and after all could not bring him to the ground!"[58] Here Weems was bringing up a theme common in many paintings of Washington, especially as he led his troops to victory.[59] Weems describes the death of Washington as an apotheosis: "Swift on angels' wings the brightening saint ascended; while voices more than human were heard (in Fancy's ear) warbling through the happy regions, and hymning the great procession towards the gates of heaven. His glorious coming was seen far off, and myriads of mighty angels hastened forth, with golden harps, to welcome the honoured stranger."[60] If all this seems fevered and overblown today (Bryan says that it sounds like a burlesque of the elevated style of Homer or Milton),[61] it was a product of the early nineteenth century and received as the most popular book of its day. Elite artists such as Barralet and Constantino Brumidi later depicted similar scenarios of the great Washington ascending to or enthroned in heaven. Poets described his incorporation into the Olympian pantheon, and Jonathan Mitchell Sewell's "Festival Song" proclaimed him the equal of Jove.[62] Weems's portrayal of Washington was "in line with the religious and ethical code of the ordinary public that he wished to reach. . . . the poor man's Washington, not the aristocrat's and definitely not the scholar's or the critic's."[63]

Weems's *Life of Washington* was reprinted eighty times over the years, and parts of it were regularly used in Sunday School lessons. It was also widely used in private-school curricula, and most significantly, parts of it were incorporated into the *McGuffey Readers,* the mostly influential elementary school textbook in America from the nineteenth to the early twentieth century.

Besides the story of the cherry tree and the prayer at Valley Forge, not much Weemsiana remains in popular culture today. Still, Parson Weems should be credited with a major role in shaping the myth of Washington. Although his book is obviously not great literature, his style of lively narration and sure sense of the symbolic gave him great influence. He manages to combine a slightly irreverent attitude with a profound love and respect (if not adoration) for his subject. In the course of the tale, he yokes together stories of the young Washington (for which there were no historical sources) and a powerful sense of the grand destiny of his subject. That is why Grant Wood's sly painting of the legend of the cherry tree, referred to earlier, is such a perceptive cultural comment on the myth-making capacity of the nation and its surrogate, Weems (see Figure 20). The Parson stands outside the curtain, inviting us to peer into the window of his mythic imagination, like a forerunner of Walt Disney.[64]

If this is a fair summary of the myth of the hero, how is his story portrayed in the city of Washington? Unsuccessfully, at first, with the ill-fated paintings and sculptures mentioned earlier, then enigmatically, with the eventual erection of the Washington Monument. Already in August 1783, the Continental Congress resolved that "an equestrian statue of General Washington be erected at the place where the residence of Congress shall be established." Then in 1790, when Washington had just assumed the presidency, he became involved with the planning of the capital, to be named for him. Although president of the new republic, his role as the victorious General Washington was still uppermost in the minds of most Americans. Pierre L'Enfant's original plan was to represent the man he so admired in an equestrian pose on the bank of the Potomac exactly at the spot where a line drawn south from the president's house intersected a line drawn west from the Capitol. But funds were insufficient, and Washington himself rejected what he considered a nonessential expense. In hindsight, all these circumstances were probably fortunate, for it is hard to imagine that a really significant work could have been produced at that period in U.S. history. And the lack of any fitting memorial would eventually goad the nation into erecting the monument that exists today.

At Washington's death, Representative John Marshall proposed a memorial inside the Capitol.[65] Predictably, decades of debate ensued, and it was only as the centennial of Washington's birthday approached in 1832 that a mausoleum was approved under the Capitol rotunda for the remains of both George and Martha. But John Augustine Washington, a nephew of Bushrod and owner of Mount Vernon, where the two were buried, refused to allow their remains to be moved from the property. So these plans, too, came to nothing, but did result in the commissioning of the much reviled Greenough statue.

In 1833 the Washington Monument Society was organized with the purpose of providing a worthy memorial to the great hero. Its first president was John Marshall, then the venerable and powerful chief justice of the Supreme Court who had established the court's equality with the executive and legislative powers. Hoping to raise 1 million dollars, the society promoted the contribution of one dollar by all citizens. But by 1836 it had

FIGURE 20 Grant Wood, *Parson Weems's Fable*. Oil on canvas, 1939. Amon Carter Museum, Fort Worth, Texas, painting no. 1970.43.

raised only $28,000, just enough to sponsor a design competition for the memorial, which they hoped would spur interest in the project. Perhaps it was Washington's lofty place among the Founding Fathers that made the tower structure seem a fitting memorial, but as early as 1816 a contributor to the *North American Review* had advocated "a column" as most appropriate because "only in that form could America surpass the whole world." Such typical American bombast was expressed even more blatantly by the sculptor Hiram Powers in 1845, who proposed a tower with a figure on top so large that "the features would be recognizable fifty miles away." Those who opposed the monument often couched their opposition in the observation that no monument could adequately express America's veneration for Washington and that therefore none was needed.

Among the designs proposed in the competition was one by the prominent architect Robert Mills, leading exponent of the Greek Revival in America, who would later build the Treasury building and the National Patent Office (now the National Museum of American Art and National Portrait Gallery). It included an obelisk with a blunt capstone, the shaft to be surrounded by an elaborate colonnaded pantheon to house the statues of American heroes of the Revolutionary era. Above the main doorway, Mills planned an international extravaganza, an image in the Roman style, a colossal thirty-foot toga-clad Washington (the lesson of Greenough had not yet been learned), sitting in a Greek battle chariot driven by an Etruscan Winged Victory and drawn by Arabian steeds. Overall, it was "classical," as then understood.

Again, fortune smiled on the nation, and funds were insufficient for such an elaborate undertaking. Only in 1848, when $87,000 had been collected, was construction able to begin. Rejecting any elaborations, the stated objective was simply to build a 500-foot obelisk on the spot chosen by Congress in 1795 for a monument to the Revolution, the same site chosen by Major L'Enfant for the equestrian statue to the president. President Polk presided at the ceremony of laying the cornerstone on July 4, accompanied by a host of Washington notables including Dolly Madison, Mrs. Alexander Hamilton, and three future presidents: James Buchanan, Andrew Johnson, and a little-known congressman from Illinois, Abraham Lincoln. The ceremony was led by the grand master mason, who used the same silver trowel used by George Washington in laying the cornerstone of the Capitol in 1793. Robert C. Winthrop, speaker of the House, gave the principal address eulogizing Washington.

Despite the auspicious beginning, the history of the project was one of delays, congressional infighting, vandalism (Know Nothings stole and destroyed a commemorative stone donated by the Vatican and even co-opted control of the society itself for a few years), stoppages caused by insufficient funds, and the disruptions of the Civil War. In 1853 the "stump" of the unfinished monument stood at about 150 feet above grade, where it remained for more than thirty years. Just as Congress was about to help out with an appropriation of $200,000, the Know-Nothing episode occurred and work ceased. Mark Twain derisively compared the stump of the monument to "a factory chimney with the top broken off." This bit of history is still visible in the change of color in the marble just at the level where construction ceased in 1853.

In attempting to revive the moribund Monument Association in 1866, Andrew Johnson summoned all of his rhetorical powers, urging that the obelisk "rise higher and higher until it shall meet the sun in his coming and his last parting ray shall linger and play on its summit."[66] Congress was not persuaded. It was only as the centennial of independence approached in 1876 that the legislators were finally driven to act, appropriating funds and passing a law providing for the completion and maintenance of the monument. Army engineers strengthened the foundation, and by another stroke of good fortune the U.S. minister to Italy and architectural authority George Marsh sent advice on the proportions of a true classical obelisk. It should have the exact proportions of a height ten times the diameter of its base. This design change resulted in the elegant proportions of the obelisk today. The aluminum capstone was put into place on the graceful pyramidion on December 6, 1884, and the monument was dedicated on Washington's birthday, February 22, 1885, by President Chester Arthur.

The main speech was composed for the occasion by the aged Robert C. Winthrop, who had spoken at the laying of the cornerstone thirty-seven years earlier. He had used the first occasion to emphasize Washington's selection by Providence and the successful continuation of the noble experiment begun under Washington, while "prostrate thrones and reeling empires this day bear witness to the shock!" In 1885, against the background of the Civil War, he stressed *Union,* seeing an apt metaphor of the United States in the monument itself. As the stones of the obelisk are "held firmly in position by their own weight and pressure," so they "will ever be an instructive type of the national strength and grandeur which can only be secured by the union of 'many in one.'"[67] *E pluribus unum.*

Is this monument appropriate to commemorate the character and significance of George Washington? His contemporaries held a range of opinions about his character, the majority of which were positive if not adulatory. At one end of the spectrum are the worshipful panegyrics of family members like Bushrod Washington and George Washington Parke Custis, friends John Marshall and George Mercer, and others.[68] At the other end of the spectrum are comments that range from the occasional sour remarks of John Adams to the vituperative comments of Republican opponents during Washington's second term. Moncure Conway wrote in 1892 that until Andrew Johnson no president went out of office "so loaded with odium."[69] Bryan's study of Washington in American literature from 1775 to 1865 is probably the most complete catalogue of views of Washington, evaluating his portrayal in oratory, biography, verse, drama, and fiction. Yet he too is forced to admit that, in the end, Washington's mythic stature prevents a fully accurate assessment of his character.

In summing up we can probably do no better than recall Jefferson's famous description. Although he could have viewed Washington as a Federalist and thus a political opponent, the passage of time (and likely the demise of the Federalist Party) enabled Jefferson to describe him, in a letter to his friend Walter Jones dated January 2, 1814, in the following measured words:

I think I know General Washington intimately and thoroughly; and were I called on to delineate his character, it should be in terms like these.

His mind was great and powerful, without being of the very first order . . . and as far as he saw, no judgment was ever sounder. It was slow in operation, being little aided by invention or imagination, but sure in conclusion. . . . Perhaps the strongest feature in his character was prudence, never acting until every circumstance, every consideration, was maturely weighed; refraining if he saw a doubt, but, when once decided, going through with his purpose, whatever obstacles opposed. His integrity was most pure, his justice the most inflexible I have ever known, no motives of interest or consanguinity, of friendship or hatred, being able to bias his decision. He was, indeed, in every sense of the words, a wise, a good, and a great man. His temper was naturally high toned; but reflection and resolution had obtained a firm and habitual ascendancy over it. If ever, however, it broke its bonds, he was most tremendous in his wrath. . . . His heart was not warm in its affections; but he exactly calculated every man's value, and gave him a solid esteem proportioned to it. Although in the circle of his friends, where he might be unreserved with safety, he took a free share in conversation, his colloquial talents were not above mediocrity, possessing neither copiousness of ideas, nor fluency of words. In public, when called on for a sudden opinion, he was unready, short, and embarrassed. . . . His education was merely reading, writing and common arithmetic, to which he added surveying at a later day. . . . On the whole, his character was, in its mass, perfect, in nothing bad, in a few points indifferent; and it may truly be said, that never did nature and fortune combine more perfectly to make a man great, and to place him in the same constellation with whatever worthies have merited from man an everlasting remembrance. For his was the singular destiny and merit, of leading the armies of his country successfully through an arduous war, for the establishment of its independence; of conducting its councils through the birth of a government, new in its forms and principles, until it had settled down into a quiet and orderly train; and of scrupulously obeying the laws through the whole of his career, civil and military, of which the history of the world furnished no other example. . . . These are my opinions of General Washington, which I would vouch at the judgment seat of God, having been formed on an acquaintance of thirty years.[70]

These words appear to be a fair and accurate assessment. Comments about him by contemporaries as well as later writers convey the same general impression: that there was a perfect, almost miraculous symmetry between the man and the historical situation. Although he was surrounded by a host of luminous fellow Founding Fathers—Franklin, Jefferson, Hamilton, Adams, Madison, and others—popular sentiment is that no one of them could have possibly accomplished what he did: "The history of the world furnished no other example." Or to say it in Saul Padover's words: "The towering character of the man—that compound of Calvinistic morality and aristocratic obligation—enabled him to play the commanding role that he did in the early years of the United States. . . . If there ever was an indispensable leader at a critical moment in history, it was George Washington. In the formative years of the American republic, roughly between 1776 and 1796, the man, the moment, and the crisis coincided."[71]

The perfect symmetry of man and historical moment are somehow reflected in the perfect proportions of the monument. James Russell Lowell's poem on Washington would not have corresponded with Mills's original conception of the monument, but it resonates nicely with the monument we have today:

> Minds strong by fits, irregularly great,
> That flash and darken like revolving lights,
> Catch more the vulgar eye unschooled to wait
> On the long curve of patient days and nights
> Rounding a whole life to the circle fair
> Of orbed fulfillment; and this balanced soul
> So simple in its grandeur, coldly bare
> Of draperies theatric, standing there
> In perfect symmetry of self-control,
> Seems not so great at first, but greater grows
> Still as we look, and by experience learn
> How grand this quiet is, how nobly stern
> The discipline that wrought through lifelong throes
> That energetic passion of repose.[72]

It is appropriate that the first president is represented on Washington's mythic stage by a giant obelisk rather than the equestrian statue first envisioned by Pierre L'Enfant. Words like "lofty," "pure," "simple," "balance," and "harmonious" are constantly used to eulogize Washington. The elemental form, lapidary quality, and marmoreal white of the monument are appropriate to the character of the man and expressive of "quiet" and of the "energetic passion of repose." Daniel Webster, too, saw the analogy between monument and man. He called attention to it in his oration at the dedication of another obelisk, the Bunker Hill monument to Washington. It was, he said, "by its uprightness, its solidity, its durability, . . . no unfit emblem of his character."[73]

Joseph Hudnut, architect and theorist, once imagined himself in Washington standing before the monument, interrogating it. "There is really no limit to the effrontery of these obelisks," he says. "They will recite any story, confirm any lie, exalt any authority." Hudnut was a modernist, and modernist architects have generally been bitter in their criticism of the backward-looking classical architecture of the U.S. capital. Hudnut's change of heart is then all the more remarkable. Suddenly the appropriateness of the obelisk strikes him:

> In spite of all I said the imperturbable monument faced me down, declaring itself the perfect simulacrum of our first president. . . . Not only is that structure very tall and very heavy: it is also very simple. It speaks to me not only of that which is powerful and that which is eternal but also of that which is elemental. A single crystal of stone . . . . Its language is direct and requires the intervention neither of text nor apology; it does not withhold itself for the sophisticated or the learned; we apprehend it at our first glance and without debate. The obelisk, sheer abstraction of a spire, is as catholic as prayer.[74]

Over the course of U.S. history, George Washington has played various roles for citizens: the honored general and revered president in his lifetime, canonized at death and then transformed according to the needs of each generation: sugar-coated and domesticated in the 1876 commemorations, lifted in the reign of Benjamin Harrison to regal splendor, made into a courtly dandy later in the 1890s, reduced to an "ordinary Joe" in the complacent Harding era, debunked in the 1920s, acclaimed as a communist, fascist, or capitalist during the next decade. He was, in the end, whoever patriotic citizens wanted him to be. And toward the end of the twentieth century, enlisted by various groups for trendy purposes, Washington "had suddenly become a very eighties kind of guy."[75]

In the light of such kaleidoscopic shifts, the monument retains its value as a steady corrective, recalling qualities that, in Hudnut's words, require neither "text nor apology." Unlike most of the other architectural monuments of Washington, D.C., the great obelisk has resisted changing meanings rather successfully. It remains a mute but overwhelming presence, suggesting some enduring meaning that binds together past and present, even accommodating the radical pluralism that marks America today. Like the man it memorializes, its great secret is silence.

CHAPTER 6

The Jefferson Memorial

Image of Enlightenment Faith

LOOKING SOUTH across the tidal basin on a sunny day, the Jefferson Memorial appears as a brilliant gem of white marble. I might call it

> . . . a shape that shines, . . .
> . . . so wrought and innocent of imprecision
> That a man who hoped to be a man, and be free
> Might enter in, and all his mind would glow
> Like a coal under the breath, in that precinct
> Where the correctness of our human aspiration
> Has body and abides and bespeaks the charmed space.[1]

So Robert Penn Warren has Jefferson describe his beloved Maison Carrée in France, and the words seem an even better summary of the Jefferson Memorial (see Figure 21).

The building looks small from my distant vantage point, pure, simple and almost textbookish in its classical form, "an exquisite work of perfectly proportioned architectural sculpture with primary architectural impact from afar."[2] John Russell Pope used the classical forms that Jefferson had chosen for Monticello and the University of Virginia and reduced them to their essentials, a pantheon with a portico: "A brilliant design . . . . at once a terminus and an open, midspace focal point."[3] The Jefferson is unique among all the Washington memorials because it is immediately comprehensible to the viewer. "The aim of the Grecian," says a nineteenth-century writer, "is to bring all the parts within the compass of the mind."[4] That is exactly what Pope has done.

Approaching more closely, the visitor realizes that the memorial is not small at all. It simply stands in isolation from the Mall, across the tidal basin, and apart from other structures that might place it in proper scale. It is a massive building, even though it was reduced by one-third from the size

FIGURE 21 Jefferson Memorial across the tidal basin. Photo by the author.

originally proposed by the Jefferson Memorial Commission. Although both inside and outside are visible simultaneously, the building still creates the sense of awe evoked by many large and beautiful structures, secular and sacred.

Speaking of the library Jefferson designed at the University of Virginia, Vincent Scully says that the architect "fills something less than half its height with two lower floors and endows the resultant open space above them with the proportions of the Pantheon. In that space . . . we do indeed feel placed in the center of the world. Through the wide windows a great axis is felt, running through our own bodies down the lawn, while the dome opens its image of the heavens above us in the light."[5] These words are even more true of the Jefferson Memorial. With its openings to north, east, south, and west, its glowing dome to suggest the sky, and standing upon its massive round terrace, the structure creates a feeling of "cosmic connection" to nature outside and the universe beyond.

This temple to clarity is a fitting memorial for the man who hated Plato, his metaphysics, his idealizations, his mysticism. There is nothing esoteric or secretive here, no dim interior such as the visitor will find at the Lincoln Memorial. The temple is flushed with the hard light of day. The intentions of Pope are in perfect harmony with the thought of Jefferson. This memorial's openness, simplicity, clarity, and light perfectly exemplify Louis I. Kahn's definition of architecture, "the material realization of silence and light."[6]

Approaching from any one of the four directions one sees the Jefferson sculpture standing at the center of the ensemble, looking north toward the White House. One critic calls him a "canary in his peristyled bird cage." Perhaps he is more like an Asian god in his shrine. The building, reduced to its basic elements, is like a Chinese palace or temple, simply a roof supported by pillars, standing on a massive platform. There are no walls, just four panels of stone, facing northeast, southeast, southwest, and northwest, which carry the inscriptions chosen by the commission to highlight what they considered Jefferson's principal contributions to U.S. history.

The Jefferson Memorial is important because it is the site in Washington that most clearly expresses the meaning of the Revolutionary period, "the one component of our past," says Michael Kammen, "that we have not, at some point or other, explicitly repudiated."[7] For most Americans, the Revolution is a noncontroversial phenomenon. This memorial sets forth in straightforward visual images and memorable quotations the essential story of the birth and childhood of the nation. Like most births, it evokes thoughts of freshness, the beginning of something entirely new in the world: confidence in the promise of a political and religious spring after centuries of oppression. It is entirely fitting that the favorite postcard image of this memorial is one surrounded by the cherry blossoms in spring. And just as the cherry blossoms quickly fade and fall, the optimism of the Revolutionary euphoria soon faded into the ordinary air of commercial crises, war, party strife, and a gathering crisis over slavery. But the memorial still reminds Washington visitors of the nation's hopeful, even euphoric, origins.

The Thomas Jefferson Memorial Commission decided in 1936 that this building should not be utilitarian—a museum, a conference center, or anything of the sort.[8] Its purpose should be to glorify and celebrate the ideal of freedom and the man Americans identify as its most eloquent spokesman. "I have sworn upon the altar of God eternal hostility against every form of tyranny over the mind of man" are the words proclaiming Jefferson's passionate commitment to this idea, and they encircle the inside frieze beneath the dome. This expression is one of the few uncontestable truths he enunciated. If every other principle of Thomas Jefferson can be contradicted by something he said or did at another time, this one cannot. He is the "Apostle of Freedom" in the eyes of Americans, and perhaps not much more than that for the majority.[9] As is the case with most public memorials, this one offers no hint of critique but simply celebrates the person for whom it was erected and the ideals he represents.

The memorial integrates inside and outside, the human and natural worlds, in its architecture. Most architecture suggests protection from the elements. This building suggests openness to them. The statue of Jefferson can be clearly seen from any of the four cardinal directions. As his image stands inside and light pours in through the colonnades, contact is established with the natural world outside.

Nature was extremely important to the Virginia planter. It provided the context for the unique religious sensibility characteristic of Jefferson and his circle (American Enlightenment thinkers like Benjamin Rush, Thomas Paine, David Rittenhouse, William Barton, and Joseph Priestley), who saw nature as a "Bible" revealing the Creator's sacred order. In contrast to the Jeffersonians, Puritan thinkers of an earlier period had often seen nature as the realm of Satan. Describing the landing of the Pilgrims at Plymouth harbor, for example, William Bradford recalled the terror of "a hidious & desolate wilderness full of wild beasts & wild men."[10]

By the early eighteenth century, Boston minister Cotton Mather was foreshadowing the change that would come with the Enlightenment. He asked his listeners to look at nature as a second book of Revelation, manifesting the wonderful works of God in its mineral, vegetable, and animal kingdoms. Nature was God's book, a "vast organized blueprint setting down god's wisdom in rational terms."[11] Jonathan Edwards reported that a mystical experience, "looking up on the sky and clouds," increased his sensitivity to things divine: "God's excellence, his wisdom, his purity and love, seemed to appear in everything; in the sun, moon, and stars; in the clouds, and blue sky; in the grass, flowers, trees; in the water, and all nature."[12] These modifications in the Puritan outlook helped prepare the way for the philosophy of the Founding Fathers, who looked upon the book of nature rather than the Bible as a more accurate revelation of the mind of the Creator.

Yet the divine experienced by American Enlightenment thinkers was less personal and immediate than the God worshiped by Puritans. For Jeffersonians, impressed with the discoveries of Galileo and Newton, nature was marked by a marvelous order, and in this natural order the characteristics and intentions of God could be discerned. The natural and moral order were expressions of the same God, the laws discovered by Newton comparable to the social norms by which all men should be considered equal and "endowed by their Creator with certain inalienable rights." This meant that the Creator had given everyone a sense of right and wrong that is "as much a part of his nature as the sense of hearing, seeing, feeling." Whenever Jefferson talks "of God's design as manifested in men's natures, it is to stress their fittedness for life with each other."[13]

Jefferson was specifically criticized for basing his philosophy on "nature," especially by conservative Christian ministers. Slavery advocate W. J. Grayson called the Declaration of Independence "an infidel production" because "it deduces rights in the social state from the state of nature; or in other words, appeals to nature for the exhibition of the principles of social science."[14] Exactly. Perhaps Thomas Paine put it most forcefully: "But some, perhaps, will say: Are we to have no Word of God—no revelation? I answer, Yes; there is a Word of God; there is a revelation. THE WORD OF GOD IS THE CREATION WE BEHOLD and it is *this word,* which no human invention can counterfeit or alter, that God speaketh universally to man."[15]

Jefferson's political principles were based on natural law, which he believed was implanted in the world by the Creator. Jefferson spent his entire life "on the threshold," meditating on the relationship between nature and culture. He "studied the logic, the order, the perfection of the natural world, sought to impose something of that same order and perfection on the social and political and the moral world."[16] Although "nature" meant many different things in the Enlightenment, its chief use was as "an engine of attack on the authority of tradition."[17] Its principles, discernible to human reason, were Jefferson's license for overthrowing the old agents of authority he hated so much: the monarchy, the aristocracy, the priestly hierarchy. In this appeal to nature, he was standing solidly in the mainstream of eighteenth-century thought, which saw nature as "the grand alternative to all that man had made of man; . . . upon her solid ground therefore . . . must all the religion, the ethics, the politics, the law, the art of the future be constructed."[18]

Jefferson was not so much a lover of "wild nature" (his excursion to the top of Natural Bridge on his Virginia property gave him a "violent headache") as he was of the tamed nature of neatly tended fields and vineyards. When he traveled through southern France he seemed altogether unaware of the rugged beauty of the Alps but paid close attention to types of soil, local crops, orchards, cheese-making, the culture of vineyards, even the small sounds of rustic evenings, frogs croaking and nightingales singing.[19] It was through a parallel attraction that he carefully noted every monument of classical architecture, even fragments and ruins, while ignoring the great Gothic cathedral as he passed through Cologne. He must have sensed something of what Benjamin Silliman said in 1830, that the aim of Gothic style is "to confound the attention, and while the powers of the mind are thus weakened, to bring it completely under its control."[20] Neoclassical architecture, in contrast, set the mind *free* by giving it *control.*

Nature in its many forms became part of Jefferson's vocabulary and the tools of his thinking. He called on natural metaphors for political use, envisioning the relationship between the states and the federal government like that between the "planets and the sun." Human genius was divinely given, "like seeds of genius which nature sows with even hand . . . which need only soil and season to germinate."[21]

As the single image that captured Jefferson's varied qualities and activities, Merrill Peterson chose the picture of Jefferson at Monticello, where he stood in a "portico facing the wilderness."[22] There he lived by a "natural economy joined to a natural morality, an aesthetics bound to nature, a private life of natural affection, the whole within a natural political order." Summing it up, Miller asserts:

> Nature was Jefferson's myth for all purposes, a flexible idea that gathered together his deepest beliefs. It was uncritically accepted, pervasively invoked. Nature was the source of all that existed and all that was worthwhile . . . the means to the discovery of truth, to understanding the good and the beautiful, and to a life of liberty and prosperity.
>
> Jefferson's God was the creator of nature. Nature itself was thereby invested with divinity.[23]

The ambivalent image of Jefferson standing in the portico at Monticello is appropriate. While the philosopher gazed boldly outward, he was still protected under the eaves. He may not have shuddered at the wild peaks of Saint Gotthardt, as did the classicist Winckelmann when passing through the Alps, but his eye regularly chose calmer vistas, in both the natural world and the human heart. Perhaps the essential power of the image is best recaptured in Washington, where he stands sheltered in his shrine, on a humanly contrived spit of land between the tidal basin and the Potomac, gazing across the gentle slopes of the Mall toward the White House lawn.

The land on which the memorial stands did not exist in the Washington of L'Enfant. But in 1901 the McMillan Commission changed the triangular core of the capital plan. The perpendicular sides of the triangle would now intersect at the Washington Monument and continue on to two new sites, on which the Lincoln Memorial would be built in 1922 and the Jefferson Memorial in 1943. This new design changed L'Enfant's central triangle into a cross.

According to a government estimate, some 2 million visitors visit the Jefferson Memorial each year. Most know him as the author of the Declaration of Independence and the third president of the United States. Perhaps the majority of Americans know little more than that, and often what they think they know is erroneous. Jefferson, like Washington, has become an icon, a peg on which to hang whatever positive attributes may be the favorites of the writer or speaker. According to an Associated Press article, an Oregon jail banned the wearing of briefs after the inmates had used them to clog the toilets. Only a single prisoner complained, claiming it was his constitutional right to wear underwear. Sheriff Dave Burright said: "I don't remember Thomas Jefferson putting anything about underwear in the Constitution." Burright's answer probably reflects the conventional understanding of most Americans that somehow Jefferson should be credited with establishing the individual rights and freedom enjoyed by citizens, though of course as ambassador to France he was not even present at the time the Constitution was being written.

As the Jefferson Memorial opens to the four cardinal directions, it also offers the visitor four perspectives through which to view the hero it celebrates. Along with the window of nature, there are the sculptural image, the architecture, and the quotations engraved on the walls. All four concepts, taken together, contribute to an understanding of Jefferson's significance. At the same time they transform the past, shaping it into the contemporary myth of Jefferson that visitors find so appealing when they visit the memorial. Because it celebrates the theme of the Revolution and founding of the nation, it represents an important element of American self-understanding. What myth did the Memorial Commission intend to create with the Jefferson Memorial? What does it communicate about Jefferson to those who visit? As Emerson said of nature, another mute partner in dialogue, "Let us interrogate the apparition."

How to view the apparition through its four windows has been, in one sense, the subject of a long and contentious dialogue in the history of Western culture about how nature, art, architecture, and words are to be understood and interpreted. Plato's words about painting may be applied to sculpture and architecture as well: "The painter's products stand before us as though they were alive: but if you question them, they maintain a most majestic silence." The great philosopher was skeptical of art and its message, just as he was wary of poetry, the "maker of lies." Aristotle, in this case, represents the counterpoint to Plato. He was more receptive to the power of image to represent reality, saying that "the soul never thinks without a mental picture."[24]

These two contrasting viewpoints have generated a long history of disputation. Despite an eighth-century outburst of iconoclasm, the first 1,500 years of Christianity were an affirmation of the Aristotelian principle that right thinking was generated by accurate images. The art of the great churches was called the bible of the illiterate. At the beginning of the fourth century, Bishop Eusebius of Caesarea said that "the evidence of our eyes makes instruction through the ears unnecessary," and in the thirteenth century Bishop Durandus of Mende affirmed that "[Images] move the mind more than descriptions; . . . in churches we pay less reverence to books than to images and to pictures."[25] With the Reformation, iconoclasm again had its day, and there was a shift to word as the most trustworthy bearer of truth. Martin Luther said: "The ears are the only organs of a Christian." The success of the Protestant effort may be seen in a petition, signed by group of Strasbourg burghers, which read in part: "We see all images as evil, for they appeal not to the perfected Christians but to the weak and those whom the word has not yet possessed."[26]

In Revolutionary America, led by Founding Fathers who despised the Papacy and rejected the political and religious views of Roman Catholicism, the Protestant worldview had become dominant. In such a religious climate it was natural that faith in word and scripture replaced the reliance on art.[27] As the disgusted Italian artist Antonio Canova remarked, "You English see with your ears."[28] Thus, the word may provide the best window through which to discern the intentions of the Jefferson Memorial Commission. The words carry the message and shape the myth for the visitor. To contradict Bishop Durandus, perhaps we Americans pay more reverence to books than to statues and architecture. At least consciously.

Yet if the Founders and subsequent Americans have been worshipers of the word, we should be even more alert to the more subtle power of art and architecture. If their effect is absorbed in a place below the level of conscious processes of thought, it may be all the more effective. As Ruskin said, "Great nations write their autobiographies in three manuscripts, the book of their deeds, the book of their words and the book of their art. Not one of these books can be understood unless we read the two others, but of the three the only trustworthy one is the last."[29]

Charles Moore, as chair of the Washington Commission of Fine Arts from 1915 to 1937, was one of the most influential shapers of monumental Washington in the twentieth century. He learned Ruskinian thought from his mentor at Harvard, Charles Eliot Norton, who maintained that architecture revealed "the moral temper and intellectual culture of the various races."[30] Because Thomas Jefferson was such a "sphinx," the art and architecture of this memorial convey truths about him more profound than the simple messages of the inscriptions.

The sculptural image created by Rudolph Evans seems to make a straightforward statement. The Thomas Jefferson portrayed is a commanding figure: sixteen feet tall with a scroll in hand (presumably the Declaration of Independence), he seems mature and confident as he faces the future (see

Figure 22). The statue is more expressive of his rugged yeoman ideal than of the "other" Jefferson, the cosmopolitan who loved French wines and Parisian furniture. Confidence and determination come to mind as the characteristics of the man portrayed by this thirty-ton statue of bronze. It is the same confident Jefferson shown on our nickel coins and on the old three-cent postage stamp, both minted in 1943, the bicentennial of the birth of Jefferson and the same year the Jefferson Memorial was dedicated by Franklin Roosevelt. Seeing this determination, one can almost hear the trumpet-like proclamation of Jefferson in his letter late in life to John Adams: "The flames kindled on the 4th of July 1776 have spread over too much of the globe to be extinguished by the feeble engines of despotism. On the contrary they will consume those engines, and all who work them."[31]

Given the bloody despotisms of the twentieth century, these sentiments appear naive, almost adolescent. Michael Kammen called this period of American history "a season of youth." But why would the Founders not be confident in the late eighteenth century? Jefferson and his circle had a faith that the human mind could comprehend Divine Reason and discover the holy order of the universe imparted at creation. Part of this order was the equality of humans and their right to political self-determination.

Jefferson believed that all species had been created at the beginning and that none could become extinct.[32] The frugality implied in this understanding—nothing wasted, nothing squandered—appealed to Jefferson: "As We are poor We ought to be Oeconomists."[33] The natural order, ordained with such perfect economy, would endure, and it was the task of humans to imitate the Author of Nature and apply that thrifty and stable pattern to their social and political arrangements.

Jefferson's choice of classical architecture was based on the same principles. Unlike their European counterparts, it was the good fortune of the American political philosophers to be able to shape their revolutionary ideas into a permanent political entity. The Evans statue conveys this confidence in human reason and its naive political syllogisms, which all reach the same conclusion: that democracy is the form of government the Creator destined for the human race. As the Jacksonian democrat George Bancroft said, democracy is the "voice of God as it breathes through the people."[34] *Vox populi, vox dei.*

Architecture was an abiding passion of Jefferson's. It reflects his ideals, even the economy of form and simplicity of expression just indicated. The Creator was for him above all a great architect. Beyond its utilitarian purposes, Jefferson understood architecture's metaphoric capacity to express his deepest personal and aesthetic ideals as well as his political and cultural

FIGURE 22 Rudulph Evans, sculpture of Thomas Jefferson, Jefferson Memorial.
Courtesy of the Library of Congress.

hopes for the new republic. In the vast majority of his writings, Thomas
Jefferson was cool, reserved, and dispassionate. That is why the following
passage jumps out of his collected writings like an unexpected frog. He was
touring southern France where he saw an ancient Roman building, the Maison Carrée. "Here I am, Madame," he said, describing the experience in a

letter to the Comtesse de Tesse, "gazing whole hours at the Maison Carrée, like a lover at his mistress."[35] So smitten was he that he proposed the building as the model for the new Virginia statehouse in Richmond in 1789, "the first positive step toward American cultural independence."[36] Taking no chances on his drafting skills, he had a small model for the statehouse made and sent to America so there could be no mistake about what he was suggesting (see Figure 23). In a letter to Madison, he wrote that the Maison Carrée was "one of the most beautiful, if not the most beautiful and precious morsel of architecture left us by antiquity . . . it is very simple, but is noble beyond expression."[37] One of the most influential spokesmen for neoclassicism in the eighteenth century, Sir John Soane, urged a return to the architecture of the ancients, especially to the "primitive model" of the Greeks. Thus contemporary architecture would rest on the same "great Primitive Principle" that the architecture of the ancients had. It would be founded on "the immutable laws of Nature and Truth." [38] Looking at the Maison Carrée today, one wonders how it could have drawn such a passionate response from Jefferson. A twentieth-century critic remarks: "I cannot explain the complacency of the Virginia legislators, willing to compress their explosive energies in that tight little box which the American ambassador sent them from Paris."[39] But for Jefferson, the tight little box was crammed with significance. It had become for him an icon perfectly embodying the simplicity and elegance of the classical ideal.

Pierson describes the earliest form of neoclassical architecture in America as traditional or Federal—that is, connected with Boston, the Federalist Party, conservatism, and England. As Jefferson despised Williamsburg's architecture, he also rejected the Federal style and favored the newer style, which Pierson calls the "idealistic phase" of neoclassicism. This phase came to be connected with Virginia, Jefferson, and France, though it reached back to Rome and Greece for its inspiration. Jefferson's preference led to an architectural independence from England just as the Declaration of Independence had signaled political independence. Although he was not at first given the credit he deserved, Jefferson is now acknowledged as the "father of architecture" in English America. His role in the evolution of American architecture "was as decisive as his role in the formation of American democracy; and the two are inseparable."[40]

The neoclassicism Jefferson loved was marked by clarity of line, simplicity of form, noble conception, and restraint in color. He perceived a congruence between this style of architecture, his personal ideals, and his conceptions of democracy. One of the most eloquent expositors of neoclassicism was a French priest, the Abbé Laugier, who in 1773 theorized that classical

FIGURE 23 Model for the Virginia Statehouse. Thomas Jefferson and Charles-Louis Clérisseau, 1786. The Library of Virginia.

architecture went back to "first principles." He imagined that the earliest form of human architecture was the primitive hut, having four tree trunks as "pillars," sloping branches forming the gable, and horizontal branches from trunk to trunk completing a "pediment."[41] Therefore the Doric Greek temple was the simplest, though sophisticated, development of this most primitive or elemental architecture of the human house. In reconnecting with this elemental simplicity, neoclassicism was in contact with a powerful truth, completely consistent with Jefferson's belief that human cultural expressions should be in accord with natural law: "The efforts to equate order in architecture with order in nature, such as Laugier's insistence upon that which is 'natural and true, wherein all is reduced to simple rules and executed according to great principles,' were in fact attempts to equate the origins of architecture with natural law."[42] In favoring classical architecture Jefferson was selecting not just a style that appealed to him, but one that he believed was in harmony with the fundamental principles of the universe, implanted by the Creator at the beginning, as compelling as the truths of physics discovered by Newton. In that sense, for him, classical architecture expressed eternal principles.

Since it conforms to these principles, the Jefferson Memorial serves as reminder of this sense of the rediscovery of ancient and pure sources of human culture. After the passage of thousands of years, the Founding Fathers and their enlightened generation believed that they had recovered the truths, first hinted at in Greece and Rome, that men could govern themselves, that the authority for government came from the people governed to their ruler, and not vice versa. It was an audacious thought. After some 6,000 years of human history, someone had finally got it right. This knowledge of human destiny was not, in their view, a gradual evolution, the culmination of a slow process of change, but a true revolution. Later in their lives Jefferson and Adams agreed that the real revolution was not the war but an event that happened in men's minds. Other than the short-lived experiments in the ancient classical world, this political idea was unheard of. It was like a new dawn on the human race, containing within it the power that marks the initial heady stages of all great revolutions.

We should not be insensitive to the deep spiritual significance of ideas of renewal and rebirth. Every religious tradition has celebrated the power inherent in beginnings, providing periodic ceremonies of renewal, rebirth, and revitalization to tap their power. In the minds of participants, the 1770s was a turning point in human history when something altogether new was created. The old had become vitiated and had to be destroyed. "Revolutions always seemed a way of giving government back to the Creator—of wiping the slate clean of distorted and obsolete human designs, so that the divine pattern might become visible," says Boorstin of Jeffersonian thought.[43]

Jefferson, despite his own obvious relish of Europe's architecture, literature, food, and wines, had lamented its decadent aristocracy, its degenerate ways, its corrupt and oppressive political systems. American youth, he thought, should not go to Europe for their education but remain in America where the sturdy spartan mores would not be exposed to the degeneracy of the old world. Writing to his friend John Banister in 1785 about the education of Banister's son Mark, Jefferson said:

> Why send an American youth to Europe for education? . . . Let us view the disadvantages. . . . If he goes to England, he learns drinking, horse racing, and boxing. . . . He acquires a fondness for European luxury and dissipation, and a contempt for the simplicity of his own country. . . . It appears to me, then, that an American coming to Europe for his education, loses in his knowledge, in his morals, in his health, in his habits, and in Happiness.[44]

The new system was not just a political change but a total rejection of the past. It was a transformation into a fresh and powerful system more in keeping with the order of nature and nature's God, the *novus ordo seclorum* declared on the Great Seal of the United States. The Latin phrase implies not just a "new order" but a "new age." In all these phrases and ideas—the return to the beginning, the power of renewal, the coming of a new age—we hear echoes of ancient religious themes that gave the Revolutionary impetus much of its power. Although often seen as a secular or antireligious movement, Revolutionary democracy was just the opposite: a new religious vision of the world, though often at variance with traditional Christianity. In setting aside a connection with any specific religion, the Founding Fathers were able to tap the power of dynamic religious scenarios that have stimulated social change since the beginning of history. They were not just dismantling the superstructure of an old political system or going through the tired process of rearranging old elements; they were creating something new from the bottom up. Or so they thought. As Jefferson wrote to Priestley: "We can no longer say there is nothing new under the sun. For this whole chapter in the history of man is new."[45]

Religious scenarios of rebirth and renewal were meant to recapture the prestige of beginnings as the time of exceptional power, purity, and perfection. Every major religious tradition has celebrated them, often in conjunction with rites commemorating creation at New Year's festivals, enthronement or coronation ceremonies, temple building or rebuilding, and similar events. We find such rituals in ancient Mesopotamia, among Christians, Jews, and Hindus as well as in many nonliterate traditions.[46] Since much of traditional culture was in fact not new but the repetition of time-honored patterns, the ritualistic celebration of renewal had the effect of making them new. Revolutions touch on this religious source of power.

The American Revolutionary movement had both elements, a sense of return to archetypal but fragile periods of democracy in the history of Greece and Rome, but also a sense by the participants of the utter originality of what they were proposing. Their language and rhetoric clearly reflect this strong sense of something momentous, a clean break with past forms and the foundation of a new order. Robert Rantoul Jr., reflecting on the meaning of the Revolution, wrote in 1833: "The independence of the United States of America is not only a marked epoch in the course of time, but it is indeed the end from which the new order of things is to be reckoned. It is the dividing point in the history of mankind; it is the moment of the political regeneration of the world."[47] Rantoul's statement is full of words with ancient religious connotations: "epoch," "the end," "new order of things," "regeneration." What more appropriate phase could have been chosen to express this idea than *novus ordo seclorum*? Jeffersonians had, as Boorstin observes, "a sense of living at the beginning of history."[48]

Paradoxically, among the Founding Fathers, it was the "atheist" Thomas

Paine who most clearly expressed the religious dimension of the Revolution. He described monarchic tyrannies as the loss of an original perfect phase of human history, a garden of Eden. "The palaces of Kings are built upon the ruins of the bowers of paradise," he said in *Common Sense.*[49] When asked, rhetorically, by some doubters who the king of America was, Paine answered, "He reigns above." In 1775, thinking about a charter to unite the colonies, he asked that "it be brought forth placed on the divine law, the Word of God; let a crown be placed there on, by which the world may know, that so far as we approve of monarchy, that in America the law is king."[50] He saw the Revolution as an act of rebirth and renewal, the initiation of something entirely new: "We have it in our power to begin the world over again. A situation, similar to the present, hath not happened since the days of Noah until now. The birthday of a new world is at hand."[51]

Again in *The American Crisis,* he exclaims with missionary fervor: "To see it in our power to make a world happy—to teach mankind the art of being so—to exhibit, on the theatre of the universe a character hitherto unknown—and to have, as it were, a new creation intrusted to our hands, are honors that command reflection, and can neither be too highly estimated, nor too gratefully received."[52] No missionary went forth to proclaim the Gospel with greater religious fervor than Thomas Paine as he preached revolution and democracy. Contrary to accusations by his critics, one motive for Paine's writing *The Age of Reason* was his alarm at the growth of atheism. He began the tract with a statement of his creed: "I believe in one god, and no more; and I hope for happiness beyond this life. I believe in the equality of man; and I believe that religious duties consist in doing justice, loving mercy, and endeavoring to make our fellow-creatures happy."[53]

Paine and Jefferson were both Deists. They believed not that God is remote and uninvolved in his creation—the usual understanding of Deism—but that He is everywhere visible in the universe: "Creation is the Bible of the Deist." Paine felt that Christianity and other institutional religions brought about sectarianism and strife because of their priesthoods and dogmas, while Deism with its wordless "Bible" did the opposite. It united: "The Creation speaks a universal language, independently of human speech or human language, multiplied and various as they be."[54] Jefferson had always supported Paine and voiced similar sentiments, and he too was called an "atheist" by his enemies. What Paine and Jefferson represent is not atheism or secularism but a religious revolution. They saw themselves rejecting human interpretations, anthropomorphisms, fables, and dogmas that divide humans, and turning toward a universal religion, beyond dogmas, that would unite them. Even science became a religious pursuit for them, a methodical and painstaking examination, more demanding than scriptural exegesis, of nature itself: "It is an inconsistency scarcely possible to be credited that . . . held it to be *irreligious* to study and contemplate the structure of the universe that God has made."[55]

Sometimes, in contemplating the spirit of the Enlightenment, writers have placed too much emphasis on the element of intellect. In Enlightenment America, it was the moral sense that was paramount. Jefferson did not believe that all human beings were equal intellectually or spiritually, but he did believe that they were equal in moral endowment because all possessed a human conscience. Nor did he believe that humans could always be convinced intellectually of the truth through the arguments of the mind, but he did believe humans would know the moral truth from the conscience implanted in them. On that basis they could know what was right and be inclined to do it.

Two years before he died, Jefferson recalled to Adams their efforts to articulate the principles of the Revolution: "We had no occasion to search into musty records, to hunt up royal parchments, or to investigate the laws and institutions of a semi-barbarous ancestry. We appealed to those of nature, and found them engraved on our hearts."[56] There in the human heart he found the basis for the Declaration of Independence and his hopes for the national future. When the Thomas Jefferson Memorial Commission and the Washington Commission for Fine Arts planned the memorial in the 1930s, they struggled with the complex and controverted question of the meaning of Thomas Jefferson. Even choosing a sculptor and model for the statue proved difficult. For one thing, although Houdon had done a bust in the eighteenth century, and a few statues had been erected to him subsequently, nothing of any monumental significance was produced before the twentieth century. This neglect might be interpreted benignly as expressing the view that "no monument raised by a grateful posterity was necessary or adequate to celebrate his fame," or perhaps more realistically, that he was such a controversial figure that no great impetus existed to celebrate him. The fact was that for nearly every great stand he took "on principle" one can find him, at some other time in his life, denying that principle in either his words or his actions. His reputation rose and fell periodically over the hundred years between his death and the beginnings of the movement to give him a national memorial.[57]

At his death Jefferson was eulogized as a veritable sign of the blessing of Providence on the land. He and John Adams, fellows in the Revolutionary cause, later bitter political enemies, and finally reconciled in the later years, had died on the same day, within five hours of each other. That day was

July 4, 1826, the fiftieth anniversary of the proclamation of the Declaration of Independence. All over the land, people marveled at this miraculous omen. When John Quincy Adams, then president, reached his home in Quincy, family members told him that the instant his father expired "a clap of thunder shook the house" and "a splendid rainbow arched immediately over the heavens." JQA later declared in an official proclamation that the two simultaneous deaths certified that their work in founding the republic was "Heaven directed" and confirmed the belief that the nation was under the special care of a kind Providence: "In this most singular coincidence, the finger of Providence is plainly visible! It hallows the Declaration of Independence as the Word of God, and is the bow in the Heavens, that promises its principles shall be eternal, and their dissemination universal over the Earth."[58]

But once the soaring hymns of apotheosis had died down and the *general* adulation was forgotten, it rapidly became clear that in regard to *specific* issues, the two Founders were quite different. Although Adams's positions were clear, there was no unequivocal Jeffersonian position or principle to provide guidance to his followers. The third president could be quoted on both sides of almost every issue. For example, Andrew Jackson appealed to the authority of Jefferson as he ran against John Quincy Adams, vowing to dismantle the national bank. Jefferson had certainly fought against Alexander Hamilton on the issue of a national bank. Yet opponents of Jackson could point out that when Jefferson took office he did nothing to curtail the bank's power, and after the Louisiana Purchase he in fact authorized the establishment of the bank in New Orleans.

On the issue of slavery, abolitionists in Congress could point to many statements of Jefferson's lamenting or condemning it. At the same time, Southern supporters could point to his stand on limiting the powers of the federal government, his support of states' rights, and the fact that Jefferson was himself a slave holder, passing all but five of his slaves on to his heirs in his will. Both Lincoln and Douglas quoted Jefferson in their famous debates. On nearly every major issue contested in Congress, Jefferson could be quoted to support either side. As the *Niles' Weekly Register* complained on April 7, 1832, "What *principle* in the political ethics of our country might not be *sanctioned* AND refuted by the writings of Mr. Jefferson?" Unlike his old antagonist Hamilton, who consistently represented one set of values, the paper said Jefferson "was protean, capable of infinite reinterpretation within the shared faith of the American people."

Jefferson's reputation fell to its lowest ebb during the Civil War, while that of Hamilton, his antagonist, rose accordingly. The strong federalism of the latter appeared as Solomonic wisdom in comparison with the divisive states' rights views of Jefferson. American commentators saw that Lincoln, though he admired Jefferson and quoted his principles, was acting like a Hamiltonian in his use of force to hold the federal union together. James A. Garfield, later president, began to study the works of Hamilton during this period and in 1865 asserted in Congress that "the fame of Jefferson is waning, and the fame of Hamilton is waxing, in the estimation of the American people."[59]

By the end of the nineteenth century, Jefferson had been brought back into the political fray. He was predictably quoted by both sides during the era of American imperialism, the anti-imperialists stressing his insistence on "the consent of the governed," while imperialists like Teddy Roosevelt could point out how he "grabbed" Louisiana without the consent of Congress and ruled it for a time like a colony. Senator Hoar imagined Jefferson holding two documents in his hands, one the Declaration of Independence, the other the Louisiana Purchase, and posed the question: "Does his left hand know what the right was doing?" In the context of the Jefferson Memorial, the question might well have been posed: "Does he have the Declaration of Independence in his hand, or the Louisiana Purchase?"

By the 1930s the Depression had subverted the reputation of Hamilton and the see-saw accordingly raised Jefferson to new heights of popularity. The New Deal of FDR jettisoned most Jeffersonian principles in action while heaping honors upon him in words, ironic retribution to the third president, who died as he had lived "in the odor of phrases."[60] In other words, Franklin Roosevelt "killed Jeffersonian philosophy" and atoned for it by building a great memorial for him. At the same time the Republicans were also reclaiming him, using his anti–Supreme Court positions, for example, in their fight against Roosevelt's packing of the Court and to combat FDR's decision to run for a third term. Both parties piously laid wreaths on Jefferson's grave on July 4, 1938. In fact, Jefferson was adopted during this decade by all shades of the political spectrum, from the far right American Liberty League to the Communist Party on the left.

How Jefferson was able to appeal to such radically opposed constituencies is an interesting question. One Jefferson scholar ventures the opinion that Jefferson's "magic" worked because "we permit it to function at a rarified region where real-life choices do not have to be made." Jefferson "floats above the fray," he says, "like a dirigible hovering over a football stadium flashing words of inspiration to both sides." Unlike Madison, Jefferson's fondest political topic "was not the artful arrangement of government power but rather the cordoning off of a region where no government could exist." Fixing their gaze on an object of such elusiveness, "ordinary Americans carried around expectations and assumptions about what Jefferson symbolized that were infinitely more powerful than any set of historical facts."[61]

In the 1930s there could be little opposition to building a memorial to Jefferson, particularly in the later stages of construction when World War II pitted the United States against two aggressive totalitarian enemies. World War II was understood by most Americans as a struggle for freedom and democracy against tyrannical foes, and Jefferson as the "Apostle of Freedom" was the natural icon to focus the patriotic sentiments of all Americans.[62] The controversies that arose were not over the idea of a memorial, but over almost every detail of its execution: where it should stand, how large it should be, what it should look like, what style of architecture, what sculpture, and so on.

Representative John Boylan of New York presented a joint resolution to Congress on June 24, 1934, calling for the establishment of a commission to plan a permanent memorial to Jefferson in Washington, D.C. Two days later, with the support of FDR, the joint resolution passed, creating the Jefferson Memorial Commission whose composition sounded like a recipe for disaster: three members to be appointed by President Roosevelt, three by the Senate, three by the House, and three by the Thomas Jefferson Memorial Foundation. In fact the members chosen generally presented a united front, circling their conservative wagons against all critics. Four different sites for the memorial were considered, with final choice going to a site in conformity with the McMillan plan, where the axis drawn south from the White House would intersect an imaginary extension of Maryland Avenue. This decision created, or completed, the cruciform plan that now constitutes the ceremonial center of Washington.

Because Congress had passed an appropriation of $3 million for the memorial in June 1936 and had put the Jefferson Memorial Commission in complete control, the initial decision about what style to employ was made easily. The commission was dominated by Fiske Kimball, who insisted on the selection of John Russell Pope as architect, without any competition, as the last exponent of American classicism. Pope was then employed in building the National Gallery of Art on the Mall, and he offered two classical plans, one cruciform and the other similar to the National Gallery, a pantheon with a portico. The pantheon design was accepted in February 1937 but was immediately criticized by the Washington Fine Arts Commission, the group charged with maintaining the artistic integrity of the U.S. capital. Though also classically oriented, this body was not as rigidly classical in taste as Kimball and Pope. They held out for a simpler and more original design, more in keeping with the nature of the site chosen.

The commission's decision to accept Pope's pantheon design aroused a much stronger reaction among contemporary architects and theorists such as Talbot Hamlin, Joseph Hudnut, and Lewis Mumford. It was called "an empty shell," "a pretentiousness and falsehood to symbolize the search for truth," "a cadaver," "a pompous pile," "a senile sham." Frank Lloyd Wright said that if Jefferson were alive he would be the first to condemn this "stupid erudition mistaken in his honor."[63] Along with differing aesthetics, the debate between architectural conservatives and progressives hinged on the perennial question of how to interpret the spirit of Thomas Jefferson. This task proved no easier for architects than it had been for politicians, historians, or biographers. Should his preference for the classical be taken as definitive, as a perpetually valid expression of his love of the simple, elemental, and essential in the order of nature and the human spirit? Or was Jefferson's mind better expressed in another idea of his, that all societies need a revolution every twenty years or so, and that no generation can legislate (or memorialize) for following generations? Of course, with politicians deeply involved, the debate was not always restricted to a discussion of such high-minded principles. Republicans felt that a New Deal memorial to Jefferson was blasphemous (they were thinking of the small-federal-government, states'-rights, anti-Court Jefferson) unless he was shown "with tears streaming down his cheeks." In the end, the debates over the representation of Jefferson for the memorial were as inconclusive as those of the previous century.

In addition, it was rumored that the new memorial would cause the destruction of most of the beloved cherry trees in its vicinity. Women of Washington chained themselves to the trees, vowing to die rather than allow the destruction of the trees. Because of the uproar, Congress blocked the appropriation of funds in early 1938. The Fine Arts Commission then suggested a new design, an open memorial in which the Jefferson statue would stand in the middle of a circle, the north quarter open to the White House, the south to the Potomac, and the east and west defined by two peristyle colonnades, like parentheses enclosing the circle in which Jefferson stood. The Memorial Commission accepted this plan but it was quickly discovered that it was a rehash of Pope's sketch for a proposed Theodore Roosevelt memorial. Since the architect had just died and his widow forbade any modifications of his design, the commission went back to the pantheon design. Backed by the now impatient FDR, this was the design finally adopted. At the cornerstone laying on November 21, 1938, Franklin Roosevelt delivered a short address in which he recognized Jefferson for three achievements: drafting the Declaration of Independence, writing the Virginia Statute for Religious Freedom, and rendering his services "in establishing the practical operation of the American Government as a democracy and not an autocracy."[64] The report of the commission for the following year makes careful note of the fact that only 171 of 1,700 cherry trees in the vicinity would have to be moved or cut and that 1,000 additional trees would be planted.

The next problem was the sculpture. The commission chose Rudulph Evans's model for the Jefferson statue with similar autocratic spirit. Although the commissioners declared an open competition and selected an art jury to judge the submissions, in the end they and Roosevelt disregarded the jury and simply chose Evans, working with him until he produced the strong though conventional Jefferson they favored. Three commissioners, headed by Senator Elbert Thomas of Utah, then selected the four inscriptions for the wall panels. The selection of passages from the Declaration of Independence was inevitable, and appropriate, although somewhat manipulated:

> We hold these truths to be self-evident: that all men are created equal, that they are endowed by their creator with certain inalienable rights, among these are life, liberty and the pursuit of happiness. That to secure these rights governments are instituted among men. We . . . solemnly publish and declare, that these colonies are and of right ought to be free and independent states . . . and for the support of this declaration, with a firm reliance on the protection of divine providence, we mutually pledge our lives, our fortunes and our sacred honor.[65]

Opposite this passage, on the northwest wall panel, are words from the Virginia Statute for Religious Freedom:

> Almighty God hath created the mind free, all attempts to influence it by temporal punishments or burthens . . . are a departure from the plan of the holy author of our religion . . . no man shall be compelled to frequent or support any religious worship or ministry or shall otherwise suffer on account of his religious opinions or belief, but all men shall be free to profess and by argument to maintain, their opinions in matters of religion. I know but one code of morality for men whether acting singly or collectively.

The southeast panel quotes Jefferson's letter to Samuel Kercheval of July 12, 1816, stating his conviction that, although he is not a believer in frequent changes in laws and constitutions, such "changes in laws and institutions must go hand in hand with the progress of the human mind." This quotation is the least stirring of the four presented and plunges the reader into the old Jeffersonian controversy: are the institutions of the Revolutionary era, especially the Declaration of Independence and the Constitution, icons that must be maintained in the form then given, or are they open to radical change? As usual, Jefferson can be quoted to support either opinion.

Up to this point, the choice of quotations is appropriate and true to Jefferson's own desires. For his own gravestone he chose to be remembered for three things: the Declaration of Independence, the Virginia Statute for Religious Freedom, and his founding of the University of Virginia (representing his lifelong interest in education). But the words quoted on the northeast wall are disturbing. The two selections that constitute it, the first about slavery and the second about education, do not fit together, and there is no indication on the wall that they are taken from two separate writings that treat entirely different subjects. The last two sentences about public education, taken from a letter to George Washington (January 4, 1786), are unexceptionable: "Establish the law for educating the common people. This it is the business of the state to effect and on a general plan." But the initial words bring a somber note into this monument to the light, clarity, and optimism of the Enlightenment. They are the snake in the garden. Taken from Jefferson's *Notes on Virginia*, they begin:

> God who gave us life gave us liberty. Can the liberties of a nation be secure when we have removed a conviction that these liberties are the gift of God? Indeed I tremble for my country when I reflect that God is just. That his justice cannot sleep forever. Commerce between master and slave is despotism. Nothing is more certainly written in the book of fate than that these people are to be free.

Jefferson's own attitude toward slavery, as already indicated, can only be described as ambiguous. He was theoretically opposed to it. Yet his own estates were dependent on slavery, and unlike George Washington, who planned and saved carefully so that his slaves could be freed at his death, Jefferson freed only two, one year after his death, and three others at a later time; he left the rest of his many slaves still in bondage to his heirs.[66] These ambiguities of the historic Jefferson have been obscured, and the quotations leave us with an idealized Jefferson, the great figure of the champion of liberty.

There is no doubt that Jefferson was ideologically opposed to slavery. In the same place from which the inscription was taken, Jefferson reflected on two evils resulting from the institution of slavery. The rights of the slaves themselves have been trampled on, he says, and if a slave can ever have a country in this world, "it must be any other in preference to that in which he is born to live and labor for another." The effect on the masters is equally devastating, he said, for "the whole commerce between master and slave is a perpetual exercise of the most boisterous passions, the most unremitting despotism on the one part, and degrading submission on the other." Slavery ruins family education, for the child begins to imitate his parent in cruelty: "The parent storms, the child looks on, catches the lineaments of wrath, puts on the same airs in the circle of smaller slaves, gives a loose to the worst of passions, and thus nursed, educated, and daily exercised in tyranny, cannot but be stamped by it with odious peculiarities."[67]

A few years later, responding to questions from a French encyclopedist, M. de Meusnier, he recalled his earlier hopes of inserting an amendment to the Slave Law of Virginia that would call for the slaves' eventual emancipation. He expressed clearly the tragic irony of the situation:

> What a stupendous, what an incomprehensible machine is man! who can endure toil, famine, stripes, imprisonment, and death itself in vindication of his own liberty, and, the next moment be deaf to all those motives whose power supported him through his trial, and inflict on his fellow men a bondage, one hour of which is fraught with more misery, than ages of that which he rose in rebellion to oppose.[68]

Perhaps his views of African Americans changed. Jefferson had described slaves in his *Notes on Virginia* as inferior to whites in a number of ways. Their dark skin, he said, was less capable of showing varieties of emotions, their hair was inferior in quality, they had a "strong and disagreeable odor" (because, he said, they urinated less frequently than whites). He catalogued their inferiorities according to his personal observations, prejudices, stereotypes, and suppositions of the "science" contemporary to him.[69] At the same time, he claimed that blacks were equal to whites in bravery, in strength of memory, and in morality. Later in his life, when the talented, black, self-taught surveyor and astronomer Benjamin Banneker sent to him an almanac he had produced, Jefferson replied: "No body wishes more than I do to see such proofs as you exhibit, that nature has given to our black brethren, talents equal to those of the other colors of men, and that the appearance of a want of them is owning merely to the degraded condition of their existence, both in Africa and America."[70] And to Henri Gregoire, who had written a book called *Literature of Negroes,* he admitted that his views on blacks were based on very limited observation: "Be assured that no person living wishes more sincerely that I do, to see a complete refutation of the doubts I myself have entertained and expressed on the grade of understanding allotted to them by nature and to find that in this respect they are on a par with ourselves."[71]

It would be pointless here to prolong the debate on Jefferson's attitude toward slavery. The commissioners who chose the quotation for the memorial no doubt wanted to reflect their own condemnation of slavery and belief in the equality of all before the law. They also assumed that in doing so they would have the assent of most American people. Here again the "history" presented in the memorial is more concerned with the present of the 1930s than with the past. But in order to appeal to Jefferson as a sort of precursor of abolition, the commissioners had to carefully stop their quotation right in the middle of Jefferson's sentence, the full text of which reads as follows: "Nothing is more certainly written in the book of fate, than that these people are to be free; nor is it less certain that the two races, equally free, cannot live in the same government. Nature, habit, opinion have drawn indelible lines of distinction between them."

Perhaps Jefferson kept his own slaves for reasons of simple economy: his expensive European purchases and his inability to economically manage his own estate. Though he often preached frugality, "he himself—with his books, chefs, retinues of servants, and extravagant trappings (80 crates of French furniture)—could never manage to live within his own income, and in his movings-about would insist on extensive remodelings of every house he stayed in, no matter how briefly."[72] He simply could not afford to free his slaves. Although Jefferson protested that "nobody will be more willing to encounter every sacrifice" for the abolition of slavery, John Quincy Adams was closer to the truth about him when he remarked that Jefferson was not inclined to be a martyr. Although he held advanced ideas, he was not, to quote Richard Hofstadter, "in the habit of breaking lances to fulfill them."[73] He was also frightened by the potential social conflict if blacks were freed, as the full quotation above indicates. He once used a telling metaphor to describe the continuing institution of slavery: "we have the wolf by the ears. We can neither continue to hold on nor let go."

Whether Jefferson felt guilty about the conflict between his expressed ideas of human equality and his holding of slaves we cannot know. He rarely expressed his more tender inner feelings or self-doubt in public writing or even private letter. One exception is found in his letter to Maria Cosway, a married woman with whom he fell in love while in France. There in his famous dialogue between head and heart, he gives the last word to the latter. The heart reprimands the head: "my friend, as far as my recollections serves me, I do not know that I ever did a good thing on your suggestion, or a dirty one without it."[74] Perhaps, in the issue of slavery, the heart simply had no chance to be heard.

In the end there is still a validity to the commissioners' choice of this amputated quotation. Whatever Jefferson meant by "all men are created equal," the phrase has become one of the great seminal ideas of Western history, and as a metaphorical seed sowed in receptive soil, it has taken on an independent existence, somehow separate from the man who planted it. Once germinated, it grew, matured, and bore fruit in its own way. If a farmer who plants a seed is to be given credit for his farm and his orchards, then perhaps Jefferson should also get the credit for the outcome of his idea by the 1930s, when the memorial to him was built, and for the far greater extension of that idea that has occurred since. It is a metaphor that Jefferson the gentleman farmer might have appreciated.

In an early entry in *Notes on Virginia,* Jefferson tells of climbing to the top of Natural Bridge, which he owned at the time, and the terrible headache that suddenly seized him as he looked over "into the abyss." It has such grandeur from below, he noted (like a lofty idea, a theory, a principle), but it inspires horror from above, where one looks down at the distant earthly reality. Perhaps that striking experience also bears within it an accurate metaphor for his views of slavery. When landowner and slaveholder Thomas Jefferson looked down at the reality of slavery, he peered all too accurately into the abyss of the future and wrote a passage almost Lincolnesque in its prophetic tone and beautiful but grim cadences. He saw two possible courses for the nation, one too hopeful, the other thoroughly ominous:

> We must await, with patience, the workings of an overruling providence, and hope that this is preparing the deliverance of these, our suffering brethren. When the measure of their tears shall be full, when their groans shall have involved heaven itself in darkness, doubtless, a god of justice will awaken to their distress, and by diffusing light and liberality among their oppressors, or, at length, by his exterminating thunder, manifest his attention to the things of this world, and that they are not left to the guidance of a blind fatality.[75]

With the rumbling of that dark prophecy in our ears, we leave the axis of the Enlightenment, of the Founding Fathers and their "season of youth," and move to the axis of memory, where mystic chords sound more somber tones for a later period of civil bloodshed, a time of "exterminating thunder."

The Jefferson Memorial, when viewed from a distance, seems to float like a mirage over planes of water. On a foggy day it can disappear into the white air. Its apparent lapidary solidity is gently mocked by the cherry blossoms falling from the trees that the women of Washington fought to save in 1938. There is no direct approach to this place. Like the winding paths of an oriental garden, the ways to this monument are roundabout, inviting the stroller to reflection and thoughtful preparation before arriving at its steps.

Unlike its complete subservience to human design elsewhere in this city of baroque and classical magnificence, nature at the Jefferson Memorial clings to some minimum of control. I find myself grateful to the women of Washington, those earliest ecological guerrillas, who made a statement for nature in chaining themselves to the flowering cherries. If there is a sense of unreality about this monument, it is found not in their idealism but in the adolescent imagination of the whole "season of youth," in the dream of freedom and democracy, in the belief in the special virtues and nobility of American cultivators of the agrarian utopia, and in the role given them by "an overruling Providence," to be a model for all the world.

PART III

The Axis of Memory

FIGURE 24 Map of Washington, D.C., the Mall axis emphasized. Map reproduced courtesy of Travel Graphics International.

From Arlington Cemetery to the Capitol

It is Easter Sunday 1998. Despite the spirit of the day, I am aware of the somber character of this axis. I am beginning my walk at the imaginary extension of L'Enfant's Mall axis in Arlington, Virginia. From this vantage point my eye travels back to the Lincoln Memorial, the Washington Monument, and the Capitol, a distance of almost three miles. It will be a long march to the Capitol.

Despite its sober connotations, Arlington Cemetery is a popular destination for visitors. More than 245,000 members of the armed services and their family members are buried here, but most visitors and tourists come to see the graves of the famous—the Kennedys, Oliver Wendell Holmes, Commander Richard Byrd, Joe Louis, Audie Murphy, and of course the Unknown Soldiers honored by the changing of the guard. I sit in the reception center, among hundreds of visitors, watching how many pass respectfully by a life-sized photograph of the astronauts who died on the mission of the Space Shuttle *Challenger*. Included are a black man and two white women. The display symbolizes what most Americans want to believe about their nation: that it is the land of opportunity for all, the "last best hope of earth."

I walk to the Custis-Lee Mansion to see the grave of L'Enfant just below it, overlooking the river and the core of the city he designed. The old home once belonged to the Washington family and then to the Lees, and is located at the western end of a tangential axis created by the Arlington Memorial Bridge, which connects it to the Lincoln Memorial. The bridge yokes together Lincoln and Lee, North and South, a symbolic attempt by city planners to heal the wounds of the Civil War. I follow this axis back to Washington, across Memorial Bridge.

Joining the Easter crowds, I climb the stairs of the Lincoln Memorial and turn to take in the view of the reflecting pool and the Mall beyond it. Like the vista from the Capitol, this is a tour de force, with the white image of the Washington Monument lying flat on the blue of the reflecting pool.

Inside the building I try to get a sense of why so many visitors have come here. Many of them, perhaps the majority, are foreign tourists: Chinese, Japanese, Indians, Middle Easterners, Hispanics, Malays, and many others impossible for me to identify. I am reminded that Lincoln is not just a great American president but an international hero. I look at the faces gazing up at the avuncular Lincoln and wonder what they are thinking, and just then I hear a person ask her companion, in broken English, "He five dollar?"

There is a difference between the way the Lincoln and Jefferson Memorials affect observers. Visitors stroll around the Jefferson, glancing at his statue in the center, most taking time to read the four short quotations on the walls. I see very few people actually reading the Gettysburg Address or the second inaugural address on the walls here. My guess is that almost no one can figure out the Jules Guerin murals above them. I ask three people at random. None knows what they mean. The attention of most is fixed on the immense seated Lincoln. They stare at it, some for a surprisingly long time. Here it is the image, not the words, that engrosses the visitors.

The past is still alive here. An overweight gray-haired man, with his back deliberately turned to the Gettysburg Address, fumbles his way through the text. His wife, facing him, helpfully supplies the words when his memory fails. Finally he struggles through to the last sentence, "of the people, by the people, for the people, shall not perish from the earth," and exclaims to his wife: "Damn! It's been a long time since I was in the seventh grade." He shakes his head, mystic chords of memory clearly overtaxed.

Unlike the confident Jefferson, Lincoln's image is pensive. He sits in the subdued light of the cella, his face thoughtful, evoking the trials that lifted him to heroic status. The brightness and optimism of the Enlightenment are long forgotten, overwhelmed by memories of a tragic Civil War. This statue and building, with its murals and inscriptions, have a daunting task. It is their job to explain the meaning of that bloodiest of wars, for if the dead are to be honored, then the cause for which they fought must be an honorable one. But if the causes of the two parties were diametrically opposed, how can both be honorable? Did they fight over slavery, or was it over preserving the Union? If, as the Great Seal claims, Providence had favored the beginnings of this American experiment in democracy, where was God during the Civil War? It took Lincoln's tortured biblical musings and his soaring rhetoric to begin to deal with these questions, but the answer is muddied in the ambiguities of this memorial. Mostly, it is simply a mausoleum to a martyr.

Across the street I come to the Vietnam Memorial, with a task just as daunting: to commemorate not only a war that divided the nation, but one that the United States lost. Every war memorial must attempt to answer a question: why did so many have to die? The statue of three soldiers at the entrance to the memorial space makes a conventional statement: these men served and fought courageously. But that statement still begs the question: fought for what? The black granite wall designed by architect Maya Lin gives a mute and mysterious answer. Like a myth, the wall does not offer a rational answer but recounts the story without flinching. Its two angled walls make a mythic claim, one pointing east toward the monument to Washington, the other west toward the memorial to Lincoln, reminding visitors that whatever answer they find here must relate to those two men and what they represent.

As I walk forward into the memorial space, the path slopes down. I feel that I am reliving the history of the war, the TV news reporting ever higher body counts. As I descend, the wall rises next to me, and the names of the dead on the black marble multiply. I am in a pit, the rows of names rise higher than my head. At the vertex of the two walls I feel overwhelmed by the magnitude of suffering. A few people are weeping, touching their loved ones' names with their fingertips, making rubbings of the names to take home, to North Carolina, Oklahoma, Michigan. Then I walk on, relieved as the path rises, the wall grows shorter, and the number of names diminishes. Perhaps prompted by the spirit of the day, Easter Sunday, I feel as if I have entered a grave and risen from it.

The Vietnam Memorial fulfills its purpose like no other in Washington, its statement the opposite of every other architectural statement made in this city of dominant white memorials. Even the Lincoln, which was to be "horizontal" to contrast with the vertical Washington obelisk, is overwhelmingly grand, lofty on its platform, pure white in its marble. Did Maya Lin deliberately make her memorial play yin to the yang of all the other memorials in the city? It is low, a gash in the earth, dark-faced, receptive, and humble, in contrast to their height, their brightness, their dominant and proud exteriors. It reaffirms the strength of the earth and thus seems an appropriate answer to the questioning of our most unpopular war. It is maternal, a place of tears and remembering lost children.

I follow the Mall east, passing through the area proposed as a site for a World War II memorial. I find myself hoping it will not be built there. It would interrupt the precious open space around the Washington Monument, where it is all right to lie in the sun, play ball games, and toss a Frisbee. We need these activities to relieve the gravity created by so many war memorials on the Mall.

I continue walking down the Mall, east of the Washington Monument, thinking of the throngs of people who have gathered here over the past few decades: groups seeking civil rights, racial equality, economic rights, women's rights, gay rights, justice for their causes, and a share in the American dream. In a way that L'Enfant, Washington, and Jefferson could never have envisioned, this place has become an agora for protest, a forum for declamation and contestation. To claim a place on the Mall is to claim a role in the evolving national mythology.

At the east end of the Mall is a vast white tent specially erected for two Easter worship services. The 3:00 service is in progress as I enter to an enthusiastic rendition of "The Joy of Giving" by the choir of the Metropolitan Baptist Church. I am handed a program and find my somber mood reinforced by the title: "Resurrection '98, Easter Sunday, April 12, 1998: Proclaiming a Resurrection Faith for a Crucified City." As I leave, I ask an usher what is meant by a "a crucified city." Hardly a pause: "you know, drugs, violence, and . . . nonrepresentation."

I walk past the Grant Memorial and up the stairway to the Capitol, going around the Senate side. On the east steps of the Capitol are hundreds of Easter lilies arranged to form a cross. Next to them stands a risen Jesus. Should this lift my spirits? I remember seeing this same man two days earlier, crowned with thorns, carrying his cross down Pennsylvania Avenue, surrounded by a small band of appropriately dressed soldiers and mockers. Now, though he is wearing the same burlap robe, his crown of thorns is gone. But he looks singularly glum for a man risen from the dead. I ask Jesus what church is sponsoring this display. None, he says. He refers me to a well-dressed woman wearing a white, broad-brimmed Easter hat. She can answer your questions, he says, in a way that makes me wonder if he is playing his role out of conviction or because he is paid by the well-dressed woman. She tells me that she and her friends have produced this pageant and the display of lilies every Easter for many years.

Next to the white passion-play mummers is a shabbily dressed black man, a street person. He sits with his homemade "broadside," which says: "Lost my health in World War II, had a bad heart HI-Blood pressures gout cuttard & more. I am one of the black dogs had no right to go to war only difference between slave and an animal is a slave is treated worse than an animal." Here, at the very center of national life, the past and present of the nation come together: human rights, slavery, wars, protest, and ever-present religion. For some, this great land of freedom is no picnic ground. And yet this homeless man is allowed to be here, to lay a guilt trip on the thousands of pilgrims who come to the "Temple of Democracy." I look above him and find my epiphany in the three allegorical figures on the pediment. One figure represents America, the two below her Justice and Hope. Hope points to America, but America says look to Justice. That's the message. Our hope depends on doing justice. America has been here a long time, since the days of John Quincy Adams, pointing patiently toward Justice. She is not pointing toward a military triumph or toward economic prosperity, but toward Justice, which has gradually become more inclusive since 1825, when Adams fussed over the decoration of this pediment. Justice is an abstract virtue that must be given content by each generation of citizens. The jury is still out, and always will be I suppose, while the experiment goes on.

CHAPTER 7

Memento Mori

The Lincoln Memorial and the Honored Dead

SOMETIMES IT TAKES an outsider to see the truth. Fei Xiaotong, an eminent Chinese anthropologist of the mid-twentieth century, once remarked that he felt sorry for Americans because they had no ghosts. Besides referring to the contrast between the ways Chinese and Americans treat the deceased, he also meant that Americans had little sense of history, with "no attachment to any place as all were alike."[1] Admittedly, compared with the Chinese, Americans have a cavalier attitude toward their dead and in their mobility are less connected to specific places. Native Americans had noted this too. In the famous words attributed to Chief Seattle: "The ashes of our ancestors are sacred and their final resting place is hallowed ground, while you wander away from the tombs of your fathers without regret. . . . Your dead cease to love you and the homes of their nativity as soon as they pass the portals of the tomb. They wander off beyond the stars, are soon forgotten and never return."[2]

If there is anywhere Americans can refute charges that they neglect their ancestors, it is in Washington, D.C., where there are ghosts aplenty that receive the continuous attention of multitudes of pious visitors each year. There the shades of Founding Fathers and later heroes linger, commemorated in sculpture, celebrated in engraved quotations, buildings, and memorials, and housed in the graves of Arlington Cemetery. Between John F. Kennedy's death in 1963 and the year 1971, some 28 million visitors had visited the "eternal flame" marking his grave.[3] Americans and foreign tourists also visit the dead at the memorials on the western half of the Mall: those to Lincoln, the Vietnam and Korean Wars, and now Roosevelt. Each memorial celebrates the "honored dead" but at the same time calls up the unexorcised ghosts that still haunt the memories of the American people. And since the words "these honored dead" are Lincoln's words, it is fitting that the major monument at this end of the axis is the memorial dedicated to Abraham Lincoln.

Although the memorial does not house the grave of Lincoln, it has the feeling of a mausoleum. It stands in sharp contrast to the Jefferson Memorial, which is flooded with light and charged with the atmosphere of youthful hopes and dreams. The Lincoln Memorial speaks the wisdom of age, admitting light only from the eastern entry and through the dim ceiling light. Daniel Chester French's seated Lincoln is somber and pensive, the very image of a Christ-like martyr who had to suffer along with his people for the tragic flaw the Founders had left in the Constitution, the "peculiar institution" of slavery.

When James Buchanan delivered his inaugural address on March 4, 1857, from the Capitol steps, astute listeners might have shaken their heads at his wishful thinking. The Kansas-Nebraska Act had left the determination of whether to legalize slavery up to the people of the new territory, and when it was thrown open to settlement, "settlers from both slave and free states rushed into the area and engaged in bloody combat in their struggle to determine Kansas' status." The conflict appeared even in the halls of Congress. After Senator Charles Sumner indignantly delivered a speech he called "The Crime against Kansas," he was attacked and beaten almost to death by a Democratic representative from South Carolina, Preston Brooks. Buchanan's inaugural speech, however, noted complacently that "when the people proclaimed their will [during the election], the tempest at once subsided and all was calm."[4]

In fact the storm was just about to break. Two days after Buchanan's inauguration, the Supreme Court delivered the Dred Scott decision, which unleashed a storm of controversy. Ruling against Scott and declaring the Missouri Compromise unconstitutional, it seemed to imply that slavery must be accepted in *every* state of the Union. But John Brown's antislavery raid at Harper's Ferry, Virginia, in 1859 frightened the South, and Lincoln's election confirmed Southerners' fears. On December 20, 1860, South Carolina voted to secede from the Union and was soon followed by Alabama, Mississippi, Florida, Georgia, Louisiana, and Texas. On the same day, Buchanan, called by a contemporary "the personification of evasion, the embodiment of an inducement to dodge,"[5] wrote to a friend complacently, "I have never enjoyed better health or a more tranquil spirit than during the past year. All our troubles have not cost me an hour's sleep or a single meal."[6] Franklin Pierce had said in 1856, when denied the nomination of his party, "men are dwarfs, principles alone are abiding," but in the early 1860s it seemed that neither men nor principles could be found to save the Union. In 1862, historian Francis Parkman wrote in despair: "Out of three millions, America found a Washington, an Adams, a Franklin, a Jefferson, a Hamilton; out of twenty millions, she now finds none whose stature can compare with these."

To his contemporaries, Lincoln appeared to be cut from the same cloth as temporizers like Millard Fillmore, Franklin Pierce, and James Buchanan. The insults heaped upon him at the time read like a litany composed in a zoo. Lincoln was called "a slang-whanging stump speaker," "that giraffe," "a half-witted usurper," a "mole-eyed" monster, "the present turtle at the head of government," "the head ghoul at Washington," the "original gorilla," a baboon, a long-armed ape, an "abolitionist orang-outang," a poor horse that *must be led,* the Kentucky mule, and a "joke incarnated." He was described as stupid, unfit, dazed, foolish, uneducated, a political coward, and also its opposite, a dictator. The impatient abolitionist Wendell Phillips called him, in a much-quoted phrase, a "first-rate *second-rate* man."[7] Some of these insults came from men in his own party, who found him timid, unsure, and unequal to the task before him. "Oh, for an hour of Jackson," cried some Republicans.[8] Leaving aside the calumnies, the author reporting much of this vituperation sums up the situation more soberly: "To most men of his own day Lincoln seemed neither liberal nor conservative statesman; he was simply a rather ineffectual president. It is hard to remember how unsuccessful Lincoln's administration appeared to most of his contemporaries."[9]

His rise to eminence was sudden and dramatic. The same newspapers that found him incompetent in 1864 suddenly discovered after April 15, 1865, that "Lincoln had been the greatest man in the world."[10] Union victories in late 1864 helped. His tragic death was immediately seen as a martyrdom and was the single most important factor in his rapid canonization: "Indeed, it was the manner and timing of Lincoln's death, more than anything else, that made a hero of him."[11] It also prevented him from having any connection with the political snarls soon to emerge in the period of Reconstruction. By the centennial of Lincoln's birth in 1909, Russian author Leo Tolstoy, arguably the most famous man in the world at the time, said of him: "Of all the great national heroes and statesmen of history, Lincoln is the only true giant."[12] Tolstoy went on to describe the amazing penetration of his fame to remote places, telling of meeting a Muslim chieftain in the remote Caucasus Mountains who said of Lincoln: "He was a hero. He spoke with the voice of thunder; he laughed like the sunrise and his deeds were strong as the rock and sweet as the fragrance of roses."

This image of the noble and beloved Lincoln, greater than life, is the figure revered today in the Lincoln Memorial. By the time this shrine was planned, the Great Emancipator's canonization had taken place. The story of how and why this happened is a long and complicated one, with many areas still open to scholarly debate. More has been written on Lincoln, according to James McPherson, than on any other figure in Western history save Jesus and Shakespeare.[13] There are more than three hundred books and articles on the subject of Lincoln's religion alone. At the risk of oversimplifying the story, let me try to outline what I take to be the most important element in the religious dimension of Lincoln's canonization and enshrinement on the Mall.

Few would deny that the Civil War was the greatest crisis to face the United States since its founding. Henry James had said that the real U.S. history began with it. The war obviously threatened the dissolution of the Union, with the first secession opening the door to others and to a potential splintering into an indefinite number of regions bound together by social patterns or sectional interest. The nation had begun some four score and seven years earlier, a noble experiment in republican government that the Founders thought would become a light to the whole world, testimony to the idea that ordinary people could rule themselves. At no time since 1783 did this fundamental ideal seem more at risk. Since that time, two French republics had fallen, and numerous republican governments had come and gone in Latin America. The hopes of 1848 in Europe had been dashed. The "brave experiment" launched in Philadelphia "seemed fragile indeed in this world bestrode by kings, emperors, czars, dictators, theories of aristocracy, and unequality." Most Northerners, at least, shared Lincoln's conviction that the fate of democratic government hung in the balance.[14] He used melodramatic language to express this, calling the United States the "last best hope of earth." In fact, representatives of the old order abroad were delighted at the South's insurrection. The *Times* of London bid good riddance to the Union and its republicanism, wishing success to the Confederacy. Emperor Napoleon III stated with ill-concealed relish that "the work of George Washington has come to an end." King Leopold of Belgium described the Lincoln administration as "the most rank Radicalism" and thought its victory, "in collaboration with Europe's revolutionaries, might undermine the very basis of the traditional social order of Europe."[15]

Lincoln saw himself as heir to the ideals of the Founders, with the responsibility to protect the ongoing "brave experiment." Unlike his debating partner Douglas, he would not sit by and allow a minority of states to dissolve the Union. As he said in his second inaugural address, one of the parties "would *make* war rather than let the nation survive, and the other would *accept* war rather than let it perish, and the war came." Although he accepted the bloody struggle, it went on far longer and took many more casualties than he or anyone else anticipated. At Gettysburg alone, there were more than 50,000 killed and wounded. The enormity of the war cried out for an explanation.

Today, if Americans revere Lincoln, it is not because he waged war fearlessly but because he convinced them that the war was unavoidable, a tragic necessity. He thought about it incessantly, not just tactically and militarily, but asking the deeper questions of why it happened and why it continued so long with the loss of so many lives, and what, after all, it meant. He spoke of God's will in a letter to a Quaker: "Surely he intends some great good to follow this mighty convulsion, which no mortal could make, and no mortal could stay."[16] The "suffering and pain that tore at the nation's life . . . cried aloud for some interpretation."[17] Of all those who sought to make some sense of this terrible event, Lincoln's own interpretations today seem the most compelling. Yet as Edmund Wilson has pointed out, if we can place ourselves at the time of the Civil War, "we realize that it was not at all inevitable to think of it as Lincoln thought." His molding of public opinions was a matter of "style and imagination as well as of moral authority, of compelling argument and obstinate will."[18] That is to say, Lincoln, like Elizabeth Bishop's great artist, has taken the "incoherent fragments," history's ruins, and from them "made creations."[19] He created the story that most Americans accept as the best telling of the Civil War, and in the process created the myth of his own life. "The Civil War is, to most Americans," says Garry Wills, "what Lincoln wanted it to mean."[20] It is not inaccurate to say that Lincoln "won the war with metaphors."[21]

Hidden behind the awkward persona, Lincoln had remarkable abilities that allowed him to succeed in this task. His mind was analytical, rational, logical. He was a consummate politician. He had great rhetorical skills that he honed as he gained more experience. He had the gift of a disarming humor. He had an innate appreciation of the power and poetry of language, which was enhanced by his reading (and hearing) of Shakespeare and the King James Bible. But I think the principal reason Americans have allowed him to shape the meaning of the Civil War and to reshape the myth of the United States is that they perceive that he did it out of the crucible of his own experience. The inner crisis he experienced as he pondered the mysteries of the war somehow reflected the outer crisis experienced by the country he led. Like a biblical prophet, his personal sufferings resulted in a public message, and many people who heard his words were prepared to believe that he did indeed speak for God, an "American Isaiah, or Jeremiah, or St. Paul."[22]

The Civil War was catastrophic, bringing death and suffering into the lives of most families in the nation. But its critical proportions were enlarged not just by the bloodshed but through its challenging of the foundational myth by which Americans understood their national existence. If I am correct that there was a strong messianic element in the Founders' ideals, amounting to a religious mission to the world, then the Civil War posed an obvious question: why is the mission not succeeding? Because the question is based on a religious premise, it would require a religious response. That is what Lincoln provided. Though he joined no church, he shared in the deepest religious sensibilities of ordinary American people and was able to frame his answer in a language that spoke to their condition.

As the war began, Lincoln was absorbed with the problem of preserving the Union. He shared the Founders' almost mystical belief in the sacredness of the union of the states, which Jefferson had called "the last anchor of our hope." Madison had defended it with a passionate plea in his political testament of 1834, "Advice to My Country." The sanctified notion of the Union gathered momentum in the decades after the nation's founding, reaching its climax in the high idealism of Lincoln. Even Alexander Stephens, the vice president of the Confederacy, admitted that "with Lincoln the Union rose to the sublimity of religious mysticism."[23] He knew that slavery was the problem, but for him, at least at first, it was the dependent not the independent variable. In taking his constitutional oath to preserve the Union, Lincoln very likely thought in terms similar to those propounded by John Witherspoon, a signer of the Declaration of Independence, that such an oath is "an appeal to God, the Searcher of hearts, for the truth of what we say, and always expresses or supposes an imprecation of his judgment upon us, if we prevaricate."[24]

Yet despite his clear perceptions of duty, Lincoln seemed to be in an impossible position. In the initial stages of the crisis Lincoln was all too aware of the Madisonian problem, which is the touchstone of democracy: how to preserve the delicate balance between the competing interests that faced him: slave states, free states, radical and conservative Republicans, Unionist and secessionist Democrats (all but the last represented in his own cabinet), abolitionists and proslavery factions, gradual and immediate emancipators, executive and congressional power, federal and state authority, to mention just some of them. He said at one point that "if slavery is not wrong, nothing is wrong." Yet though personally against it, he added, "I have never understood that the Presidency conferred upon me an unrestricted right to act officially upon this judgment and feeling."[25] That is to say, Lincoln was the president of a democracy, not a dictator. Radical abolitionist William Lloyd Garrison said of Lincoln that he "moved slowly in the right direction, needed 'spurring on to yet more decisive action,' but was moving as fast as public opinion allowed."[26]

His own political convictions simply did not leave him the option of "the radical leader" whose "singleness of purpose" freed him from responsibility to many competing constituencies. Garry Wills points out in his study of leadership that freedom of responsibility to many competing interests allowed such a radical as Harriet Tubman to singlemindedly pursue an unswerving purpose: leading slaves to freedom. [27] William Lloyd Garrison, who initially stood ready to burn the Constitution because it countenanced slavery, was like Tubman. As he said at the end of his introduction to Frederick Douglass's autobiography:

> Reader! are you with the man-stealers in sympathy and purpose, or on the side of their down-trodden victims? If with the former, then are you the foe of God and man. If with the latter, what are you prepared to do and dare in their behalf? . . . Come what may—cost what it may—inscribed on the banner which you unfurl to the breeze, as your religious and political motto—"NO COMPROMISE WITH SLAVERY? NO UNION WITH SLAVEHOLDERS!"[28]

Lincoln's position, in contrast, left him in the condition Wills describes as "the general immobility induced by 'balanced' leaders." He could go only as far as his perception and shaping of public sentiment allowed him to go. He could not be satisfied with attracting a committed minority to his cause, but had to seek to form a majority position.

As the crisis deepened and the casualties mounted, Lincoln began to think of the war in more clearly religious terms. Many historians have noted this, but no one has put it more accurately than Harriet Beecher Stowe. After the interview in which Lincoln is supposed to have said, "So you're the little woman who wrote the book that made this great war," she offered the following appraisal of the president:

> We do not mean to give the impression that Lincoln is a religious man in the sense in which that term is popularly applied. We believe he has never made any such profession, but we see evidence in passing through this dreadful national crisis he has been forced by the very anguish of the struggle to look upward, where any rational creature must look for support. No man in this agony has suffered more and deeper, albeit with a dry, weary, patient pain, that seemed to some like insensibility.[29]

Americans, as commentators from Tocqueville on have noted, are among the most religious peoples in the world. Lincoln was able to connect with this defining characteristic more successfully than any other American president before or since. As he sought to understand the tragedy of the war himself, he was able to interpret it for his people. Although the Founders had also been religious, their Enlightenment faith was a rational confidence in what they considered the general principles of "natural religion" rather than revealed religion. Lincoln's own thought moved along the paths of revealed religion, and he used the language of the Bible with an almost Shakespearean sense of rhythm and vocabulary. He spoke a language that resonated in the souls of most Americans. What one scholar said of the Revolutionary generation was even more true of Lincoln's time: "Ordinary people might be uncomfortable with the complex language of republicanism but could identify with a biblical language that tapped their sense of identity as a religious and ethical people."[30]

Although Lincoln probably was in general agreement with the religious views of Washington and Jefferson, his religion embraced complexities. The conflict had taken on such immense proportions that the Founders' "natural religion" was incapable of providing an adequate response. The war had broken the bounds of the rational, moving into the realm of the absurd, the catastrophic, the unthinkable. It was Armageddon, the dark sinfulness of human nature unleashed in the heart of the promised land. The eighteenth-century theologian Jonathan Edwards might have said that Americans were "sinful souls in the hands of an angry God." Americans were convicted under sin, literally experiencing a kind of "damnation" as they looked at the bloodshed around them. In single battles like Antietam and Gettysburg they saw more casualties than the nation had sustained in all previous wars combined. It was hell, and Lincoln gradually turned toward the tragic concepts and somber resonance of biblical discourse to understand the catastrophe and to seek ways of explaining it to his people.

It was not a calculated move on his part that impelled him to do so. He seemed driven to it. He did not simply apply biblical terms to concepts otherwise derived. The Bible provided a structure for his thinking, helping him to see what the questions were as well as suggesting answers. Beyond mere terminology he appealed to underlying concepts and scenarios from Jewish and Christian resources: sin and salvation, pollution and purification, creation and renewal, the inherent mystery of human actions and the inscrutable will of God, suffering, death, and resurrection. The ideas of Julia Ward Howe in the "Battle Hymn of the Republic"—"the grapes of wrath," "the terrible swift sword"—Lincoln expressed in more nuanced but still stirring and profound phrases of divine judgment. But he also adopted the theological hope of spiritual regeneration: "Our republican robe is soiled, and trailed in the dust. Let us repurify it. Let us turn and wash it white, in the spirit, if not the blood, of the Revolution."[31]

His appeal to the Founding Fathers, especially to the words of the Declaration of Independence, was like an appeal to Scripture, and he was often able to yoke the two in ingenious and compelling juxtapositions. Indeed, he turned the Declaration into an American scripture, calling it "the sheet anchor of our principles." In his objection to the Kansas-Nebraska Act, which countenanced slavery in the new territories, he said:

> Let us re-adopt the Declaration of Independence, and, with it, the practices and policy which harmonize with it. Let north and south—let all Americans— let all lovers of liberty everywhere—join in the great and good work. If we do this, we shall not only have saved the Union, but we shall have so saved it as to make and keep it forever worthy of saving. We shall have so saved it that the succeeding millions of free happy people, the world over, shall rise up and call us blessed to the latest generation.[32]

He not only recalled Mary's words heralding the birth of the Savior ("henceforth all generations shall call me blessed"); he also revealed the crux of his dilemma during the war and the reason for his change of mind. In view of the disaster of the bloody war, saving the Union was not enough. The Union had to be kept "forever worthy of saving." Some great good had to be sought to balance the obvious enormity of evil. And that good was to be the ending of slavery.

In order to do this, Lincoln had to place a higher priority on the Declaration of Independence than on the Constitution. He excused the latter for countenancing slavery with the explanation, offered during his debates with Douglas, that the Founders had hidden slavery in the document "just as an afflicted man hides away a wen or a cancer, which he dare not cut out at once, lest he bleed to death; with the promise, nevertheless, that the cutting away may begin at the end of a given time."[33] But the Declaration of Independence had said that "all men are created equal," and ignoring what the phrase may have meant for Jefferson and the others who signed the document, Lincoln would take it literally: "if all men are created equal, they cannot be property." He would use the occasion of the Gettysburg Address to make his official reinterpretation of the phrase and canonize it for the future. The nation was conceived in liberty, he said, and dedicated to the proposition that all men are created equal. Those who had died at Gettysburg did so so that the nation, so conceived, might live. Those remaining needed to carry on the work they had so nobly begun, taking increased devotion to the cause "for which they gave the last full measure of devotion; that we here highly resolve that these dead shall not have died in vain; that this nation, under God, shall have a new birth of freedom; and that government of the people, by the people, for the people, shall not perish from the earth."

As Moses had called upon the people of Israel to reaffirm their commitment to God, Lincoln called upon Americans to renew their commitment to the promise of the Founders and to reactivate its power in their own times. From that time on, most Americans have accepted Lincoln's interpretation of the meaning of the war and for the terrible bloodshed have sought absolution in the thought that the disaster was necessary to end slavery. Even the ex-slave Frederick Douglass, who did not always approve of Lincoln's policies, caught this image and said that the Lincoln who "began by playing Pharaoh . . . ended by playing Moses."[34]

At Gettysburg, Lincoln both reinterpreted the Declaration of Independence and cleansed the Constitution, altering it from within, appealing from its letter to its spirit. What he did, says Garry Wills, was "one of the most daring acts of open-air sleight-of-hand ever witnessed by the unsuspecting. Everyone in that vast throng of thousands was having his or her intellectual pocket picked." Perhaps Wills borrowed that image from states' rights advocate and Lincoln critic Willmoore Kendall, who complained that we should not allow Lincoln to "steal the game," wrenching a single proposition from the Declaration and making it "our supreme commitment." In so doing, Kendall observes, Lincoln has made his Gettysburg Address more influential than the Declaration by determining how we read it.[35]

All metaphors, if pushed too far, become misleading. While expressing the audacity of Lincoln's interpretation, the image of a pickpocket working the crowd covers only one aspect of the event. A more comprehensive metaphor to describe what happened on that occasion would be that of a high priest solemnly expounding a sacred text and reinterpreting it to apply to a contemporary situation. The Supreme Court has done this many times, and presidents have done it before and since Lincoln, but none with so much authority and such far-reaching implications. Besides connecting with the Founders and reinterpreting their meaning, Lincoln baptized them into the religious discourse of ordinary American Christians. As the poet Robert Lowell said at the Gettysburg centennial in 1963, "By his words, he gave the field of battle a significance that it had lacked . . . he left Jefferson's ideals of freedom and equality joined to our Christian sacrificial act of death and rebirth."[36]

Lincoln indeed worked magic with his words. Even his enemies felt their power and knew their religious source. M. E. Bradford, one of his fiercest critics, recently accused him of being a "country hustler," a "self-made Caesar," creating an imperial presidency, all the while "wrapping up his policy in the idiom of Holy Scripture, concealing within the Trojan Horse of his gasconade and moral superiority an agenda that never would have been approved if presented in any other form." The *Chicago Times,* reacting to the Gettysburg Address, also expressed irritation at the net of words Lincoln had thrown, complaining that the central issue was the Union as enshrined in the Constitution, not equality. One senses in the angry reactions of critics the frustration of trying to oppose mere logic to poetry. Lincoln supports his assertions with rational arguments, but he does more than that. Here, at Gettysburg, was eloquence, "here was an ear keenly tuned to the music of the English language; here were intellectual grasp and moral urgency; here was great emotional power under firm artistic control. Here, in short, was the mastery that we associate with genius."[37] Trying to combat such eloquence was difficult. How do you argue against metaphor, music and myth? "Lincoln argues, but he also casts a spell; and what can a rebuttal do to incantation?"[38]

Slavery was dead, its death sentence announced on the first day of the same year, 1863, in the Emancipation Proclamation. Despite its guarded tone, its totally uninspiring character, and the fact that it applied only to slaves in areas under Confederate control (and thus, as critics have pointed out, freeing *no one*), it was the beginning of the end for "the peculiar institution." As John Hope Franklin has said: "The tragedy of this republic was that as long as human slavery existed its base had a fallacy that made it both incongruous and specious. The great value of the Emancipation Proclamation was that in its first century it provided the base with a reinforcement that made it at long last valid and worthy."[39] Lincoln's new interpretation of the Declaration of Independence as applying to all human beings was later officially confirmed when the thirteenth amendment was ratified on December 6, 1865: "Neither slavery nor involuntary servitude, except as a punishment for crime whereof the party shall have been duly convicted, shall exist within the United States, or any place subject to their jurisdiction."

It was left to the second inaugural address to take up the theological questions with which Lincoln had struggled so long. In a letter to Albert Hodges in Kentucky, he wrote, "If God now wills the removal of a great wrong, and wills also that we of the North as well as you of the South, shall pay fairly for our complicity in that wrong, impartial history will find therein new cause to attest and revere the justice and goodness of God."[40] He expressed that idea with greater eloquence in the second inaugural. Lincoln the theologian draws out the inference and its full religious implication: "All knew that this interest [slavery] was the cause of the war." Both sides "read the same bible and pray to the same God, and each invokes His aid against the other."

> The Almighty has his own purposes. "Woe unto the world because of offenses; for it must needs be that offenses come, but woe to that man by whom the offense cometh." If we shall suppose that American slavery is one of those offenses which, in the providence of God must needs come, but which, having continued through His appointed time, He now wills to remove, and that He gives to both North and South this terrible war as the woe due to those by whom the offense came, shall we discern therein any departure from those divine attributes which the believers in a living God always ascribe to Him. Fondly do we hope, fervently do we pray, that this mighty scourge of war may speedily pass away. Yet, if God wills that it continue until all the wealth piled by the bondsman's two hundred and fifty years of unrequited toil shall be sunk, and until every drop of blood drawn with the lash shall be paid by another drawn with the sword, as was said three thousand years ago, so still it must be said "the judgments of the Lord are true and righteous altogether."[41]

Charles Francis Adams, diplomat and son of John Quincy Adams, often disapproved of Lincoln; but he said that the second inaugural provided "for all time the historical keynote" of the Civil War.[42] Its words take on additional power when it becomes clear that they are not a self-righteous condemnation of the South or a simple reiteration of the Deuteronomic theology that good will be rewarded and evil punished. As Lincoln said in a later comment on his second inaugural, "whatever of humiliation there is in it falls most directly on myself, I thought others might afford for me to tell it."[43] Lincoln touches on the imponderable offenses that "must needs come," and the mystery of the divine will: "The Almighty has his own purposes." He had made it clear on more than one occasion that both North and South, and he himself, stood under divine judgment. All were in complicity with slavery. Proclaiming April 30, 1863, as a day of fasting and humiliation, he called upon the entire nation to acknowledge its guilt and pray for "the pardon of our national sins."[44] In this light, the final peroration of the second inaugural may be seen not as patronizing and sentimental, but as an absolute requirement because of mutual guilt for the institution of slavery: "With malice toward none, with charity for all, with firmness in the right as God gives us to see the right, let us strive on to finish the work we are in, to bind up the nation's wounds, to care for him who shall have borne the battle and for his widow and his orphan, to do all which may achieve and cherish a just and lasting peace among ourselves and with all nations."

It is often pointed out that Lincoln's common origins were a source of strength and one of the reasons for his success. Thomas Jefferson had described the yeoman farmer whose sense of real morality was more trustworthy than the professional moralist: "Those who labor in the earth are the chosen people of God, if ever He had a chosen people. . . . Corruption of morals in the mass of cultivators is a phenomenon of which no age nor nation has furnished an example."[45] After the procession of two Virginia patricians and a Boston Brahmin, the idea struck a chord again in the popularity of Andrew Jackson as the unsophisticated and incorruptible man from the West. Abraham Lincoln would become the epitome of it: the common man who could rise to unparalleled heights of wisdom, morality, and greatness. He could combine the paradoxical characteristics of being "awkward, amiable, robust, rail-splitting, story-telling, frontier folk hero, *and* the towering figure of the Great Emancipator and Savior of the Union, a man of sorrows, Christ-like in his character and fate."[46] Poet Percy Mackaye wrote on the centennial of Lincoln's birth: "He stands forth / 'Mongst nations old—a new world Abraham, / The patriarch of peoples still to be."[47] There is something peculiarly American in this juxtaposition: the unpolished, simple, and good person who rises to eminence because of his transcendent qualities. In this understanding of his character there developed an intimate connection between his personal qualities and the myth of America. He became "the representative of the nation."[48]

Needless to say, the man-of-the-people theme drew also on New Testament motifs, for a woodworking rail-splitter is not so different from a carpenter. Both were of ordinary origins, men of sorrows; the iconography of the suffering Christ, so familiar to nineteenth-century Americans and used once before for George Washington, became even more visible in Lincoln as the war continued. The deepening lines of anguish in the visage of Lincoln, recorded by photography over the four years of his presidency, seemed to confirm the torment in his mind over the deaths of "soldier boys," blue and gray. Then the assassination by a traitor on Good Friday placed the final seal of resemblance on his life. He died to save his people.

By the time the Lincoln Memorial Commission was formed in the first decade of the twentieth century, Lincoln had already been purged of all ambiguity in the popular mind and stood at the pinnacle of the American pantheon of national heroes. Some historians caviled, but the verdict of literary figures was all but unanimous: Walt Whitman, James Russell Lowell, Carl Sandburg, Vachel Lindsay, and Edwin Markham all saw him as the quintessential American hero. Only Edgar Lee Masters reviled him. When historians of the period brought up problems and ambiguities, the response of literary figures may be generally summed up by H. L. Mencken's response to criticism of Sandburg's portrait of Lincoln: "Are the facts all respected? Is the narrative satisfactory to the professors of Lincolnology? To hell with the professors of Lincolnology!"[49]

Revisionist historians such as J. G. Randall, Claude Bowers, and Howard Beale asked whether the Civil War was really necessary. They questioned Lincoln's motives, documented his dilatory movements toward emancipation, and called attention to the racism of his black "colonization" ideas and his dubious plans for reconstruction. Southern sympathizers like Lyon Gardiner Tyler called Lincoln the cause of the war, the father of the horrors of Reconstruction, "legislative robbery, negro supremacy over their masters, cheating at polls, rape of white women, lynching and the acts of the Ku Klux Klan."[50] Still, Lincoln's reputation gradually improved in the South as he was credited with saving the Union and his phrase "malice toward none" came to be seen as promising a much more just reconstruction than actually materialized. Even Jefferson Davis said that his death had been "a great misfortune to the South." The gradual rise of Lincoln as a Southern hero is suggested in a 1937 speech given to the Georgia Daughters of the Confederacy by their historian Dolly Blount Lamar: "Let the world know of the wisdom, the kindness, and the justice of the great President of the Confederate States of America, Abraham Lincoln!" Just a slip, she said later.[51]

All told, the criticisms of Lincoln were an insignificant ripple on the surface of his overwhelming popularity. He never went through the ups and down of public esteem that Jefferson did. Movements to erect statues and build memorials to honor Lincoln began early and scarcely abated for a hundred years after his death. Friends and associates formed the National Lincoln Monument Association, which was incorporated by Congress in 1867. Clark Mills submitted a design, which ultimately failed for a number of reasons, among them its probable immense cost and complicated iconography, and perhaps because it included the idea of emancipation. Illinois erected a grand monument in Springfield in 1874, and Hodgenville, Kentucky, enshrined the putative log cabin of his home inside an elegant Greek temple designed by John Russell Pope in 1909. Augustus St. Gaudens did a statue of him that became the centerpiece for Lincoln Park in Chicago.

In Washington the impetus for the earliest monument to Lincoln came from freed slaves. The Freedman's Monument, a sculpture by Thomas Ball, shows Lincoln emancipating a slave who kneels at his feet (see Figure 25). It was dedicated in Lincoln Park east of the Capitol on April 14, 1876, with

FIGURE 25 Thomas Ball, emancipation monument. Courtesy of the Library of Congress.

most of the money for the memorial coming from former slaves who served in the Union army. The major address was given by Frederick Douglass, whose honesty on the occasion was a refreshing contrast to the adulatory prose usual at such events. "Truth compels me to admit," he said, that Lincoln was not in the fullest sense "either our man or our model." In other words, he was preeminently the white man's president. Looking at the white faces in the crowd, he said, "you are the children of Abraham Lincoln. We are at best his step children; children by adoption, children by force of circumstances and necessity."[52] Perhaps Douglass was a bit irritated by the abject slave in Ball's sculpture. His servile position was later noted by black art critic Henry Murray, who interpreted it to mean that the freed slave had no real appreciation of his new status other than that of a person who has escaped punishment. He is still a slave.[53]

The drive for a national memorial for Lincoln did not gather momentum until the first decade of the twentieth century. A crucial event was the formation of the McMillan Commission to plan for the overall development of Washington. Its charge was to recapture the grandeur of L'Enfant's original vision and to rescue the city from its chaotic state at the beginning of the century. This plan is examined more thoroughly in the next chapter. It is important to mention here because it called for a Lincoln monument to be located on the site it now occupies. It was to be, in fact, "the key to the symbolism of the new Mall." Because it planted "the seed that grew into Henry Bacon's temple in Potomac Park a decade later, the work of the McMillan Commission is a turning point in our story."[54] But between the seed and the fruition was a decade of false starts that included two years of acrimonious debate between 1911 and 1913.

The major issues of contention were the nature and location of the memorial and who would design it. The principal official players in the struggle were the Commission of Fine Arts, appointed by President Taft in 1910 to oversee the aesthetic aspects of the development of the Capital according to the McMillan plan; and the Lincoln Memorial Commission established by Congress on February 11, 1911, "to procure and determine upon a location, plan, and design for a monument or memorial in the city of Washington, District of Columbia, to the memory of Abraham Lincoln, subject to the approval of Congress."[55] As indicated by the last phrase, the third player was Congress itself. A few years earlier, a congressionally appointed committee had authorized Representative James T. McCleary of Minnesota to visit Europe to research ideas on a similar commemorative project. He returned, ironically, with a thoroughly American idea, though he clothed it in a Roman toga. He suggested building an Abraham Lincoln Memorial Highway from Washington, D.C., to Gettysburg, Pennsylvania (inspired, he said, by Rome's Appian Way). It would be dynamic, continually changing, and it would reflect Lincoln's common origins while highlighting his visit to the site where American soldiers, both blue and gray, "exhibited valor unsurpassed in the annals of military prowess."[56] McCleary's idea appealed to the burgeoning automobile lobby, as well as to related industries and interests.

McCleary's idea lost momentum in Congress at the time but remained a latent option. The Commission of Fine Arts was clearly in favor of the Potomac site suggested by the McMillan plan, as were most members of the Lincoln Memorial Commission. But one member of the latter commission, the powerful speaker of the House, Joseph "Uncle Joe" Cannon, was dead set against it. "So long as I live I'll never let a memorial to Abraham Lincoln be erected in that God damned swamp," he said, referring to the newly reclaimed land on the shore of the river.[57] As a Republican and Illinois representative with personal memories of Lincoln, he felt that he had special insight into what would be fitting. To avoid the Potomac shore, he proposed one site after another, forcing the commission to consider other locations— Meridian Hill on Sixteenth Street north of the White House, several sites near the Capitol, and the Old Soldiers' Home at the terminus of North Capitol Street. Each of these locations had its advocates.

Both commissions were reluctant to propose an architectural competition to design the memorial, and Henry Bacon became the consensus choice as architect to plan a design for the Potomac site. But again Uncle Joe objected, pushing a resolution through the Memorial Commission asking that architect John Russell Pope submit designs for the Sixteenth Street and Old Soldiers' Home locations to be examined along with Bacon's. Ultimately, at a highly charged meeting January 22, 1912, the Memorial Commission chose Bacon's design and the Potomac site. Again Uncle Joe's opposition managed to delay the decision. The commission reaffirmed the Potomac site on February 3 but asked John Russell Pope to also submit plans for the memorial on that site. The delays allowed proponents to resurrect in Congress the idea of a highway to Gettysburg, and bitter debates went on simultaneously in the House of Representatives.

An examination of the voting shows some sectional animosity, with those favoring the Potomac site hoping to erase the divisive memory of the battlefield. Yet what is most significant in the House debate is that both sides argued that their proposals would work toward a reconciliation between North and South. From the tenor of the proposals it is evident that this would be accomplished by ignoring the idea of emancipation and civil rights. Representative Graham of Illinois wanted to wipe out the remembrance of "that awful field of carnage" and focus on the life of Lincoln, who above all wanted to "save the union." Frank Nye, also of Illinois, wanted to commemorate the "larger national love" that Lincoln represented, the "blending of the blue and the grey." J. Thomas Heflin of Alabama also favored the Potomac site, seeming to intuit that a ninety-mile highway risked conveying multiple messages, while a site in Washington could impress the tourist with one clear message about Lincoln to carry back home. Had Lincoln lived, he said, the South would not have known the horror of Reconstruction, but "the two sections, bravely fighting for what they believed to be right, would have been bound together sooner in the ties of everlasting love and union."[58]

Supporters of the memorial highway called Henry Bacon's design for the memorial a symbol of death that rendered the American ideals of justice and equality "embalmed and ossified." Yet even they emphasized that the highway would immortalize not just Lincoln but the "dauntless heroism of the citizen soldiers of American," who on the famous battlefield "proved to themselves and to all world that they were one in race, one in courage, and one in destiny." The phrase "one in race" was ominous, indicative of the "romance of reunion," which was the leitmotif of the reconciliation between North and South after the Civil War. As Eric Foner remarks, "The retreat from Reconstruction went hand in hand with broad acceptance, North and South, of a romantic image of the Civil War as a family quarrel among white Americans in which both sides fought valiantly for noble principles."[59] Once the bitterness of Reconstruction had passed, reconciliation was the one "safe" area for celebration, while any rhetorical forays into the meaning of the Civil War itself were fraught with danger. When one representative suggested that Congress also authorize a memorial to Jefferson Davis, Representative Benjamin K. Focht of Pennsylvania angrily replied, "We are not going to forget that those heroic men who came out of the North and West and fought to the death for a principle were altogether right and, with Lincoln, will live in memory as patriots as long as liberty endures." Focht had challenged the fragile "romance of reunion" and received no applause for his remarks. Finally, on March 5 and 6, Representative William P. Borland's bill proposing a memorial highway was rejected by the House Appropriations Committee because it would cost too much money, and on that note the bill died.[60] On April 16, the Lincoln Memorial Commission formally chose Henry Bacon over John Russell Pope as architect.

The idea of Lincoln as an American hero and savior of the nation was in Bacon's mind from the time when he first surveyed the project. He immediately realized the symbolic potential of the newly emphatic axial structure provided by the McMillan plan and saw the Capitol as the chief symbol of U.S. government, with the Washington monument dedicated to its founder and the Lincoln to its savior.[61] The hero would be presented as a godlike figure, his memorial building a religious shrine. In its isolation the memorial would create an atmosphere of timelessness and tranquillity, separated from the scramble of daily life. Bacon was quoted as saying that the "principle of seclusion is an old one. At the height of achievement in Greece is found the Athena, in the Parthenon, and one of the seven wonders of the world was placed within the Temple of Zeus at Olympia."[62] Proponents of a mausoleum- or shrine-like memorial quoted Lincoln's former personal secretary and early biographer John Hay: "As I understand it, the place of honor is on the main axis of the plan. Lincoln of all Americans next to Washington deserves this place of honor. He was of the immortals. You must not approach too close to the immortals. The monument should stand alone, remote from the common habitations of man, apart from the business and turmoil of the city; isolated, distinguished and serene."[63]

The Lincoln Memorial, as finally approved, achieved consensus by ignoring the controversies surrounding the meaning of the Civil War. Emancipation would be downplayed. The purpose of the memorial would be to reaffirm the reunion of the states. The thirteen steps to the main platform represented the original states, the thirty-six pillars of the peristyle the number of states at the time of Lincoln, and the forty-eight festoons on the entablature or attic story would represent the number of states when the memorial was built. Bacon introduced his design to the commission, proposing that "the Memorial to Lincoln take the form of a monument symbolizing the Union of the United States of America."[64] Observers did not miss the point. One wrote a letter to the editor of the *Washington Star*, praising the design as expressing the "real purpose" of the memorial: to commemorate Lincoln as the "father of the 'reunion' of these States and of their lasting unity as an indissoluble nation."[65]

The words carved above the Daniel Chester French statue say only, "In this temple, as in the hearts of the people for whom he saved the Union, the memory of Abraham Lincoln is enshrined forever" (see Figure 26). Bacon's friend Royal Cortissoz, who provided this text for the inscription, wrote to him that he wanted words simple enough that people could carry them away in their memory. Furthermore, he added, by avoiding the issue of slavery, the inscription would provide common ground for both North and South: "By saying nothing about slavery you avoid the rubbing of old sores."[66]

Generally, Bacon's design met with great favor. But one prominent Washingtonian told William Howard Taft that the memorial was "a picture of gloom, . . . in effect an immense mausoleum." A few also attacked the elegance of Bacon's classical design as inconsistent with the populist tendencies and common origins of Lincoln. Modernists like Louis Sullivan vilified the building. Gothic revivalist architect Ralph Adams Cram said of it: "There is scant harmony between the gaunt, ill-proportioned figure, the cadaverous visage with its distorted modelling, the awkward carriage, the absurd clothing, and this classical fane which suggests only the perfect bodily forms, the chiselled faces, the noble vesture of Athenian gods and hierarchs and

FIGURE 26 Daniel Chester French, sculpture of Abraham Lincoln, Lincoln Memorial.
Courtesy of the Library of Congress.

athletes."[67] Yet Cram's response was not entirely negative, for he also realized that the memorial passed the test of "beauty," and if it lacked a certain
"vitality," still "Mr. Bacon was supremely right, to go back to the finest
things we can find in some period of the past when art was an integral part
of life."[68]

Bacon wanted the Lincoln Memorial to appeal to both head and heart. The statue in the central cella would speak to the emotions, and the texts on the north and south walls to the intellect. What message do visitors to the memorial take away with them? Those who take the time to read the Gettysburg Address will see the words "a new nation conceived in liberty and dedicated to the proposition that all men are created equal," and they will be asked "whether that nation or any nation so conceived and so dedicated can long endure." They will recall that slavery was an issue. Those who read the longer second inaugural address will see that "colored slaves" concentrated in the South "constituted a peculiar and powerful interest. All knew that this interest was the cause of the war." They will also read the following terrible words: "Yet, if God wills that it [the War] continue until all the wealth piled by the bondsman's two hundred and fifty years of unrequited toil shall be sunk, and until every drop of blood drawn with the lash shall be paid by another drawn with the sword, as was said three thousand years ago, so still it must be said 'the judgments of the Lord are true and righteous altogether.' "

Slavery and emancipation issues are therefore not completely ignored by the memorial but are embedded in long texts that most visitors do not read carefully.[69] And Guerin's murals, above and surrounding these texts, although they include an illustration of emancipation, are so complicated in their allegorical treatment that almost no visitor would recognize the theme. One mural illustrates the reconciliation of enemies, the other emancipation. In fact, as more than one critic has pointed out, the "emancipated slaves" of the mural above the Gettysburg Address do not even look like American blacks. The murals are also so dull in color and mounted so high on the walls that the limited lighting makes them nearly impossible to see clearly.

If "Union" is the main message conveyed by the memorial, it was clearly the leitmotif of the ceremonies and speeches given at its ceremonial dedication on Memorial Day, May 30, 1922. Estimates of the crowd range from 35,000 to 50,000 people (see Figure 27). Among them were Lincoln's only surviving son, Robert, Joseph Cannon (presumably eating his words), President Harding, Chief Justice Taft, and Dr. Robert R. Moton, successor to Booker T. Washington as president of the Tuskegee Institute. Prayers of invocation and dedication were offered, and a poem was read by Edwin Markham; Moton gave the major address, which was followed by Taft's presentation of the memorial and Harding's speech of acceptance.

Moton began his address with the striking analogy of two ships, the *Mayflower* at Plymouth and "another ship" that had already arrived at Jamestown: "The first was to bear the pioneers of freedom, freedom of

FIGURE 27 Dedication of the Lincoln Memorial, May 30, 1922. Courtesy of the
Library of Congress.

thought and freedom of conscience; the latter had already borne the pioneers
of bondage." Moton declared that the claim of greatness for Lincoln "lies
in this, that amid doubt and distrust, against the counsel of chosen advisors,
in the hour of the Nation's utter peril, he put his trust in God and spoke the
word that gave freedom to a race and vindicated the honor of a Nation
conceived in liberty and dedicated to the proposition that all men are created
equal."[70]

Taft began his words with a skillfully written eulogy of the character of
Lincoln, then summarized the history of the quest to build the memorial,
praised those who had most contributed to its planning and building, and
concluded with the following peroration: "Here is a shrine at which all can
worship. Here an altar upon which the supreme sacrifice was made in the
cause of Liberty. Here a sacred religious refuge in which those who love
country and love God can find inspiration and repose." Taft said nothing
about emancipation.

Harding's rambling address, predictably, was the least successful of the
three. He did mention emancipation but chose to subordinate it to Lincoln's
great end, which was "maintained union and nationality." Emancipation,
said Harding, was a means to that end.

The dedication ceremonies were full of religious references, trading on Lincoln's nature and the religious character of the shrine. The Lincoln statue sat on its throne like Zeus in his temple at Olympia. Against strong opposition Royal Cortissoz had insisted on using the word "temple" in his inscription behind the seated Lincoln, realizing that it best described his friend Bacon's conception of the memorial. One participant in the ceremonies that day wrote to Bacon of his experience: "By sheer accident if not through divine guidance, I stood at the western end of the water feature of your work, saw and heard the service and rose with you into a plane of spiritual elation I shall not ask providence to grant again." As the *New York Sun* said in reporting the event, it would be "the place where the cults of Lincoln shall centre."[71]

But there was also symbolic dissonance. In one of the monumental ironies of American history, the crowds who came to honor the man who emancipated the slaves were confined in segregated seating. Even Dr. Moton was ushered off to the area for blacks on the far left side of the memorial. This was reported by the African American newspaper *New York Age,* as were the efforts of some blacks, including the secretary-treasurer of Howard University, to sit in the designated white areas. The newspaper complained, mildly enough, that this was the last occasion "where the color line should have been drawn." The mainline white-owned newspapers did not report on these ironies.

As a comment on the meaning of the Civil War, the Lincoln Memorial is simply the most prominent example of what became the standard anodyne for forgetting the pain of the battlefield, the divisive issue of slavery, and the still unsettled issue of racial equality. Kirk Savage has done a wide-ranging study of Civil War memorials in the communities of the nation, both Northern and Southern.[72] The nation was hard pressed to devise a suitable method of commemorating that most cataclysmic event in its history. Besides the generally accepted need to observe filial piety and remember the dead, some reason had to be sought to counterbalance and justify the enormous and obvious evil of the loss of life. Two reasons suggested themselves, both evident in the words and writings of Lincoln himself: to end slavery and to preserve the Union. The first proved too divisive, and the second seemed to beg the question since, without the abolition of slavery, reunification would simply have returned the nation to the status quo ante.

In the end, the many local Civil War memorials ignored both of these reasons. Northern and Southern communities seem to have arrived at the same solution. Some memorials simply recorded the names of the heroic dead. If sculpture was featured at all, it was of white and Anglo-Saxon soldiers, "always erect and unwounded," thus overcoming the "memory of bodies violated and destroyed" by shifting the emphasis to courage and loyalty. The memorials celebrated the soldier before the battle or the survivor after the battle. When the "cause" is mentioned on the memorials, it is "Union" for the North or "the State" for the South, thus avoiding the bitterly contested issues and fixing on loyalty to higher authority, a safe enough ideal. In summary, local memorials commemorate and celebrate the unity of white antagonists, Northern and Southern, reconciled in their mutual courage and loyalty to their ideals.

The Lincoln Memorial was born in compromises of the Jim Crow period and nourished in the imperial ambitions of early-twentieth-century America. It did not confront the difficult issues. It glorified Lincoln but was also a monument to contemporary political aspirations. Lewis Mumford said of it in 1924: "one feels not the living beauty of our American past, but the mortuary air of archeology. . . . Who lives in that shrine, I wonder—Lincoln or the men who conceived it: the leader who beheld the mournful victory of the Civil War, or the generation that took pleasure in the mean triumph of the Spanish-American exploit, and placed the imperial standard in the Philippines and the Caribbean?"[73] But the Lincoln Memorial has had a history far different perhaps than its creators envisioned. As Savage remarks, "the cultural contest that monuments seem to settle need not end once they are built and dedicated."[74]

Monuments have a way of changing, and even reversing, the meanings initially given to them. Years pass, events occur at them, and one day when the fog lifts over the Potomac we see a different memorial. In this sense the memorializing of Washington is truly mythic, not just incorporating "original meanings" but embracing new meanings with symbolic potential to incorporate the significance of a changing history. As Lindsay Jones says, "even the simplest buildings invariably both transcend and subvert the deliberate intentions of their designers."[75] Any myth is the summation of "the given" of its original structure and the "the imputed," arising from the needs of those who receive the myth and reinterpret it.

Abraham Lincoln personally hoped to eliminate slavery, and it is not difficult to celebrate his leadership in the process of emancipation. Yet at the same time he had many deep-seated racist attitudes and he said quite clearly that he was not aiming at racial equality. He advocated "colonization" of blacks elsewhere because of his doubts that the two races could live together in harmony. Yet the Lincoln presented at the memorial in Washington is not, in the end, the historical man but the myth that he has become. Americans of the late twentieth century, having lived through some forty years in the struggle for civil rights and racial equality, now look to Lincoln as the patron saint and symbol of this and other related ideals. The white "Mr. Smith" in *Mr. Smith Goes to Washington* renews his courage to fight for noble goals at the foot of Lincoln. In Ralph Ellison's posthumously published novel *Juneteenth*, a group of elderly black folk respond to the Lincoln Memorial in exactly the same spirit. Failing in their attempt to see a senator, they face "the great sculpture with bowed heads" and are seen "praying quietly within the Lincoln Memorial."[76] This is not only legitimate but also inevitable. It is an expression of the natural process of myth-making, which does not mean arbitrary fabrication but its opposite, a necessary embodiment of truth. It is possible to trace this process not only in the life and death and "afterlife" of Lincoln but also in the history of the Lincoln Memorial from its ironic dedication to the present. In the events that have taken place there, the songs sung, the speeches made, and the prayers offered, Americans have woven a new fabric of meaning, rendering the Lincoln Memorial a symbol of black freedom, and more generally of racial equality and of resistance to all the forces of oppression.[77]

The first major event in the chronology of this changing mythology occurred in 1939. In that same year, Senator Theodore G. Bilbo, a white supremacist from Mississippi, had introduced the "Greater Liberia Act," which he claimed would fulfill Lincoln's "noblest aspiration," to repatriate blacks to Africa. But events were moving in another direction. Marian Anderson, the internationally acclaimed contralto, had never performed in the nation's capital. When her agent, Sol Hurok, attempted to secure Constitution Hall as the venue, the Daughters of the Revolution, who owned the building, refused because of her race. An uproar ensued. Eleanor Roosevelt resigned her membership in the DAR. Walter White, director of the National Association for the Advancement of Colored People (NAACP) went to the Department of the Interior and reserved the Lincoln Memorial for Anderson's performance. "Oh, my God," he thought, "if we could have her sing at the feet of Lincoln!" Secretary of the Interior Harold Ickes gave his approval, as did FDR. The issue that everyone had tried to avoid at the memorial's dedication some fifteen years earlier, now came forward, front and center. Ickes, in introducing Anderson, underscored the significance of the event and its setting. Lincoln had given his life to free the slaves, he said, and now, at his memorial, "glorious tribute is rendered to his memory by a daughter of the race from which he struck the chains of slavery." Anderson, accompanied by Ickes on the piano, opened the concert with the "Star Spangled Banner" and followed it with "America the Beautiful" (see Figure 28). The Lincoln Memorial was on its way to being reconfigured into a

FIGURE 28 Marian Anderson concert, Easter Sunday 1939. Courtesy of the Library of Congress.

symbol of racial equality. As black leader Mary McLeod Bethune said, "Through the Marian Anderson protest concert we made our triumphant entry into the democratic spirit of American life." The concert began to rescript the meaning of the Lincoln Memorial as an icon for civil rights.[78]

The 1950s and 1960s were decades of radical change. The Supreme Court's *Brown v. Board of Education* decision in 1954 required desegregation of the public schools. In 1957, Martin Luther King Jr. organized a Prayer Pilgrimage to Washington to urge the government to enact civil rights legislation. Some thirty thousand gathered in front of the Lincoln Memorial to hear King and others speak. Mahalia Jackson sang "I Been 'Buked and I been Scorned," which was so true, said Langston Hughes, that "even Abe Lincoln's statue nodded his head."

President Eisenhower took no official notice of the event but later proposed the first civil rights legislation in Congress in eighty-two years, and when Governor Orville Faubus resisted school desegregation in Little Rock, Eisenhower sent federal troops to enforce the order. By the time of the Kennedy administration it was evident that the Supreme Court's order that desegregation proceed at "all deliberate speed" was being widely ignored. King proposed to JFK that he issue a second emancipation proclamation on its centennial in 1963. The president, not wishing to alienate his southern sup-

FIGURE 29 Martin Luther King Jr. March on Washington and rally, August 28, 1963. Courtesy of the Library of Congress.

port, ignored King's suggestion. But Kennedy did finally send a bill to Congress to secure desegregation in interstate transportation, protect black voting rights, and hasten school desegregation. King organized a march on Washington to lobby for passage of the bill, and on August 28, 1963, some two hundred thousand marchers gathered in front of the Lincoln Memorial to hear speeches, sing songs, and offer prayers. The final speech was delivered by Martin Luther King Jr., and unlike most of the other speakers, he connected the event with Lincoln. Not "one hundred years ago" but

> Fivescore years ago, a great American, in whose symbolic shadow we stand today, signed the Emancipation Proclamation. This momentous decree came as a great beacon of hope to millions of Negro slaves who had been scarred in the flame of withering injustice. It came as a joyous daybreak to end the long night of their captivity. . . . I have a dream that one day this nation will rise up and live out the true meaning of its creed: We hold these truths to be self-evident that all men are created equal.[79]

Standing on the steps of Lincoln's temple, King reinterpreted the myth of Lincoln. By reclaiming the interpretation of his Gettysburg Address, King carried his dream back to Jefferson and the Founders, as Lincoln had done before him. "When the architects of our republic wrote the magnificent words of the Constitution and the Declaration of Independence," he said, "they were signing a promissory note to which *every American* was to fall heir" (my emphasis). This event was the culmination of the process by which the memorial's meaning was changed from celebrating the "reunion of white brothers" as Taft, Harding, and its original builders had emphasized, to celebrating Lincoln as the father of racial equality. King was picking the people's pockets as boldly as Lincoln had done one hundred years earlier at Gettysburg. In doing so, he was probably speaking as much to white as to black Americans. "This speech, more than any other single event," it has been said, "legitimized the ongoing black revolution in the eyes of most Americans and came to symbolize a historic national turning point, lifting King into the pantheon of great American heroes."[80] Like Lincoln's, his words "I have a dream" were not to be rebutted by mere logic.

Merrill Peterson notes a gradual diminution in the Lincoln cult since the early 1960s, perhaps because the country faces problems beyond racism and equality for which Lincoln's myth offers no ready solution. In 1991, more people visited the Vietnam than the Lincoln Memorial. Yet whenever a poll asks who was the greatest president, Lincoln always comes out first.[81] In confirmation of the esteem in which he is held, we should consider one other memorial, the animated robot portraying Lincoln created by Walt Disney Enterprises for the New York World's Fair in 1964 and later installed at Disneyland. Although the wax image, seen by millions, delivered a five-minute message composed of excerpts from his most famous speeches, initially it said nothing about slavery.[82] In 1991 Disney announced that it intended to replace the Lincoln exhibit with an attraction featuring Kermit the Frog. It is comforting to know that there was such an outcry from both patrons and employees that Disney rescinded its decision. As one twelve-year-old protestor said, with some sense of proportion, "Lincoln was president, Kermit is a frog."[83]

CHAPTER 8

The Changing Meaning
of the National Mall

THERE IS an inherent deception in Washington. To the occasional visitor, the city of illusion seems not to change. Its memorials preserve an immutable heritage that goes back to the Founding Fathers, the image of the "eternal capital of an eternal republic."[1] This illusion is, of course, the source of its power and confirms the success of its commemorative architecture. Said the architect Louis I. Kahn, "Monumentality in architecture may be defined as a quality, a spiritual quality inherent in a structure which conveys the feeling of eternity, that it cannot be added to or changed."[2]

When I first visited Washington in the 1950s as a high-school senior, it did seem eternal. The "temps"—rows of hastily constructed World War I and II buildings that lined the northern and southern edges of the Mall— were there, but I did not even notice them. The Jefferson Memorial, which seemed to me as ancient as Hadrian's tomb, had been completed less than thirteen years earlier. I was a victim of the deception that Jefferson was a revered Founder whose exalted place in the national pantheon of heroes had been secure from the beginning, as unassailable as the canonized saints in the churches of my Catholic upbringing. There were no Vietnam, Korean, or FDR Memorials. The Lincoln Memorial looked the same in 1955 as it did in 1964, when I next visited the capital. I did not realize that the civil rights march and Martin Luther King's "I have a dream" speech there in 1963 had changed it forever. The planners and architects of Washington wanted it to be a Rome, a Babylon, a Beijing—an eternal city—and in many ways they succeeded. Washington is as unchanging as the Constitution, as ephemeral and contingent as the latest decision of the Supreme Court. The physical changes, over its more than two hundred years of history, are re-markable enough, but the changes of meaning behind the immutable facades are more remarkable and dramatic. As Kirk Savage remarked, the stories told by monuments "are not necessarily what the monuments were intended to tell us. To make the monuments speak again we must question the often bland surface they show the world."[3]

Nowhere has the Washington kaleidoscope shifted more significantly than in that area called the Mall. Anyone who examines the plan of L'Enfant for this area west of the Capitol and south of the president's house will see a resemblance between his original idea and the Mall of today. This similarity belies the fact that there never was a L'Enfant mall and obscures the substantial changes that have occurred in the public space that connects the Capitol and the White House.[4] Even after the area had assumed its present shape under the guidance of the McMillan Commission unseen changes continued on the grassy avenue and behind the mask of its buildings, especially after the 1960s. I am referring to more than construction and demolition or the change of landscaping from romantic to neoclassical. Like the Lincoln Memorial, the Mall may look approximately the same in the early twenty-first century as it did in 1960, but the shift of meaning in both has been profound.

L'Enfant's plan, probably based on Versailles and the Paris of his day, envisioned the Mall as an urban avenue lined with public buildings. In a letter to George Washington he described it as "a place of general resort," lined by theaters, assembly halls, academies, and "all sort of place[s] as may be attractive to the l[e]arned and afford diver[s]ion to the idle."[5] At the same time, he introduced into this sophisticated urban milieu a picturesque element, calling for the artful planting of trees to define the green expanse and taking advantage of the natural features of the landscape, the knolls, the watercourse (the Tiber), the low areas, and the Potomac River. Thus Pamela Scott calls it a baroque plan on paper but modified by picturesque elements, a unique design in which natural and artificial were to be balanced.[6]

Although many plans were suggested over the next half-century for the improvement of the Mall, neither they nor L'Enfant's original conception was ever implemented. It remained essentially a wasteland—part tidal swamp, part undeveloped fields. Flocks of sheep and herds of cattle grazed there. "Figure to yourself," wrote a congressman in 1807 after falling from his horse midway between the White House and the Capitol, "a man almost bruised to death, on a dark, cold night, in the heart of the capital of the United States, out of sight or hearing of human habitation, and you will have a tolerably exact idea of my situation."[7] Because Washington was a regional center for the slave trade, pens were built in the Mall area to house hundreds of slaves. As late as 1850 a group of citizens wrote a petition to the House of Representatives complaining of its use for private vegetable gardens, the storage of lumber and firewood, and occasionally "for rubbish of an offensive and unsightly kind." As Washington's population grew (it doubled between 1840 and 1860) the Tiber became increasingly foul and polluted: "What is known today as the Ellipse was a fetid swamp; created by sewage from the executive mansion. Waste from the Patent Office and Post Office emptied into the canal that ran along the northern side of the public grounds."[8] Joseph Varnum, a lawyer and grandson of a former Revolutionary officer who later served in both houses of Congress, wrote in 1848: "Every one who has gazed upon the landscape to be seen from the Western front of the capitol, must have observed the large tract of waste ground, between Pennsylvania and Maryland Avenues, extending from the front of the capitol to the Potomac. . . . It is not generally known, even to the members of Congress, that this is the national mall—. . . . a very small outlay in planting trees, and laying out walks and drives, would make it a second Champs-Elysees."[9]

By mid-century, Varnum's writings were part of a new impetus to improve the long-neglected Mall. Construction had begun on two projects, the Smithsonian building and the Washington Monument. The Compromise of 1850 banned the slave trade in the District of Columbia. Three wealthy and influential citizens of Washington approached Millard Fillmore with the idea to landscape the Mall, and Andrew Jackson Downing was hired the following year to develop a plan for its improvement. From the beginning, Downing's concepts envisioned gardens that would parallel the functions of the Smithsonian in promoting educational, scientific, moral, and democratic purposes. They would be "a public museum of living trees and shrubs," not restricted as a preserve of the powerful and wealthy but open to all. His public parks, like art galleries, free libraries, and public schools, would be developed for all citizens to enjoy. They would take up "popular education where the common school and ballot box leave it," lifting up "the working man to the same level of enjoyment with the man of leisure and accomplishment."[10] Downing's blueprint for the Mall called for five discrete but related gardens that together would cover the whole area. He conceived them in the romantic style, the trees and vegetation thick and naturally planted, with meandering paths and many vistas. He saw "no positive beauty in the straight line," although he did acknowledge that it could be "expressive of power." His desire, rather, was to provide a multifaceted experience for the individual citizen.[11]

Downing's premature death in 1852 was a primary reason his plans were not implemented. Hopes of realizing his comprehensive plan were then further sabotaged in 1854 when the Baltimore and Ohio (B&O) Railroad was allowed to extend its tracks through the Mall all the way to the foot of

Capitol Hill. Beginning in 1848, the area around the emerging Washington Monument became a large construction site with all its attendant clutter. By the time of the Civil War only the grounds of the White House and the area around the Smithsonian Institution were landscaped at all. The rest lay "unkempt and forgotten." Over the next decades, more areas were reclaimed from neglect, but "fragmentation of the Mall continued so that by the end of the century, the mall consisted of a series of seven separate parks or gardens, each representing different governmental bureaus, each with its own architect and gardeners, and each responsible to independent congressional committees." [12]

Still, Downing's influence was decisive in two respects: Like L'Enfant, he realized that the Mall could have lasting national significance. Both had aimed at a use of space in service of democracy, not as a resort for the wealthy. As one writer described it in 1877, "This mall is set out in great forests of oaks and pines, low seats for lovers, and little by-paths for baby carriages and nurses, in fact, it is an enchanted forest with castle-like structures, and ten months out of the year, is sweet with fragrant flowers and song of birds." [13] Both planners shared democratic ideals. L'Enfant called his Mall "a place of general resort," and Downing said, in a burst of populist enthusiasm: "Open wide, therefore, the doors of your libraries and picture galleries, all ye true republicans! . . . Plant spacious parks in your cities, and unloose their gates as wide as the gates of morning to the whole people." [14] In setting down the romantic style for the Mall, Downing was striving for an educational effect, the intellectual and moral improvement of those who frequented it. For the rest of the nineteenth century, the romantic style associated with Downing governed the development of the Mall, tapping some of the same spiritual yearnings for a human relationship to nature that inspired the transcendentalism influential in America at that time. Thomas Huxley had said, "To a person uninstructed in natural history, his country or a seaside stroll is a walk through a gallery filled with wonderful works of art, nine-tenths of which have their faces turned to the wall. Teach him something of natural history, and you place in his hands a catalogue of those which are worth turning around." [15] Downing and the romantic gardeners who followed him meant to do just that.

The beginning of the twentieth century brought plans for a major change to the character of the Mall, a dramatic reversal indicative of the emergence of the United States as a world power. With the capital's centennial year approaching, the American Institute of Architects proposed that a board of experts be appointed to study plans and suggest ways to improve the Mall. The Mall of the late nineteenth century was "cluttered." The Botanic Gardens and the B&O Railroad terminal were located on the Mall just below the Capitol. Among the pillared neoclassical buildings of Washington, two medieval interlopers appeared, like barbarians at the border, the old post office and the original Smithsonian building, the latter jutting into the Mall area itself. Along the north side, the slums of Pennsylvania Avenue and the Central Market intruded.[16]

Senator James McMillan, chair of the Senate Committee on the District of Columbia, sponsored legislation to create a body officially called the United States Senate Park Commission—though it would generally be called the McMillan Commission because of the senator's support for its work. Its head and energizing force was Daniel Burnham, the mastermind behind the creation of the "White City" for the World's Columbian Exposition in Chicago in 1893. Burnham seemed the ideal choice to lead a committee whose purpose was to revitalize L'Enfant's plan for the city. He thought along the same grand lines as L'Enfant. His most characteristic statement was "Make no little plans. They have no magic to stir men's blood."[17] The committee eventually included landscape architect Frederick Law Olmsted Jr., Charles McKim, who had worked with Burnham in Chicago, and the most respected American sculptor of his day, Augustus St. Gaudens.

To prepare themselves for their work, the committee (minus St. Gaudens, who was too infirm to accompany the group) traveled to Europe to visit sites they presumed had influenced L'Enfant, such as Paris and Versailles, as well as some others of their own choosing, including Hampton Court in England, Schönbrunn near Vienna, and Rome. In the last, especially, they "were brought face to face with things eternal. . . . The fleeting, the transitory, the ephemeral . . . all seemed to drop out of mind, leaving a desire to discover and to use in the work of a new nation those forms which have satisfied age after age of men."[18] A better paraphrase of the sentiments of Thomas Jefferson could hardly be imagined. After their return, the group worked quickly and for the most part congenially to produce a comprehensive plan that would guide the development of the Mall in the twentieth century. It received general approbation, though it was definitely not a slavish attempt to resurrect L'Enfant. The commission transformed the nature of the Mall from an urban phenomenon to a natural green space, segregated from the rest of the city, a place where people could seek release from the stress of urban life and experience "a little touch of the outside country."[19] It transformed L'Enfant's grand processional avenue into a *tapis vert*, a parklike enclosure at the core of the city, closed off instead of open. As architectural critic (and member of the later Commission of Fine Arts) Elbert Peets pointed out, "L'Enfant, when Washington was a forest, dreamed of the Mall as a fashionable Parisian avenue, while the [Senate Park] Commission of 1901, with a big city spreading all about them, dreamed of the Mall as a quiet sanctuary from the city's noise and bustle."[20] Perhaps the commission remembered the passionate pleas of Senator Charles Sumner years earlier, who had called for preserving the Mall as a park to function as the lungs of the city.[21]

Yet within this secluded public space the McMillan Commission envisioned an expansive monumental core, with buildings of grandeur to reflect the new image of the United States as a world power (see Figure 30). Influenced by the White City of the Chicago World's Columbian Exposition, the revitalization of Washington offered "an opportunity for the unbridled expression of imperial pomp and glory," said one critic. Another pointed out that "in L'Enfant's day, the political and architectural allusions had been to republican Rome. In the era of McKinley, Roosevelt, Burnham, and McKim, the rhetoric and rationale were unabashedly imperial."[22] Gone were the meandering paths and informal bowers of the Downing era. At the very beginning, Olmsted Jr. was ready to modify Olmsted Sr.'s more informally picturesque plans for the Capitol grounds as he contemplated the overall character of the Mall. His proposals for it would take many years to realize, but his plans were prophetic:

> When I speak of the importance of treating the Mall in such a way as to relate strongly and visibly to the Capitol, I do not mean merely, or necessarily that a straight road should be slashed down the middle of it. . . . A different and more agreeable treatment would be a sort of compound "boulevard," marked by several parallel rows of trees with several pavements and turf strips. Such an avenue was that of the Champs Elysées. . . . The axis of the Capitol should neither be ignored by the use of a wiggling road and confused informal planning, nor should it be marked by a mere commonplace boulevard, but by an impressively broad and simple space of turf, with strong flanking masses of foliage and architecture and shaded driveways.[23]

Olmsted, Burnham, and McKim were just as didactic as their predecessors, but now the lesson to be taught was that the United States was an imperial power with international responsibilities. The Mall must reflect the status of the nation.

Although the McMillan Plan was well received by politicians, architects, and the press, it was slow to be implemented. Behind the delay was the same problem that had hindered the development of the capital since the days of Washington and Jefferson, what Henry Adams described as the "contrast

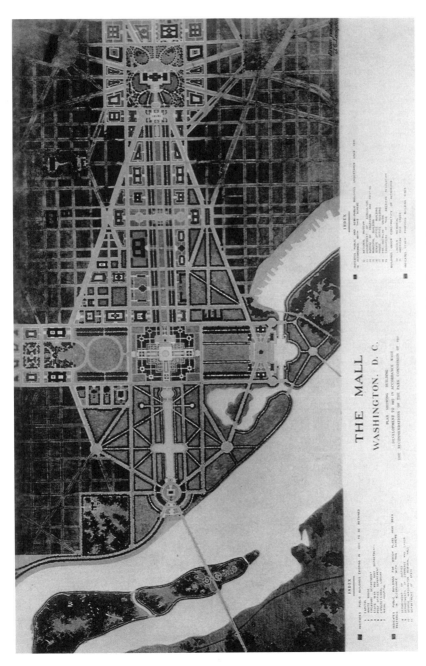

between the immensity of the task and the paucity of means." Still, from 1910 on, with the appointment of the Commission of Fine Arts as a watch-dog, the recommendations of the McMillan Commission carried decisive weight. The redesigned Mall, expressive of the spatial mastery of an imperial government, would gradually become the physical expression of a new na-tionalism. It would become the spatial-architectural equivalent of a world-dominant Anglo-Saxon culture, the North American division, which many saw as destined to be the vanguard of an evolutionary development bringing democracy to the rest of the world. The Founding Fathers had thought this would occur through the influence of example and the light of reason, but it now acquired evangelical motivation and employed more aggressive meth-ods than the Founders had ever contemplated.

The same year that the McMillan Commission prepared its report, Wil-liam McKinley gave his inaugural address. Somewhat "unexpectedly," the American victory in the recently completed "splendid little war" with Spain had given the United States an empire. It was God's will, McKinley had explained during his campaign, that the United States should accept this burden and annex the Philippines and other territories ceded by Spain, ed-ucate them, "uplift and civilize them, as our fellow-men for whom Christ also died."[24] His failure to note that most of the people in these territories were already Christians of the Roman Catholic persuasion was simply an-other example of the assumption of the Protestant, northern European su-periority rampant at that time. As Michael Kammen has pointed out, "a strident belief in Anglo-Saxon supremacy had provided a potent theme ever since the 1840's, but reached its apogee during these very years, 1885–1915."

There was, however, a lag between these changing cultural conceptions and their expression in the plan for Washington—that is, long years between proposal and realization. The commission understood this from the begin-ning, and when Senator McMillan reported to the Senate on January 15, 1902, he admitted that the work was a stupendous task "much greater than any one generation can hope to accomplish." But if adhered to over time, he insisted, the city's development would keep "pace with the national ad-vancement, until it become the visible expression of the power and taste of the people of the United States."[25] Piece by piece, monumental architecture rose to define the Mall—the Lincoln Memorial (1922), the National Ar-chives (1935), the Department of Agriculture (1937), the National Gallery of Art (1941), the Federal Triangle cluster, and the Jefferson Memorial (1943). Slowly the "wiggling lines" of the romantic gardens were straight-ened to make the Mall an impressive and uninterrupted vista.

The two-hundred-year development of the Mall may be roughly divided into four periods of about fifty years each. Each period was inaugurated by a pronouncement that seems to capture the spirit that would guide its direction during the half-century to follow. Thomas Jefferson initiated the first period, roughly 1800 to 1850, when he said that nothing much need be done but "cut out the 'superabundant plants'" and let nature itself then dictate the form that landscape should take.[26] And so the first fifty years saw the Mall as essentially a wasteland, grazed by animals, at its best reminding the resident politicians of America's great natural beauty, paradisal qualities, and abundant natural resources. As Jefferson said in his first inaugural address, we are "separated by nature and a wide ocean from the exterminating havoc of one quarter of the globe," a kind of hidden garden, separated from Europe and its decadence by the dispensation of nature and nature's God. At its worst, the Mall was a thicket and a dump during this fifty-year period.

The second period, from 1850 to 1900, was inaugurated by Andrew Jackson Downing's design, which called for deliberate human intervention. The derelict Mall was transformed into a romantic and picturesque series of gardens, with indigenous vegetation planted in natural formations and traversed by winding pathways to provide multiple scenic perspectives. The third period, inaugurated by Frederick Law Olmsted's call to eliminate the informal plantings and "wiggling" pathways, returned the Mall to the formal condition envisioned by L'Enfant and made it more harmonious with the highly formal architecture that surrounded it. Daniel Burnham clearly expressed the philosophy of the commission when he expounded the following guiding principle: "We do not feel that [the Mall] can with propriety be left in its natural state. We do not think that in the midst of a great city, which has formality all about it, that informality should become the rule. We think with the capitol at one end and the Monument at the other, which are the most formal things in the world, the treatment between these structures should be equally formal."[27]

But what of the most recent half-century? Superficially it may seem to be a gradual realization and mere continuation of the McMillan plan of 1902. The "temps" were finally removed under the prodding of Richard Nixon; Pennsylvania Avenue was revitalized, formalized, and monumentalized. The Commission of Fine Arts gave its approval to the Vietnam, Korean, and FDR Memorials, undertakings not envisioned in the McMillan plan but generally in keeping with its intentions. But the appearance of continuity is only partly accurate. In certain ways the Mall has been radically changed since the mid-twentieth century, not in its physical form but in how it is used and in the symbolism it now holds. This change reflects some of the radical changes, social and political, that have occurred since the 1960s and 1970s. Frederick Law Olmsted Jr. would certainly recognize the Mall today and very likely be pleased with its appearance, but he would be truly astonished at the uses to which it is now given. The Mall has gone from being a place where citizens gather as passive spectators, receiving "instruction" from the noble monuments, the museums, and the memorial sculpture (although they still do all these things), to being a place where active participants struggle to be heard in an agora, a forum where protesting and demonstrating groups contend to make their voices heard at the center of the nation, seeking the right to interpret the American myth.

We may get some notion of the radical nature of these changes by considering some of the critical reactions to the McMillan plan. One of the most articulate architectural critics was Elbert Peets, quoted earlier. Initially satisfied with the plan, he later came to feel that it would produce a bucolic landscape, pleasant to the eye but essentially empty of human life and vitality. "The sheep have gone," he pointed out wickedly, "but their aesthetic preferences prevail." He wanted to see the Mall lined with benches, lamp standards, and flagpoles flying the colors of every country in the world, more in the mode of L'Enfant's plan as he understood it, a grand majestic avenue where visitors could hear "the fife and drum and see the gay flags of peace."[28] Peets's words, deemed radical critique at the time, now seem not just harmless, but naive and old-fashioned in the light of what the Mall has become. More recently, Rom Landau, a policy expert and an artist, complained of the potentially deadening effect of Washington's immense and ubiquitous monumentalism, which can overwhelm the visitor by its superhuman scale. Although positive about Washington on the whole, Landau warned:

> The man who stands overawed and ennobled in front of the profoundly moving Lincoln Memorial, views it in the same spirit of reverence that might flood his being as he contemplates a sunrise or a magnificently rolling sea. It is right that he should feel dwarfed and insignificant. But is it reasonable to expect him to measure up to an equally monumental architecture while adding up figures, filling in Income Tax returns, or crossing the corridor to visit the W.C.?[29]

His criticism, like Peets's, seems mild and harmless, grist for the mill of discussion in an architectural seminar rather than an issue to trouble public emotions.

My tidy scheme of changes every fifty years breaks down with the most recent period, because the upheavals that have occurred mostly had their beginning not at mid-century, but in the 1960s and 1970s. And it is not easy to identify the statement of a single individual that set forth the program for change. My choice would be Martin Luther King's "I have a dream" speech in 1963, which so deliberately reached back to the sacred documents and invoked the ideals of Lincoln and Jefferson as criteria by which to judge the present. Using the same resonant rhetoric as Lincoln, he extracted a promissory note to which "every American was to fall heir," the inalienable rights of life, liberty, and the pursuit of happiness. His dream, he said, was "deeply rooted in the American dream."

Like Lincoln, King used the poetic language of the Bible to good effect, ending the litany of the "I have a dream" section with the hope that "every valley shall be exalted, every hill and mountain shall be made low, the rough places will be made plain, and the crooked places will be made straight, and the glory of the Lord shall be revealed." Then in the final section he invoked a patriotic song, "My country 'tis of thee," and created the litany "let freedom ring," ending with the words of a Negro spiritual, "Free at last! free at last! thank God Almighty, we are free at last!"

If Lincoln had ended slavery and implicitly led the nation toward the distant goal of racial equality, then King called for that racial equality and implicitly led the nation toward a further goal, the multiculturalism we have today. He was mostly talking of blacks and whites, but there was a hint of more, a direction that became clearer as other disenfranchised groups heard and acted upon what his words implied. He spoke of a nation where "little black boys and black girls will be able to join hands with little white boys and white girls and walk together as sisters and brothers." He looked forward to a day when "all God's children" could sing together, "black men and white men, Jews and Gentiles, Protestants and Catholics." Although he did not include the expanded list of multiculturalism current today, he planted its seeds. This civil rights march, and the many similar demonstrations that followed it, were part of a sea change in American society, an opening to new or forgotten voices that did not so much leave an architectural mark on the landscape of commemorative Washington as recast the way Americans would understand the architecture that was already there. Perhaps the best confirmation of the change effected by King is the tenor of the speeches at the Million Man March of October 16, 1995. There Minister Louis Farrakhan, whose prominence can be traced to a black supremacist group, took his theme from the U.S. Constitution, "toward a more perfect union." The great question is, he said, standing before the Capitol, "out of the many Asians, the many Arabs, the many Native Americans, the many

Blacks, the many people of color who populate this country, do you mean for them to be made into the one?"[30]

People often say that a visitor can learn much about U.S. history from a trip to Washington. Yet the capital presents the visitor with precious few historical facts. Rather, the city projects a series of powerful visual images that become deeply imprinted upon the visitor's memory: the enigmatic obelisk that dominates the city, the vast sweep of the Mall, the purposeful Jefferson in his rotunda on the tidal basin, the wise and pensive Lincoln in his religious shrine. The Capitol and White House have become unavoidable icons, reinforced daily on TV news programs, paper currency, postage stamps, and logos, fixed in memory as national symbols. What Washington projects is not history so much as myth, a selective story as dependent upon forgetting as it is upon remembering. It tells the story, collectively created over the past two hundred years and recalled to us in most of the presidents' inaugural addresses, that the United States is a paradigm of democracy for the world. This myth, despite the disruption of the Civil War, received overwhelming confirmation until the mid-twentieth century, with World War II as its dramatic canonization, a war in which the United States took the leading role in defeating two totalitarian aggressors.

Then came the changes: an ambiguous war in Korea that stopped communist aggression there but ended in a stalemate, an unpopular war in Vietnam that ended in defeat, the threat of Marxist governments in the Soviet Union and China, racial and gender conflicts, the beginnings of protest by new minority groups. This sea change was reflected on the Mall in two ways, first by the large number of marches and demonstrations that have been staged there since the time of Martin Luther King. The National Geographic Society has published a chart showing a total of 853 of marches, rallies, sit-ins, and vigils in Washington between 1963 and 1985.[31] First were the civil rights marches, which reached a peak of forty-five in 1968. During the next few years demonstrations and protests against the Vietnam War predominated: there were thirty-five in 1969, fifteen in 1970, sixty-two in 1971, and forty in 1972. Soon other movements began to use Washington as a national forum, for protests over specific domestic and foreign policies and for demonstrations focusing on abortion, the environment, women's rights, Indian rights, gay rights, and other issues. Many of the major speakers at these events used the symbolism around them to situate their message within the mythology of the nation, but few as successfully as Martin Luther King in 1963. Of course there had been previous demonstrations in Washington— by Coxey's Army in the 1890s, later by the Bonus Army, the Ku Klux Klan, animal lovers, and others (see Chapter 2), but not in the same number or frequency as in the period since the 1960s.

Perhaps there is nothing earth-shattering about the fact that the government allows virtually anyone to demonstrate on the Mall. To some, their protests appear to be harmless and ineffectual. Daniel Boorstin has said of such protests, "The messages change (and seldom are heard where it counts) but the messengers keep coming, reminding us that in this city *everybody* can say his piece, even if nobody listens."[32] Contrary to this cynicism, I would say that the overall effect of all these demonstrations has been substantial. If democracy has changed, then *some* of the right people, at least, have listened.

A second manifestation of these radical changes may be tracked in the changing role of the Smithsonian, whose monumental buildings stand as sentinels along the edges of the Mall. Besides the general role given it by the bequest of James Smithson—the commitment to the "increase and diffusion of knowledge"—it has gradually taken on a more specific role as the quasi-official interpreter of American history and culture. This second stage of the museum's development began in 1858 with the acquisition of the U.S. government collection formerly housed at the U.S. Patent Office, "a shrine celebrating American mechanical ingenuity."[33] Since then, the Smithsonian has become the official "theologian" of the American myth, a role visible in the enhanced interpretative functions of the Museum of American History, the Museum of American Art, the National Portrait Gallery, and the National Air and Space Museum. In the process, the Smithsonian went from mid-nineteenth-century "cabinet of curiosities" to purveyor, arbiter, and even challenger of the national mythology. The third stage has developed under the influence of cultural changes since the mid-1960s. The Smithsonian has become an "idea-driven museum" in which the curators are required to confront a wide range of social, political, ethical, and cultural issues as they seek to develop relevant exhibits.[34]

Until the 1960s, the Smithsonian's museums presented exhibitions that portrayed realities from traditional perspectives derived from European and American scholarship of the past few hundred years. They were the curators and conservers of the views of the elite leaders of the dominant and mostly Anglo-Saxon race that had founded the nation. By the early twentieth century, much of Asia, Africa, and the Middle East were under the strong influence, if not the direct control, of Europe and the United States. Not that these elites always agreed with each other (the mission of the two-party system is to provide disagreement), but the arguments were always *their* arguments, framed in *their* terms, and presented from *their* points of view.

Even the displays of "primitive" and "oriental" cultures were objectified according to the categories, analyses, and perspectives of these same cultural leaders. The museums of the Smithsonian were not exhibiting the reality of such exotic cultures but their constructions by Western scholars, missionaries, and travelers. "In the 1940s, 1950s and 1960s," points out museum historian Mike Wallace, "America's history museums drowsed happily on the margins of a go-ahead culture, tending their gentle artifacts, perpetuating regnant myths in which Africans, women, immigrants and workers figured as supporting actors or not at all."[35] For more than a hundred years it was assumed that this method and this dominant perspective simply represented the "truth," a narrative whose veracity was almost as certain as the conclusions of science.

Then in the 1970s and 1980s, says Wallace, "came rude poundings at the door." Since then, the Smithsonian has been profoundly affected by the "new social history," with "its focus on history from 'the bottom up' and its inclusion of previously marginal voices." Not a cosmetic change, this new approach has had a major impact on museum research, collecting policies, and exhibitions.[36] Curators became aware that they were displaying a perspective, a point of view—though as the understanding of the dominant Western culture, it seemed quite compelling, especially to those who shared that culture. Edward Linenthal points out that some of the Smithsonian curators were convinced that they could "play a role in reflecting and mediating the claims of various groups, and perhaps help construct a new idea of ourselves as a nation."[37]

These changes in the Smithsonian's mission were part of a national phenomenon occurring at many museums where history was presented. Although slaves constituted half the population of "historic" colonial Williamsburg, that tourist attraction for years presented itself as "white only." If anyone brought up the question of slavery, docents were instructed to gloss over the issue as quickly and innocuously as possible and move on briskly to the Chippendales in the next room. Today, blacks have become part of the scene, and a Williamsburg living history program has even reenacted an eighteenth-century slave auction.[38] Even the quintessentially establishment Walt Disney Enterprises, with its seemingly invincible optimism and tendency to sanitize U.S. history, succumbed. Florida's Epcot Center, in its twenty-minute capsule history of America from the Pilgrims to the present, includes mention of Frederick Douglass, Susan B. Anthony, and John Muir to help people understand that problems of race, gender, and the environment were more than mere blips in the otherwise smooth course of national progress.[39]

It was when the Smithsonian began to hear other voices, see through others' eyes, and display other points of view that its troubles began. Tackling the race issue, the National Museum of American History (NMAH) presented the African American perspective in "Field to Factory: Black Migration 1915–1940." In another exhibit it dealt with Japanese American experience in detention camps and on the battlefield in World War II. It also developed an exhibit called "American Encounters," which explored the complex story of conflict and compromise between Native Americans, Africans, Asians, and Europeans in America, showing how the interactions between these groups affected one another other and contributed to the constitution of the nation's identity. The Smithsonian's Natural History Museum, for the Columbus commemoration in 1992, exhibited "Seeds of Change," which included the perspective of those for whom the explorer's coming meant pestilence, servitude, and death. NMAH addressed issues of class with "Symbols and Images of American Labor" and gender with "Men and Women: A History of Costume, Gender and Power" and "Parlor to Politics: Women and Reform, 1890–1925."[40] Many people were unhappy with these forays into contemporary social issues, since they often implied a critique of the dominant culture. For example, from the European-American point of view the anniversary of Columbus's landing in the "New World" was an event to be celebrated, the moment when the history of the Western hemisphere "began." From the perspective of Native Americans, it was in nearly every sense the opposite: an unmitigated disaster, in some sense the "end of history" with the decimation of indigenous societies (literally—nine-tenths of the population was destroyed during the next one hundred years) and the destruction of many of the Native cultures. Clearly, any exhibition that attempted to portray the significance of Columbus would have to take both points of view into account. Yet many did not wish to see the other point of view. As one editorialist put it with refreshing candor: "Where did the old principle that winners write history go?"[41]

The two exhibits that have caused the greatest controversy to date were "The West as America" and the *Enola Gay* exhibit on the fiftieth anniversary of the atomic bombing of Hiroshima. Although the Columbus exhibit offended many, it did not directly attack the central myth of the United States. Columbus was a figure "before creation," a Roman Catholic and idealized precursor figure unconnected with the religious ideology of British Protestantism responsible for the founding of the nation. "The West as America" at the National Museum of American Art was a collection of major artworks reflecting American ideas of the West as presented in 164 paintings, drawings, photographs, sculptures, and prints. Some of the artists, such as Frederick Remington, Caleb Bingham, Alfred Bierstadt, Thomas Moran, and George Catlin were well known, others obscure. Taken together, their works provided what many Americans have accepted as accurate and authentic images of the West, and thereby contributed an important element to the nation's self-understanding.

The curators chose to interpret most of the art of the exhibit analogously rather than literally. Accordingly, the Capitol murals of Columbus's landing in the West Indies and De Soto's discovery of the Mississippi are not really about those putative events, but about the nineteenth-century conquest of the West. Since the paintings show how the discoverers brought the blessings of civilization to the New World, their real meaning is to document how the pioneers brought the same blessings to the West. The paintings of Remington, Russell, and Schreyvogel, ostensibly depicting the true West of the nineteenth century, are in fact about the twentieth-century urban and industrial culture of the East when the paintings were made, commentaries on the conflict between "old Americans" and the hordes of unwashed immigrants.[42] In other words, the curators had rather aggressively taken on the task of reinterpretation. The West was not seen as the stage for the providential sweep of the United States to its "natural" border, the Pacific Ocean, a place of majestic scenery, essentially uninhabited, waiting to be claimed for civilization and Christianity as part of the ethos of pioneer nation-building. Rather, the "exhibition labels present the unvarnished truth of conquest and exploitation," the decimation of Indian tribes and the environmental degradation of the landscape that resulted from the greed of the pioneers.[43]

The reaction against the exhibit was often furious. The *Wall Street Journal* labeled it "an entirely hostile ideological assault on the nation's founding and history," in which "the show's creators outdid one another in absurdity with commentaries attacking the Pilgrims as capitalists lacking 'true pioneer spirit,' the Western settlers as rapacious brutes, and the founding and development of America generally as a criminal capitalist venture."[44] Addressing Smithsonian director Robert McCormick Adams at a congressional hearing, Senator Ted Stevens of Alaska criticized the museum's "political agenda." Later Stevens admitted that he had not seen the exhibit but had heard that historian Daniel Boorstin had left the following message in the museum's guestbook after *he* had seen it: "A perverse, historically inaccurate, destructive exhibit. No credit to the Smithsonian."[45] *Time*'s reviewer called the exhibit "prosecutorial, and often unfairly so. The walls are laden with tendentious 'educational' labels, seemingly aimed at 14 year olds."[46]

Having seen the exhibit myself, I can say that although I generally agreed

with its revisionist tenor, I did feel that it was tendentious and overly didactic. William Truettner, curator of the exhibit, himself admitted this. "We
wrote too aggressively for a museum audience in a tone that was too declarative," Truettner said later, adding, "Were I to do it over again I would
be a little more temperate in our arguments."[47] Yet generally speaking, I
think the principle behind the exhibit's interpretations is unassailable: with
so-called "historical" paintings, the critic must pay as much attention to the
context of the time of its painting as to the time of the action depicted *in*
the painting.

Emmanuel Leutze's giant *The Storming of the Teocalli by Cortez and His
Troops* (84¾ × 98¾ in.), painted in 1848, is one of the most convincing
examples of this principle in application (see Figure 31). The dramatic tableau is based on a passage in William H. Prescott's *Conquest of Mexico*
(1843), and Leutze took many of the architectural motifs on the altar from
drawings by Frederick Catherwood, who had carefully studied and drawn
Mayan temples in the Yucatan. Even though these motifs were therefore
from the wrong native group, they still reflected an attempt at a kind of
authenticity. The painting was commissioned by Amos Binney, a wealthy
Boston scientist, who may have known Prescott.

The painting shows armored Spanish troops storming an Aztec
stepped-pyramid altar on which a barbaric sacrifice is about to take place.
A native priest with knife clenched in his mouth holds an infant over a
steaming cauldron. Aztec warriors are resisting, but they will obviously be
defeated. Why would Leutze and his patron be interested in an event that
took place two centuries earlier? Quite obviously because the United
States was fighting a war with Mexico between 1846 and 1848 and the
"conquest of Mexico" was of current interest. The curators suggest that
the idea of a European group conquering a native opponent would also be
a contemporary issue because the Eastern pioneers were at that time
swarming all over the West. Some justification was needed for taking the
land from the Indians. The painting was making a clear point: a more advanced civilization is entitled to conquer a backward one. As Prescott had
said, we cannot lament the fall of a barbaric empire that reduced its subjects "to the rank of the brutes that perish." He also carefully drew a parallel with the nineteenth century, noting that the bloody ceremonies and
torture by the Aztecs "were not the spontaneous suggestions of cruelty, as
with the North American Indians; but were all rigorously prescribed in
the Aztec ritual."[48]

The curators made an additional point about the *Storming of Teocalli*,
suggesting that Leutze was doing more than just asserting the European right

FIGURE 31 Emmanuel Leutze, *The Storming of the Teocalli by Cortez and His Troops*. Wadsworth Atheneum, Hartford. Ella Gallup Sumner and Mary Catlin Sumner Collection.

to conquer the Aztecs (and the analogous right of Americans to conquer the Indians). The Spaniards are not in fact portrayed heroically. They are dressed in dark uniforms and clad in black armor, an ominous and frightening phalanx surging up the stepped altar. One soldier is greedily ripping jewelry from the neck of a slain Indian. Another, near the top of the platform, grips an Indian child by the foot and is about to hurl the infant to its death. Since they too are portrayed as barbarians, Leutze's point is almost too obvious to spell out: a more advanced civilization (the Anglo-Saxon) is entitled to conquer a lesser one (the Hispanic).

The museum visitors' response to this exhibit was overwhelming, both positive and negative. One angry visitor wrote: "An exhibit of revisionist bulljive, made by anemic, analytical academics who shed no blood, sweat, or tears in the frontier of the West." Another wrote: "I loved this exhibit. I think the approach, the stimulation to thinking, the challenge of easy assumptions, is like a fresh wind blowing." Many of the comments responded to other comments, creating a kind of ongoing dialogue of visitors. If the purpose was to stimulate thinking and promote discussion, the exhibit was an unqualified success.

An even more "explosive" incident in the hallowed halls of the Smithsonian was the proposed exhibit about the *Enola Gay*, the B-29 Superfortress that dropped the first atom bomb on the Japanese city of Hiroshima. The controversy over the Smithsonian exhibit, which lasted from mid-1994 until the spring of 1995, was so bitter that media wits and punsters could not resist using air-war metaphors to describe it, contriving headlines such as: "Fresh fallout from Hiroshima bombing," "After a five-month strafing of political correctness," "Exhibit nuked," "Veterans blast air museum," etc. Reportorial hyperbole aside, the uproar was unprecedented. As the most popular of the Smithsonian Museums with some 8 million visitors annually, the National Air and Space Museum (NASM) was the preeminent interpreter of U.S. military history and political ideology. It had once before raised some hackles with an exhibit that demythologized air combat in World War I but was in no way prepared for the storm of protest over the proposed *Enola Gay* exhibit.[49]

Briefly summarized, the chronology of events is as follows. In 1993, NASM shared plans and an initial script for the exhibit with the Air Force Association. The AFA met with museum officials over a period of months but ultimately decided that the script was unbalanced and "politically correct" and that it was not likely to be changed substantially by the NASM curators. In mid-March 1994, the Air Force Association went public, issuing a press release criticizing the upcoming exhibit. By August and September outrage was being expressed in newspapers all over the country. In the meantime, NASM expressed its willingness to work with its critics, meeting first with the AFA and later with representatives of the American Legion. Congress became involved in August, with Representative Peter Blute leading a group of eighteen Republicans and six Democrats in criticizing the proposed exhibit. NASM rewrote the script four times between May and October but was never able to completely satisfy its critics. By October a committee of academic historians, together with peace organizations, criticized the fifth script for "a transparent attempt at *historical cleansing*" and deplored the congressional intrusion into an area they believed deserved the protection of academic freedom. Finally, under increased threat of congressional funding cuts, I. Michael Heyman, the new director of the Smithsonian, scrapped the exhibit as planned and arranged a scaled-down version with little beyond the display of the fuselage of the *Enola Gay*. In an open letter to the Smithsonian staff and the public, he said: "I have concluded that we made a basic error in attempting to couple an historical treatment of the use of atomic weapons with the 50th anniversary commemoration of the end of the war."[50] On May 2, Martin Harwit, the administrator behind the exhibit, retired as head of NASM.

The proposed exhibit raised many valid historical issues. Why did President Truman authorize the bombing? Was it to end the war quickly with the fewest casualties, as the veterans' groups insisted; or was it to demonstrate U.S. power to the Soviets, as some historians suggested? Was it a combination of these and other motives? How many casualties would have resulted from a land invasion of Japan? What hypothetical numbers did Truman use to make his decision? Would the Japanese have surrendered sooner if the United States had not demanded unconditional surrender? Could a demonstration bomb have been dropped in Tokyo Bay or some sparsely populated area? Why was the *second* bomb dropped at Nagasaki? All of these questions are regularly posed and debated in academic settings all over the country. But in the context of the *Enola Gay* exhibit and the celebration of the fiftieth anniversary of the end of World War II, they assumed a new importance, especially in view of the way the controversy between veterans' groups and the Smithsonian was portrayed in the media.

First, media coverage usually favored the veterans' perspective. Of 500–600 pieces published in newspapers and magazines on the exhibit, about 150 were impartial, usually "news" features that presented part of both sides of the controversy. Only about thirty supported the Smithsonian's exhibit as originally conceived. About 175 directly attacked it in op-ed pieces or quoted only the views of its opponents in news reports. By the end of the episode, many historians who had originally supported the exhibit had become critical of the Smithsonian's placation of the veterans' groups. The media hurled charges of "political correctness" and "revisionist history" incessantly at the Smithsonian. The second charge is puzzling, since revision is what historians always do. Some idea of the unfairness of most of the coverage can be gathered from the constant use of a single sentence included in the first script as proposed by the museum. The offending sentence had been dropped by the second script, but that did not stop the critics from quoting it for the duration of the controversy. Highlighted in its full context:

In December 1941, Japan attacked U.S. bases in Pearl Harbor, Hawaii, and launched other surprise assaults against allied territories in the Pacific. Thus began a wider conflict marked by extreme bitterness. *For most Americans, this war was fundamentally different than the one waged against Germany and Italy—it was a war of vengeance. For most Japanese, it was a war to defend their unique culture against Western imperialism.* As the war approached its end in 1945, it appeared to both sides that it was a fight to the finish.

"It was those two sentences," say two analysts of the press coverage, "endlessly repeated by the media outside their original context, that did the most damage to the museum's credibility."[51] The museum curators were trying to express both American and Japanese perspectives in those two sentences, while press coverage made it seem that they were expressing their own point of view. The same analysts offer many other examples of unfair lifting of quotes out of context.

Besides the verbal "red flags" naively waved by the original script, a moral issue irritated the veterans' groups and their political allies. Most of them would have liked the exhibit to end when the bomb bay doors flew open, but the museum intended to force visitors to view the results on the ground. By showing vividly the effects of the explosion—shadows on the surface indicating where bodies were vaporized, the melted lunch box of a young Japanese girl, mangled religious objects—the curators pushed viewers to confront the morality of dropping the bomb. This was the last issue those who planned to celebrate the end of World War II wished to consider. The *Enola Gay*'s commander, Paul Tibbets, said in a press release, speaking for veterans, "The million or so of us remaining will die believing that we made the world a better place as a result of our efforts to secure peace that has held for almost 50 years." Tom Crouch, the curator most responsible for the exhibit, had said at about the same time in a letter to Martin Harwit, "Do you want to do an exhibition intended to make the veterans feel good, or do you want an exhibition that will lead our visitors to think about he consequences of the atomic bombing of Japan? Frankly I don't think we can do both."[52] Perhaps he and Secretary Heyman were right—that it is not possible to celebrate a victory and raise questions about the morality of nuclear weapons in the same exhibit.

The *Enola Gay* exhibit was far more contentious than "The West as America." It was easily the most controversial museum exhibit in American history, and we are still left with the task of explaining the bitterness it unleashed. To take a single example, one columnist accused the curators of being dumb as well as arrogant, "weird and sick individuals. Some strange compulsion inside them causes them to hate themselves, hate their country, hate their heritage and hate their history."[53] By early 1995, opponents knew that the Smithsonian was on the ropes. They were demanding unconditional surrender and the equivalent of a war crimes trial—that is, an investigation and purge of the Smithsonian. Nine days later *Time* published an editorial excoriating "the corruption of our institutions of national culture," and ending with a call to cut off the Smithsonian's public subsidy. "Let heads, and agencies, roll." Finally, Representatives Sam Johnson, Peter Blute, and seventy-nine other members of the House asked for Martin Harwit's resignation.[54]

Why did the exhibit stir up such a maelstrom of passionate opposition? This is the question that must be answered if we are to understand the role of the Smithsonian on the Mall. Referring to the change in the philosophy of museums in the 1980s and 1990s, Edward Linenthal says that "NASM curators became ever more acutely aware of the need to change their institution *from a temple to a forum.*"[55] In that phrase, Linenthal has identified the crux of the issue. Spelling out this insight more fully, Mike Wallace suggests that we think of museums, and especially the national museums of Washington, as religious institutions that maintain the nation's sacred relics and preside as censors or interpreters of the nation's most cherished truths. People attend museums for similar reasons that they attend a church service, to reinforce their most deeply held beliefs and commitments. The last thing they want is iconoclasm, exhibits that "dismantle the mythic dramas that give meaning and value to their lives."[56] Seeing the ordinary museum in this way would be an exaggeration, perhaps, but not the Smithsonian. During the *Enola Gay* controversy, opponents of the museum's planned exhibit constantly called for it to return to this earlier function.

The curators' new approach says, in effect, that the buildings of the Smithsonian, formerly functioning as the shrines housing the sacred history of the nation, should now reflect the awareness that sacred history is *an interpretation* from a certain perspective, one among other possible ways of looking at the same series of events. Americans have been as resistant to rethinking their history as Christians and Jews to questioning the constitutive events of their religious past. For American patriots, the "true" story is the narration of the gradual realization of the ideals of the Founders, in which evidence to the contrary, like slavery and imperialism, were considered aberrations: "The holy nation thus acquired a holy history. A conspiracy of myth, history, and chauvinism served to create an ideology as the dominating historical motif against which all history would resonate."[57]

Another way of putting the point is that critics of the museum want it to return to simply celebrating conventional patriotic understandings of the nation's history. Their phraseology indicates both the wish for this reversion and their intuition of the religious dimensions of the museum's earlier role. It is the business of the Smithsonian, said the *Wall Street Journal,* "to tell the nation's story." The *World War II Times* remarks plaintively, of the curators, "one wonders how such mind-set people [*sic*] ever attained such high positions at the Smithsonian, which we always thought was almost a sacred guardian of our Nation's rich traditions and heritage." An editorial in the *Atlanta Constitution* spoke of the Smithsonian as "a bastion of tradition," its exhibits displayed "in settings that border on worship." Sensing this nostalgia on the part of critics, one museologist says that the public must know that although museums "are places of commemoration and reverence, sacred spaces that allow the public to revel in tradition and celebratory episodes," they are much more than that: institutions that "contextualize, inspire, challenge, prod, and stimulate." While it is valid to look upon them as "temples," and "cathedrals" and wonderful "nation's attics," he says, they must also be places of scholarship and interpretation where "celebration can often co-exist with controversy."[58] New museums, like the proposed Native American and African American museums, will be fashioned in the midst of similar controversies, as was the Holocaust Museum, which opened in 1993.[59] Despite the setback resulting from the *Enola Gay* exhibit, that is clearly the direction in which museums will go in the future.

The *Enola Gay* debate stirred passions because it challenged American self-understanding as the instrument of divine Providence, its role as the white knight whose mission was to bring democracy and freedom to the world. It took what had always been described, in the face of the Vietnam debacle, as the one incontestably "good war" and raised questions about it. The critics would not be mollified unless every doubt and every shadow were removed from the interpretation. They wanted the war and its bloody conclusion described in black and white terms, with no shades of gray. American history has been haunted by a powerful religious tendency first found in Zoroastrianism, which was absorbed into Judaism, Christianity, and Islam. It divided the world into forces of good and evil, those loyal to God and to Satan, and saw the purpose of life as a great struggle against unadulterated evil, a battle to the death between darkness and light. The clearest recent expression of this dualistic concept was Ronald Reagan's description of the Soviet Union, not long before it collapsed and Russians suddenly became our friends, as "the evil empire." It is the way most Americans think. Tom Webb, in the Washington bureau of the *Wichita Eagle,* wrote a story about the *Enola Gay* exhibit featuring the views of Ben Nicks, a seventy-five-year-old veteran B-29 pilot. He and his colleagues found the Smithsonian's plans troubling, wrote Webb: "To win World War II, the nation demanded—and received—immense sacrifice in a black-and-white, life-or-death struggle. Today, from a distance of two generations, even 'The Good War' contains shades of gray."[60] But for the true believer, sacred truth does not come in "shades of gray."

CHAPTER 9

Back to the Capitol

Artists' Voices

BENJAMIN PERLEY POORE, nineteenth-century gossip and raconteur, related the following incident. A Menominee chief named Grizzly Bear was taken into the Capitol rotunda to see the recently completed bas-reliefs above the four doors. Indicating the *Landing of the Pilgrims* over the east door, which shows a brave welcoming a Pilgrim family with a gift of corn, he said: "There Ingen give hungry white man corn." Then turning to the north door, which showed Penn's treaty with the Indians, he said: "There Ingen give white man land." Next he indicated the relief over the west door, which showed Pocahontas saving the life of Captain John Smith, and said: "There Ingen save white man's life." Finally, turning to the relief over the south door, which shows Daniel Boone about to stab an Indian while his foot rests on the dead body of another, "And there white man kill Ingen. Ugh!" (see Figure 32).[1]

Two nineteenth-century guidebooks to the Capitol relate the story of another Native American response to the Boone relief. A group of Winnebagos visited Washington after selling their land in Wisconsin to the federal government and being relocated to Iowa. They were described as "noble looking fellows," clothed and ornamented "in a warlike manner with scalping knives and tomahawks." When they visited the rotunda of the Capitol, the relief of Boone killing the Indian caught their attention. According to one of the guidebooks, the tribesmen formed a semicircle and after "scrutinizing and recognizing every part of the scene . . . they raised their dreadful war-cry and ran hurriedly from the hall."[2]

Although couched in the condescending style of the period, these stories, and the reliefs to which they refer, reprise most of the major themes in the history of relations between white settlers and Native Americans. The Indians are brave and noble, warlike and fearful, generous and sly, equal and inferior, powerful in battle but abjectly defeated, wise counselors and helpless children. They are, in the art of the Capitol, whatever the whites who

FIGURE 32 Enrico Causici, *Conflict of Daniel Boone and the Indians, 1773*, relief sculpture, Capitol rotunda. Architect of the Capitol.

painted, sculpted, or wrote about them needed them to be at the time. They also appear to have been much more perceptive than most of the ordinary tourists who pass through the rotunda and barely take note of the reliefs. The art of the Capitol spoke to the Indians loud and clear, and they did not like what they heard.

The pilgrimage route I describe in this book begins at the Capitol and follows the major axes of ceremonial Washington. In focusing on sites that have become part of the protocol of national ritual, I omitted everything but the memorial core. In the first chapter I considered the Capitol as the architectural center of the city plan as designed by L'Enfant. Having completed my prescribed circuit, I now return to the Capitol to consider the messages of its art. Some of the messages are clearly deliberate, some more likely the unconscious expression of ideas and viewpoints held by those who sponsored, funded, and fashioned the art. Either way, the art speaks, perhaps more clearly than the architecture and planning, telling us much about the attitudes of those most closely involved in its creation, and revealing the part they played in constructing the national mythology as it is projected by the city. Unlike the multicultural richness of the Smithsonian museums' displays, the art of the Capitol seems quite narrow to the visitor today, almost exclusively reflecting the culture of the nineteenth century when most of it was created. To provide a sense of the changes that have taken place, I conclude this chapter with a survey of the responses of poets and novelists to capital and Capitol. At the last stop on my self-devised pilgrimage, these views stand as a summary of recent changes in the capital and as an argument for the mutability of its symbolism.

Much of the Capitol's art can be considered a response to historical crises and ideological challenges. Art is rarely innocent, especially when designed for a highly charged center of political power. A careful study of the art of the Capitol shows two issues of particular concern to the artists and their sponsors, the break with Great Britain and relations with Native Americans. Perhaps surprisingly, since it was the most serious of all the crises in U.S. history, the Civil War and its concomitant issue of slavery and racial equality are absent from the Capitol's art. Like the designers of the Lincoln Memorial, political leaders believed the issue so painful and divisive that it could not be directly addressed. Most of Constantino Brumidi's decorative program for the Capitol was undertaken and executed after the Civil War (until his death in 1880), but no hint of that struggle or of emancipation and civil rights appears in his work.[3] His rotunda frieze, continued by his successor Filippo Costaggini in the years 1880 to 1888, depicts a series of events beginning with the landing of Columbus and ending with the Mexican War.

It was only in the early 1950s that Allyn Cox, in finally completing the Brumidi frieze, added three more events, including a segment called *The Civil War* (see Figure 33). Predictably it showed nothing about slavery or emancipation but depicted a Yankee and a Confederate soldier shaking hands. More recent crises, like the Vietnam War, are completely absent from the artistic and decorative program.

Of the two crisis themes that *are* addressed in the art of the Capitol, the break with Britain was an extremely serious issue before and during the Revolutionary War. The rebellion against the crown was frequently spoken of in terms that suggested family tension: familial disruption, fratricidal strife and the rebellion of child against parent. As Jefferson's original words in the Declaration of Independence proclaimed: "These facts have given the last stab to agonizing affection, and manly spirit bids us to renounce for ever these unfeeling brethren."[4] The metaphor of parricide was used after the destruction of King George III's statue in New York, a dramatic action that expressed violent feelings toward a father figure. Because the concept of family was the very lingua franca of the discourse of revolution on both sides of the Atlantic, its constant use highlighted the agonizing seriousness of the act of declaring independence.[5] Occasionally writers even used the grisly metaphor of dismembering a body to express the break with Britain.[6] But by the early nineteenth century the issue was less problematic. The Declaration of Independence, the Revolutionary War, the writing of the Constitution, and the life of Washington are prominent in the thematic art of the Capitol, not because they were unsettled issues but because they were the constitutive events in the sacred history of the new nation. They are a declaration that the unthinkable act, the destruction of the family relationship, was in fact a necessity. The rotunda, with four paintings of these now mythic beginnings by John Trumbull, is the major repository of art dealing with this theme. On February 6, 1817, Congress authorized the paintings and specified their content: "four paintings commemorative of the most important events of the American Revolution, to be placed, when finished, in the Capitol of the United States."[7] Over the next seven years Trumbull completed four paintings that depicted the beginning of the revolution in the *Signing of the Declaration of Independence* (1819), a major turning point of the war in *The Surrender of General Burgoyne at Saratoga* (1822), the victory in *The Surrender of Cornwallis at Yorktown* (1820), and *Washington Resigning His Commission as Commander in Chief of the Army* (1824), which confirmed that the government would be a democracy, not a monarchy. A prominent depiction of the signing of the Constitution was not added until Howard Chandler Christy's twenty-by-thirty-foot painting was installed at the top of the east stairway of the House wing in 1940.

FIGURE 33 Allyn Cox, frieze painting, Civil War section, Capitol rotunda. Architect of the Capitol.

Belonging to this same category of paintings about the founding of the new republic are the many images of George Washington in the Capitol. The most prominent is Brumidi's *Apotheosis of George Washington,* a fresco covering the canopy of the rotunda dome. The major figures in the painting are about fifteen feet tall, but the dome is so high above the viewer that it is difficult to make out the details of the artist's work. Brumidi was careful not to repeat Greenough's mistake of presenting Washington naked, but the result is incongruous. Brumidi used classical drapery to cover the lower half of Washington's body, while clothing his upper body in a Revolutionary War uniform. The allegorical figures on the outer ring are testimony to American achievements in six areas: arts and sciences, marine developments, commerce, mechanics, and agriculture. The *Apotheosis* suggests that the American solution to the perennial problem of the relationship of the federal government to the states has received celestial approbation. Washington is surrounded by thirteen blithe maidens, symbolizing the harmony of the original states. They hold a banner reading *e pluribus unum*. Below him an armed Liberty strikes down Tyranny and Royal Power. With her sword and shield of stars and stripes, she is strikingly similar to Thomas Crawford's Liberty atop the dome, who also has *e pluribus unum* as her motto.

As of December 1974, there were 677 works of art in the Capitol, as listed in a catalogue published for the U.S. bicentennial: 132 portraits; 54 paintings; 77 busts; 102 statues; 90 reliefs; 137 frescoes, murals and lunettes; 29 pieces outside the building, and 57 miscellaneous items (capitals, clocks, windows, etc.).[8] Since remembering and forgetting are equally important in framing a historical narrative, this collection is suggestive both for what it contains and for what it omits.

First, it is obvious that the Capitol is a men's club. Before the nineteenth century it was simply taken for granted that women were of the private, not the public sphere. The physical layout of the capital and the art of the Capitol tell the same story of separate spheres for men and women, gendered so that "the role of republican wife and mother [is] within the home."[9] Of the 667 works of art, only ten feature real women (there are a few allegorical female figures). Four of these deal with the story of Pocahontas, who saved the life of Captain John Smith, but the Indian maid is celebrated because she accepted white culture, not because she is a woman.[10] Four others are sculptures in Statuary Hall donated by the states: Esther Morris, a Wyoming judge; Dr. Florence Sabin, a Colorado physician; Maria Sanford, a Minnesota educator; and Frances Willard, an Illinois educator. There is a painting in the Senate wing showing Mrs. Rebecca Motte heroically directing Generals Francis Marion and Henry "Lighthorse Harry" Lee to burn down her mansion to dislodge the British. She is the only woman whose image was commissioned by the federal government. Finally, there is the memorial to the pioneers of the women's suffrage movement, Elizabeth Cady Stanton, Susan B. Anthony, and Lucretia Mott. This sculpture, donated in 1921 by the National Women's Party, shows the three leaders with their upper bodies emerging from a large block of marble (see Figure 34). It was received in the rotunda for a few months and then installed in the crypt, where it remains today. No woman artist had work represented in the Capitol until Vinnie Ream received a commission to create the statue of Lincoln that stands in the rotunda.[11]

In contrast, Native American subjects are portrayed with striking frequency. Thirteen paintings, two busts, two statues, four reliefs, seven frieze vignettes, two wall paintings, three external sculpture groups, and one miscellaneous piece feature Indians as a central or important element of the

FIGURE 34 Adelaide Johnson, memorial to the pioneers of the women's suffrage movement (Elizabeth Cady Stanton, Susan B. Anthony, Lucretia Mott). Architect of the Capitol.

work. Some of these are among the most prominent and easily visible works in the Capitol. Since the great majority of the Capitol's art addresses no issue at all but simply commemorates individuals in sculpture, relief, or painting, the number of works dealing with Native Americans is remarkable. The sheer numbers indicate that the issue is one that occupied the minds of those who built and decorated the Capitol.

The problem of European-Indian relations is complex, but the major issue may be stated simply. In 1492 perhaps 12 million Native peoples occupied North America from the Atlantic to the Pacific and north of the Rio Grande. Over the next few centuries approximately nine-tenths of the Native population was eliminated, the results of wars between settlers and Indians, as well as some intratribal warfare. Alcohol took its toll, but most died from diseases borne by white settlers to which the Natives had no immunity.[12] Four hundred years later, most of the tribes had become extinct, and those remaining were confined to reservations on the most undesirable land on the continent. The obvious question was how the Europeans, the agents of this disaster, justified their aggressive behavior. Or, stating the question in another way, what moral or legal right did the Europeans have to the land they had taken? Even though they had rationalizations that answered these questions, the surprising frequency of this theme in the art of the Capitol suggests that political leaders were not completely comfortable with the conventional reasoning. I do not wish to suggest that there was some vast conspiracy to rationalize the European conquest, although there were some deliberate attempts to do so. Most often it was an unconscious process reflecting ideas of widespread currency in the nineteenth century.

The "Indian problem" had been an issue since the establishment of the new nation, alluded to constantly in presidential inaugurals and other formal summations of the state of the Union. George Washington mentioned Indian hostility in his first annual address to Congress, urging the protection of settlers on the "Southern and Western frontiers," and, if necessary, taking steps "to punish aggressors." The issue runs like a leitmotif through all eight of his annual messages to Congress, his concerns as much to protect the Indians from the depredations of white settlers as to protect the whites from hostile Indian attacks.[13] As he said in his seventh message of December 8, 1795, "To enforce upon the Indians the observance of justice it is indispensable that there shall be competent means of rendering justice to them."

The "Indian problem" appeared before Trumbull's four paintings were installed as Charles Bulfinch was attempting to arrange for relief panels over the four doors of the rotunda. They were completed between 1825 and 1827, and all deal directly with the relations of white settlers and indigenous people. Two were done by Enrico Causici, one by Antonio Capellano, and one by Nicholas Gevelot. These are the four reliefs to which Chief Grizzly Bear reacted with such disgust. The Capellano panel presents the scene of Pocahontas saving Captain Smith. Two muscular braves hold clubs ready to beat him to death, one with a foot on the recumbent man's thigh. Pocahontas stretches her arms out in supplication, a gesture that also shields Smith from their blows. In the middle stands Chief Powhatan holding his hand high telling the braves to desist. The relief depicts three common Indian stereotypes—the benevolent Native who helps the settler, the fierce savage who threatens the settler, and the noble and heroic leader. To make sure we recognize the "noble savage," Capellano drapes Powhatan in a toga-like garment to equate him with a figure from the classical past.

Causici's first effort was the *Landing of the Pilgrims* (see Figure 35). A

FIGURE 35 Enrico Causici, *Landing of the Pilgrims, 1620*, relief sculpture, Capitol rotunda. Architect of the Capitol.

family of three disembarks at Plymouth; the father leads while the mother looks to heaven with gratitude. The benevolent Indian sits on the rock, extending an ear of corn to welcome the pilgrims, with two more ears at his feet, indicating plenty. The sculptor has managed to treat the Indian paradoxically. While he is shown to be friendly yet strong, his lower position indicates subservience and inferiority to the Europeans. Causici's second effort was the famous (or infamous) *Conflict of Daniel Boone and Indians.*

Boone is the paradigm for European encroachment, the intrepid pioneer who heads for the wilderness willing to fight with the Indians to make a place for himself and his followers. One Indian is already slain. The second, muscular and with a fierce scowl on his face, has his tomahawk raised to strike. But Boone holds his gun in place to block the savage blow and with his right hand is about to plunge a knife into his enemy. The outcome is certain, showing the futility of the Native Americans trying to stop the whites in their movement westward.

Gevelot's panel shows the idea of reasonable, nonaggressive Europeans, represented by William Penn conferring with a Delaware Indian chief and his adviser. Penn, wearing his familiar Quaker hat, is somewhat over-shadowed by the muscular and animated Indians. Penn's treaty with the Indians was always taken as a model of peaceful cooperation, and Gevelot has conveyed the point that this is a relationship of mutual respect. Penn and the chief shake hands as equals in sealing their agreement. On the other hand, the Indians are depicted as "children of nature." They are naked ex-cept for their animal skins, and their feathery headdresses mirror the thick vegetation above them. They are clearly still a part of nature, while Penn, with his hat and long frock coat is a representative of civilization (see Figure 36). Although three of the four reliefs show positive relations between whites and Indians, the Boone relief reflects the antagonism of contemporary conflicts between the two races. In 1828, the year after the Boone panel was installed, Andrew Jackson reversed the assimilation policy of previous ad-ministrations and vigorously pursued "removal" as a solution to the Indian problem.

Critical reaction to the relief panels was generally favorable. Not sur-prisingly, the Boone panel was praised as superior to the others. Architect Robert Mills probably spoke for most viewers when he praised Causici's rendering of the intrepid hero, "whose cool resolution and self-possession are strongly contrasted with the ferocity and recklessness of the savage." There were a few dissenting voices, however. Representative Tristram Burges argued that the Boone panel "very truly represented our dealing with the Indians, for we had not left them even a place to die upon." Represen-tative Henry Wise imagined how Indians would interpret the reliefs and not unlike Grizzly Bear said: "We give you corn, you cheat us of our lands; we save your life, you take ours," and concluded that the reliefs were "a pretty faithful history of our dealing with the native tribes."[14] All four of the relief themes are repeated in the Brumidi-Costaggini grisaille frieze in the dome above.

The concern of the nation with unity is addressed ceaselessly in the art

FIGURE 36 Nicholas Gevelot, *William Penn's Treaty with the Indians, 1682*, relief sculpture, Capitol rotunda. Architect of the Capitol.

and architecture of the Capitol. While the divinized Washington in the dome is surrounded by the spirits of thirteen happy states in heaven, the situation on earth was otherwise. The same four relief panels represent four sections of regional interest: the North, especially Massachusetts (Pilgrims landing); the Mid-Atlantic states, especially Pennsylvania (Penn's treaty); the South, especially Virginia (Pocahontas); and the newly emergent West (Boone).

FIGURE 37 John G. Chapman, *Baptism of Pocahontas at Jamestown, Virginia, 1613,* painting, Capitol rotunda. Architect of the Capitol.

Conflict was soon to erupt into the open in the nullification crisis, with South Carolina threatening secession in 1832. Although civil war was averted by Henry Clay's compromise tariff reform bill, the continuing uneasiness led to strenuous efforts to create symbols of unity in the Capitol.

After ten years the four blank spots on the walls of the rotunda began to bother congressmen. In 1836 they passed a measure that called for "historical pictures serving to illustrate the discovery of America; the settlement of the United States; the history of the Revolution; or of the adoption of the Constitution,"[15] in other words, major events constituting the sacred history of the republic. Surprisingly, the committee formed to select the artists followed none of the suggestions of Congress but the first. The four committee members appointed were all ardent expansionists, and although they left the specific subjects up to the artists, it may not have been entirely accidental that the paintings eventually chosen seemed to support this purpose.

John Chapman's *Baptism of Pocahontas at Jamestown, Virginia, 1613* was completed in 1840. Since the release of a Walt Disney movie about Pocahontas in 1995, Chapman's painting has offered Capitol guides an entrée into the usually inaccessible world of children's interests. The painting has more human interest than any of the other paintings. Pocahontas's family attends the ritual, their faces expressing a wide range of emotions in

FIGURE 38 Robert W. Weir, *Embarkation of the Pilgrims at Delft Haven, Holland, July 22, 1620*, painting, Capitol Rotunda. Architect of the Capitol.

response to the event. Pocahontas, dressed in a European's white dress and bathed in light, is described in an early government guide to the painting as one of the "children of the forest" who has been "snatched from the fangs of barbarous idolatry" (see Figure 37). Two Indians, Pocahontas's uncle and sister, look with interest and receptivity toward the baptism. Nantequaus, the son of Powhatan, stands regal and proud, looking away from the event. His face is in the shadows, as is that of Opechankanough, another uncle, who sits defiantly on the floor of the church. It was he who later broke the peace and led a massacre at the Jamestown settlement. At a period when the government was following a policy of Indian removal, the message of the painting is clear: unless they are willing to be absorbed into white civilization, the Indians are too warlike to live with. Conflict is inevitable and peace can only come with their relocation.

Chapman's Pocahontas painting brings a religious dimension to the issue of European-Indian relations, though we sense that it is secondary to the idea the heroine has accepted European culture. In Robert Weir's *Embarkation of the Pilgrims at Delft Haven, Holland, 22 July 1620*, religion is the central issue (see Figure 38). Weir shows the Pilgrims on board the *Speedwell*, praying for their safe journey back to England and from there over to America (in the leaky *Mayflower*). As the Pocahontas painting celebrates

Virginia and the Jamestown colony, this one glorifies Massachusetts and the Plymouth plantation. Although the Pilgrims landed at Plymouth after Jamestown, Plymouth gradually became the premier mythological place of the nation's founding, since it was not blemished by an association with slavery. Robert Winthrop, in a 1939 speech in New York, glorified this plantation as the place where the country was formed and molded and the whole hemisphere "shaken." Led by the "Great Master," he said, the settlers created a "civilized society on this whole northern Continent of America." Their coming was often compared to the Israelites' arrival in the Promised Land, and like these forebears, they often resorted to arms to make themselves a place. Weir has the Pilgrims' armor and weapons in a prominent place at front and center in the picture. As that quintessential New Englander Robert Lowell put it:

> Our fathers wrung their bread from stocks and stones
> And fenced their gardens with the Redman's bones;
> Embarking from the Nether Land of Holland,
> Pilgrims unhouseled by Geneva's night
> They planted here the Serpent's seeds of light.[16]

Fourteen years after the Pilgrims' arrival, governor of the colony John Winthrop would say that God "cleared our title to this place" by sweeping away the Indians with a smallpox epidemic. As Darwin put it, with typical understatement, "Wherever the European had trod, death seems to pursue the aboriginal."[17]

The last two paintings, John Vanderlyn's *Landing of Columbus* and William H. Powell's *Discovery of the Mississippi by DeSoto,* are similar in conception and meaning. Columbus represents the most remote beginnings of the nation and De Soto the opening of the West, so once again these four paintings represent regional interests. Both works show Europeans entering a natural region, almost like gods, while the native inhabitants cower at their feet or cluster at the edges of the clearing. The representatives of religion appear in both paintings, especially the Powell, which has DeSoto's men planting a huge crucifix while friars pray. The official pamphlet describing the Columbus painting describes how the Indians almost disappear as they merge with their surroundings, in retreat before the "mysterious strangers" who appear "as beings of a higher order." A reporter for the *National Intelligencer* described the DeSoto painting with refreshing candor, as conveying "the great ideas of the submission of the Indian tribes, and the important part played by religion, allied with force, in the conquest of the New World."[18]

With the installation of the Powell painting in 1855, the essential decoration of the rotunda was complete. Congress had earlier commissioned the statue of Washington by Horatio Greenough, discussed in Chapter 5. It remained in the rotunda from 1841 until 1843, then was placed outside in a prominent place facing the east entrance to the Capitol. It has two small figures, Columbus and an Indian chief, standing on the rear corners of the throne seat of Washington. The three figures represent, once again, important events in a mythic history. Columbus is shown as a Greek philosopher contemplating a small globe, the image of wisdom and scientific knowledge. The Indian chief, explained Greenough, represents "what state our country was in when civilization first raised her standard there." He leans dejectedly, perhaps already aware of his fate and that of his people. The message is the same as that of the paintings, the inevitability of the conquest of the continent by a higher civilization.

Two statues that once stood prominently on each side of the main steps to the Capitol's east door are now in storage, having been acknowledged as an embarrassment. But they are worth discussing as crass examples of the victorious expansionist sentiment. Designated to grace the cheek blocks of the main stairway to the Capitol, the sculptural groups were to be commissioned by Congress. Representative James Buchanan promoted his friend, sculptor Luigi Persico. William Preston and John Calhoun both promoted Greenough. In the end, the task was divided and the two sculptors met in Italy to discuss size and themes, and to select marble. When completed, the two sculptural groups rehearsed the same themes depicted inside the Capitol. Persico's *Discovery of America* is the most arrogant rendering of this familiar theme in the Capitol collection. Columbus is shown as an older man, bearded, grim, and severe, striding forward to take possession of a continent while holding a globe of the earth in his upraised right hand. Cowering below him is an Indian maiden, with no adornment but a small cloth (see Figure 39).

When the vulnerability of the land and the helplessness of its inhabitants were the theme, artists of the Capitol usually represented the idea with a young maiden or a defeated brave. Persico uses the maiden's vulnerable sexuality as an analogy—she is as subject to Columbus as the "virgin continent" is to the will of European conquerors. A lunette painting by Brumidi in the Senate wing reflects the same idea. In this case a youthful Columbus stands on the shore, next to an Indian woman. The *Santa Maria* floats on the bay behind them. The young woman is seated on a rock, dressed in almost Middle Eastern fashion. Columbus smiles as he lifts the edge of her shawl to look at her face, a not very subtle symbol of his access to her, and of unimpeded European access to the continent (see Figure 40).

FIGURE 39 Luigi Persico, *Discovery of America,* sculptural group. In storage. Architect of the Capitol.

Greenough's sculptural group *The Rescue* was installed in 1853, nine years after Persico's Columbus. It shows a pioneer fighting to defend his family from an Indian attacker (see Figure 41). The pioneer's wife, holding an infant, crouches at the back corner of the pedestal. Although the Indian brave looks strong and holds a tomahawk in his hand, there is no doubt about the result of the fight. The pioneer will overpower him. The theme of

FIGURE 40 Constantino Brumidi, *Columbus and the Indian Maiden*, painting, Senate wing, U.S. Capitol. Architect of the Capitol.

the white woman held captive by Indians, as old as America itself, had become a common one in the nineteenth century, appealing to prurient interests and suggesting the forbidden act of miscegenation.[19] Greenough in this case shows the pioneer intervening to prevent the capture. In the inevitable clash between the Natives and the settlers, there was no doubt who would be the eventual victors. These two statues are classic statements of the idea of "manifest destiny," the belief of nineteenth-century republicans that they were destined by Providence to occupy the land between the Atlantic and Pacific Oceans. After the war with Mexico, this goal was close to fulfillment. As Representative William Sawyer pointed out in defending the annexation of the Oregon Territory, "We received our rights [title to the Oregon Territory] from high Heaven—from destiny." Columbus was "the agent Heaven employed to place us in possession," he claimed, and "we have the right to every inch" of the continent. Representative James E. Belser had actually referred to Greenough's sculpture as providing "an instructive lesson" to support the extension of the nation to the Pacific.[20]

There was no doubt as to the meaning of these two sculptural groups. A reviewer for *Bulletin of the American Art-Union* wrote of *Rescue* in 1851:

FIGURE 41 Horatio Greenough, *Rescue,* sculptural group. In storage. Architect of the Capitol.

The thought embodied in the action of the group, and immediately communicated to every spectator is the natural and necessary superiority of the Anglo-
Saxon to the Indian. It typifies the settlement of the American continent, and
the respective destinies of the two races who here come into collision. . . . His
[the pioneer's] countenance is indignant, yet dignified; . . . there is nothing vin-

dictive or resentful in it; the cloud of passion has passed from the surface of that mirror of high thoughts and heroic feelings, and the severity of its rebuking force is a shade saddened and softened by the melancholy thought of the necessary extinction of the poor savage, whose nature is irreconcilable with society.[21]

In belated recognition of a change in sentiment, the two sculptural groups were finally removed during the Capitol extension that began in 1958. The Indian Reorganization Act of 1934 acknowledged, "We took away their best lands; broke treaties, promises, tossed them the most nearly worthless scraps of a continent that had once been wholly theirs." As early as 1939 a resolution proposed that Greenough's *Rescue* be "ground to dust, and scattered to the four winds, that no more remembrance may be perpetuated of our barbaric past." Two years later the House considered a joint resolution suggesting that the *Rescue* group "now disgracing the entrance to the Capitol" be replaced by a statue of one of the great Indian leaders famous in American history. In 1976 a crane attempting to move *Rescue* to a new storage area accidentally dropped it. *Discovery of America* is still in storage unharmed.

There are three other examples of iconography on the exterior of the Capitol worthy of examination—the sculptural groups in the pediments over the main east entrance, the House wing, and the Senate wing. The earliest of these is Luigi Persico's *Genius of America*, which was commissioned and installed during the presidency of John Quincy Adams (see Figure 42). During the extension of the Capitol in 1959, Persico's badly deteriorated sandstone original was removed and an exact copy in marble installed. It has pride of place, certainly, covering the portico through which most visitors to the Capitol must pass. Waiting in long lines to enter the building, thousands of tourists have ample opportunity to examine this icon. Whether they do, or having done so they actually understand it, is questionable. It is, frankly, a yawner, one more example of the classical decor found all over this city with its petrified forest of classical columns and ubiquitous pediments.

The *Genius of America,* however, despite its trite components, is in my opinion not just an architectural centerpiece but a culmination of national mythology. It is an expression of what Lincoln meant by the "better angels of our nature." Yet to appreciate it the viewer must patiently interrogate the three allegorical figures with their classical drapery and stereotyped symbols—the shield and spear, the eagle, the scales of justice, the anchor of hope. The meaning proposed is lofty, the heart of the nation's self-declared

FIGURE 42 Luigi Persico, *Genius of America*, east central pediment, U.S. Capitol.
Architect of the Capitol.

ideals. But it is accessible only if one gets beyond the outworn and overused
symbols. John Quincy Adams thought the project to decorate the pediment
very important, appointing a commission of three to preside over a national
competition. The commission included William Thornton, the designer of
the original Capitol, and Adams himself was deeply involved in the selection
process. There were thirty-six submissions, but none of them adequately
expressed what Adams was seeking, nothing less than "a new national mythology."

Bulfinch, the Capitol architect, reported that Adams "disclaimed all wish
to exhibit triumphal cars and emblems of Victory, and all allusions to heathen mythology, and thought that *the duties of the Nation or Legislators
should be impressed in an obvious and intelligible manner.*"[22] When he even-

tually approved Persico's design, he traded one set of conventional allegories for another. At first he was not completely satisfied with the sculptor's plans and convinced him to remove Hercules and the fasces, which had too much heathen mythology for his taste, and to incorporate instead the scriptural image of Hope with an anchor. Besides being drawn to biblical symbolism, he was in both cases downplaying the ideas of force and military power, although he did not insist that they be eliminated altogether. Adams also wanted the pediment design to include the two key dates of the nation's sacred history, July 4, 1776, and March 4, 1789. The final result is a tableau of three female figures. The central one is the "Genius of America," representing the nation. At her right side are the shield and spear of war and the wreath of peace, with "July 4, 1776" inscribed within it. On her left side is the eagle. Adams described the eagle as "indifferent in the drawing; better, but not good, in the model." On the actual pediment, however, he liked it, calling it the "the pouncing bird." To the left of America is the figure of Justice, holding her scales in one hand and the scroll of the Constitution in the other, with the date of its ratification, March 4, 1789. Adams's Hope is on the right, one hand on the anchor.

Although I believe the work suffers from an excess of conventional allegory, its underlying meaning is both simple and profound, conveyed by the gestures in the relief. The viewer's eye first falls on the right side, where Hope points upward toward America, a gesture that says America is the hope of the world. This was the belief of the Founding Fathers, echoed in Lincoln's "last best hope of earth," repeated by many inscriptions in memorial Washington. America is in turn pointing toward Justice, and that is the eye's final resting place. In the same letter mentioned above, Bulfinch explained the meaning of the relief concisely—"the whole [is] intended to convey that while we cultivate *Justice* we may *hope* for *success*." This is "the duty of the Nation," expressed in "an obvious and intelligible manner." A sentence later Bulfinch added, "It is intended that an appropriate inscription shall explain the meaning and moral to dull comprehensions."[23] The "appropriate inscription" was never provided.

The second pediment design to be put in place was Thomas Crawford's *Progress of Civilization*, installed over the entrance to the Senate extension in 1863. It is nearly as offensive as Greenough's *Rescue*, celebrating the expansion of the United States "from sea to shining sea" at the expense of the original inhabitants. Perhaps because it is high above the viewer, complex, and difficult to understand, there has been no serious attempt to remove it. Montgomery Meigs was the immediate supervisor of the extension at the time, working under Jefferson Davis, secretary of war in the Franklin

Pierce administration. Seeking to obtain appropriate art for the blank pediments on the new extensions, Meigs wrote a letter to Crawford and Hiram Powers suggesting that they consider the theme of racial conflict in submitting plans for it. "Our history of struggle between civilized man and the savage, between cultivated and wild nature," he thought, would appeal "to the feelings of all classes."[24] Native Americans were obviously not among the classes he had in mind.

Like Persico, Crawford designed a pediment showing a female allegorical symbol of America in the center, with a similar eagle at her side (see Figure 43). On her left are the figures representing the early days of America, first a pioneer cutting down a tree (a commonly used symbol for the progress of civilization), then an elegiac Indian group, indicating those about to be displaced. On her right Crawford depicted evidence for the glorious triumph of European culture, figures of a soldier, a merchant, two youths, a schoolmaster and child, and a mechanic. They evince confident accomplishment and progress in the fields of commerce, industry, education, and agriculture. In contrast, the Indian figures on America's left are pictures of dejection and defeat. A small Indian boy returns from the hunt with some small game, a symbol of a way of life that was ending. From Jefferson on, the policy of the government was to urge the Indians to adopt farming and abandon hunting, which required too much space and hindered Euro-American expansion. President Monroe expressed it unequivocally: "The hunter state can exist only in the vast uncultivated desert. It yields to the . . . greater force of civilized population; and, of right, it ought to yield, for the earth was given to mankind to support the greater number of which it is capable; and no tribe or people have a right to withhold from the wants of others, more than is necessary for their support and comfort."[25] Ironically, even tribes that did develop a prosperous agricultural economy, as the Cherokees did, fared no better at the hands of an expansive nineteenth-century nation than the tribes that refused to abandon their hunting and gathering life.

Next to the boy sits a brave, his head propped on his hand, a figure of depression. His passivity contrasts with the energetic pioneer to his right, cutting down a tree. To his left is an Indian woman holding her infant protectively, and next to them a grave mound. Crawford explained that the demeanor of the brave represents his "despair and profound grief resulting from the conviction of the white man's triumph," and that the grave was "emblematic of the extinction of the Indian race." No one could miss the message. The *Crayon*'s review of Crawford's pediment in 1885 explained: "His tribe has disappeared, he is left alone, the solitary off-shoot of a mighty race; like the tree-stump beside him he is old and withered, already the axe

FIGURE 43 Thomas Crawford, *Progress of Civilization,* Senate pediment, U.S. Capitol. Architect of the Capitol.

of the backwoodsman disturbs his last hours; civilization and Art, and agriculture . . . have desecrated his home."[26]

The idea that the Indians were fated to vanish was already well established by the time of Crawford's work. One of the most vigorous purveyors of the notion was George Catlin, who in the 1830s took upon himself the mission of "preserving" them. His romanticism conceived the Indians as noble savages, "the bold, intrepid step—the proud, yet dignified deportment of Nature's Man, in fearless freedom, with a soul unalloyed by mercenary lusts."[27] His goal was not to save the actual tribes, however, but to paint them authentically so that their *memory* would be forever preserved. They are a doomed and dying race, their term of existence nearly expired, a sad but unavoidable fact. "Catlin replayed this lament tirelessly. Reading his narrative is very much like attending an endless funeral service; one drifts off for a moment and returns to find the eulogy still in progress."[28] Catlin became a nineteenth-century "star," completing a gallery of some 400 Indian paintings and taking them on a tour of the United States and Europe. He made every effort to sell his gallery to the government. Sympathetic friends in Congress introduced numerous resolutions, between 1838 and 1852, to purchase his collection, echoing the common sentiment: the Natives "are receding before the advancing tide of our population, and are probably destined, at no distant day, wholly to disappear; but [Catlin's] collection will preserve them."[29] Although none of the resolutions was successful, both Catlin's paintings and the most of the tribes he was all but burying have survived.[30] The sense of tragedy Catlin and other contemporaries felt at the demise of the Indians is captured in Crawford's sculptures.

The message of *The Progress of Civilization,* which now seems like an outrage, was generally taken for granted by nineteenth-century Americans. A recent popular pictorial guide to the Capitol says blandly that Crawford's relief depicted "a concept that would be thought offensive today but was not considered so in Crawford's day: the ascendancy of the white race over the Indians."[31] Nineteenth-century Americans did not think of "culture" as a highly complex system of language, art, technology, and thought patterns with a logic and integrity of its own. The regnant logical ordering system was much simpler, a bipolar view of civilization poised against savagery. Most white Americans of the day thought about the subject in a series of mutually exclusive categories:

> Carrying associations of both nobility and violence, savagery was mankind's childhood. . . . [It] meant hunting and gathering, not agriculture; common ownership, not individual property owning; pagan superstitions, not Christianity; spoken languages, not literacy; emotion, not reason. Savagery had its charms but was fated to yield before the higher stage of civilizations represented by white Americans. . . . [Yet] all the cultural understanding and tolerance in the world would not have changed the crucial fact that Indians possessed the land and that Euro-Americans wanted it.[32]

The *Progress of Civilization* can therefore be judged an accurate expression of American attitudes during a period of aggressive expansion in the 1840s and 1850s, whether at the expense of Mexico or of the Indians. The rationale for both was the same: the inevitable ascendancy of a higher civilization over a lower one, with the added moral vision of bringing the higher values to those at the lower stage. As President Buchanan said of the Mexican War, it was not prosecuted for conquest but as a means to bestow upon others "the same blessings of liberty and law, which we ourselves enjoy." From this it is a short step to Jefferson Davis, who said of the war, with charming candor, "I hold that in a just war we conquered a large portion of Mexico, and that to it we have a title which has been regarded as valid ever since man existed in a social condition—the title of conquest."[33]

For a variety of reasons the pediment over the House entrance remained undecorated until 1916. Meigs had urged both Crawford and Hiram Powers, the Cincinnati sculptor, to submit designs for the two pediments. Powers refused, not wishing to submit his work to politicians for approval. He was also angered because Congress had refused to purchase his allegorical statue *America*. Having first depicted a female figure of America holding a liberty cap aloft on a pike, he had run afoul of Jefferson Davis's well-known allergy to any headgear that might hint at the idea of emancipation. More moderate members of Congress agreed, realizing that southern representatives would never accept any art that suggested it. Edward Everett and others advised Powers of his "inconsistency," since freedom was an original condition in the United States, not a matter of emancipation. Powers appeared to acquiesce but then substituted an even more offensive symbol, the America figure trampling on manacles! Congress, needless to say, never purchased the statue.

Another respected sculptor, Henry Kirke Brown, submitted an unsolicited design for the House pediment when Meigs assured him than any submission from an artist of his reputation would be given serious consideration. But Brown made the egregious gaffe of including in it a black slave sitting on a cotton bale. He tells of his audience with Montgomery Meigs:

> The Capt. [Meigs] on looking at my design for some moments placed his finger on the (figure) of the slave. I felt its significance at once and saw that my hopes of introducing him into the composition were vain.
>
> After long and careful looking he said: I do not think it would do to represent a slave in the pediment, it is a sore subject and upon which there is a good deal of feeling. I think no southerner would consent to it—but I [Brown] interposed—that it is an institution of the country. How else can it be represented? He [Meigs] said the South talked of it as the greatest blessing both for slave and master, but that they did not like to have it alluded to, and I was advised to avoid so fruitful a subject of contention, and yet he could not see how else the south could be represented.[34]

Brown eliminated the slave, but in the end Meigs rejected his design anyway.[35] Numerous other designs were submitted over the next years. None was accepted, and it was not until 1916 that Paul Wayland Bartlett's *Apotheosis of Democracy* was installed in the House pediment. It represents the idea that democracy, protected by a vigilant and prepared Peace, has resulted in the unprecedented growth of agriculture and industry, the two groups symbolically depicted in the pediment. In the center stands an allegorical female representing Peace protecting genius. At the unveiling, Bartlett described it as follows:

"Peace," an armed "Peace," stands erect, draped in a mantle which almost completely hides her breast-plate and coat of mail; her left arm rests on her buckler, which is supported by the altar at her side. In the background is the "olive tree of peace." Her right arm is extended in a gesture of protection over the youthful and winged figure of "Genius," who nestles confidingly at her feet, and holds in his right hand the torch of "Immortality."[36]

Another yawner. Observers, however, contrasted Bartlett's peaceful vision of America with the convulsions in Europe going on at the time. While the "incidental destruction of industries and antiquities" took place in Europe, Bartlett's pediment called attention to "a figure of Peace protecting Genius on the front of its Capitol—now, when the rest of the world is engaged in war."[37]

The phrase "apotheosis of democracy" may be taken as a shorthand expression of the central mythology of the United States, that democracy, like a goddess, would eventually triumph everywhere, and it was the duty of the United States to ensure this final victory. The Founding Fathers had certainly believed in the nation's unique destiny, even melodramatically insisting that if we failed there might not be another chance. And yet for them the mission was to provide a *model* for emulation while avoiding entangling alliances. They would have been astonished at a later America's willingness to *impose* democracy by force of arms. They would have also been shocked at the way Christianity had become embedded in the mission. In 1885 the clergyman Josiah Strong had written in *Our Country* that the Anglo-Saxon race was the representative of two great ideas, civil liberty and "*spiritual Christianity.*" He claimed as another characteristic of Anglo-Saxons "an instinct or genius for colonizing." "Does it not look," he asked, "as if God were not only preparing in our Anglo-Saxon civilization the die with which to stamp the peoples of the earth, but as if he were also massing behind that die the mighty power with which to press it?"[38] Speaker of the House Champ Clark presented a milder expression of this version of history at the dedication of Bartlett's pediment. He ended his speech with a reaffirmation of the mission of the nation, with reference to Bartlett's theme: "Our mission in the world has been to carry government of the people, by the people, and for the people to the ends of the earth as missionaries . . . and we have worked at it faithfully. . . . We here and now finish the Capitol building. May it stand forever as the emblem and symbol of a free people, and may our missionary work never end until all people everywhere are free."[39] Within a short time, under the "evangels of democracy" Woodrow Wilson and his secretary of state William Jennings Bryan, the nation would be fighting in Europe for "democracy" and actively intervening in Mexico, Central America, and the Caribbean. They believed American supremacy was absolutely necessary there, intervening as a "good neighbor rescuing his helpless friends from foreign dangers and internal disorders."[40]

There are many other significant works of art in the Capitol, most of which reaffirm these same themes. Paintings in the House and Senate wings document battles and commemorate important historical events. Emmanuel Leutze's *Westward the Course of Empire Takes Its Way* is a massive work (twenty by thirty feet) hanging in the west stairway of the House wing. It is an epic confirmation of the myth of settling the West, showing a group of pioneers reaching the valley of California bathed in the evening glow of the setting sun. There is a series of nine paintings of Indian life by Seth Eastman, inspired by the same preservationist sentiment that moved George Catlin. Eight show aspects of the "good Indian" life unrelated to Euro-Americans. One resurrects the image of the savage barbarian. Called *Death Whoop*, it shows a brave triumphantly holding up the scalp of a settler he has just killed, the skinned head painfully evident (see Figure 44). The *First Reading of the Emancipation Proclamation*, the only piece of art in the Capitol that addresses the issue of slavery, hangs in the west stairway of the Senate wing.

Each piece of art in the Capitol may be said to present its creator's voice and convey some message. But because each one was either commissioned or accepted by the government, the artists were all to some degree censored. The purpose of much of the art of the Capitol is national self-justification, and with that as a major motivation, it is not difficult to understand why most of its art does not rise above the mediocre. Moreover, since the art program was virtually completed by the late nineteenth century, much of it does not speak to contemporary issues.

In order to explore some of the more recent issues, I here consider some uncensored responses to the Capitol and to the city as a whole, particularly the work of writers and poets. Nineteenth-century authors including Charles Dickens, Anthony Trollope, Mark Twain, Walt Whitman, Henry Adams, Henry James, and others responded chiefly to the aesthetics of the city. Dickens took the "City of Magnificent Distances" and turned it into the "City of Magnificent Intentions." Twain also aimed his sardonic wit at Washington. Satirizing, for example, the pretensions of the city, he described the half-completed Washington Monument towering "out of the mud—sacred soil is the customary term. . . . With a glass you can see the cow-sheds about its base, and the contented sheep nibbling pebbles in the desert solitudes that surround it, and the tired pigs dozing in the holy calm of its protecting shadow." Trollope was generally scornful of Washington. He called the

FIGURE 44 Seth Eastman, *Death Whoop*, painting, Longworth House Office Building. Architect of the Capitol.

Smithsonian building "bastard Gothic." Whitman, in constrast, was captivated by the city, evoking "the White House of future poems, and of dreams and dramas, there in the soft and copious moon—the gorgeous front, in the trees, under the lustrous flooding moon, full of reality, full of illusion—the forms of the trees, leafless, silent, in trunk and myriad-angles of branches under the stars and sky—the White House of the land, and of beauty and night."[41]

Henry Adams described the slow development of the city with mordant wit: "As in 1800 and 1850, so in 1860, the same rude colony was camped in the same forest, with the same unfinished Greek temples for workrooms, and sloughs for roads. . . . Right or wrong, secession was likely to be easy where there was so little to secede from."[42] But Adams was more interested in observing the workings of power in the city from his grand home just across Lafayette Park from the White House. In *The Education of Henry Adams* he remarks that his aunt could not guess "—having lived always in Washington,—how little the sights of Washington had to do with its interest." For Adams, "Washington was the inside track of those in the know, in command." His best friend was John Hay, formerly Lincoln's private secretary and later secretary of state under McKinley and Roosevelt. Yet in his novel *Democracy,* Adams did express a disjunction between the perfection of monumental Washington and the corruption of politics as actually practiced there. Madeline Lee, the book's heroine, moves from New York to Washington. Fascinated with the city's political life, she seeks to plumb its mysterious workings and perhaps make a moral contribution. Her sister, baffled by this interest, writes derisively, "Haven't you got to the heart of the great American mystery yet?" By the end of the novel, Madeline is thoroughly disillusioned and cries out for the unattainable perfection of monumentality: "I want to go to Egypt, democracy has shaken my nerves to pieces. Oh, what a rest it would be to live in the Great Pyramid and look out forever at the pole star."[43]

Henry James spent some time in Washington between longer periods of sojourn in Europe. He saw two faces to the city, the official city of buildings and monuments as a kind of stage prop, merely the backdrop to a city of exciting social intercourse. But there was a dissociation between the two, with the human conversation "overweighted by a single Dome and overaccented by a single Shaft—this loose congregation of values seemed, strangely, a matter disconnected and remote, though remaining in its way portentous and bristling all incoherently at the back of the scene."[44] The social groups he referred to were not the "lower orders." They existed in the rarefied atmosphere of certain Washington social clubs, the most brilliant of which was the "Five of Hearts," whose membership included Henry Adams, John Hay, and prominent geologist Clarence King. So James's other face of Washington was "the quite majestic fact of the city of Conversation pure and simple, and positively of the only specimen, of any such intensity, in the world." At the same time James parodied the snobbery of the "Five of Hearts" in his story "Pandora," where he has Bonnycastle (the Adams character) airily suggesting to his wife, "Hang it, there's only a month left; let us be vulgar and have some fun—let us invite the President."[45] Adam's *Democracy* has the same scornful attitude toward the uncultured president (said to be a composite of Lincoln, Grant, and Hayes).

Twentieth-century writers have been more critical in their impressions of monumental Washington, aiming their comments not so much at aesthetic failures as at the gap between ideological aspiration and reality, questioning the national myth itself. In Willa Cather's novel *The Professor's House* a character describes his feelings toward the Capitol as follows: "I stood for a long time watching the white dome against the flashing blue sky, with a *very religious feeling*" (emphasis added). He has just arrived for his first visit to the city and senses the ancient awe that gave birth to imperial capitals, but soon feels overwhelmed by the oppressive power and regimentation such monumentality implied. As a man from the West he finally cries out, "I wanted nothing but to go back to the mesa and live a free life and breathe free air, and never, never again to see hundreds of little black-coated men pouring out of white buildings."[46] William Carlos Williams, in his poem "It Is a Living Coral," developed a far more negative image of the capital. He calls the "living coral" of the Capitol and the "coral islands" of the capital "agglomerations of skeletons, symbols of the violence that helped to forge the American Republic." The city is like a vast coral reef, which builds its superstructure upon the successive layers of the calcified bodies of the dead creatures beneath.[47]

Elizabeth Bishop, as consultant at the Library of Congress, wrote a poem called "View of the Capitol from the Library of Congress," which conveys the inability of the traditional patriotic symbolism to convey its meaning:

> Moving from left to left, the light
> is heavy on the Dome, and coarse.
> One small lunette turns it aside
> and blankly stares off to the side
> like a big white old wall-eyed horse.

From the window of her office she sees the Air Force band playing a concert on the steps of the Capitol, but her view and hearing are partly obstructed,

"The giant trees stand in between," intervening, their leaves like little flags "feed their limp stripes into the air, and the band's efforts vanish there." All the conventional symbols fail. "The gathered brasses want to go/ *boom—boom.*"[48]

Robert Lowell's "July in Washington" conveys a similar elegiac impression of mid-twentieth-century Washington. He refers to the circles and starburst patterns of the L'Enfant plan, visioning Washington as the center of the world: "The stiff spokes of this wheel / touch the sore spots of the earth. . . . On the circles, green statues ride like South American / liberators above the breeding vegetation."

> The elect, the elected . . . they come here bright as dimes,
> and die dishevelled and soft.
> We cannot name their names, or number their dates—
> circle on circle, like rings on a tree—
> but we wish the river had another shore,
> some further range of delectable mountains, . . .

Lowell had at first supported Roosevelt in World War II; then when the indiscriminate bombing of civilians began he wrote a letter to the president announcing that he would not register for the draft. He was sent to prison. In 1967 Lowell returned to Washington to join with thousands of others in a protest against the Vietnam War. In "The March I" he expresses the same disillusionment with the city:

> Under the too white marmoreal Lincoln Memorial,
> the too tall marmoreal Washington Obelisk,
> gazing into the too long reflecting pool,
> the reddish trees, the withering autumn sky,
> the remorseless, amplified harangues for peace—

It is a poem of depression, the memorial architecture excessive, and even the normally positive colors of autumn transmuted into symbols of negation. Although he shares their antiwar sentiments, he finds the speeches irritating.[49]

Stanley Kunitz's poem on Lincoln describes Washington as the place where the emancipator's dream has been denied.

> Mr. President,
> in this Imperial City
> awash in gossip and power,

where marble eats marble
and your office has been defiled,
I saw piranhas darting
between rose-veined columns,
avid to strip the flesh
from the Republic's bones.
Has no one told you
how the slow blood leaks
from your secret wound?[50]

On the grounds of the Soldiers' Home, where Lincoln and his family so often went to escape Washington's summer heat, black writer Jean Toomer went in the evenings to reflect. In his book *Cane,* considered a masterpiece of the New Negro Renaissance, he describes his experience there. Like Madeline in Henry Adams's *Democracy,* he saw the contrast between the ideal, as represented by the monuments, and the reality of social and political life. He seems to seek an escape from ugly realities in the city by speaking from a vantage point above it: "The ground is high. Washington lies below. Its light spreads like a blush against the darkened sky. Against the soft dusk sky of Washington. And when the wind is from the South, soil of my homeland [he came from Georgia] falls like a fertile shower upon the lean streets of the city." Langston Hughes, a black poet who also lived in Washington for a period, felt the same nostalgia for the South, where, despite Jim Crow realities, there was a human dimension lacking in the capital. The character in "Po' Boy Blues" says

When I was home de
Sunshine seemed like gold.
When I was home de
Sunshine seemed like gold.
Since I came up North de
Whole damn world's turned cold.[51]

As John Dos Passos wrote in 1943 in *The State of the Nation,* Washington was after all "a town of lonely people."

A few years ago I took a group of university students to Washington as part of a course on sacred cities. Afterward, in a class discussion, one black student said of the capital that it had not offered much she could relate to. In the monumental core, perhaps only the Lincoln Memorial would qualify, and that particularly because of its later history. Black poet Rita Dove writes of standing at the Lincoln Memorial and looking toward the Washington monument and the city as a whole:

> A bloodless finger pointing to heaven, you say,
> is surely no more impossible than this city:
> A no-man's land, a capital askew
> a postcard framed by imported blossoms—
> and now this outrageous cue stick
> lying, reflected, on a black table.[52]

Because the reflecting pool is too short to reflect the entire Washington monument, Dove's image of it, without pyramidion, gains credibility. The poet either transmutes the blue to black or sees it at night, but in any case her poem negates the beauty of the postcard view, hers the voice of a black and a woman and thus doubly excluded from the power structure represented by the city.

I began the previous chapter with Chief Seattle's famous observation on whites' disconnection from the place their ancestors are buried. In the same speech, the chief says:

> The very dust under your feet responds more lovingly to our footsteps than to yours, because it is the ashes of our ancestors, and our bare feet are conscious of the sympathetic touch, for the soul is rich with the life of our kindred. . . . When the last Red Man shall have perished, and his memory among white men shall have become a myth, these shores shall swarm with the invisible dead of my tribe. . . . At night when the streets of your cities and villages shall be silent, and you think them deserted, they will throng with the returning hosts that once filled them and still love this beautiful land.[53]

Though these sentiments may seem both romantic and implausible in the context of Euro-American culture, they are straightforward enough in a traditional culture that practices some form of ancestor worship. They simply reiterate the mythic belief that the departed are still present in some real sense near the places where they lived and died. Joy Harjo, contemporary Native American poet, writes in "The Myth of Blackbirds" about her own spiritual awakening to this belief in Washington, D.C.[54] Until very recently, Native Americans had never shared in the justice promised by the myth of America. Harjo explains her disgust with the "terrible symbolism" of the city, describing how it was impossible for her to approach the Bureau of Indian Affairs or the Justice Department without seeing the "red blood streaming under the white marble" of the grand architecture. It is rather, for her, the "city of death," a "city of disturbed relativity."

Harjo's great-great-grandfather was Chief Menawa, who led a Creek revolt that was crushed by Andrew Jackson in 1813. "They have disappeared from the face of the earth," said Jackson of the Creeks, reporting to his superior officer after the battle. The poet knows they have not disappeared, though she is aware that for white culture the Creek myths "are simply lies." She goes to Washington with a lover, also a Native American, and they visit the shores of the Potomac by night: "We fled the drama of lit marble in the capital for a refuge held up by sweet, everlasting earth." There they become aware of the presence of their ancestors, whom Jackson had confidently believed "disappeared from the face of the earth."

> They form us in our deep sleep of exhaustion as we make our way through the world of skewed justice, of songs without singers.

> I embrace these spirits of relatives who always return to the place of beauty, whatever the outcome in the spiral of power.

She experienced the reawakening of her ancestors in this most unlikely setting because they "always return to the place of beauty." As Harjo had explained elsewhere, "I know when I write there is an old Creek within me that often participates." Before the Jamestown plantation, the area around the present site of Washington had been a place of Indian settlement and tribal gathering. A former head of the Map Division of the Library of Congress suggested that President Washington chose the Potomac site for the U.S. capital because "in the early days of Virginia history the great Indian tribe of Algonquins met at stated times in the land located between the Potomac river and its Eastern Branch, just as Congress does now, to make laws and discuss national affairs."[55] Others, more hardheaded, would say that Washington chose the site because he thought he could make a killing by developing the upper Potomac as the water link to the West. The site was in any case important to tribes before the arrival of the Jamestown settlers.[56] It is as good a myth as any of the regnant official accounts, as Harjo was aware. She ends her poem, "thankful to the brutal city . . . to the ancestors who do not forget us in the concrete and paper illusion." She accomplishes what Elizabeth Bishop (quoted in the Introduction) asked of her artist: "out of ruins, you have made creations." She understands the power of poetry and myth: "Hatred can be turned into something else, if you have the right words, the right meanings." Then she adds a kind of explanatory coda, after the poem: "I believe love is the strongest force in this world, though it doesn't often appear to be so at the ragged end of this century. And its appearance in places of drought from lovelessness is always startling."[57]

If a Native American, battered by the iconography of the Capitol and the symbolism of the ceremonial core, can still find hope and affirmation in Washington, then there is no denying the provisional quality of the city's meaning. Harjo's creativity is testimony to the tenaciousness of the mythic imagination. Seen in that light, calling Washington "a myth in stone" may be misleading, since the stuff of its symbols is clearly composed of a more malleable material and always open to new interpretations. What Pauline Maier said of the Declaration of Independence is equally true of the symbolic power of the national capital: its ultimate authority rests "less in law than in the minds and hearts of the people, and its meaning changes as new groups and new causes claim its mantle, constantly reopening the issue of what the nation's 'founding principles' demand."[58] Previously excluded groups may claim it. John Quincy Adams's "Genius of America" points to justice as the key to the nation's future. As an abstract concept, its content is always open to reinterpretation, as are the decisions of its official guardian, the Supreme Court. The Mall, as Jeanne Houck points out, "carried a built-in suggestion that a stage was being provided, . . . a locality for redefinitions." Its spatial logic "created an immense landscape that challenged people to find a place for themselves there."[59] The space must be claimed, as Frederick Douglass did when he said: "It is our national center. It belongs to us, and whether it is mean or majestic, whether arrayed in glory or covered with shame, we cannot but share its character and its destiny."[60]

Notes

INTRODUCTION

1. Quoted in H. Paul Caemmerer, *The Life of Pierre Charles L'Enfant* (Washington, D.C.: National Republic, 1950; reprint, New York: Da Capo Press, 1970), 128.

2. John W. Reps, *Washington on View: The Nation's Capital since 1790* (Chapel Hill: University of North Carolina Press, 1991), 20.

3. Ibid., 60.

4. The story of the selection of the site for the capital is well documented in Kenneth R. Bowling, *The Creation of Washington, D.C.: The Idea and Location of the American Capital* (Fairfax, Va.: George Mason University Press, 1991).

5. *Universal Asylum and Columbian Magazine,* March 1792. Meridional line means the line drawn south from the polestar perpendicular to the east-west line of the sun's path. This surveyor's method reflects archaic patterns of determining directions and establishing a capital's centrality. It was used in the building of royal cities in many ancient cultures.

6. Fred J. Maroon, *The United States Capitol* (New York: Steward, Tabori and Chang, 1993), 43. The quotation has been repeated countless times, but historians have tried in vain to verify it.

7. Lynda Lasswell Crist, ed., *The Papers of Jefferson Davis* (Baton Rouge: Louisiana State University Press, 1989), 6:6–7; William C. Davis, *Jefferson Davis: The Man and His Hour* (New York: HarperCollins, 1991), 237.

8. Letters to Meigs of March 18, 1856, and October 18, 1855, Records of the Architect of the Capitol, Washington, D.C., Curator's Office.

9. Kirk Savage, *Standing Soldiers, Kneeling Slaves: Race, War, and Monument in Nineteenth-Century America* (Princeton, N.J.: Princeton University Press, 1997), 116, 31.

10. Glenn Brown, *History of the United States Capitol* (Washington, D.C.: Senate Document no. 60, 56th Congress, 1st session, U.S. Government Printing Office, 1900, 1903; reprint, New York: Da Capo Press, 1970), 2:138.

11. Victor Turner and Edith Turner, *Image and Pilgrimage in Christian Culture: Anthropological Perspectives* (New York: Columbia University Press, 1978), 106.

12. On civil religion as the state religion of the United States, see Robert Bellah,

"Civil Religion in America," *Daedalus* 96 (Winter 1967): 1–21. After this seminal article, there was a spate of scholarship on civil religion. R. B. Mathisen reviews the later course of the discussion; see "Twenty Years after Bellah: Whatever Happened to American Civil Religion?," *Sociological Analysis* 50 (1989): 129–46.

13. Quoted in Pamela Scott, *Temple of Liberty: Building the Capitol for a New Nation* (New York: Oxford University Press, 1995), 3.

14. Philip S. Foner, ed., *Basic Writings of Thomas Jefferson* (Garden City, N.Y.: Halcyon House, 1944), 807.

15. Quoted in Caemmerer, *The Life of Pierre Charles L'Enfant*, 134.

16. Lewis Mumford, *The City in History: Its Origins, Its Transformations, and Its Prospects* (New York: Harcourt, Brace and World, 1961), 29–35.

17. Jacquetta Hawkes, *History of Mankind: Cultural and Scientific Development* (New York: New American Library, 1965), 1:47.

18. So fundamental were these concerns in traditional culture and so foreign to contemporary patterns of thought that the historian of religions Mircea Eliade marshaled a whole lexicon of strange classical terms to express them: *omphalos, axis mundi, orientatio, templum, imago mundi, in illo tempore, imitatio dei*; see Mircea Eliade, *Patterns in Comparative Religion*, trans. Rosemary Sheed (Cleveland: World, 1963).

19. Caemmerer, *The Life of Pierre Charles L'Enfant*, 11–24.

20. "Monumental Spaces," in Richard Longstreth, ed., *The Mall in Washington, 1791–1991* (Washington, D.C.: National Gallery of Art, 1991), 25–26.

21. Michael Kammen, *People of Paradox: An Inquiry Concerning the Origins of American Civilization* (Ithaca, N.Y.: Cornell University Press, 1980), 217.

22. Catherine Bell, *Ritual Perspectives and Dimensions* (New York: Oxford University Press, 1997), 130.

23. Lindsay Jones, *Twin City Tales: A Hermeneutical Reassessment of Tula and Chichen Itza* (Niwot, Colo.: University Press of Colorado, 1995), 16. Jones's book is a useful corrective and supplement to the more classic "essentialist" interpretations of cities such as Mircea Eliade and Paul Wheatley. Jones's insistence that architecture must not be studied in isolation, but as a partner in an architectural/ritual event (see 186–200), is amply illustrated by the present book. See especially Chapters 7–8.

24. Social scientists paid little attention to the phenomenon of pilgrimage until Victor Turner began writing about it in the 1970s, especially (with Edith Turner) in *Image and Pilgrimage*. Since then the floodgates have opened, pilgrimage conferences have been held, books and articles written about pilgrimage in general as well as its expression in particular cultures. A corrective to Turner's emphasis on the *communitas* effect of pilgrimage is provided by J. Eade and M. Sallnow in *Contesting the Sacred: The Anthropology of Christian Pilgrimage* (London: Routledge, 1991). Roger Friedland and Richard Hecht have located the meaning of sacred sites not in the experience of community but in political struggles: "Power is written and re-written from and at the center"; see "The Bodies of Nations: A Comparative Study of Religious Violence in Jerusalem and Ayodhya," *History of Religions* 38, no. 2 (November 1998): 149. Two general comparative studies are Alan Morinis, *Sacred*

Journeys: The Anthropology of Pilgrimage (Westport, Conn.: Greenwood Press, 1992); and Simon Coleman and John Elsner, *Pilgrimage: Past and Present in the World Religions* (Cambridge, Mass.: Harvard University Press, 1995). Area studies include the writings of Surender Bhardwaj, Diana Eck, Alan Morinis, and James J. Preston on Hindu pilgrimage traditions; Susan Naquin, Yu Chunfang and Raoul Birnbaum on pilgrimage in China; F. E. Peters has written on pilgrimage in Judaism and Islam. Recent writings in American studies have opened the door to interpreting American sites as laden with sacred values, tending to blur the distinctions between sacred and secular, pilgrimage and tourism. See, for example, works by historians John F. Sears, *Sacred Places: American Tourist Attractions in the Nineteenth Century* (New York: Oxford University Press, 1989), and Edward Linenthal, *Sacred Ground: Americans and Their Battlefields* (Urbana: University of Illinois Press, 1991). As the Turners had said earlier, "a tourist is half a pilgrim, if a pilgrim is half a tourist" (20).

25. Wilbur Zelinsky, *Nation into State: The Shifting Symbolic Foundations of American Nationalism* (Chapel Hill: University of North Carolina Press, 1988), 180.

26. One reviewer of this book called these reflections "fey," a charge to which I plead guilty. I have attempted to create a sense of the strange and a bit of the "magical" in these personal reflections as counterpoint to the potential banality of buildings and structures that have become boring and predictable national icons. As Lindsay Jones points out, citing the authority of Hans Georg Gadamer and Christian Norberg-Schultz, the act of interpretation (hermeneutics) requires disorientation and unpredictability as well as familiarity (Jones, *Twin City Tales,* 206–10). Otherwise Washington's symbolism may be neither appreciated nor understood.

27. Quoted in Joseph Rykwert, *The Idea of a Town: The Anthropology of Urban Form in Rome, Italy and the Ancient World* (Princeton, N.J.: Princeton University Press, 1976), 188.

28. I am taking these characteristics from J. McKim Malville, "Complexity and Self-Organization in Pilgrimage Systems," in *Pilgrimage and Complexity,* a collection of papers presented at the Indira Gandhi National Center for the Arts, New Delhi, January 5–9, 1999.

29. Turner and Turner, *Image and Pilgrimage,* 25. The authors stress the democratic and populist, even anarchical character of pilgrimage, 31–32.

30. Robert Penn Warren, *Brother to Dragons: A Tale in Verse and Voices* (New York: Random House, 1953), xii.

31. Elizabeth Bishop, "Objects and Apparitions," in *The Complete Poems, 1927–1979* (New York: Farrar, Straus and Giroux, 1983), 75.

32. Jones, *Twin City Tales,* 194.

REFLECTIONS: FROM THE CAPITOL TO THE WHITE HOUSE

1. *American Heritage History of the Revolution* (New York: American Heritage / Bonanza Books, 1971), 214–15.

CHAPTER 1. CAPITAL AND CAPITOL

1. Melvin Yazawa, "Republican Expectations: Revolutionary Ideology and the Compromise of 1790," and Kenneth R. Bowling, "A Capital before a Capitol: Republican Visions," in Donald R. Kennon, *A Republic for the Ages: the United States Capitol and the Political Culture of the Early Republic* (Charlottesville: University Press of Virginia, 1999), give a good summary of the contention over the nature of the federal city at the time and the question of whether to have such a city at all. In *The Creation of Washington, D.C.,* Bowling discusses the acrimonious debates over the location of the capital.

2. Reps, *Washington on View,* 16.

3. Edmund Bacon, *The Design of Cities* (New York: Viking Press, 1967), 13.

4. Bowling, *The Creation of Washington, D.C.,* 5.

5. Ibid., 8.

6. Ibid.

7. Ibid., 163–67 and 103. Rush and Adams were both opponents of slavery.

8. The account is taken from Julian P. Boyd et al., eds., *The Papers of Thomas Jefferson,* 27 vols. to date (Princeton, N.J.: Princeton University Press, 1950–), 17: 205–8. Jefferson later gave another account of the same incident in the *Anas* that was much more antagonistic to Hamilton while defensive about his own role in the affair. Scholars do not doubt that the incident occurred. The argument is whether this dinner agreement actually provided the margin of congressional victory for the residence and assumption bills. See Jacob E. Cooke, "The Compromise of 1790," *William and Mary Quarterly,* 3d ser., 27 (1970): 523–45, and the critique by Kenneth R. Bowling, "Dinner at Jefferson's," in the following issue, 3d ser., 28 (1971): 629–48, which includes Cooke's rebuttal.

9. Bowling, *The Creation of Washington, D.C.,* 168 ff.

10. Caemmerer, *The Life of Pierre Charles L'Enfant,* 127–28.

11. Frederick Gutheim, *Worthy of the Nation: The History of Planning for the National Capital* (Washington, D.C.: Smithsonian Institution Press, 1977), 17.

12. Ibid., 146.

13. Ibid., 149.

14. These two quotations are taken from a memoir written to Washington on August 19, 1791, to accompany his "plan" for the city.

15. Mumford, *The City in* History, 403–4.

16. Stanley Elkins and Eric McKitrick, *The Age of Federalism* (New York: Oxford University Press, 1993), 180.

17. Jefferson disliked even the embellishments of Christopher Wren in London and his imitators in America. When the architect for the Capitol, Benjamin Latrobe, proposed a cupola to allow light into the rotunda area, Jefferson objected that it was not found in Greek and Roman architecture but was "an Italian invention . . . one of the degeneracies of modern architecture." Saul Padover, *Thomas Jefferson and the National Capital* (Washington, D.C.: U.S. Government Printing Office, 1946), 387.

18. Lois Craig, *The Federal Presence: Architecture Politics, and Symbols in the United States Government Building* (Cambridge, Mass.: MIT Press, 1978), xv.

19. Gutheim, *Worthy of the Nation,* 13.

20. Joseph Ellis, *American Sphinx* (New York: Alfred A. Knopf, 1997), 173.

21. Quoted in Marc Egnal, *A Mighty Empire: The Origins of the American Revolution* (Ithaca, N.Y.: Cornell University Press, 1988), 337. Scholars have acknowledged the role of the First Great Awakening of the 1740s in creating a sense of community and solidarity in the American community, which included belief in "the providential religious meaning of the American colonies in world history." Robert Bellah and Philip Hammond, *Varieties of Civil Religion* (New York: Harper and Row, 1980), 13.

22. Mary-Jo Kline, ed., *Alexander Hamilton: A Biography in His Own Words* (New York: Newsweek, 1973), 144.

23. Saul Padover, *The Complete Madison: His Basic Writings* (New York: Harper and Row, 1953; Millwood, N.Y.: Kraus Reprint, 1973), 309, 345.

24. Catherine Albanese, *Sons of the Fathers: The Civil Religion of the American Revolution* (Philadelphia: Temple University Press, 1976), 6. Their success in the war, she suggests, had much to do with their having a myth, a story, which the loyalists lacked (14).

25. Ellis, *American Sphinx,* 185.

26. Padover, *Jefferson and the National Capital,* 460–61.

27. Richard S. Patterson and Richardson Dougall, *The Eagle and the Shield: A History of the Great Seal of the United States* (Washington, D.C.: Department of State Publications, 1976), provides a complete history of the background, development, and uses of the Great Seal.

28. It is not certain whether the symbolism was meant to be specifically Masonic. There is no evidence that either William Barton or Charles Thompson, the two most responsible for the final design of the seal, was a Mason. It is more likely that they were using well-established artistic conventions of the time, quite apart from Masonic symbolism. See Patterson and Dougall, *The Eagle and the Shield,* 529–32.

29. Ibid., 84–85.

30. The classical sources of the phrases *annuit coeptis* (Virgil's *Aeneid*) and *novus ordo seclorum* (Virgil's *Eclogue IV*) are discussed in ibid., 88–91.

31. Quoted in Sidney Mead, *The Lively Experiment: The Shaping of Christianity in America* (New York: Harper and Row, 1963), 77.

32. Patterson and Dougall, *The Eagle and the Shield,* 552.

33. Ibid., 402–3. Wallace said, perhaps facetiously, that the Great Seal first seized his attention when he was browsing through a Department of State publication on the subject, and he took the *novus ordo seclorum* to refer to the New Deal!

34. Paul F. Norton, *Latrobe, Jefferson and the National Capitol* (New York: Garland, 1977), 262.

35. Michael Kammen, *Mystic Chords of Memory: The Transformation of Tradition in American Culture* (New York: Alfred A. Knopf, 1991), 165.

36. Quoted in Patterson and Dougall, *The Eagle and the Shield,* 552, 554.

37. John Wilson, *Public Religion in American Culture* (Philadelphia: Temple University Press, 1979), 29.

38. Reprinted in Charles Moore, ed., *Park Improvement Papers* No. 9, Government Printing Office, 1903, 157–66. The author was probably Stephen Hallet, and his essay was very likely influenced by L'Enfant himself. See Pamela Scott, "L'Enfant's Washington Described: The City in the Public Press, 1791–1795," *Washington History* 3, no. 1 (Spring/Summer 1991): 97–111.

39. Clifford Geertz, *Local Knowledge: Further Essays in Interpretive Anthropology* (New York: Basic Books, 1983), 122–23.

40. *The Federalist*, No. XIV, November 30, 1787, in Padover, *The Complete Madison*, 59–60.

41. Matthew Edney, "Cartographic Culture and Nationalism in the Early United States: Benjamin Vaughan and the Choice for a Prime Meridian, 1811," *Journal of Historical Geography* 20, no. 4 (1994): 384.

42. Padover, *Jefferson and the National Capital*, 160.

43. Edney, "Cartographic Culture," 391–92.

44. Gutheim, *Worthy of the Nation*, 18.

45. William V. Cox, ed., *Celebration of the One Hundredth Anniversary of the Establishment of the Seat of Government in the District of Columbia* (Washington, D.C.: Government Printing Office, 1901), 127.

46. "Annual Report of the War Department for the Fiscal Year Ended June 30, 1898"; "Report of the Chief of Engineers, Part 6." The Monument is 370 feet east and 123 feet south of the actual intersection of the two axes.

47. National Capital Planning Commission, *Extending the Legacy: America's Capital for the 21st Century* (Washington, D.C., 1996), 19, clearly states the goal: "The Capitol once again becomes the symbolic center of the city, as L'Enfant intended, with its power radiating outward in all directions."

48. Silvio Bedini, "The Survey of the Federal Territory: Andrew Ellicott and Benjamin Banneker," *Washington History* 3, no. 1 (Spring/Summer 1991): 76–96. See "Boundary Markers of the Nation's Capital: A Proposal for Their Preservation & Protection," A National Capital Planning Commission Bicentennial Report, Washington, D.C., Summer 1976, 8; and Michael G. Shackelford and David R. Doyle, "GPS Resurvey of the D.C. Boundary Stones," *ACSM Bulletin* 126 (June 1990): 29–32, for the current condition of the stones.

49. Ellicott's survey of the entire district is reproduced in Reps, *Washington on View*, 15. Half of Ellicott's perfect square disappeared when the Virginia territory was retroceded to the state in 1846.

50. Reps, *Washington on View*, 60. Bowling, *The Creation of Washington, D.C.*, 231 ff.; Elkins and McKitrick, *The Age of Federalism*, 174 ff. Arnebeck's long book *Through a Fiery Trial: Building Washington 1790–1800* (Lanham, Md.: Madison Books, 1991), describes the long and sordid story of the land speculation.

51. Arnebeck, *Through a Fiery Trial*, 452.

52. Quoted in ibid., 524.

53. Bowling, *The Creation of Washington, D.C.*, 233.

54. Reps, *Washington on View*, 48. The author has collected a large number of comments, both positive and negative, by visitors to the city.

55. Ibid., 66.

56. Ibid., 164, 172.

57. David L. Lewis, *District of Columbia: A Bicentennial History* (New York: W. W. Norton, 1976), 19.

58. Pamela Scott, "'This Vast Empire': The Iconography of the Mall, 1791–1848," in Longstreth, *The Mall*, 39.

59. Quoted on pp. 1–2 of the guide to the Library of Congress exhibition *Temple of Liberty: Building the Capitol for a New Nation,* Madison Gallery, February 24–June 24, 1995.

60. *Washington, D.C.: A Smithsonian Book of the Nation's Capitol* (Washington, D.C.: Smithsonian Books, 1992), 77.

61. Ibid., 29.

62. Reps, *Washington on View*, 20.

63. Ibid.

64. Ibid., 22.

65. Ibid., 20.

66. Constance McLaughlin Green, *Washington: A History of the Capital 1800–1850* (Princeton, N.J.: Princeton University Press, 1976), 5, relates that the original seventeenth-century owner of the land was named "Pope" and that he named his plantation "Rome" and the creek "Tiber."

67. Brown, *History of the United States Capital*, xix.

68. Charles Moore, introduction to ibid., xx.

69. Henry Adams, *History of the United States,* quoted in David Grimsted, "'Conglomerate Rock': The American Nation and Capitol in Its Greatest Work of History," in Kennon, *A Republic for the Ages*, 468.

70. *Temple of Liberty*, 4–5.

71. Ibid., 21.

72. Len Travers, "'In the Greatest Solemn Dignity': the Capitol Cornerstone and Ceremony in the Early Republic," in Kennon, *A Republic for the Ages*, 159. The article is a good summary of the religious dimensions of the Masonic contributions to the capital and Capitol.

73. Ibid., 173–74.

74. Ibid.

75. Norton, *Latrobe*, 27 ff., gives the major problems of the building, as described by Latrobe.

76. Craig, *The Federal Presence*, 41.

77. Ibid., 34.

78. Letter to Nathaniel Ingram, September 1813, quoted in Craig, *The Federal Presence*, 37.

79. Craig, *The Federal Presence*, 31.

80. Alan Gowans, *Styles and Types of North American Architecture: Social Function and Cultural Expression* (New York: HarperCollins, 1992), 85; Zelinsky, *Nation into State*, 211.

81. Quoted in Scott, *Temple of Liberty*, 97.

82. Mead, *The Lively Experiment*, 72, 1–2.

83. Albanese, *Sons of the Fathers*, 128.

84. Paul Wheatley, in *The Pivot of the Four Quarters* (Chicago: Aldine, 1971), describes the cosmic symbolism of ancient Chinese capitals and compares them with similar areas of "primary urban generation," such as Mesopotamia, Egypt, the Indus Valley, Mesoamerica, the central Andes and southwestern Nigeria; Joseph Rykwert, in *The Idea of a Town*, 163–87, extends the analysis to tribal cultures.

85. Wheatley, *The Pivot*, 423–51.

86. Charles H. Long, *Significations* (Philadelphia: Fortress Press, 1986), 99.

87. Yifu Tuan, *Man and Nature*, Commission on College Geography Resource Paper No. 10, Association of American Geographers, Washington, D.C., 1971, 26. On center symbolism, see Mircea Eliade, *The Myth of the Eternal Return, Images and Symbols,* and *Patterns in Comparative Religion.* See discussion in Long, *Significations*, 68–74.

88. Garry Wills, *Inventing America: Jefferson's Declaration of Independence* (Garden City, N.J.: Doubleday, 1978), 129.

89. Geertz, *Local Knowledge*, 124. Emphasis mine.

90. Bernard Bailyn, interviewed in *Humanities* 19, no. 2 (March/April 1998): 23.

91. Joseph Hudnut, *Architecture and the Spirit of Man* (Cambridge, Mass.: Harvard University Press, 1949), 23, 25.

92. I refer here to the critiques of Washington in Elkins and McKitrick, *The Age of Federalism;* and in James M. Banner Jr., "The Capital and the State: Washington, D.C. and the Nature of American Government," in Kennon, *A Republic for the Ages,* 64–86.

93. Alfred Kazin, *A Writer's America: Landscape in Literature* (New York: Alfred A. Knopf, 1988), 193–94.

94. Arnebeck, *Through a Fiery Trial*, 622.

CHAPTER 2. A BALANCING ACT

1. Robert A. Rutland, *James Madison and the Search for Nationhood* (Washington, D.C.: Library of Congress, 1981), 3; Padover, *The Complete Madison,* 8.

2. Ada Louise Huxtable, *Architecture, Anyone?* (Berkeley: University of California Press, 1986), 195–201.

3. Richard B. Morris, *Witnesses at the Creation: Hamilton, Madison, Jay and the Constitution* (New York: Holt, Rinehart and Winston, 1985), 96–97.

4. Jack N. Rakove, *Original Meanings: Politics and Ideas in the Making of the Constitution* (New York: Random Vintage Books, 1997), 336.

5. Padover, *The Complete Madison,* 335.

6. Letter of October 17, 1788, in ibid., 339.

7. Elkins and McKitrick, *The Age of Federalism,* 6–7.

8. Discussion in Long, *Significations,* 98–99.

9. Gerardus Van der Leeuw, *Religion in Essence and Manifestation,* trans. J. E. Turner, 2 vols. (New York: Harper Torchbooks, 1963), 1:23–28. An introduction to the study of religion that makes use of the hermeneutic category is Amanda Porterfield, *The Power of Religion* (New York: Oxford University Press, 1998).

10. Gary Lease, quoted in Ivan Strenski, "Religion, Power, and Final Foucault," *Journal of the American Academy of Religion* 66, no. 2 (Summer 1998): 346.

11. Anthony Giddens, *A Contemporary Critique of Historical Materialism,* Vol. 1: *Power, Property, and the State* (London: Macmillan, 1981), 145–46.

12. See the summaries in Victor (Avigdor) Hurowitz, *I Have Built You an Exalted House: Temple Building in Light of Mesopotamian and Northwest Semitic Writings* (Sheffield, England: JSOT Press, 1992).

13. Herodotus, *The Persian Wars,* trans. George Rawlinson (New York: Modern Library, 1942), 97–98. The God was Marduk, whom Herodotus calls "Zeus Belus."

14. Paul Lampl, *Cities and Planning in the Ancient Near East* (New York: George Braziller, 1968), 18–19, and illustrations 33–36.

15. See Johanna Broda, David Carrasco, and Eduardo Matos Moctezuma, *The Great Temple of Tenochtitlan: Center and Periphery in the Aztec World* (Berkeley: University of California Press, 1987).

16. Lawrence Vale, *Architecture, Power, and National Identity* (New Haven, Conn.: Yale University Press, 1992), 43.

17. The comparison here follows information provided in Jeffrey F. Meyer, "The Eagle and the Dragon: Comparing the Designs of Washington and Beijing," *Washington History* 8, no. 2 (Fall/Winter 1996–97): 4–21. For more complete information on Beijing, see idem, *The Dragons of Tiananmen: Beijing as a Sacred City* (Columbia: University of South Carolina Press, 1991).

18. Arthur Waley, trans., *The Analects of Confucius* (New York: Vintage Books, 1968), 193.

19. Albert Speer, *Inside the Third Reich,* trans. Richard and Clara Winston (New York: Macmillan, 1970), 103.

20. Ibid., 153.

21. Ibid., 158.

22. Quoted in Geoffrey Broadbent, "Neo-Classicism," *Architectural Design* 49, nos. 8–9 (1979): 2.

23. Huxtable, *Architecture, Anyone?,* 292.

24. In Carol M. Highsmith and Ted Landphair, *Pennsylvania Avenue: America's Main Street* (Washington, D.C.: American Institute of Architects Press, 1988), 8–9.

25. Padover, *The Complete Madison,* 86.

26. William G. McLoughlin, "The Role of Religion in the Revolution: Liberty of Conscience and Cultural Cohesion in the New Nation," in Stephen G. Kurtz and James H. Hutson, *Essays on the American Revolution* (Chapel Hill: University of North Carolina Press, 1973), 199–200.

27. Padover, *The Complete Madison,* 348.

28. *National Gazette,* January 19, 1792, quoted in Padover, *The Complete Madison,* 335.

29. Mead, *The Lively Experiment,* 88.

30. Pauline Maier, *American Scripture: Making the Declaration of Independence* (New York: Alfred A. Knopf, 1997), 34.

31. John Ferling, *John Adams: A Life* (Knoxville: University of Tennessee Press, 1992), 36.

32. Elkins and McKitrick, *The Age of Federalism,* 313.

33. Adrienne Koch, *Power, Morals, and the Founding Fathers: Essays in the Interpretation of the American Enlightenment* (Ithaca, N.Y.: Cornell University Press, 1961), 82.

34. Lester J. Cappon, *The Adams-Jefferson Letters: The Complete Correspondence between Thomas Jefferson and Abigail and John Adams,* 2 vols. (Chapel Hill: University of North Carolina Press, 1959), 2:334.

35. Rakove, *Original Meanings,* 248. The best expression of orthodoxy on the separation of powers is in Madison, *Federalist 51.*

36. Robert G. McCloskey, *The American Supreme Court,* 2d ed., rev. Sanford Levinson (Chicago: University of Chicago Press, 1994), 23 ff.

37. Koch, *Power, Morals,* 60.

38. Morris, *Witnesses at the Creation,* 233.

39. Letter to George Washington, in Rakove, *Original Meanings,* 52, 182, 184.

40. Padover, *The Complete Madison,* 13.

41. Cappon, *The Adams-Jefferson Letters,* 2:573.

42. P. Foner, *Basic Writings of Jefferson,* 635.

43. Elkins and McKitrick, *The Age of Federalism,* 536–37.

44. Henry Steele Commager, *Jefferson, Nationalism and the Enlightenment* (New York: George Braziller, 1975), 138, 147.

45. Padover, *The Complete Madison,* 179.

46. Rakove, *Original Meanings,* 279.

47. Michael Kammen, *A Machine That Would Go of Itself: The Constitution in American Culture* (New York: Alfred A. Knopf, 1987), 55, 58.

48. Morris, *Witnesses at the Creation,* 187; Rakove, *Original Meanings,* 5.

49. Rakove, *Original Meanings,* 335–36.

50. James Stirling Young, *The Washington Community, 1800–1828* (New York: Columbia University Press, 1966), xi–xii.

51. Ibid., 3–5.

52. Ibid., 78.

53. See Reps's discussion, *Washington on View,* 7.

54. *Equal Justice under Law: The Supreme Court in American Life* (Washington, D.C.: Foundation of the Federal Bar Association, 1965), 15.

55. See McCloskey, *The American Supreme Court,* on the significance of *Marbury vs. Madison;* Jefferson's letter to William Johnson (Supreme Court justice 1804–34), in P. Foner, *Basic Writings of Jefferson,* 780–81. The Court, in fact, declared no congressional law unconstitutional until the Dred Scott case in 1857.

56. McCloskey, *The American Supreme Court,* 16.

57. *Equal Justice under Law,* 10.

58. McCloskey, *The American Supreme Court,* xi, 8–9.

59. Zelinsky, *Nation into State,* 245.

60. Robert Bellah and Philip Hammond, *Varieties of Civil Religion* (New York: Harper and Row, 1980), 75–76.

61. Scott, *Temple of Liberty,* 48.

62. For a concise summary of the shifting locations of the Court and a description of its final magnificence in the Cass Gilbert Building across from the Capitol, see Pamela Scott and Antoinette J. Lee, *Buildings of the District of Columbia* (New York: Oxford University Press, 1993), 123–24, 138–39.

63. Young, *The Washington Community,* 76. See the description in Kammen, *A Machine,* 85.

64. Scott, *Temple of Liberty,* 75.

65. Kammen, *A Machine,* 267.

66. Ibid., 268–69.

67. Arnebeck, *Through a Fiery Trial,* 52, says, "To denote the freedom of the judiciary from political influence," the avenues from Judiciary Square would not run to Capitol or president's house.

68. Quoted in Gutheim, *The Federal City,* 26.

69. William Seale, *The President's House: A History,* 2 vols. (Washington, D.C.: White House Historical Association, 1986), 1:237–38.

70. James Carroll, *An American Requiem: God, My Father, and the War That Came between Us* (Boston: Houghton Mifflin, 1996), 32.

71. Highsmith and Landphair, *Pennsylvania Avenue,* 94 ff.

72. Daniel Boorstin, *Cleopatra's Nose: Essays on the Unexpected* (New York: Random House, 1994), 74.

73. Highsmith and Landphair, *Pennsylvania Avenue,* 88.

74. Zelinsky, *Nation into State,* 78.

75. Seale, *The President's House,* 1:238.

76. Boorstin, *Cleopatra's Nose,* 74.

CHAPTER 3. A "NATIONAL CHURCH" AND ITS HOLY SCRIPTURES

1. Kammen, *A Machine,* 127.

2. Kammen, *People of Paradox,* 176.

3. Jean-Jacques Rousseau, *The Social Contract and Discourses*, trans. G. D. H. Cole (New York: E. P. Dutton, 1950), 139.

4. Mead, *The Lively Experiment*, 64.

5. Isaac Kramnick and Lawrence R. Moore, "Is the U.S. Constitution Godless?" *Chronicle of Higher Education*, March 29, 1996, A68.

6. The scholarship on "civil religion" is immense. Bellah's original article is "Civil Religion in America," *Daedelus* 96 (Winter 1967): 1–21. For summaries of the issue, see George A. Kelly, "Civil Religion," in *Politics and Religious Consciousness in America* (New Brunswick, N.J.: Transaction, 1984); and Robert Nisbet, "Civil Religion," in *Encyclopedia of Religion*, ed. Mircea Eliade (New York: Macmillan, 1987), 3:524–27.

7. J. Paul Williams, *What Americans Believe and How They Worship*, 3d ed. (New York: Harper and Row, 1969), 89.

8. Ernst Cassirer, *The Myth of the State* (New Haven, Conn.: Yale University Press, 1946), 137–39.

9. Quoting Otto von Gierke in Lippmann's *Essays in the Public Philosophy;* see Williams, *What Americans Believe*, 483. Mill's aphorism is quoted on page 10 of the same work.

10. Reps, *Washington on View*, 22.

11. Ibid., 86.

12. Ibid., 86, 98.

13. Douglas E. Evelyn and Paul Dickson, *On the Spot: Pinpointing the Past in Washington, D.C.* (Washington, D.C.: Farragut, 1992), 104.

14. Scott and Lee, *Buildings*, 381.

15. *Guide to Washington Cathedral* (Washington, D.C.: National Cathedral Association, 1983), 5, 8.

16. A brochure, "Washington National Cathedral: 'A Great Church for National Purposes,' " distributed free during the early 1990s, makes this connection explicit: "A Church for the Nation: every president since Theodore Roosevelt has come to Washington National Cathedral; Helen Keller and Woodrow Wilson are buried here, and the Rev. Dr. Martin Luther King Jr. delivered his last Sunday sermon from the Canterbury pulpit."

17. Laura Bergheim, *The Washington Historical Atlas* (Rockville, Md.: Woodbine House, 1992), 221.

18. Ibid., and photo, 21.

19. *Washington: City and Capital:* Federal Writers' Project (Washington, D.C.: U.S. Government Printing Office, 1937), 469. Philip Frohman, chief architect of the cathedral for fifty years, expressed the hope that the cathedral would become "the Westminster Abbey of America"; see *Guide to Washington Cathedral*, 23.

20. Scott and Lee, *Buildings*, 176.

21. Kammen, *People of Paradox*, 217.

22. Quoted in Kammen, *A Machine*, 46.

23. Kammen, *Mystic Chords*, 75; idem, *A Machine*, 72–73.

24. Carl Becker, *The Declaration of Independence: A Study in the History of Political Ideas* (New York: Vintage Books, 1970), 194.

25. Garry Wills's *Inventing America* is an exegesis, phrase by lofty phrase, of the document. Carl Becker has a chapter, "The Literary Qualities of the Declaration," 194–223.

26. Maier, *American Scripture,* 160. The author gives an overview of the Declaration's march from obscurity to canonical status, 154–208. I am following her account.

27. Wills, *Inventing America,* 335.

28. Maier, *American Scripture,* 189.

29. Ibid., 205–6.

30. Carl Van Doren and Carl Carmer, *American Scriptures* (New York: Boni and Gaer, 1946). The quotation is from the Preface.

31. Ibid., 9.

32. Morris, *Witnesses at the Creation,* 188.

33. Philip S. Foner, ed., *The Complete Writings of Thomas Paine,* 2 vols. (New York: The Citadel Press, 1945), 396, 398.

34. Kammen, *A Machine,* 340 ff., describes this and other such surveys.

35. In a feature article for the *New Yorker,* quoted in Kammen, *A Machine,* 224.

36. Saul K. Padover, *The Washington Papers: Basic Selections from the Public and Private Writings of George Washington* (New York: Harper and Brothers, 1955), 232.

37. Egnal, *A Mighty Empire,* 333.

38. Letter to Lafayette, in Padover, *The Washington Papers,* 243; Farewell Address, 311.

39. Kammen, *A Machine,* 45, xviii.

40. Foner, *Basic Writings of Jefferson,* 750–51. Jefferson then goes on to propose his odd theory of generational change every nineteen years. Wills discusses the theory in *Inventing America,* 124 ff.

41. Quoted in Martin E. Marty, *Religion and Republic: The American Circumstance* (Boston: Beacon Press, 1987), 142.

42. Ibid., 33.

43. Quoted in Sidney Mead, "Christendom, Enlightenment and the Revolution," in Gerald Brauer, ed. *Religion and the American Revolution* (Philadelphia: Fortress Press, 1976), 31–32.

44. Marty's views, summarized below, are taken from the chapter "Scripturality: The Bible as Icon in the Republic," in Marty, *Religion and Republic,* 140–65.

45. Ibid., 151.

46. Ibid., 142.

47. His biographer, Francis Russell, quoted in Robert S. Alley, *So Help Me God: Religion and the Presidency, Wilson to Nixon* (Richmond, Va.: John Knox Press, 1972), 45.

48. Dickinson W. Adams, ed. *Jefferson's Extracts from the Gospels* (Princeton,

N.J.: Princeton University Press, 1983); photocopies of Jefferson's actual texts, 135, 297.

49. Quoted in Kammen, *A Machine,* 38.

50. Ibid., 205–8.

51. Ibid., 254, 308.

52. Kammen, *Mystic Chords,* 573 ff.; and James Gregory Bradsher, "Taking America's Heritage to the People: The Freedom Train Story," *Prologue* 17 (1985): 229–45. Most of the information that follows is taken from these two sources.

53. The others were the Treaty of Paris, the Northwest Ordinance, the Emancipation Proclamation, the Gettysburg Address, and the Tokyo Surrender.

54. Bradsher, "Taking America's Heritage to the People," 240.

55. Ibid., 244.

56. Albanese, *Sons of the Fathers,* 202.

57. Maier, *American Scripture,* introduction, xii. The phrases quoted are taken from the official statements in the Reports of the Librarian of Congress; see 244 n. 5.

58. Kammen, *A Machine,* illustration 20.

59. Maier, *American Scripture,* introduction.

60. Kammen, *A Machine,* 230.

61. David Morgan, *Visual Piety: A History and Theory of Popular Religious Images* (Berkeley: University of California Press, 1998), 11.

CHAPTER 4. THE WHITE HOUSE AND PRESIDENTIAL RELIGION

1. Ferling, *John Adams,* 255.

2. Thomas Hobbes published his translation of Thucydides, according to Robert Kaplan, to demonstrate how democracy, among other factors, was responsible for the decline of Athens. See Robert Kaplan, "Was Democracy Just a Moment?" *Atlantic Monthly,* December 1997, 64.

3. Koch, *Power, Morals,* 99.

4. *Federalist Papers 18–20,* in Padover, *The Complete Madison,* 64–79.

5. Ibid., 62.

6. Cappon, *The Adams-Jefferson Letters,* 1:213.

7. P. Foner, *Basic Writings of Jefferson,* 724.

8. Charles C. Thach Jr., *The Creation of the Presidency, 1775–1789: A Study in Constitutional History* (Baltimore: Johns Hopkins University Press, 1969), 22.

9. P. Foner, *Basic Writings of Jefferson,* 558.

10. Letter of April 16, 1787, in Padover, *The Complete Madison,* 186.

11. Daniel Boorstin, *The Americans: The National Experience* (New York: Vintage Books, 1965), 203.

12. Herbert J. Storing, in Thach, *The Creation of the Presidency,* v.

13. Rakove, *Original Meanings,* 257.

14. Ibid., 101.

15. *The Federalist 48*, in Padover, *The Complete Madison*, 169.

16. P. Foner, *Basic Writings of Jefferson*, 564.

17. Ibid., 564.

18. Thomas E. Cronin, ed. *Inventing the American Presidency* (Lawrence: University of Kansas Press, 1989), 73–74.

19. P. Foner, *Basic Writings of Jefferson*, 578.

20. Thach, *The Creation of the Presidency*, 173, 177.

21. Merrill D. Peterson, *The Jefferson Image in the American Mind* (New York: Oxford University Press, 1960), 290–91.

22. Cronin, *Inventing the American Presidency*, 309.

23. Mumford, *The City in History*, 35.

24. Garry Wills, *Cincinnatus: George Washington and the Enlightenment* (Garden City, N.J.: Doubleday, 1984), 129.

25. John A. Schutz and Douglas Adair, eds., *The Spur of Fame: Dialogues of John Adams and Benjamin Rush, 1805–1813* (San Marino, Calif.: Huntington Library, 1966), 60–61.

26. Seale, *The President's House*, 1:5.

27. Ibid.

28. Ferling, *John Adams*, 303.

29. Seale, *The President's House*, 1:7.

30. Ibid., 18.

31. William Ryan and Desmond Guinness, *The White House: An Architectural History* (New York: McGraw-Hill, 1980), 22.

32. Ibid., 9.

33. Seale, *The President's House*, 1:27.

34. Ibid., 33.

35. Ferling, *John Adams*, 303.

36. Young, *The Washington Community*, 45.

37. Ferling, *John Adams*, 170.

38. Ibid., 304.

39. Seale, *The President's House*, 1:85.

40. Young, *The Washington Community*, 169. Jefferson's critique of regal ceremonialism in the previous administrations may be found in his letter, late in life, to Martin Van Buren, in P. Foner, *Basic Writings of Jefferson*, 795 ff.

41. Cronin, *Inventing the American Presidency*, 329.

42. Seale, *The President's House*, 1:103.

43. Padover, *The Complete Madison*, 343.

44. C. Green, *Washington*, 82.

45. Benjamin Perley Poore, *Reminiscences of Sixty Years in the National Metropolis*. 2 vols. (Philadelphia: Hubbard Brothers, 1886), 94.

46. Seale, *The President's House*, 1:222.

47. Young, *The Washington Community*, 187–88; Adams's troubles are

described in Paul C. Nagel, *John Quincy Adams: A Public Life, a Private Life* (New York: Alfred A. Knopf, 1998), 296–323.

48. Young, *The Washington Community,* 216, 248.

49. Robert V. Remini, *Andrew Jackson and the Bank War: A Study in the Growth of Presidential Power* (New York: W. W. Norton, 1967), 177.

50. Ibid.

51. J. Wilson, *Public Religion,* 59–61.

52. The quotations from the inaugurals of Washington through Kennedy are taken from *The Inaugural Addresses of the American Presidents: From Washington to Kennedy,* annotated by Davis Newton Lott (New York: Holt, Rinehart and Winston, 1961). The quotations from the inaugurals of Lyndon B. Johnson through Bill Clinton may be found at www.cc.columbia.edu/acis/bartleby/inaugural/pres57.html.

53. Padover, *The Washington Papers,* 243.

54. Aaron Goldman, "The Word of God: Presidential Inaugural Addresses," *America* 175 (November 16, 1996): 11, lists what he calls "euphemistically strained renditions": Almighty Being, the smiles of heaven, Supreme author of all Good, Power, Divine Being, Beneficent Being, almighty ruler of the Universe, Omnipotence.

55. James H. Smylie, "Providence and Presidents: Types of American Piety in Presidential Inaugurals," *Religion in Life* 35, no. 2 (Spring 1966): 270–82.

56. Deut. 28:1–2, 15 Revised Standard Version.

57. See the inaugural addresses of Herbert Hoover, Franklin Roosevelt, Harry Truman, John F. Kennedy, Lyndon Johnson, Richard Nixon, Jimmy Carter, Ronald Reagan, George Bush, and Bill Clinton.

58. Cronin, *Inventing the American Presidency,* 299.

59. Robert J. Donovan, *The Assassins* (New York: Popular Library, 1964), 107.

60. Don E. Fehrenbacher, *Lincoln in Text and Context: Collected Essays* (Stanford, Calif.: Stanford University Press, 1987), 174.

61. Bell, *Ritual Perspectives,* 130.

CHAPTER 5. THE WASHINGTON MONUMENT

1. Clint W. Ensign, *Inscriptions of a Nation: Collected Quotations from Washington Monuments* (Washington, D.C.: Congressional Quarterly, 1994), 7.

2. Charles F. Bryan Jr., in William M. S. Rasmussen and Robert S. Tilton, *George Washington: The Man behind the Myths* (Charlottesville: University Press of Virginia, 1999), vii.

3. Wills, *Cincinnatus,* xix.

4. Hudnut, *Architecture,* 18.

5. Sigfried Giedion, *The Eternal Present: The Beginnings of Architecture* (Washington, D.C.: Bollingen Pantheon Books, 1964), 345, 379.

6. Marcus Cunliffe, *George Washington: Man and Monument* (Boston: Little, Brown, 1958), 4.

7. Letter to Francis Hopkinson, in Padover, *The Washington Papers,* 85–86.

8. Wendy C. Wick, *George Washington: An American Icon* (Washington, D.C.: Smithsonian Institution Exhibition Service, National Portrait Gallery, 1982), 4.

9. Mark Edward Thistlethwaite, *The Image of George Washington: Studies in Mid-Nineteenth-Century American History Painting* (New York: Garland, 1979), 4.

10. *Washington: City and Capital,* 216.

11. Quoted in Scott, *Temple of Liberty,* 103.

12. William Alfred Bryan, *George Washington in American Literature 1775–1865* (Westport, Conn.: Greenwood Press, 1970), 84.

13. Gustavus A. Eisen, *Portraits of Washington.* 3 vols. (New York: Robert Hamilton and Associates, 1932), 3:759–61. Eisen's three volumes are the standard work on the paintings of Washington.

14. Ibid., 791.

15. Frances Davis Whittemore, *George Washington in Sculpture* (Boston: Marshall Jones, 1933), 24–26.

16. Ibid., 29.

17. Eisen, *Portraits of Washington,* 1:12.

18. Boorstin, *The Americans,* 353. So canonized was the work of Stuart that two other painters, Carl H. Schmolze and J. L. G. Ferris, painted Washington being painted by Gilbert Stuart. Karal Ann Marling, *George Washington Slept Here: Colonial Revivals and American Culture, 1876–1986* (Cambridge, Mass.: Harvard University Press, 1988), 10–11.

19. Quoted in Marcus Cunliffe, *In Search of America: Transatlantic Essays, 1951–1990* (New York: Greenwood Press, 1991), 180.

20. Quoted by Rembrandt Peale, in Eisen, *Portraits of Washington,* 1:312.

21. Ibid., xvii.

22. Ibid., 299.

23. Ibid., 2:410.

24. Ibid., 3:815.

25. Cunliffe, *George Washington,* 189.

26. Ibid., 122.

27. Marling, *George Washington Slept Here,* 9.

28. Eisen, *Portraits of Washington,* 3:902.

29. Peter H. Gibbon, quoted in the *Charlotte Observer,* Sunday, December 7, 1997, C1.

30. Wills, *Cincinnatus,* 96.

31. Padover, *The Washington Papers,* 7.

32. Wills, *Cincinnatus,* 102.

33. Padover, *The Washington Papers,* 391. The title of Paul Longmore's book, *The Invention of George Washington* (Charlottesville: University Press of Virginia, 1999), "calls attention to Washington's conscious and purposeful role in that process [of becoming a myth], his intentional shaping of his public and historic self" (ix).

34. David Gerald Orr, "The Icon in the Time Tunnel," in Ray P. Browne and Marshall Fishwick, *Icons of America* (Bowling Green, Ohio: Popular Press, 1978), 18.

35. George Washington Green, ed., *The Works of Joseph Addison,* 6 vols. (New York: G. P. Putnam, 1854), 1:399–400.

36. Letter to Colonel Lewis Nicola, in Padover, *The Washington Papers,* 194.

37. See G. W. Green, *Cato,* in *The Works of Joseph Addison,* 423. My emphasis.

38. Wills, *Cincinnatus,* xix–xx.

39. Thistlethwaite, *The Image of George Washington,* 84, 102.

40. Bryan, *George Washington,* 10, 13.

41. Howard N. Rabinowitz, "George Washington as Icon, 1865–1900," in Browne and Fishwick, *Icons of America,* 70.

42. Bryan, *George Washington,* 58, 85, 62.

43. Cunliffe, *George Washington,* xxxix.

44. Bryan, *George Washington,* 73; Rufus Griswold, quoted on 118. It seems that Washington's actual relations with his mother were neither very warm nor frequent; Rasmussen and Tilton, *George Washington,* 181–84.

45. Senator George F. Hoar, at a speech in Washington, November 1900, in Cox, *Celebration,* 127.

46. Mason L. Weems, *The Life of Washington,* ed. Marcus Cunliffe (Cambridge, Mass.: Harvard University Press, 1962), 55–57.

47. Whittemore, *George Washington in Sculpture,* 83.

48. Van der Leeuw, *Religion,* 2:654.

49. Wills, *Cincinnatus,* 225.

50. Quoted in John Dillenberger, *The Visual Arts and Christianity in America: The Colonial Period through the Nineteenth Century* (Chico, Calif.: Scholars Press, 1984), 115.

51. Padover, *The Washington Papers,* 213–14.

52. Giedion, *The Eternal Present,* 99.

53. Weems, *The Life of Washington,* 12.

54. Ibid.

55. Ibid., 53.

56. Padover, *The Washington Papers,* 175; See similar expressions on 130, 204, 258. Longmore, 29–33, treats his growing confidence in Providence as the keystone of Washington's religious faith.

57. Marling, *George Washington Slept Here,* 1–8, notes the iconic similarity of the general in prayer at Valley Forge to the many portraits of Christ praying in Gethsemane.

58. Ibid., 42. Later he has the returning British troops acknowledge that "God fought for Washington" (116).

59. Thistlethwaite, *The Image of George Washington,* 71–79.

60. Weems, *The Life of Washington,* 168.

61. Bryan, *George Washington,* 95.

62. Ibid., 145.

63. Ibid., 95.

64. Grant Wood's motivation in doing this painting was entirely sincere. Considering this and similar myths in danger of being lost, "his goal was to help preserve the story in the American imagination." Rasmussen and Tilton, *George Washington*, 14.

65. The history of attempts to build a memorial to Washington may be found in Frederick L. Harvey, *History of the Washington National Monument and Washington National Monument Society* (Washington, D.C.: U.S. Government Printing Office, 1903); and briefly in Scott and Lee, *Buildings*, 100–102.

66. Harvey, *History of the Washington Monument*, 74.

67. For the text of Winthrop's speech, see ibid., 242.

68. Eisen, *Portraits of Washington*, 3:890 ff., gathers thirty-one descriptions of his appearance and character by contemporaries, with emphasis on his physical appearance.

69. Bryan, *George Washington*, 12.

70. P. Foner, *Basic Writings of Jefferson*, 722–24.

71. Padover, *The Washington Papers*, 7–8.

72. Quoted in Bryan, *George Washington*, 169.

73. Peterson, *The Jefferson Image*, 98.

74. Hudnut, *Architecture*, 18–23.

75. Marling, *George Washington Slept Here*, 338. I am shamelessly compressing a wealth of detailed information on the changing reputation of Washington documented in the author's excellent book, especially 56, 118–21, 143, 241, 250ff, 374 ff., 387–88.

CHAPTER 6. THE JEFFERSON MEMORIAL

1. Robert Penn Warren, *Brother to Dragons: A Tale in Verse and Voices* (New York: Random House, 1953), 40.

2. Scott and Lee, *Buildings*, 102.

3. Richard Grey Wilson, "High Noon on the Mall: Modernism versus Traditionalism, 1910–1970," in Longstreth, *The Mall*, 153.

4. Benjamin Silliman, quoted in Dillenberger, *The Visual Arts*, 86.

5. Vincent Scully, *New World Visions of Household Gods and Sacred Places: American Art and the Metropolitan Museum of Art, 1650–1914* (Boston: Little, Brown, 1988), 64.

6. Ibid., 175.

7. Michael Kammen, *A Season of Youth: The American Revolution and Historical Imagination* (New York: Alfred A. Knopf, 1978), 15.

8. Peterson, *The Jefferson Image*, 425.

9. J. W. Cooke, "Jefferson on Liberty," in Frank Shuffelton, ed. *The American*

Enlightenment (Rochester, N.Y.: University of Rochester Press, 1993), 281, discusses the remarkably consistent but shifting emphasis on freedom in Jefferson's thought.

10. Catherine L. Albanese, *Nature Religion in America: From the Algonkian Indians to the New Age* (Chicago: University of Chicago Press, 1990), 34.

11. Jeske, in Shuffelton, *The American Enlightenment,* 61.

12. Albanese, *Nature Religion,* 41–43.

13. Wills, *Inventing America,* 202–3, 189.

14. Peterson, *The Jefferson Image,* 166.

15. *The Age of Reason,* in P. Foner, *The Complete Writings of Thomas Paine,* 2:482.

16. Commager, *Jefferson,* 83.

17. Charles A. Miller, *Jefferson and Nature: An Interpretation* (Baltimore: Johns Hopkins University Press, 1988), 7.

18. Basil Willey, *The Eighteenth Century Background: Studies on the Idea of Nature in the Thought of the Period* (New York: Columbia University Press, 1961), 2. As Willey points out, the idea of a *controlling* law of nature had been common in the Middle Ages, but by the seventeenth and eighteenth centuries it had ceased to be a *regulating* principle and became mainly a *liberating* principle.

19. "Travel Journals," in P. Foner, *Basic Writings of Jefferson,* 242 ff.

20. Dillenberger, *The Visual Arts,* 86.

21. See also Miller, *Jefferson and Nature,* 114, 63.

22. Peterson, *The Jefferson Image,* 446.

23. Miller, *Jefferson and Nature,* 251.

24. Plato, *Phaedrus* 275d; Aristotle, *De Anima* 432a.17; quoted in Margaret R. Miles, *Image as Insight: Visual Understanding in Western Christianity and Secular Culture* (Boston: Beacon Press, 1985), 140, 190.

25. Quoted in Miles, *Image as Insight,* 49, 66.

26. Ibid., 95, 104. Miles summarizes the movement against images, and the Roman Catholic reaction, 95–125.

27. Dillenberger, *The Visual Arts,* 16, maintains that the bias against art was rooted in cultural as well as religious attitudes: "English life and religion, Puritan and Non-Puritan alike, reflect a literary predilection, and art is either not on the horizon of consciousness or is accorded a secondary role."

28. Ibid., 12.

29. Quoted in Kenneth Clark, *Civilization: A Personal View* (New York: Harper and Row, 1969), 1.

30. Wilson, "High Noon," in Longstreth, *The Mall,* 156.

31. Letter of September 12, 1821, in Cappon, *The Adams-Jefferson Letters,* 2:575.

32. Boorstin, *The Americans,* 41–53.

33. Cappon, *The Adams-Jefferson Letters,* 1:72.

34. Peterson, *The Jefferson Image,* 84.

35. William H. Pierson, Jr. *The Colonial and Neoclassical Styles* (New York: Oxford University Press, 1970), 295.

36. Ibid., 295, 297.

37. Ibid., 296.

38. Ibid., 339.

39. Hudnut, *Architecture*, 51. Robert Penn Warren, in *Brothers to Dragons*, has his own persona reply to Jefferson's enthusiastic praise of the building: "I call it cold and too obviously mathematical" (40).

40. Ibid., 286; On Jefferson as the father of American architecture, see Peterson, *The Jefferson Image*, 395 ff. Jefferson's influence on the Capitol is documented in the Stillman and Brownell articles in Kennon, *A Republic*, 271, 401.

41. Broadbent, "Neo-Classician," 5.

42. Pierson, *The Colonial and Neoclassical Styles*, 209.

43. Boorstin, *The Americans*, 204.

44. Commager, *Jefferson*, 118.

45. Boorstin, *The Americans*, 237.

46. Mircea Eliade, *Myth and Reality* (New York: Harper Torchbooks, 1963), 21 ff.

47. Kammen, *A Season of Youth*, 51.

48. Boorstin, *The Americans*, 238.

49. P. Foner, *The Complete Writings of Thomas Paine*, 1:5. This and the following quotations from Paine are all taken from this edition.

50. Ibid., 29.

51. Ibid., 44.

52. Ibid., 231.

53. Ibid., 464.

54. Ibid., 482.

55. Ibid., 495.

56. P. Foner, *Basic Writings of Jefferson*, 788.

57. The summary that follows is based on Peterson, *The Jefferson Image*, 229 ff.

58. Paul C. Nagel, *John Quincy Adams: A Public Life, a Private Life* (New York: Alfred A. Knopf, 1998), 312; Peterson, *The Jefferson Image*, 5–6.

59. Peterson, *The Jefferson Image*, 223.

60. F. S. Oliver, quoted in ibid., 339. Oliver was a British biographer of Alexander Hamilton.

61. Ellis, *American Sphinx*, 8–10, 109.

62. Peterson, *The Jefferson Image*, 9–10. Peterson discusses here what freedom may have meant for Jefferson.

63. Ibid., 426, 429.

64. Report of the Thomas Jefferson Memorial Commission, Washington, D.C., June 1, 1939, 4.

65. The mangling of this quotation occurred mostly because only 325 letters could be used on each panel, but also because FDR wanted the last line of the document included (which ironically was appended not by Jefferson but by Richard Henry Lee or an unknown member of Congress between July 2 and July 4, 1776). See Maier, *American Scripture*, 209–11.

66. "Jefferson's Will," in P. Foner, *Basic Writings of Jefferson*, 808–10.

67. Ibid., 160; Patrick Henry, who also had slaves, was just as eloquent an opponent of slavery, calling it "as repugnant to humanity as it is inconsistent with the Bible and destructive of liberty." James W. Loewen, *Lies My Teacher Told Me* (New York: New Press, 1995), 139.

68. P. Foner, *Basic Writings of Jefferson*, 239.

69. Ibid., 144–46.

70. Ibid., 601.

71. Ibid., 682. All such Jeffersonian musings seem especially ironic in view of the evidence uncovered by the DNA sleuths, which has convinced most scholars that Jefferson fathered at least one of his slave Sally Hemings's children.

72. Elkins and McKitrick, *The Age of Federalism*, 205; Kammen, *A Season of Youth*, 94.

73. Elkins and McKitrick, *The Age of Federalism*, 205.

74. P. Foner, *Basic Writings of Jefferson*, 543.

75. Ibid., 239.

CHAPTER 7. MEMENTO MORI

1. R. David Arkush and Leo O. Lee, *Land without Ghosts: Chinese Impressions of America from the Mid-Nineteenth Century to the Present* (Berkeley: University of California Press, 1989), 177-80.

2. Taken from the earliest version, recorded by Dr. Henry Smith, quoted in Rudolf Kaiser, "Chief Seattle's Speech(es): American Origins and European Reception," in Brian Swann and Arnold Krupat, eds. *Recovering the Word: Essays on Native American Literature* (Berkeley: University of California Press, 1987), 518-21.

3. Zelinsky, *Nation into State*, 95.

4. *The Inaugural Addresses*, 110-11.

5. Garry Wills, *Certain Trumpets: The Call of Leaders* (New York: Simon and Schuster, 1994), 50.

6. Seale, *The President's House*, 1:358.

7. David Donald, *Lincoln Reconsidered: Essays on the Civil War Era* (New York: Random Vintage Books, 1961), 61-62, 74; and Cunliffe, *In Search of America*, 188.

8. Merrill Peterson, *Lincoln in American Memory* (New York: Oxford University Press, 1994), 10.

9. Donald, *Lincoln Reconsidered*, 128.

10. Ibid., 60.

11. Christopher Alexander Thomas, *The Lincoln Memorial and Its Architect Henry Bacon (1866-1924)* (Ph.D. dissertation, Yale University, 1990), 289.

12. Merrill D. Peterson, in James M. McPherson, ed., *"We Cannot Escape History": Lincoln and the Last Best Hope of Earth* (Urbana: University of Illinois Press, 1995), 158.

13. Quoted in Philip Shaw Paludan, *The Presidency of Abraham Lincoln* (Lawrence: University of Kansas Press, 1994), 365.

14. McPherson, *"We Cannot Escape History,"* 2-3.

15. Ibid., 5-6.

16. Edmund Wilson, *Eight Essays* (Garden City, N.J.: Doubleday Anchor Books, 1954), 196.

17. William J. Wolf, *The Religion of Abraham Lincoln* (New York: Seabury Press, 1963), 115.

18. E. Wilson, *Eight Essays,* 189.

19. See Elizabeth Bishop's poem in the introduction to this book.

20. Garry Wills, *Lincoln at Gettysburg: The Words That Remade America* (New York: Simon and Schuster, 1992), 38.

21. Peterson, *Lincoln,* 396.

22. Wolf, *The Religion of Abraham Lincoln,* 24-25.

23. Zelinsky, *Nation into State,* 241; Stephens quoted in J. Wilson, *Public Religion,* 197. In Gore Vidal's engaging historical novel *Lincoln* (New York: Ballantine Books, 1984), Lincoln's secretary John Hay reflects that "few men could fathom Lincoln's passion for the Union, which had become, for him, the ultimate emblem of all earthly if not heavenly divinity" (449).

24. Smylie, *Providence and Presidents,* 271.

25. Ibid., 134.

26. Paludan, *The Presidency,* 262.

27. Wills, *Certain Trumpets,* 48.

28. In Frederick Douglass, *Narrative of the Life of Frederick Douglass* (1845; N.Y.: Dover reprint, 1995), xiii.

29. Philip B. Kunhardt Jr. et al., *Lincoln: An Illustrated Biography* (New York: Alfred A. Knopf, 1992), 235.

30. Linda Kerber, "The Revolutionary Generation: Ideology, Politics, and Culture in the Early Republic," in Eric Foner, *The New American History* (Philadelphia: Temple University Press, 1997), 45.

31. Wills, *Lincoln,* 88.

32. Donald, *Lincoln Reconsidered,* 231; see also Wills, *Lincoln,* 89.

33. Wills, *Lincoln,* 101.

34. Peterson, *Lincoln,* 29.

35. Wills, *Lincoln,* 38, 146-47.

36. Peterson, *Lincoln,* 372.

37. The first two quotations in this paragraph are from Don E. Fehrenbacher, *Lincoln in Text and Context: Collected Essays* (Stanford, Calif.: Stanford University Press, 1987), 210-11 and 286.

38. Wills, *Lincoln,* 89.

39. John Hope Franklin, *The Emancipation Proclamation* (New York: Doubleday, 1963), 154.

40. Kunhardt et al., *Lincoln,* 239.

41. *The Inaugural Addresses,* 126.

42. Smylie, *Providence and Presidents,* 277.

43. Paludan, *The Presidency,* 25.

44. Wolf, *The Religion of Abraham Lincoln,* 162-64.

45. P. Foner, *Basic Writings of Jefferson,* 161.

46. Fehrenbacher, *Lincoln,* 96.

47. Peterson, *Lincoln,* 187.

48. Houck, "Written in Stone," 151.

49. Peterson, *Lincoln,* 277-78.

50. Ibid., 253. Peterson's book is a detailed treatment of the reputation of Lincoln from his death to the late twentieth century.

51. Ibid., 255; see also Fehrenbacher, *Lincoln,* 97.

52. Peterson, *Lincoln,* 60.

53. Freedman Henry Morris Murray, *Emancipation and the Freed in American Sculpture* (Washington, D.C.: Published by the author, 1916), 28. The checkered history of the effort to build the Freedman's Memorial, with all its ironies, complexities, and contradictions, is told in an illuminating chapter by Kirk Savage in *Standing Soldiers,* 89-128.

54. Thomas, *The Lincoln Memorial,* 360, 334.

55. Public Law No. 346, quoted in ibid., 679.

56. Thomas, *The Lincoln Memorial,* 155.

57. Ibid., 371.

58. Houck, "Written in Stone," 176–97 passim.

59. E. Foner, *The New American History,* 102-3.

60. Thomas, *The Lincoln Memorial,* 535 ff.

61. Scott and Lee, *Buildings,* 103-4. Bacon's own account of the memorial is in Edward F. Concklin, *The Lincoln Memorial, Washington* (Washington, D.C.: U.S. Government Printing Office, 1927), 40-43.

62. In the *New York Tribune,* January 7, 1912, cited in Thomas, *The Lincoln Memorial,* 477.

63. Quoted in Houck, "Written in Stone," 159.

64. Thomas, *The Lincoln Memorial,* 497.

65. Ibid., 515.

66. Ibid., 624.

67. *Washington: City and Capital,* 334.

68. Thomas, *The Lincoln Memorial,* 649-51.

69. Washington critic Elbert Peets takes the opposite point of view. He asserted in 1925 that most visitors glance at the statue and then immediately read the texts. See ibid., 655. Perhaps his view is a reflection of a pre-McLuhanesque period.

70. The texts from the dedication may be found in Concklin, *The Lincoln Memorial,* 75 ff.

71. Ibid.

72. "The Politics of Memory: Black Emancipation and the Civil War Monu-

ment," in John R. Gillis, ed., *Commemorations: The Politics of National Identity* (Princeton, N.J.: Princeton University Press, 1994), 127-49.

73. Quoted in Thomas, *The Lincoln Memorial*, 652.

74. Kirk Savage, "Politics of Memory," in Gillis, *Commemorations*, 143.

75. Jones, *Twin City Tales*, 16.

76. Ralph Ellison, *Juneteenth*, ed. John Callahan (New York: Random House, 1999), 9.

77. "Play (or conversation) is, thus, the most adequate metaphor for the interactive relationship between the pilgrim and the pyramid." This "conversation" is a "ritual-architectural event" that determines the meaning of built forms, rather than some a priori significance imparted by the original builder. Jones, *Twin City Tales*, 194-96.

78. Houck, "Written in Stone," 364.

79. www.billslater.com/mlkdream.htm.

80. For this sequence of events at the Lincoln Memorial, I follow the account in Peterson, *Lincoln*, 351-56.

81. See a poll published in *The Journal of American History* 81, no. 3 (December 1994): 1210. When asked, "What person in American history do you most admire?," 226 respondents chose Lincoln; Jefferson came in second, with 95 votes.

82. Historian Eric Foner tells of writing a letter of complaint to Disney Inc. over this omission, whereupon the corporation invited him to write a more appropriate speech for the display. *New Yorker*, May 10, 1999, 36.

83. Peterson, *Lincoln*, 380.

CHAPTER 8. THE CHANGING MEANING OF THE NATIONAL MALL

1. See the speeches of Representative Sereno E. Payne and Senator John W. Daniel, 1900, on the occasion of the Washington centennial celebration. Cox, *Celebration*, 115, 123.

2. Paul Zucker, ed., *New Architecture and City Planning* (New York: Philosophical Library, 1944; reprint, Freeport, N.Y.: Books for Libraries Press), 577.

3. Savage, *Standing Soldiers*, 8.

4. Longstreth, *The Mall*, 14. This collection of essays, celebrating the 200th anniversary of the Mall, is the best source of information on the development of the area.

5. Scott, "'This Vast Empire': The Iconography of the Mall, 1791–1848," in Longstreth, *The Mall*, 40.

6. Ibid., 40.

7. Young, *The Washington Community*, 75.

8. Therese O'Malley, "'A Public Museum of Trees': Mid-Nineteenth Century Plans for the Mall," in Longstreth, *The Mall*, 61.

9. Reps, *Washington on View*, 122.

10. Ibid., 70.

11. Ibid., 67.

12. Ibid., 72.

13. Houck, "Written in Stone," 8–9.

14. Ibid., 74.

15. Thomas Huxley, "On the Educational Value of Natural History Sciences," in *Science and Education: Essays* (New York: D. Appleton, 1894), 63.

16. Kathryn Fanning, "American Temples: Presidential Memorials of the American Renaissance" (Ph.D. dissertation, University of Virginia, 1996), 111.

17. Thomas Hines, "The Imperial Mall: The City Beautiful Movement and the Washington Plan of 1901–1902," in Longstreth, *The Mall*, 86.

18. Ibid., 87–88.

19. Gutheim, *Worthy of the Nation*, 97–98.

20. Evenson, "Monumental Spaces," in Longstreth, *The Mall*, 33.

21. Howard Gillette, review of the National Building Museum exhibit "Washington: Symbol and City," *Journal of American History* (June 1992): 210.

22. *Washington: City and Capital*, 103–4; Hines, "The Imperial Mall," in Longstreth, *The Mall*, 96. Senator Albert Beveridge defended the annexation of the Philippines on January 9, 1900: "We will not renounce our part in the mission of the race, trustee, under God, of the civilization of the world. . . . He has made us adepts in government that we may administer government among savage and senile peoples. . . . And of all our race, He has marked the American people as His chosen Nation to finally lead in the regeneration of the world." (Mead, *The Lively Experiment*, 153–54.)

23. David C. Streatfield, "The Olmsteds and the Landscape of the Mall," in Longstreth, *The Mall*, 122.

24. Charles V. LaFontaine, "God and Nation in Selected U.S. Presidential Addresses, 1789–1945," Part 2, *Journal of Church and State* 18 (August 1976): 512.

25. Reps, *Monumental Washington*, 109.

26. Miller, *Jefferson and Nature*, 116.

27. Frederick Gutheim, *The Federal City: Plans and Realities* (Washington, D.C.: Smithsonian Institution Press, 1976), 88.

28. Streatfield, "The Olmsteds," in Longstreth, *The Mall*, 136.

29. Reps, *Washington on View*, 246.

30. Haki R. Madhubuti and Maulana Karenga, eds., *Million Man March / Day of Absence: A Commemorative Anthology* (Chicago: Third World Press, 1996), 10–11.

31. *Historical Atlas of the United States* (Washington, D.C.: National Geographic Society, 1988), 235. The survey considered only those with twenty or more participants.

32. Boorstin, *Cleopatra's Nose*, 100.

33. Reps, *Washington on View*, 98.

34. Amy Henderson and Adrienne L. Kaeppler, *Exhibiting Dilemmas: Issues of*

Representation at the Smithsonian (Washington, D.C.: Smithsonian Institution Press, 1997), 1–3.

35. Mike Wallace, *Mickey Mouse History and Other Essays on American Memory* (Philadelphia: Temple University Press, 1996), 116.

36. Henderson and Kaeppler, *Exhibiting Dilemmas*, 2.

37. Edward Linenthal, "Anatomy of a Controversy," in Edward Linenthal and Tom Engelhardt, eds., *History Wars: The Enola Gay and Other Battles for the American Past* (New York: Henry Holt, 1996), 22.

38. Lonnie Bunch, "Museums in an Age of Uncertainty," *Museum News* (March/April 1995): 33.

39. Wallace, *Mickey Mouse History*, 149–50.

40. Ibid., 117 ff.

41. He was speaking of the Enola Gay exhibit, about which I go into more detail in the following text, but the same principle applies.

42. William Truettner, "Ideology and Image: Justifying Westward Expansion," in William Truettner, ed. *The West as America: Reinterpreting Images of the Frontier* (Washington, D.C.: Smithsonian Institution Press, 1991), 41.

43. Andrew Gulliford, review of the "The West as America" exhibit in *Journal of American History* 79 (June 1992): 200. I recommend this review as a balanced summary of the exhibit.

44. "Review and Outlook," *Wall Street Journal,* August 29, 1994, A10.

45. *Newsweek,* June 17, 1991, p. 79. A positive review in *Nation* then took Boorstin to task for saying in his book *The Americans* that the Western ranchers' "great opportunity was to use apparently useless land that belonged to nobody."

46. Robert Hughes, "How the West Was Spun," *Time,* May 13, 1991, 79.

47. Gulliford, Review of "The West," 204–5.

48. Truettner, "Ideology," in Truettner, *The West,* 59–63.

49. The Air Force Association has put together a three-volume documentary history of the controversy, consisting of letters and documents, press releases, media interviews, script analyses, and other material, without comment, although its own point of view is expressed in many letters and articles in the *Air Force Magazine.* I thank the AFA for providing me with these volumes.

50. I. Michael Heyman, letter of Monday, January 30, 1995.

51. Tony Capaccio and Uday Mohan, "Missing the Target: How the Media Mishandled the Smithsonian Enola Gay Controversy," *American Journalism Review* (July–August 1995): 20.

52. Internal memo of July 21, 1994.

53. Charley Reese, *News Chief,* August 24, 1994, 4A.

54. "History Hijacked," *Time,* February 13, 1995, 90.

55. Linenthal and Engelhardt, *History Wars,* 23. My emphasis.

56. Wallace, *Mickey Mouse History,* 125.

57. Marilyn B. Young, "Dangerous History: Vietnam and the 'Good War,'" in Linenthal and Engelhardt, *History Wars,* 200, quoting historian Nathan Huggins.

58. "War and the Smithsonian," *Wall Street Journal,* August 29, 1994, A10; "An Insult to Our Veterans," *World War II Times* 9, no. 5 (August/September 1994): 3; "New Attitudes on Display," *Atlanta Constitution,* May 3, 1994, A4; Bunch, "Museums in an Age of Uncertainty," 34–35.

59. Edward Linenthal, *Preserving Memory: The Struggle to Create America's Holocaust Museum* (New York: Penguin Books, 1995), describes the conceptualization, controversies, and final realization of the Holocaust Museum, located on the southern edge of the Mall. Some of the contentious issues were: Did a museum commemorating a European event belong in America at all, especially at its national center? What was the nature of the Holocaust? Was it a Jewish event or did it extend to other massacred communities—Armenians, Gypsies, Slavs, etc.? Was it essentially a religious event (as writer and Holocaust survivor Elie Wiesel believed), a mystery beyond the ability of a museum to convey, or was it simply historical and therefore secular?

60. "Enola Gay Gives Flight to Debate," *Los Angeles Daily News,* May 8, 1994, U1.

CHAPTER 9. BACK TO THE CAPITOL

1. Poore, *Reminiscences,* 1:46.

2. Vivien Green Fryd, *Art and Empire: The Politics of Ethnicity in the United States Capitol, 1815–1860* (New Haven, Conn.: Yale University Press, 1992), 35. Most of my analysis of the art of the Capitol relies on Fryd's work, together with that of William Truettner, "Prelude to Expansion: Repainting the Past," and Julie Schimmel, "Inventing the Indian," both in Truettner, *The West.*

3. One minor exception is the black face of a small boy at the right edge of *Cornwallis Sues for Cessation of Hostilities under the Flag of Truce,* now in the House members' dining room.

4. Original text given in Wills, *Inventing America,* 74–79.

5. See Kammen, *A Season of Youth,* 194 ff.

6. Maier, *American Scripture,* 29.

7. Fryd, *Art and Empire,* 12.

8. *Art in the United States Capitol,* prepared by the architect of the Capitol under the direction of the Joint Committee on the Library (Washington, D.C.: U.S. Government Printing Office, 1976).

9. Frederika J. Teute, "Roman Matron on the Banks of Tiber Creek: Margaret Bayard Smith and the Politicization of Spheres in the Nation's Capital," in Kennon, *A Republic,* 90–91. Also see Jan Lewis, "Politics and the Ambivalence of the Private Sphere: Women in Early Washington, D.C.," in Kennon, *A Republic,* 122–51.

10. Whether this famous incident happened or not is the subject of some controversy. J. A. Leo Lemay, *Did Pocahontas Save Captain John Smith?* (Athens, Ga.: University of Georgia Press, 1992), believes that it did.

11. Fryd, *Art and Empire*, 6.

12. Francis Jennings, *The Invasion of America: Indians, Colonialism, and the Cant of Conquest* (New York: W. W. Norton, 1975), 22–31. Most deaths resulted from disease. In fairness, it must be said that nineteenth-century Americans probably had little idea of the extent of this tragedy.

13. Padover, *The Washington Papers*, 266–302.

14. Fryd, *Art and Empire*, 34–35.

15. Ibid., 46.

16. Robert Lowell, "Children of Light," *Lord Weary's Castle and the Mills of the Kavanaughs* (Cleveland, Ohio: Meridian Books, 1961), 28.

17. Loewen, *Lies*, 72, 74.

18. Fryd, *Art and Empire*, 58.

19. Alex Nemerov, "Doing the 'Old America,'" in Truettner, *The West*, 303; Fryd, *Art and Empire*, 94–95.

20. Fryd, *Art and Empire*, 99–100.

21. Ibid., 101.

22. Quoted in George C. Hazelton, *The National Capitol: Its Architecture, Art and History* (New York: J. F. Taylor, 1903), 87. My emphasis.

23. Hazelton, *The National Capitol*, 87.

24. Fryd, *Art and Empire*, 112.

25. Craig, *The Federal Presence*, 112.

26. Fryd, *Art and Empire*, 116–19.

27. Patricia Nelson Limerick, *The Legacy of Conquest: The Unbroken Past of the American West* (New York: W. W. Norton, 1987), 188.

28. Ibid., 187.

29. Senator Louis Cass, 1846, quoted in Fryd, *Art and Empire*, 167–68.

30. See "The Persistence of Natives," in Limerick, *The Legacy of Conquest*, 179 ff.

31. Maroon, *The United States Capital*, 69.

32. Limerick, *The Legacy of Conquest*, 190.

33. Fryd, *Art and Empire*, 120.

34. Ibid., 201–2.

35. Thomas P. Somma, *The Apotheosis of Democracy, 1908–1916: The Pediment for the House Wing of the United States Capitol* (Newark: University of Delaware Press, 1995), 21–29, tells the full story of Brown's efforts.

36. Ibid., 96.

37. Ibid., 99.

38. John E. Semonche, ed., *Religion and Law in American History* (Chapel Hill: University of North Carolina Press, 1985), 18–19.

39. Somma, *The Apotheosis*, 100.

40. Ibid.

41. All quoted in Reps, *Washington on View*, 102, 104, 164.

42. Quoted in Craig, *The Federal Presence*, 136.

43. Henry Adams, *Novels, Mont Saint Michel, The Education* (New York: Library of America, 1983), 182.

44. Craig, *The Federal Presence*, 135, 245.

45. Lewis, *District of Columbia*, 96 ff.

46. Willa Cather, *The Professor's House* (New York: Alfred A. Knopf, 1925), 225, 236. See also Lothar Honnighausen and Andreas Falke, eds., *Washington, D.C.: Interdisciplinary Approaches* (Tübingen: A. Franke Verlag, 1993), 201.

47. Christoph Irmscher, "'This City of Disturbed Relativity': Views and Versions of Washington, D.C., from William Carlos Williams to Joy Harjo," in Honnighausen and Falke, *Washington, D.C.*, 170. I am indebted, in the ideas that follow, to the chapters by Honnighausen and Irmscher in this book.

48. Bishop, *The Complete Poems*, 69.

49. For "July in Washington," see Robert Lowell, *"Life Studies" and "For the Union Dead"* (New York: Farrar, Straus and Giroux Noonday Press, 1964), 58; for "The March I," see *Notebook* (New York: Farrar, Straus and Giroux, 1970), 54.

50. Peterson, *Lincoln*, 389.

51. Both authors quoted from D.C. History Curriculum Project's *City of Magnificent Intentions* (Washington, D.C.: Intac, 1983), 368–69.

52. Irmscher, "This City," in Honnighausen and Falke, *Washington, D.C.*, 184.

53. In Swann and Krupat, *Recovering the Word*, 521.

54. In *The Woman Who Fell from the Sky* (New York: W. W. Norton, 1994), 28. I am following the analysis of Christoph Irmscher, in Honnighausen and Falke, *Washington, D.C.*, 186 ff.

55. Philip Lee Phillips, *The Beginnings of Washington as Described in Books, Maps, and Views* (Washington, D.C.: Published for the author, 1917), 8.

56. D.C. History Curriculum Project, *City of Magnificent Intentions*, 5–7.

57. Harjo, "The Myth of Blackbirds," 30–32.

58. Maier, *American Scripture*, 214.

59. Houck, "Written in Stone," 324.

60. D.C. History Curriculum Project, *City of Magnificent Intentions*, 168.

Bibliography

Adams, Dickinson W., ed. *Jefferson's Extracts from the Gospels: "The Philosophy of Jesus" and "The Life and Morals of Jesus."* Princeton, N.J.: Princeton University Press, 1983.

Adams, Henry. *Novels, Mont Saint Michel, The Education.* New York: Library of America, 1983.

Albanese, Catherine L. *Nature Religion in America: From the Algonkian Indians to the New Age.* Chicago: University of Chicago Press, 1990.

———. *Sons of the Fathers: The Civil Religions of the American Revolution.* Philadelphia: Temple University Press, 1976.

Alley, Robert S. *So Help Me God: Religion and the Presidency, Wilson to Nixon.* Richmond, Va.: John Knox Press, 1972.

American Heritage History of the Revolution. New York: American Heritage / Bonanza Books, 1971.

Arkush, R. David, and Leo O. Lee. *Land without Ghosts: Chinese Impressions of America from the Mid-Nineteenth Century to the Present.* Berkeley: University of California Press, 1989.

Arnebeck, Bob. *Through a Fiery Trial: Building Washington, 1790–1800.* Lanham, Md.: Madison Books, 1991.

Art in the United States Capitol. Washington, D.C.: U.S. Government Printing Office, 1976.

Bacon, Edmund N. *The Design of Cities.* New York: Viking Press, 1967.

Becker, Carl. *The Declaration of Independence: A Study in the History of Political Ideas.* New York: Vintage Books, 1970.

Bedini, Silvio. "The Survey of the Federal Territory: Andrew Ellicott and Benjamin Banneker." *Washington History* 3, no. 1 (Spring/Summer 1991): 76–96.

Bell, Catherine. *Ritual Perspectives and Dimensions.* New York: Oxford University Press, 1997.

Bellah, Robert. "Civil Religion in America." *Daedalus* 96 (Winter 1967): 1–21.

Bellah, Robert, and Philip Hammond. *Varieties of Civil Religion.* New York: Harper and Row, 1980.

Bergheim, Laura. *The Washington Historical Atlas.* Rockville, Md.: Woodbine House, 1992.

Bishop, Elizabeth. *The Complete Poems, 1927–1979.* New York: Farrar, Straus and Giroux, 1983.

Boorstin, Daniel. *The Americans: The National Experience*. New York: Vintage Books, 1965.

———. *Cleopatra's Nose: Essays on the Unexpected*. New York: Random House, 1994.

Bowling, Kenneth R. *The Creation of Washington, D.C.: The Idea and Location of the American Capital*. Fairfax, Va.: George Mason University Press, 1991.

———. "Dinner at Jefferson's: A Note on Jacob E. Cooke's 'The Compromise of 1790.'" *William and Mary Quarterly*, 3d ser., 28 (1971): 629–48.

Boyd, Julian P., et al., eds. *The Papers of Thomas Jefferson*. 27 vols. to date. Princeton, N.J.: Princeton University Press, 1950–.

Bradsher, James Gregory. "Taking America's Heritage to the People: The Freedom Train Story." *Prologue* 17 (1985): 229–45.

Brauer, Jerald C., ed. *Religion and the American Revolution*. Philadelphia: Fortress Press, 1976.

Broadbent, Geoffrey, ed. "Neo-Classical." *Architectural Design* 49, nos. 8–9 (1979): 1–72.

Broda, Johanna, David Carrasco, and Eduardo Matos Moctezuma. *The Great Temple of Tenochtitlan: Center and Periphery in the Aztec World*. Berkeley: University of California Press, 1987.

Brown, Glenn. *History of the United States Capital*. 2 vols. Washington, D.C.: U.S. Government Printing Office, 1900, 1903; reprint, New York: Da Capo Press, 1970.

Browne, Ray P., and Marshall Fishwick. *Icons of America*. Bowling Green, Ohio: Popular Press, 1978.

Bryan, William Alfred. *George Washington in American Literature 1775–1865*. Westport, Conn.: Greenwood Press, 1970.

Bunch, Lonnie. "Museums in An Age of Uncertainty." *Museum News* (March/April 1995): 32–35, 58–62.

Caemmerer, H. Paul. *The Life of Pierre Charles L'Enfant*. Washington, D.C.: National Republic, 1950; reprint, New York: Da Capo Press, 1970.

Capaccio, Tony, and Uday Mohan. "Missing the Target: How the Media Mishandled the Smithsonian Enola Gay Controversy." *American Journalism Review* (July–August 1995): 19–26.

Cappon, Lester J. *The Adams-Jefferson Letters: The Complete Correspondence between Thomas Jefferson and Abigail and John Adams*. 2 vols. Chapel Hill: University of North Carolina Press, 1959.

Carroll, James. *An American Requiem: God, My Father, and the War That Came between Us*. Boston: Houghton Mifflin, 1996.

Cassirer, Ernst. *The Myth of the State*. New Haven, Conn.: Yale University Press, 1946.

Cather, Willa. *The Professor's House*. New York: Alfred A. Knopf, 1925.

Clark, Kenneth. *Civilization: A Personal View*. New York: Harper and Row, 1969.

Coleman, Simon, and John Elsner. *Pilgrimage: Past and Present in the World Religions.* Cambridge, Mass.: Harvard University Press, 1995.

Commager, Henry Steele. *Jefferson, Nationalism and the Enlightenment.* New York: George Braziller, 1975.

Comprehensive Plan for the National Capital: Federal Elements. Washington, D.C.: National Capital Planning Commission, 1989.

Concklin, Edward F. *The Lincoln Memorial, Washington.* Washington, D.C.: U.S. Government Printing Office, 1927.

Cooke, Jacob E. "The Compromise of 1790," *William and Mary Quarterly,* 3d ser., 27 (October 1970): 523–45.

Cox, William V., ed. *Celebration of the One Hundredth Anniversary of the Establishment of the Seat of Government in the District of Columbia.* Washington, D.C.: Government Printing Office, 1901.

Craig, Lois. *The Federal Presence: Architecture, Politics, and Symbols in the United States Government Building.* Cambridge, Mass.: MIT Press, 1978.

Crist, Lynda Lasswell, ed. *The Papers of Jefferson Davis.* 10 vols. Baton Rouge: Louisiana State University Press, 1989–.

Cronin, Thomas E., ed. *Inventing the American Presidency.* Lawrence: University of Kansas Press, 1989.

Cunliffe, Marcus. *George Washington: Man and Monument.* Boston: Little, Brown, 1958.

———. *In Search of America: Transatlantic Essays, 1951–1990.* New York: Greenwood Press, 1991.

Davis, William C. *Jefferson Davis: The Man and His Hour.* New York: HarperCollins, 1991.

D.C. History Curriculum Project. *City of Magnificent Intentions: A History of the District of Columbia.* Washington, D.C.: Intac, 1983.

Dillenberger, John. *The Visual Arts and Christianity in America: The Colonial Period Through the Nineteenth Century.* Chico, Calif.: Scholars Press, 1984.

Donald, David. *Lincoln Reconsidered: Essays on the Civil War Era.* New York: Random Vintage Books, 1961.

Donovan, Robert J. *The Assassins.* New York: Popular Library, 1964.

Douglass, Frederick. *Narrative of the Life of Frederick Douglass.* New York: Dover Publications, 1995.

Eade, J., and M. Sallnow. *Contesting the Sacred: The Anthropology of Christian Pilgrimage.* London: Routledge, 1991.

Edney, Matthew H. "Cartographic Culture and Nationalism in the Early United States: Benjamin Vaughan and the Choice for a Prime Meridian, 1811," *Journal of Historical Geography* 20, no. 4 (1994): 384–95.

Egnal, Marc. *A Mighty Empire: The Origins of the American Revolution.* Ithaca, N.Y.: Cornell University Press, 1988.

Eisen, Gustavus A. *Portraits of Washington.* 3 vols. New York: Robert Hamilton and Associates, 1932.

Eliade, Mircea. *Cosmos and History; The Myth of the Eternal Return.* New York: Harper Torchbooks, 1959.

———. *Images and Symbols: Studies in Religious Symbolism.* New York: Sheed and Ward, 1969.

———. *Myth and Reality.* New York: Harper Torchbooks, 1963.

———. *Patterns in Comparative Religion.* Cleveland, Ohio: World, 1963.

Elkins, Stanley, and Eric McKitrick. *The Age of Federalism.* New York: Oxford University Press, 1993.

Ellis, Joseph. *American Sphinx.* New York: Alfred A. Knopf, 1997.

Ellison, Ralph. *Juneteenth.* Ed. John Callahan. New York: Random House, 1999.

Ensign, Clint W. *Inscriptions of a Nation: Collected Quotations from Washington Monuments.* Washington, D.C.: Congressional Quarterly, 1994.

Equal Justice under Law: The Supreme Court in American Life. Washington, D.C.: Foundation of the Federal Bar Association, 1965.

Evelyn, Douglas E., and Paul Dickson. *On the Spot: Pinpointing the Past in Washington, D.C.* Washington, D.C.: Farragut, 1992.

Extending the Legacy: America's Capital for the 21st Century. Washington, D.C.: National Capital Planning Commission, 1996.

Fanning, Kathryn. "American Temples: Presidential Memorials of the American Renaissance." Ph.D. dissertation, University of Virginia, 1996.

Fehrenbacher, Don E. *Lincoln in Text and Context: Collected Essays.* Stanford, Calif.: Stanford University Press, 1987.

Feller, Richard T. *Completing Washington Cathedral: For Thy Greater Glory.* Washington, D.C.: Washington Cathedral, 1989.

Ferling, John. *John Adams: A Life.* Knoxville: University of Tennessee Press, 1992.

Foner, Eric, ed. *The New American History.* Rev. ed. Philadelphia: Temple University Press, 1997.

Foner, Philip S., ed. *Basic Writings of Thomas Jefferson.* Garden City, N.Y.: Halcyon House, 1944.

———. *The Complete Writings of Thomas Paine.* 2 vols. New York: The Citadel Press, 1945.

Franklin, John Hope. *The Emancipation Proclamation.* Garden City, N.Y.: Doubleday, 1963.

Friedland, Roger, and Richard Hecht. "The Bodies of Nations: A Comparative Study of Religious Violence in Jerusalem and Ayodhya," *History of Religions* 38, no. 2 (November 1998): 101–49.

Fryd, Vivien Green. *Art and Empire: The Politics of Ethnicity in the United States Capitol: 1815–1860.* New Haven, Conn.: Yale University Press, 1992.

Geertz, Clifford. *Local Knowledge: Further Essays in Interpretive Anthropology.* New York: Basic Books, 1983.

Giddens, Anthony. *A Contemporary Critique of Historical Materialism.* Vol. 1: *Power, Property, and the State.* London: Macmillan, 1981.

Giedion, Sigfried. *The Eternal Present: The Beginnings of Architecture.* Washington, D.C.: Bollingen Pantheon Books, 1964.

Gillette, Howard. Review of the National Building Museum exhibit "Washington: Symbol and City," *Journal of American History* 79 (June 1992): 209–12.

Gillis, John R., ed. *Commemorations: The Politics of National Identity.* Princeton, N.J.: Princeton University Press, 1994.

Goldman, Aaron. "The Word of God: Presidential Inaugural Addresses," *America* 175, no. 15 (November 16, 1996): 10–14.

Goode, James M. *The Outdoor Sculpture of Washington, D.C.* Washington, D.C.: Smithsonian Institution Press, 1974.

Gowans, Alan. *Styles and Types of North American Architecture: Social Function and Cultural Expression.* New York: HarperCollins, 1992.

Green, Constance McLaughlin. *Washington: A History of the Capital 1800–1850.* Princeton, N.J.: Princeton University Press, 1976.

Green, George Washington, ed. *The Works of Joseph Addison.* 6 vols. New York: G. P. Putnam Company, 1854.

Guide to Washington Cathedral. Washington, D.C.: National Cathedral Association, 1983.

Gulliford, Andrew. Review of "The West as America" exhibit, *Journal of American History* 79 (June 1992): 199–207.

Gutheim, Frederick. *The Federal City: Plans and Realities.* Washington, D.C.: Smithsonian Institution Press, 1976.

————. *Worthy of the Nation: The History of Planning for the National Capital.* Washington, D.C.: Smithsonian Institution Press, 1977.

Harjo, Joy. "The Myth of Blackbirds." In *The Woman Who Fell from the Sky.* New York: W. W. Norton, 1994.

Harvey, Frederick L. *History of the Washington National Monument and Washington National Monument Society.* Washington, D.C.: U.S. Government Printing Office, 1903.

Hawkes, Jacquetta. *History of Mankind: Cultural and Scientific Development.* 2 vols. New York: New American Library, 1965.

Hazelton, George C. *The National Capital: Its Architecture, Art and History.* New York: J. F. Taylor, 1903.

Henderson, Amy, and Adrienne Kaeppler. *Exhibiting Dilemmas: Issues of Representation at the Smithsonian.* Washington, D.C.: Smithsonian Institution Press, 1997.

Herodotus. *The Persian Wars.* Trans. George Rawlinson. New York: Modern Library, 1942.

Highsmith, Carol M., and Ted Landphair. *Pennsylvania Avenue: America's Main Street.* Washington, D.C.: American Institute of Architects Press, 1988.

Historical Atlas of the United States. Washington, D.C.: National Geographic Society, 1988.

Honnighausen, Lothar, and Andreas Falke, eds. *Washington, D.C.: Interdisciplinary Approaches.* Tübingen: A. Franke Verlag, 1993.

Houck, Jeanne B. "Written in Stone: Historical Memory and the Mall in Washington, D.C., 1865–1945." Ph.D. dissertation, New York University, 1993.

Hudnut, Joseph. *Architecture and the Spirit of Man.* Cambridge, Mass.: Harvard University Press, 1949.

Hurowitz, Victor (Avigdor). *I Have Built You an Exalted House: Temple Building in Light of Mesopotamian and Northwest Semitic Writings.* Sheffield, England: JSOT Press, 1992.

Huxley, Thomas. *Science and Education: Essays.* New York: D. Appleton, 1894.

Huxtable, Ada Louise. *Architecture, Anyone?* Berkeley: University of California Press, 1986.

The Inaugural Addresses of the American Presidents: From Washington to Kennedy. Annotated by Davis Newton Lott. New York: Holt, Rinehart and Winston, 1961.

Jennings, Francis. *The Invasion of America: Indians, Colonialism, and the Cant of Conquest.* New York: W. W. Norton, 1975.

Jones, Lindsay. *Twin City Tales: A Hermeneutical Reassessment of Tula and Chichen Itza.* Niwot, Colo.: University Press of Colorado, 1995.

Kammen, Michael. *A Machine That Would Go of Itself: The Constitution in American Culture.* New York: Alfred A. Knopf, 1987.

———. *Mystic Chords of Memory: The Transformation of Tradition in American Culture.* New York: Alfred A. Knopf, 1991.

———. *People of Parodox: An Inquiry Concerning the Origins of American Civilization.* Ithaca, N.Y.: Cornell University Press, 1980.

———. *A Season of Youth: The American Revolution and Historical Imagination.* New York: Alfred A. Knopf, 1978.

Kaplan, Robert D. "Was Democracy Just a Moment?" *Atlantic Monthly,* December 1997.

Kazin, Alfred. *A Writer's America: Landscape in Literature.* New York: Alfred A. Knopf, 1988.

Kelly, George A. "Civil Religion." In *Politics and Religious Consciousness in America.* New Brunswick, N.J.: Transaction, 1984.

Kennon, Donald R., ed. *A Republic for the Ages: The United States Capitol and the Political Culture of the Early Republic.* Charlottesville: University Press of Virginia, 1999.

Klapthor, Margaret Brown, and Howard Alexander Morrison. *George Washington: A Figure upon the Stage.* Washington, D.C.: Smithsonian Institution Press, 1982.

Kline, Mary-Jo, ed. *Alexander Hamilton: A Biography in His Own Words.* New York: Newsweek, 1973.

Koch, Adrienne. *Power, Morals, and the Founding Fathers: Essays in the Interpretation of the American Enlightenment.* Ithaca, N.Y.: Cornell University Press, 1961.

Kohler, Sue A. *The Commission of Fine Arts: A Brief History, 1910–1995.* Washington, D.C.: Commission of Fine Arts, 1996.

Kramnick, Isaac, and Lawrence R. Moore. "Is the Constitution Godless?" *Chronicle of Higher Education,* March 29, 1996, A68.

Kunhardt, Philip B., Jr., Philip B. Kunhardt III, and Peter W. Kunhardt. *Lincoln: An Illustrated Biography*. New York: Alfred A. Knopf, 1992.

Kurtz, Stephen G., and James H. Hutson. *Essays on the American Revolution*. Chapel Hill: University of North Carolina Press, 1973.

LaFontaine, Charles V. "God and Nation in Selected U.S. Presidential Inaugural Addresses, 1789–1945." Part 2. *Journal of Church and State* 18 (August 1976): 503–21.

Lampl, Paul. *Cities and Planning in the Ancient Near East*. New York: George Braziller, 1968.

Lemay, J. A. Leo. *Did Pocahontas Save Captain John Smith?* Athens: University of Georgia Press, 1992.

Lewis, David L. *District of Columbia: A Bicentennial History*. New York: W. W. Norton, 1976.

Limerick, Patricia Nelson. *The Legacy of Conquest: The Unbroken Past of the American West*. New York: W. W. Norton, 1987.

Linenthal, Edward T. *Preserving Memory: The Struggle to Create American's Holocaust Museum*. New York: Penguin Books, 1995.

———. *Sacred Ground: Americans and Their Battlefields*. Urbana: University of Illinois Press, 1991.

Linenthal, Edward T., and Tom Engelhardt, eds. *History Wars: The Enola Gay and Other Battles for the American Past*. New York: Henry Holt, 1996.

Loewen, James W. *Lies My Teacher Told Me*. New York: New Press, 1995.

Long, Charles H. *Significations*. Philadelphia: Fortress Press, 1986.

Longmore, Paul K. *The Invention of George Washington*. Berkeley: University of California Press, 1988.

Longstreth, Richard, ed. *The Mall in Washington, 1791–1991*. Washington, D.C.: National Gallery of Art, 1991.

Lowell, Robert. *"Life Studies" and "For the Union Dead."* New York: Farrar, Straus and Giroux Noonday Press, 1964.

———. *Lord Weary's Castle and the Mills of the Kavanaughs*. Cleveland, Ohio: Meridian Books, 1961.

———. *Notebook*. New York: Farrar, Straus and Giroux, 1970.

Madhubuti, Haki R., and Maulana Karenga, eds. *Million Man March / Day of Absence: A Commemorative Anthology*. Chicago: Third World Press, 1996.

Maier, Pauline. *American Scripture: Making the Declaration of Independence*. New York: Alfred A. Knopf, 1997.

Malville, J. McKim. *Pilgrimage and Complexity*. New Delhi: Indira Gandhi Center for the Arts, 1999.

Marling, Karal Ann. *George Washington Slept Here: Colonial Revivals and American Culture, 1876–1986*. Cambridge, Mass.: Harvard University Press, 1988.

Maroon, Fred J. *The United States Capitol*. Introduction by Daniel J. Boorstin. New York: Stewart, Tabori and Chang, 1993.

Marty, Martin E. *Religion and Republic: The American Circumstance*. Boston: Beacon Press, 1987.

Mathisen, R. B. "Twenty Years after Bellah: Whatever Happened to American Civil Religion?" *Sociological Analysis* 50 (1989): 129–46.

McCloskey, Robert G. *The American Supreme Court.* 2d ed. Rev. Sanford Levinson. Chicago: University of Chicago Press, 1994.

McPherson, James M. *"We Cannot Escape History": Lincoln and the Last Best Hope of Earth.* Urbana: University of Illinois Press, 1995.

Mead, Sidney E. *The Lively Experiment: The Shaping of Christianity in America.* New York: Harper and Row, 1963.

Meyer, Jeffrey F. *The Dragons of Tiananmen: Beijing as a Sacred City.* Columbia: University of South Carolina Press, 1991.

———. "The Eagle and the Dragon: Comparing the Designs of Washington and Beijing." *Washington History* 8, no. 2 (Fall/Winter 1996–97): 4–21.

Miles, Margaret R. *Image as Insight: Visual Understanding in Western Christianity and Secular Culture.* Boston: Beacon Press, 1985.

Miller, Charles A. *Jefferson and Nature: An Interpretation.* Baltimore: Johns Hopkins University Press, 1988.

Moore, Charles, ed. *Park Improvement Papers* No. 9. U.S. Government Printing Office, 1903, 157–166.

Morgan, David. *Visual Piety: A History and Theory of Popular Religious Images.* Berkeley: University of California Press, 1998.

Morinis, Alan. *Sacred Journeys: The Anthropology of Pilgrimage.* Westport, Conn.: Greenwood Press, 1992.

Morris, Richard B. *Witnesses at the Creation: Hamilton, Madison, Jay and the Constitution.* New York: Holt, Rinehart and Winston, 1985.

Mumford, Lewis. *The City in History: Its Origins, Its Transformations, and Its Prospects.* New York: Harcourt, Brace and World, 1961.

Murray, Freedman Henry Morris. *Emancipation and the Freed in American Sculpture.* Washington, D.C.: Published by the Author, 1916.

Nagel, Paul C. *John Quincy Adams: A Public Life, a Private Life.* New York: Alfred A. Knopf, 1998.

Nisbet, Robert. "Civil Religion." In *The Encyclopedia of Religion,* ed. Mircea Eliade. New York: Macmillan, 1987.

Norton, Paul F. *Latrobe, Jefferson and the National Capital.* New York: Garland, 1977.

Padover, Saul K., ed. *The Complete Madison: His Basic Writings.* New York: Harper and Row, 1953; reprint, Millwood, N.Y.: Kraus Reprint, 1973.

———. *Thomas Jefferson and the National Capitol.* Washington, D.C.: U.S. Government Printing Office, 1946.

———. *The Washington Papers: Basic Selections from the Public and Private Writings of George Washington.* New York: Harper and Brothers, 1955.

Paludan, Philip Shaw. *The Presidency of Abraham Lincoln.* Lawrence: University Press of Kansas, 1994.

Patterson, Richard S., and Dougall Richardson. *The Eagle and the Shield: A History of the Great Seal of the United States.* Washington, D.C.: Department of State, 1976.

Peterson, Merrill D. *The Jefferson Image in the American Mind.* New York: Oxford University Press, 1960.

———. *Lincoln in American Memory.* New York: Oxford University Press, 1994.

Phillips, Philip Lee. *The Beginnings of Washington as Described in Books, Maps and Views.* Washington, D.C.: Published for the author, 1917.

Pierson, William H., Jr. *The Colonial and Neoclassical Styles.* New York: Oxford University Press, 1970.

Poore, Benjamin Perley. *Reminiscences of Sixty Years in the National Metropolis.* 2 vols. Philadelphia: Hubbard Brothers, 1886.

Porterfield, Amanda. *The Power of Religion.* New York: Oxford University Press, 1998.

Rakove, Jack N. *Original Meanings: Politics and Ideas in the Making of the Constitution.* New York: Random Vintage Books, 1997.

Rasmussen, William M. S., and Robert S. Tilton. *George Washington: The Man behind the Myths.* Charlottesville: University Press of Virginia, 1999.

Remini, Robert V. *Andrew Jackson and the Bank War: A Study in the Growth of Presidential Power.* New York: W. W. Norton, 1967.

Report of the Thomas Jefferson Memorial Commission. Washington, D.C.: June 1, 1939.

Reps, John W. *Monumental Washington: The Planning and Development of the Capital Center.* Princeton, N.J.: Princeton University Press, 1967.

———. *Washington on View: The Nation's Capital since 1790.* Chapel Hill: University of North Carolina Press, 1991.

Rousseau, Jean-Jacques. *The Social Contract and Discourses.* Trans. G. D. H. Cole. New York: E. P. Dutton, 1950.

Rutland, Robert A. *James Madison and the Search for Nationhood.* Washington, D.C.: Library of Congress, 1981.

Ryan, William, and Desmond Guinness. *The White House: An Architectural History.* New York: McGraw-Hill, 1980.

Rykwert, Joseph. *The Idea of a Town: The Anthropology of Urban Form in Rome, Italy and the Ancient World.* Princeton, N.J.: Princeton University Press, 1976.

Savage, Kirk. *Standing Soldiers, Kneeling Slaves: Race, War and Monument in Nineteenth-Century America.* Princeton, N.J.: Princeton University Press, 1997.

Schutz, John A., and Douglas Adair, eds. *The Spur of Fame: Dialogues of John Adams and Benjamin Rush, 1805–1813.* San Marino, Calif.: Huntington Library, 1966.

Scott, Pamela. "L'Enfant's Washington Described: The City in the Public Press, 1791–1795." *Washington History* 3, no. 1 (Spring/Summer 1991): 96–111.

———. *Temple of Liberty: Building the Capital for a New Nation.* New York: Oxford University Press, 1995.

Scott, Pamela, and Antoinette J. Lee. *Buildings of the District of Columbia.* New York: Oxford University Press, 1993.

Scully, Vincent. *New World Visions of Household Gods and Sacred Places: American Art and the Metropolitan Museum of Art, 1650–1914.* Boston: Little, Brown, 1988.

Seale, William. *The President's House: A History.* 2 vols. Washington, D.C.: White House Historical Association, 1986.

Sears, John F. *Sacred Places: American Tourist Attractions in the Nineteenth Century.* New York: Oxford University Press, 1989.

Semonche, John E., ed. *Religion and Law in American History.* Chapel Hill: University of North Carolina Press, 1985.

Shackelford, Michael G., and David R. Doyle. "GPS Survey of the D.C. Boundary Stones." *ACSM Bulletin* 126 (June 1990): 29–32.

Shuffelton, Frank, ed. *The American Enlightenment.* Rochester, N.Y.: University of Rochester Press, 1993.

Smylie, James H. "Providence and Presidents: Types of American Piety in Presidential Inaugurals." *Religion in Life* 35, no. 2 (Spring 1966): 270–82.

Somma, Thomas P. *The Apotheosis of Democracy, 1908–1916: The Pediment for the House Wing of the United States Capitol.* Newark: University of Delaware Press, 1995.

Speer, Albert. *Inside the Third Reich.* Trans. Richard and Clara Winston. New York: Macmillan, 1970.

Strenski, Ivan. "Religion, Power, and Final Foncault." *Journal of the American Academy of Religions* 66, no. 2 (Summer 1998): 345–67.

Swann, Brian, and Arnold Krupat, eds. *Recovering the Word: Essays on Native American Literature.* Berkeley: University of California Press, 1987.

Thach, Charles C., Jr. *The Creation of the Presidency, 1775–1789: A Study in Constitutional History.* Baltimore: Johns Hopkins University Press, 1923–1969.

Thistlethwaite, Mark Edward. *The Image of George Washington: Studies in Mid-Nineteenth-Century American History Painting.* New York: Garland, 1979.

Thomas, Christopher Alexander. "The Lincoln Memorial and Its Architect, Henry Bacon (1866–1924)." Ph.D. dissertation, Yale University, 1990.

Truettner, William, ed. *The West as America: Reinterpreting Images of the Frontier.* Washington, D.C.: Smithsonian Institution Press, 1991.

Tuan, Yi-fu. *Man and Nature.* Commission on College Geography Resource Paper No. 10. Washington, D.C.: Association of American Geographers, 1971.

Turner, Victor, and Edith Turner. *Image and Pilgrimage in Christian Culture: Anthropological Perspectives.* New York: Columbia University Press, 1978.

Vale, Lawrence. *Architecture, Power, and National Identity.* New Haven, Conn.: Yale University Press, 1992.

Van der Leeuw, Gerardus. *Religion in Essence and Manifestation.* Trans. J. E. Turner. 2 vols. New York: Harper Torchbooks, 1963.

Van Doren, Carl, and Carl Carver. *American Scriptures.* New York: Boni and Gaer, 1946.

Waley, Arthur F., trans. *The Analects of Confucius.* New York: Vintage Books, 1968.

Wallace, Mike. *Mickey Mouse History and Other Essays on American Memory.* Philadelphia: Temple University Press, 1996.

Warren, Robert Penn. *Brothers to Dragons: A Tale in Verse and Voices.* New York: Random House, 1953.

Washington: City and Capital. Federal Writers' Project. Washington, D.C.: U.S. Government Printing Office, 1937.

Washington, D.C.: A Smithsonian Book of the Nation's Capital. Washington, D.C.: Smithsonian Books, 1992.

Weems, Mason L. *The Life of Washington.* Ed. Marcus Cunliffe. Cambridge, Mass.: Harvard University Press, 1962.

Wheatley, Paul. *The Pivot of the Four Quarters.* Chicago: Aldine, 1971.

Whittemore, Frances Davis. *George Washington in Sculpture.* Boston: Marshall Jones, 1933.

Wick, Wendy C. *George Washington: An American Icon.* Washington, D.C.: Smithsonian Institution Exhibition Service, National Portrait Gallery, 1982.

Willey, Basil. *The Eighteenth Century Background: Studies on the Idea of Nature in the Thought of the Period.* New York: Columbia University Press, 1961.

Williams, J. Paul. *What Americans Believe and How They Worship.* 3d ed. New York: Harper and Row, 1969.

Wills, Garry. *Certain Trumpets: The Call of Leaders.* New York: Simon and Schuster, 1994.

———. *Cincinnatus: George Washington and the Enlightenment.* Garden City: N.J.: Doubleday, 1984.

———. *Inventing America: Jefferson's Declaration of Independence.* Garden City, N.J.: Doubleday, 1978.

———. *Lincoln at Gettysburg: The Words That Remade America.* New York: Simon and Schuster, 1992.

Wilson, Edmund. *Eight Essays.* Garden City, N.J.: Doubleday Anchor Books, 1954.

Wilson, John F. *Public Religion in American Culture.* Philadelphia: Temple University Press, 1979.

Wolf, William J. *The Religion of Abraham Lincoln.* New York: Seabury Press, 1963.

Young, James Stirling. *The Washington Community, 1800–1828.* New York: Columbia University Press, 1966.

Zelinsky, Wilbur. *Nation into State: The Shifting Symbolic Foundations of American Nationalism.* Chapel Hill: University of North Carolina Press, 1988.

Zucker, Paul, ed. *New Architecture and City Planning.* New York: Philosophical Library, 1944; reprint, Freeport, N.Y.: Books for Libraries Press, 1971.

Index

Designer: Nicole Hayward
Compositor: Binghamton Valley Composition
Text: 9.5/13 Sabon
Display: Sabon
Printer: Southeastern
Binder: Data Reproductions